DANGEROUS HARVEST

DANGEROUS HARVEST
Drug Plants and the Transformation of Indigenous Landscapes

Edited by

Michael K. Steinberg

Joseph J. Hobbs

Kent Mathewson

UNIVERSITY PRESS

2004

OXFORD
UNIVERSITY PRESS

Oxford   New York
Auckland   Bangkok   Buenos Aires   Cape Town   Chennai
Dar es Salaam   Delhi   Hong Kong   Istanbul   Karachi   Kolkata
Kuala Lumpur   Madrid   Melbourne   Mexico City   Mumbai   Nairobi
São Paulo   Shanghai   Taipei   Tokyo   Toronto

Copyright ©2004 by Oxford Unversity Press, Inc.

Published by Oxford University Press, Inc.
198 Madison Avenue, New York, New York, 10016

www.oup.com

Oxford is a registered trademark of Oxford University Press

Library of Congress Cataloging-in-Publication Data
Dangerous harvest: drug plants and the transformation of indigenous landscapes /
edited by Michael K. Steinberg, Joseph J. Hobbs, and Kent Mathewson.
p.   cm.
Includes bibliographical references and index.
ISBN 0-19-514319-1; ISBN 0-19-514320-5 (pbk)
1. Drug traffic.   2. Narcotics, Control of.   3. Drug abuse.
I. Steinberg, Michael K., 1965–   II. Hobbs, Joseph J. (Joseph John), 1956–
III. Mathewson, Kent, 1946–
HV5801 .D246   2003
363.45—dc21   2002014779

9 8 7 6 5 4 3 2 1

Printed in the United States of America
on acid-free paper

Contents

Contributors   vii

Introduction   3
     Michael K. Steinberg

I   Background Issues

1   Drugs, Moral Geographies, and Indigenous Peoples: Some Initial
Mappings and Central Issues   11
     Kent Mathewson

2   The Stimulus of Prohibition: A Critical History of the Global
Narcotics Trade   24
     Alfred W. McCoy

II   Case Studies

3   Opium and the People of Laos   115
     Joseph Westermeyer

4   Opium Production in Afghanistan and Pakistan   133
     Nigel J. R. Allan

5 The State and the Ongoing Struggle Over Coca in Bolivia: Legitimacy, Hegemony, and the Exercise of Power 153
   Harry Sanabria

6 The Marijuana Milpa: Agricultural Adaptations in a Postsubsistence Maya Landscape in Southern Belize 167
   Michael K. Steinberg

7 Sacred and Profane Uses of the Cactus *Lophophora Williamsii* from the South Texas Peyote Gardens 182
   Clarissa T. Kimber
   Darrel McDonald

8 Desert Traffic: The Dynamics of the Drug Trade in Northwestern Mexico 209
   Eric P. Perramond

III **History and Drug Plants**

9 Cannabis in Colonial India: Production, State Intervention, and Resistance in the Late Nineteenth-Century Bengali Landscape 221
   James H. Mills

10 Suppressing Opium and "Reforming" Minorities: Antidrug Campaigns in Ethnic Communities in the Early People's Republic of China 232
   Zhou Yongming

IV **Environmental Issues**

11 Environmental and Social Consequences of Coca/Cocaine in Peru: Policy Alternatives and a Research Agenda 249
   Kenneth R. Young

12 Modern Use and Environmental Impact of the Kava Plant in Remote Oceania 274
   Mark Merlin
   William Raynor

13 The Global Nexus of Drug Cultivation 294
   Joseph J. Hobbs

Index 313

Contributors

Nigel J. R. Allan
Department of Environmental Design
University of California, Davis

Joseph J. Hobbs
Department of Geography
University of Missouri–Columbia

Clarissa Kimber
Department of Geography
Texas A&M University

Kent Mathewson
Department of Geography and
    Anthropology
Louisiana State University

Alfred W. McCoy
Department of History
University of Wisconsin–Madison

Darrel McDonald
Department of Political Science and
    Geography
Stephen F. Austin State University

Mark Merlin
Biology Program
University of Hawaii at Manoa

James Mills
Department of History
University of Strathclyde, UK

Eric P. Perramond
Department of Geography and
    Environmental Studies
Stetson University

William Raynor
Field Director
The Nature Conservancy, Pohnpei Island,
    FSM

Harry Sanabria
Department of Anthropology
University of Pittsburgh

Michael K. Steinberg
Cultural Biogeographer
U.S. Department of Agriculture
PLANTS Database
Baton Rouge, Louisiana

Joseph Westermeyer
Medical School
University of Minnesota

Zhou Yongming
Department of Anthropology
University of Wisconsin–Madison

Kenneth R. Young
Department of Geography
University of Texas at Austin

DANGEROUS HARVEST

Introduction

Michael K. Steinberg

The global drug trade and its associated violence, corruption, and human suffering create global problems that involve not only the use and abuse of substances that have traveled across great geographic spaces but also political and military conflict and policy, economic development, and indigenous and ethnic minority rights in the production regions. Drug production and eradication efforts directly affect the stability of many states and relations between states, shaping and sometimes distorting foreign policy (McCoy 1991, 1999; Bagley and Walker 1996; Meyer and Parssinen 1998; Albright 1999; Rohter 1999). Drug production and the efforts to halt it often derail national and local development (Westermeyer 1982; Smith 1992; Goodson 2001) and create potential human rights violations as small-scale producers get caught in the legal crossfire between their dangerous harvest and economic hardship (Sanabria 1992; Kent 1993; Clawson and Lee 1998). External demand and influence, not indigenous cultures, have transformed apparently simple, local agricultural activities into very complex global problems.

Psychoactive plants have always played important cultural roles in indigenous and ethnic minority landscapes. After a history of coevolution and experimentation, indigenous societies came to use psychoactive substances derived from plants in a range of religious and healing rituals. Traditional healers, or shamans, consume psychoactive plants to consult with the spiritual world in order to foretell the future and assist patients; patients ingest psychoactive substances to rid themselves of demons or diseases; and indigenous cultures use psychoactive substances in semi-ritualistic social situations to reinforce social and political bonds or simply as recreation. However, as these traditional cultures come into contact with the outside world, nonindigenous societies often mimic these practices, trying to reach a "new level of consciousness."

The poppy is an example of a psychoactive plant taken out of a traditional context and adopted by cultural outsiders for nonsacred use. In turn, globalization alters the plant's use and symbolic meaning within its traditional-use hearth area. Several chapters in this volume show that heroin, a derivative of poppies, is used and abused worldwide and in its original hearth, where the plant was once viewed as a sacred medicinal and ritualistic plant. The profane use of opium leaves a trail of destruction in its wake in the form of addicts and soaring HIV rates as the virus spreads through shared heroin needles. As Westerners bastardize the acts and rituals associated with the plants, the people and traditions in the hearth areas, where these plants were once regarded as noble, are destroyed. Eradication authorities often target indigenous farmers, along with drug traffickers, dealers, and kingpins, destroying the farmers' cultures and environments.

This militarization of psychoactive substance landscapes places indigenous cultures on the front line of the war on drugs, creating a dangerous harvest for cultures in drug plant production areas. For example, indigenous peasant farmers who produce coca in the Andean region of South America often must choose between extreme poverty and the lure of a cash crop with a steady market. However, the costs of participating in the production of coca are aerial spraying that destroys food crops, imprisonment, and violent threats from various factions that either support or attempt to suppress this economy. Present situations in Afghanistan, Burma, Colombia, and Peru provide examples of the link between psychoactive plant production centers and socially unstable, often militarized indigenous landscapes. Today, both rogue governments and rebel forces depend on the income generated by the profane use of traditional psychoactive plant substances to support their policies (Kent 1993; Cohen 1998; Steinberg 2000).

As a result of the connection among rebel groups, rogue governments, and the drug trade, drug eradication planning and policy by the United States, in particular, is an increasingly important aspect of international relations and military policy. The war on drugs is no longer viewed as a public health issue or one of personal choice. Drug eradication is now squarely in the corner of military planning and policy. The most overt example of this new eradication perspective is Plan Colombia, under which U.S. military aid inadvertently funds Colombia's war with various leftist groups who also produce drugs. Before their expulsion from Afghanistan, the Taliban regime had also benefited from a drug "tax" imposed on poppy farmers (Goodson 2001). Given the recent attacks in New York City, and the financial links between opium and the Taliban, it is likely that opium production in Central Asia will receive greater attention from U.S. military authorities. Thus the line between war and the war on drugs is becoming more and more unclear. Yet what do we (the West and especially eradication authorities) really know about those who produce the drugs that help fuel civil wars and wreak havoc in countless lives? Who are these seemingly faceless actors in this global issue, and why do they continue to produce crops that cause so much misery throughout the world, including their own homelands? As this volume will demonstrate, farmers on the production end of the global drug trade are not evil individuals who have set out to poison the West but are often people living in poor, unstable political and environmental landscapes such as those in Bolivia. These individuals have few opportunities to participate in the emerging global economy beyond the production of illicit crops such as poppies and coca. Therefore, it is the opinion of many in this volume that until we understand the plight of the drug-producing farmer, we will never successfully address one of the most difficult problems of our time, the global drug trade.

The popular media and many scholars give extensive coverage to drug use, the global drug trade, and the war on drugs. However, this coverage deals mainly with the impact of narcotics on Western society or the latest hunt for or capture of a drug kingpin in Latin America. This volume takes a different approach. Instead of examining drugs from the West's perspective, we take a bottom-up approach and analyze these issues from the perspective of the indigenous farmers whose cultures have produced psychoactive plants for centuries. Just as there are cultural costs associated with drug use in Western society, there are far-reaching consequences for indigenous societies that produce psychoactive plants. Indigenous groups face conflicts regarding cultural identity, environmental impact, public health, and human rights. This volume will examine how some indigenous peoples are confronting the consequences of the production, processing, trade, trafficking, and consumption of drugs deemed illegal by global agencies and national polities.

Because of the often pivotal role played by indigenous groups in drug plant production, this volume highlights these actors in this multibillion-dollar global industry. Again, this end of the drug pipeline is largely unknown to most people in consumer nations, and apparently even to most eradication policymakers, given their emphasis on militaristic intervention. This volume does not glorify the producers but instead demonstrates the complexity in which they live and how various circumstances have come together to entwine them in the global drug trade. These circumstances often involve pressures from poverty, pressures from repressive governments, and ethnic tensions. Until decision makers in the West understand the complicated economic, political, and ethnic circumstances in which peasant producers exist, the war on drugs will never be won but will continue to leave more casualties in its wake, both consumers and producers.

Although not every indigenous group that produces or uses psychoactive plants can be covered in this or any single volume, every major drug-plant-producing hearth region that has been altered by global demand is represented. The attempt here has been to gather contributors who write about indigenous people and psychoactive plants from a variety of disciplines, geographic regions, and times in order to reveal the complexity of the drug issues. This broad approach is important because no single region, issue, or discipline can represent or explain the many topics included under the theme of indigenous people and psychoactive plants.

This volume is unique because most chapters focus on the peasant farmers' perspective at the production end of the global drug economy. Many books and articles have been published about the global drug trade and centralized, militaristic interdiction efforts (see Celio Toro 1995; Renard 1996; Lintner 1999; Zhou 1999); however, few have been written about drug interdiction efforts from the farmers' perspectives (two exceptions are Smith 1992 and Sanabria 1993)—a critical gap.

The volume is divided into four sections. Chapters 1 and 2 provide overviews of some of the larger issues discussed throughout the volume. Chapter 1, by Kent Mathewson, presents a global overview of indigenous peoples' relations with drugs and how these practices have served both positive and destructive roles in cultural formations throughout both space and time, especially in the last five centuries — since the rise of Europe and the United States to positions of global hegemony. Chapter 2, by Alfred W. McCoy, discusses opium and coca production in the major production hearths of Southeast Asia, Central Asia, and Andean South America as well as global eradication efforts. McCoy argues that, historically, eradication efforts have had the opposite effect from their intentions. Instead of eliminating drug plant production, they have spurred production in nontargeted areas.

The second and largest section of the volume presents case studies from various cultural landscapes that are involved in various aspects of drug plant production, trade, and use. Chapter 3, by Joseph Westermeyer, provides coverage of the epidemiology of opium addiction, folk and recreational uses of opium, the social functions of opium dens, and the politics of poppies, opium, and addiction in Laos and Thailand. Chapter 4, by Nigel J. R. Allan, examines recent drug production in Afghanistan, Pakistan, and India and its influence on regional politics. Given Afghanistan's new prominence in world affairs, this chapter is important because it provides vital background information that explains the role of opium production and exports in supporting various political regimes, including the Taliban. Chapter 5, by Harry Sanabria, focuses on the ongoing struggle over coca in Bolivia and tries to explain why resistance to eradication efforts in the late 1990s and the first half of 2000, at least compared to previous years, appear to have been particularly ineffective. Bolivia, having eliminated substantial quantities of coca in the recent past, is often held up as a success in the war on drugs. Yet as this chapter will show, victory is more complicated than that in media reports. Chapter 6, by Michael K. Steinberg, examines the incorporation of marijuana into the traditional milpa agricultural system among the Mopan and Kekchi Maya of southern Belize. Marijuana illustrates the extent to which milpa agriculture has been influenced by outside economic forces. This chapter explains why farmers have incorporated marijuana into the milpa crop complex, the cultural and political changes brought about by this changing land use, and the response by eradication authorities to this new economy. Chapter 7, written by Clarissa Kimber and Darrel McDonald, examines the uses and abuses of peyote, the professional peyote suppliers, and, to a lesser extent, the role of officialdom in controlling the resource. The chapter also discusses the evolution of uses of peyote and their importance to the Native-American church. Chapter 8, by Eric P. Perramond, focuses on the transport of narcotics, mainly in the northern Mexican state of Sonora, and the problems these shipments pose for traditional cultural and environmental activities among the Tarahumara and Yaqui Indians (Tohono O'odham) in the region. Although Sonora is not a significant producer of illicit narcotics, it is a common route for their shipment into the United States.

The third section of the volume examines historical uses of illicit plant substances and eradication efforts of central governments in ethnic minority landscapes. Chapter 9, by James Mills, examines the place of cannabis in nineteenth-century peasant societies in India. This chapter first separately considers the production and consumption of preparations of Indian hemp. It then examines the interventions of the British colonial state in those processes and the reasons for the failure of the state to prohibit narcotics, which it deemed harmful. Chapter 10, by Yongming Zhou, examines antidrug campaigns in ethnic communities in the early People's Republic of China. This chapter focuses on how drug suppressions were conducted in minority areas in the 1950s by analyzing three antiopium campaigns in Yi, Tibetan, and Ewenki.

The last section of the volume examines the environmental impacts of drug plant production and the changing cultural relations with the plants in question. Chapter 11, by Kenneth R. Young, addresses the connection between coca and cocaine expansion and deforestation in indigenous landscapes. Few studies examine the environmental impacts of psychoactive plants, yet, as this chapter demonstrates, those of coca and cocaine in Peru and elsewhere in South America are profound. Chapter 12, written by Mark Merlin and William Raynor, examines the changing use and environmental impact of the kava plant (*Piper methysticum.*) in the Pacific. As this chapter documents, the recent steep rise in its use in some areas of the tropical Pacific, as well as in parts of North America and Europe, has resulted in a large increase in its cultivation. On some islands, such as Pohnpei Island, kava production already appears to have had severe impacts on native tropical flora.

It is appropriate for Joseph Hobbs to write the concluding remarks in chapter 13, because the idea for this volume stems from a conversation I had with him about his research on opium production in Egypt and a subsequent article, "Troubling Fields: The Opium Poppy," that appeared in 1998 in the *Geographical Review* (Hobbs 1998). We both agreed that although many scholars have written about various aspects of psychoactive plants, a comprehensive examination of this broad topic with a specific focus on indigenous people was missing. In this final chapter, Hobbs synthesizes some of the major points made by the authors, as well as forecasting, based on his own field experiences, such future directions as crop substitution programs, international eradication efforts, and the militarization of indigenous landscapes.

This volume will help unveil the farmer, not to glamorize those who grow drug plants but to show that there are very deep historical, cultural, and economic ties between culture and the plants in production areas.

References

Albright, M.K. 1999. Colombia's struggles, and how we can help. *New York Times*, August 10.

Bagley, B. M., and W. O. Walker III, eds. 1994. *Drug Trafficking in the Americas*. Boulder, CO: Lynne Rienner.

Celio Toro, M. 1995. *Mexico's "War" on Drugs: Causes and Consequences. Vol. 3. Studies on the Impact of the Illegal Drug Trade*. New York: Lynne Rienner.

Clawson, P. L., and R. W. Lee III. 1998. *The Andean Cocaine Industry*. New York: St. Martin's Griffin.

Cohen, Y. 1998. Cash from opium helps prop up generals. *Christian Science Monitor*, January 29.

Goodson, L. P. 2001. *Afghanistan's Endless War: State Failure, Regional Politics, and the Rise of the Taliban*. Seattle: University of Washington Press.

Hobbs, J. J. 1998. Troubling fields: The opium poppy in Egypt. *Geographical Review* 88(1): 64–85.

Kent, R. B. 1993. Geographical dimensions of the Shining Path insurgency in Peru. *Geographical Review* 83(4): 441–454.

Lintner, B. 1999. *Burma in Revolt: Opium and Insurgency Since 1948.* Thailand: Silkworm Books.

McCoy, A. W. 1991. *The Politics of Heroin: CIA Complicity in the Global Drug Trade.* Chicago: Lawrence Hill.

———. 1999. Lord of drug lords: One life as lesson for US drug policy. *Crime, Law & Social Change* 30: 301–331.

Meyer, K., and T. M. Parssinen. 1998. *Webs of Smoke: Smugglers, Warlords, Spies, and the History of the International Drug Trade.* New York: Rowman & Littlefield.

Renard, R. D. 1996. *The Burmese Connection: Illegal Drugs and the Making of the Golden Triangle. Vol. 6. Studies on the Impact of the Illegal Drug Trade.* Boulder, CO: Lynne Rienner.

Rohter, L. 1999. With U.S. training, Colombia melds war on rebels and drugs. *New York Times,* July 29.

Sanabria, H. 1992. *The Coca Boom and Rural Social Change in Bolivia.* Ann Arbor: University of Michigan Press.

Smith, M. L., ed. 1992. *Why People Grow Drugs.* London: Panos Publications.

Steinberg, M. K. 2000. Generals, guerillas, drugs, and Third World war-making. *Geographical Review* 90(2): 260–267.

Westermeyer, J. 1982. *Poppies, Pipes, and People: Opium and Its Use in Laos.* Berkeley: University of California Press.

Zhou, Yongming. 1999. *Anti-Drug Crusades in Twentieth-Century China.* Lanham, MD: Rowman & Littlefield.

I

Background Issues

1

Drugs, Moral Geographies, and Indigenous Peoples: Some Initial Mappings and Central Issues

Kent Mathewson

There are about 2,000 entities in the world today that ethnologists call societies, each with distinct cultures. Perhaps the most obvious marker, and many argue the most important, is that each of these entities has its own language. Among the other societal attributes, besides language, that can make claims to human universality, or nearly so, is the cultural use of psychoactive substances— or what commonly are referred to as simply "drugs." These range from mild stimulants such as coffee, tea, cacao, coca, and kola to stupeficients such as opium and alcohol, to hallucinogens found in mushrooms, cacti, and a number of flowering plants. Since the Mesolithic and perhaps before, the vast majority of the world's peoples have used one or more such substances for religious and related purposes. Even in their most seemingly secular contexts, drugs are often used in ritual and habitual ways that exhibit their cultural embeddedness. Increasingly the world's remaining indigenous peoples and many local folk are confronting questions and the consequences of the production, processing, trade, trafficking, and consumption of drugs deemed illegal and illicit by global agencies and national polities. Some of these substances, usually in their unrefined forms, have deep roots in local and indigenous cultures and economies. Often they serve important roles in constituting and maintaining cultural identity. With ever-increasing modernization and globalization, the circumstances and conditions under which indigenous and local peoples produce, trade, and use these substances continues to change. In turn, psychoactive substances—whether sanctioned, proscribed, or both—often serve as agents in the creation and defense of local and indigenous "moral" geographies.

The concept of moral geography (as used here) refers to both the actual and symbolic terrain upon which traditional societies elaborate their customary livelihood and belief systems, and the cognate spaces in which they defend these practices and perceptions. For most indigenous peoples, the drugs in their culture, whether sacred or profane, are manifest in both their moral economies and geographies. For some groups, drugs become defining elements in their relations with dominant cultures and polities. For others, they are less than determinate, but still play significant roles in mediating exchanges—both symbolic and material. In either case, they can serve as mechanisms of subordination, or modes of resistance, or sometimes both. We might speak, then, of the oppressive *or* the emancipatory potential of drugs for the promotion of cultural identity and the production of indigenous moral geographies.

This chapter presents a global overview of indigenous people's relations with drugs and how these practices have served both constitutive and destructive roles in cultural formations through both space and time, but especially in the last five centuries—or since the rise of Europe and its replications to positions of global hegemony. Within this broad survey, particular attention will be given the questions of scale. From individual bodies and household domains, to communities and locales, and on up through regions, nation states, realms, to the global, the scale at which drugs are collected or produced, consumed or exchanged, enframes identity issues and structures moral geographies.

One of the big surprises of the past several decades has been the challenges that recrudescent forces such as religious fundamentalism, the politics of ethnic and regional identity, and other "out-of-step" movements present to modernity's presumed trajectories. Paralleling these defections, or at least deflections, have been the upwelling and retelling of indigenous peoples' sense of their own cultural identities and the connections being made between groups. With the start of this new millennium, the plights of and the prospects for indigenous peoples have never been more visible. As part of this new awakening among indigenous people and a growing awareness of them by the world's dominant polities and populations, their collective identities and projections are no longer strictly local or even national but increasingly articulated at the global scale. These new cultural formations beget new geographies and invite revisiting old, and not so old, histories. As Michael K. Steinberg (see introduction) ably points out, the purpose of this volume is to begin to map these geographies and reexamine these histories as they relate to drugs, both illicit and sanctioned.

The purpose of this chapter is to provide some definitional groundings and suggest outlines for a broad-stroked, large-scaled sketch of drugs' import to and impact on indigenous societies. I frame these outlines, in part, in terms of what can be referred to as the "moral geography" of drugs and their traditional custodians. These moral geographies are constructed and constituted through the practices and patterns of traditional producers and users. Of course, there are also the drug geographies created and superimposed upon indigenous moral geographies by dominant groups and societies. The chapters that follow present specific cases and more detailed illustrations of both kinds of geographies, especially the second category. Therefore, it is of some value to present synoptic overviews of the historical depth and geographical extent of indigenous peoples' relations to drugs. But first, some terms need definition and some numbers and magnitudes need discussion.

Definitions

Definitions matter—increasingly so in the case of indigenity. In its original sense, indigenous simply referred to natality and location:being born in a place or native to it. Within the context of early European colonialism, it assumed more definition, coming to mean "produced, growing, or living naturally within a country or climate," as well as "native; autochthonous." As Sir Thomas Browne remarked in 1646, (this seems to be the first usage in its modern sense; see the entry for *indigenous, Compact Edition of the OED*, 1971, 1: 1417). "Although . . . there bee . . . swarms of Negroes serving the Spaniard, yet they were all transported from Africa . . . and are not indigenous or proper natives of America" In our postcolonial times, these distinctions have taken on added weight, as dispossessed and marginalized cultural groups advance claims to land and cultural legitimacy before nation-states on all continents. Geographer Stan Stevens (1997: 19) defines indigenous peoples as "those who are the 'original' or oldest surviving inhabitants of an area. They have, typically, lived in a traditional homeland for many generations—usually for many centuries. Their sense of themselves as peoples is based on that shared homeland, as well as on shared language, history, values, and customs." For Stevens, an authority on natural area conservation and cultural survival, the occupancy of a common place and its environments is paramount.

Ian McIntosh (2000: 4), of the advocacy organization Cultural Survival, points to some of the complexities that accompany the drawing of lines to define the term *indigenous*. In his definition, *indigenous* (in reference to "first peoples") has come to mean "those who maintain a collective identity through association with specific territories." This definition is somewhat less dependent on time and place than Stevens's (1997), perhaps so as not to exclude those groups with histories involving displacement or occupancies short of "time immemorial." *Indigenous* is often used interchangeably with such terms as *tribal, ethnic minority*, and *hunter-gatherer*. McIntosh points out that although these and similar terms may or may not be precisely synonymous, the more important distinctions revolve on who sets the boundaries. Powerful elites may ascribe or deny indigenous status to a minority or non-dominant group for reasons of state, or simply for its own narrower purposes.

The unevenness in the global geography of indigenes' numbers, in terms of both groups and individuals, is mirrored by the degree to which their indigenous status is recognized as such. In the lands Europeans directly colonized and often settled—such as the Americas, Australia, New Zealand, and Oceania—indigenous status is generally, even unproblematically, granted to persons and groups not descended from Europeans or the Africans and Asians they introduced. Some mixed Afro-Amerind populations such as the Garifuna of Central America or the Maroons of Suriname have ambiguous status. In Asia and Africa, where by far the largest numbers of indigenes reside, the situation is much less straightforward and often conflicted. In Asia, labels other than "indigenous"—such as "hill tribes" (Thailand), "scheduled tribes" (India), "national minorities" (China), "isolated and alien peoples" (Indonesia), and similar appellations—are applied to nondominant groups that might otherwise claim indigeneity. In Africa, only the most distinct and deeply autochthonous groups such as the Bushmen and Pygmies seem to receive the designation without discussion. As for Europe, except for a few groups such as the Saami or Lapps, the category is no longer applicable and probably has not been for centuries in most cases and countries.

The United Nations—probably the most appropriate forum for reaching agreements on these kinds of nomenclatural questions—has avoided coming to terms with a fixed definition of *indigenous*. It does, however, have a working definition that refers to five criteria: (1) self-identification, (2) historical continuity with preinvasion or precolonial societies, (3) nondominance, (4) ancestral territories, and (5) ethnic identity. In addition, there is growing agreement that indigenous groups share the experience of subjugation to the domination, exploitation, and territorial appropriation by states controlled by culturally alien peoples (McIntosh 2000: 5). Among these five criteria, the last (ethnic identity) is where customary practices may be said to reside. Traditional drug use among indigenous peoples is seldom removed from ritual behavior, usually fuses elements of religious and medicinal systems, and often serves to promote and define collective identity. The suppression or control of traditional drug use by outside, dominating groups, usually operating through state agency, can be seen at a minimum as assaults on indigenous groups' identity. Of course, the aggression usually involves more than just cultural erosion. Forms of domination, exploitation, and land alienation can all be mediated and even precipitated through drug-related interactions.

Since at least the rise of modern colonialism, dominant groups have introduced new drugs, or new forms of them, to aid in the domination, exploitation, and dispossession of indigenous peoples. One only has to think of distilled alcohol's agency in fueling the slave trade among indigenous Africans or its role in lubricating land transfers from indigenes to Europeans in North America to view only two sets of strategic exchanges within a much larger historical process. Direct transfers of drugs between imperial polities often affect indigenous peoples through the fallout in these dynamics. Perhaps the best example is the eighteenth- and nineteenth-century trade in opium between the British and Qing empires (Blue 2000; see also chapter 2 in this volume). Various national minorities and indigenous groups became both producers and consumers after Indian imports subsided and local sources were developed. Opium was a relatively novel and not widespread drug before the English and Dutch introductions.

A somewhat different situation is set in motion when a drug that was previously proscribed, though an integral element in one culture, is appropriated, redefined, and deployed for new purposes by a conquering one. Here, the best example may be coca's role within the Inca empire and its use under Spanish dominion. Under Inca rule, coca was both sacralized and monopolized by the state. Under Spanish dominion, it was secularized and deregulated, becoming a force of production. Without coca, the extraction and refining of silver in Upper Peru, in the face of declining indigenous populations, would have been much less feasible—and not nearly so successful.

These are just a few examples; the list is long, and cannot be fully explored or displayed here. In attempting to fill in some of the contours of this larger history and geography, I will discuss other examples of the roles drugs play in the domination and exploitation of indigenous peoples. Of course, there are other angles to be considered as well. In many cases, drugs play positive roles—from acting as anchors of tradition and serving as social cement to providing trade items or sources of revenue that can increase autonomy as much as they create dependencies.

Numbers

As with the question of definitions, the number of indigenous peoples thought to currently exist varies widely. McIntosh (2000: 5) suggests there are perhaps 400–500 million indigenous peoples worldwide, or about 6–8 percent of the more than 6 billion people alive today. He also points out that this figure has been growing as more members of various minorities come to define themselves as indigenous. At the same time, of course, indigenous groups continue to disappear through the processes of deculturation, dispossession, and occasionally (still), extirpation. Less than a decade ago, Jason Clay (1993: 65–68), also representing Cultural Survival, projected a total indigenous population of 600 million, or more than 10 percent of the world's population. Estimates of the number of indigenous groups are similarly fluid, with definitional questions creating much of the variance. If one were to follow nineteenth-century thinking, which placed a premium on linguistic criteria for distinguishing between ethnic and indigenous groups, then extrapolating from the number of extant languages might yield the right numbers. Most reference sources estimate that there are between 4,000 and 5,000 languages currently spoken, though estimates ranging from between 3,000 to 10,000 are encountered. The world's dominant languages would, of course, have to be excluded from the accounting to arrive at a workable figure. If one were to use language as the sole indicator, one might assume that there are at least 3,000 indigenous groups in the world today. A newer way of looking at these questions is the position that holds that all indigenous peoples and various other groupings (e.g., ethnic minorities) constitute nations, though few of these collectivities control states (Nietschmann 1988). The number of stateless nations has been estimated as high as 9,000 (Minahan 1996: xvi). Basing his estimates partly on the notion of stateless nations, Clay (1993: 65–68) suggests that over 5,000 indigenous groups could be counted. Whatever the actual numbers, it seems safe to assume the existence of several thousand groups today and more in the past, with total populations in the hundreds of millions for the past century, if not longer.

Distributions

Perhaps more salient for the subject of this volume than either absolute numbers or the estimated numbers of indigenous groups are their geographies. Increasingly, the definitions and ultimately the demographies of indigenous peoples revolve around the facts of land occupancy, past, present, and future. The International Work Group for Indigenous Affairs (IWGIA) mapped world populations of indigenous peoples in 1980 (Bodley 1994: 364). Although these figures are lower than estimates by other research and advocacy groups, they are useful for the relative ratios between regions and offer a baseline as of that year. Among the world's continents and geographical realms, with about 143 million, Asia had by far the largest population of indigenous peoples. The regional breakdown in millions is as follows: South (India) 40; East (China) 36; Southeast (including Indonesia) 35; North (Russia) 22; Southwest (from Afghanistan to Yemen) 10. As mentioned previously, the official positions on terminology held by most states in these regions would drastically reduce these numbers if tallied by the nation-states themselves.

The same holds for Africa, which followed with 14 million, divided among the Sahelian area, East Africa, and Southern Africa. Southern Africa's Bushmen are dispersed over a relatively large area, but with only 10,000 individuals, they represented less than 1 percent of the total. Oceania (including New Zealand and New Guinea) had by far the largest ratio between indigenous numbers and total population, as well as that between indigenous population and land area. With 14 million Melanesians, Micronesians, and Polynesians, more than half of the realm's population is indigenous.

South America had 11 million, 90 percent concentrated in the Andean highlands. Middle America (including Mexico) had about 10 million indigenes according to these estimates, though this figure was almost certainly conservative, as Mexico today has between 10–20 million indigenous people alone. The totals for North America (including Greenland) were about 1.5 million. Australia's indigenous population was given as 100,000. Not surprisingly, Europe had only token numbers, with about 40,000 in Scandinavia and perhaps similar numbers in northwest Russia. According to these figures the total global indigenous population in 1980 was approaching 200 million.

The United Nations declared 1993 the International Year of the Indigenous People. A number of maps and articles along the lines of "who counts and how many are there?" were published at the time in popular outlets. One from the March 1993 issue of the *World Monitor* generally doubled the IWGIA's 1980 regional figures but claimed 2,000 groups for Africa, totaling 350 million persons. None are shown for Europe, and the Pacific (minus New Guinea) was said to have 2 million. The discrepancies between these figures and the lower estimates cited earlier are doubtless due in part to the natural population increase among those groups that are generally viable. Most of the increase in numbers, however, is due to more inclusive definitions. Again, the total number of indigenous peoples probably matters less than the fact that they still persist in all of the world's major culturogeographical realms, and that in many of their regions, they are prominent, if not the dominate, components and actors.

Drugs—Definitions and Numbers

Just as with the term *indigenous* as applied to people, the definition of a drug is flexible and contextual. A commonly understood definition of a drug is a substance that produces significant changes in the body, mind, or both when consumed even in small amounts. With this definition, however, the boundaries among drugs, food, and poisons can be unclear. Indeed, some common substances such as sugar can function as both drug and food, and alcohol can be all three. Narrowing the definitional range to agents of change on the body or mind that act primarily neither as foods nor poisons still yields a large number of substances. These can be divided into the categories of therapeutic and nontherapeutic use, and then into such categories as religious, recreational, tributary, status or prestige enhancing, and so on. Here, as with the other groupings, the boundaries are not fixed.

Drugs can also be divided into groups according to their derivation. Endogenous drugs are those produced by the human body, such as endorphins and adrenaline. Natural drugs are those found in nature, mostly as compounds in plants but also some in animals. Indigenous peoples can be credited with originally discovering, experimenting with, and incorporating into their cultures almost all the known natural drugs. This list currently comprises several hundred substances, including opium, coca, and marijuana, to mention those most commonly falling under modernity's regimes of regulation and condemnation. It also embraces a large number of drugs that the same regimes tolerate or promote, such as tobacco, coffee, and tea. Perhaps the largest group involves drugs or their sources that are locally or regionally consumed. Prominent examples are kava (Oceania; see chapter 12), khat (East Africa and Arabia), betel nut (Asia and Oceania), and maté (South America). As yet not having been subjected to either vigorous global suppression or promotion, most of these kinds of drugs maintain strong indigenous cultural affiliations. Just as Coca Cola (a complex elixir of a dozen or more psychoactive substances with its sugars, caffeine, nutmeg, and decocainated coca extract) confers the symbolic status of modernity on its consumers, so kava helps constitute what it means to be an indigenous Pacific Islander.

Most naturally occurring drugs can be refined, and then they usually fall into both the illicit and therapeutic categories, for example, morphine, cocaine, and mescaline. Beyond this are the semisynthetic drugs such as heroin, a derivative of morphine, and the synthetic drugs, which have no bases in nature. Most tranquilizers and sedatives and many stimulants and painkillers are synthetic creations. None of the drugs in these last three categories have roots in indigenous knowledge systems or their agencies. Nevertheless, several—particularly heroin and cocaine—have had increasingly greater impact on the lives of indigenous peoples over the past half century, as several of the chapters in this volume demonstrate.

Yet another way to group drugs is according to their principal effects. The German toxicologist Louis Lewin published his pioneering study of drugs, which appeared in English as *Phantastica: Narcotic and Stimulating Drugs—Their Use and Abuse*, in 1931. It remains one of the most comprehensive overviews available, covering the chemistry, pharmacology, botany, ethnology, and history of drugs, as well as their role in indigenous cultures and in the medicine, psychology, psychiatry, and sociology of modern societies (Balick and Cox 1996). Lewin divided drugs into five categories: (1) euphorica ("sedatives of mental activity" such as opiates, as well as cocaine); (2) phantastica (hallucinogens such as mescaline or the nightshades); (3) inebriantia (alcohol, ether, and other chemicals that cause cerebral excitation followed by depression); (4) hypnotica (substances that induce calm and/or sleep such as kava); and (5) excitantia (stimulants that cause cerebral excitation but not consciousness alteration, such as coffee, tea, tobacco, betel nuts, and kola nuts). Since

Lewin's study the number of drugs known to science has increased manyfold. Eth-nobotanists have documented numerous plants used by indigenous peoples that were either not known to or not studied by Western science 75 years ago. At the same time dozens of new drugs, especially in the hypnotica and phantastica groups, have been created by science since the 1930s. Lewin's five categories could be in-creased to encompass some of the new discoveries, as well as new understandings of drugs' effects. Nevertheless, his taxonomy still provides a useful way to group drugs according to their effects.

In terms of indigenous peoples and their relations with natural drugs, the largest increase in knowledge has been in the phantasica group. To date, some 120 hallu-cinogenic plants have been identified worldwide (Davis 1985: 2). It is interesting that they are distributed very unevenly. More than 100 are native to the New World, the majority coming from the Neotropics. Only 15–20 have been identified in the Old World, although the Old World's natural ecological conditions are seem-ingly comparable, especially in the equatorial tropics, and it has more than twice the area. This discrepancy continues to be one of the more intriguing culture-historical questions. Both Richard Schultes (1963) and Weston La Barre (1964, 1970) seemed to have recognized this anomaly at about the same time. La Barre suggested that the shamanistic traditions of Siberia and their New World counter-parts, which place a premium on knowledge and power attained through vision quests, have a particular need not only in using psychotropic substances but also in searching for them. It is quite possible that before the spread of agriculturalists, with their more formal religions, throughout Europe, Africa, and Asia, hunter-gatherer societies had knowledge of and used a larger repertoire of psychotropics, which have been since lost to humanity. Hunter-gatherer remnants such as the Bushmen have some of the richest Old World drug use and knowledge. For what-ever reasons, even among many Amerind agriculturalists, shamanistic practices persisted until the European contact and beyond.

In addition to the 120 substances in Lewin's phantasica group, there is quite likely an equal or greater number that fit into his other four divisions. For example, there are at least two dozen plant sources of caffeine and related stimulants that in-digenous peoples have known and used; in many cases they have collected and cul-tivated these and other drugs for millennia. A complete accounting of the world's known natural drugs in their indigenous cultural contexts has not been produced—an obvious project that must be done before the global geography of indigenous peoples' relations with drugs can be comprehensively mapped. Short of this we can still look at individual drugs in particular places and contexts and derive a mosaic, although with missing parts, that is still useful for inferring the larger picture. One might hypothesize that all indigenous peoples use drugs and then move on to the daunting matter of specifying the where, when, how, and why for each group.

Drug Use—A Cultural Universal?

Various scholars have made the claim for the human universality of drug use. For example, La Barre (1980: 62) says, "There appears to be no human society so simple in material culture as to lack some sort of mood-altering drug as an escape from the workaday world." Weil and Rosen (1993: 10) state, "Drug use is universal. Every human culture in every age of history has used one or more psychoactive drugs." They add, however, that the "Eskimos" represent the one possible exception to this rule because they lacked the necessary plant sources. This may be the case, though the Inuit are reasonably recent arrivals to their current homelands and may have possessed this knowledge before they left northeastern Asia. Virtual universality of drug use seems a reasonable proposition. Conversely, few if any indigenous groups would presumably eschew drug use unless outside pressures have prohibited it. Such widespread geographical acceptance also raises questions of time: Is drug use one of the primordial human culture traits?

The various criteria proposed to define humans as a separate and unique species continue to shift. Numerous attributes ranging from tool use to speech to self-reflexivity have been proposed to define or identify the presumption of human uniqueness. The all-too-human propensity to seek out substances that provide pleasure or alleviate pain—often simultaneously—might seem to offer yet another marker. Abundant ethological evidence, both recorded and anecdotal, confirms that many animals, if given the opportunity, will consume behavior-altering agents, particularly alcohol from naturally occurring sources, as well as drugs provided in laboratories. Rather than being a diagnostic trait of *Homo sapiens'* singularity, drug use seems to be a capacity widely shared with other big-brained species, along with some not so "evolved." Both primates and elephants seem to enjoy the effects of ingesting fermented fruits if they come across them. Many other mammals will imbibe alcohol and other intoxicants with human assistance.

The defining divide may lie somewhere between intentionality and sustained efforts at procurement. It is safe to say that humans are the only animals that have consciously and systematically sought out stimulants and stupefacients, first in and from nature and then increasingly through artificial confection. This may be as good a measure as any to demarcate humans from other life-forms. In other words, *Homo faber pharmakon*, or "Man, the drug [taker] *and* maker."

If the taking and making of drugs is one measure of what it is to be human, it is also an essential human practice that has evoked an unusually wide range of deeply held convictions—both pro and con. For example, some enthusiasts of the mind-altering properties of psychoactive drugs go so far as to attribute the emergence of human cognition and consciousness to primal encounters with exogenous chemicals, particularly indoles of the tryptamine group (McKenna 1992). In a similar vein, some religious scholars have argued that humans' original capacity for numinous or spiritual awareness was sparked by these interactions. Although these lines of thought are speculative at best, and the implied species history seemingly unrecoverable and unstable, they point to one extreme in the range of claims associated with humans and their use of substances for body-mind alteration. At the other and more familiar extreme, almost all types of nontherapeutic drug use at various times and in specific places, whether for sacred or profane purposes, has been widely and routinely decried as deleterious, immoral, and "dehumanizing," if not actually devolutionary, in its consequences. The middle ground of opinion and perspectives along this continuum has been generally constricted and often beleaguered. Yet it is from these dispassionate spaces that knowledge and understanding of indigenous peoples' relations with drugs, in all of their complexities, should be examined. One such vantage point is suggested by the concept of moral geographies.

Drugs and Indigenous Moral Geographies

Modern moralists are generally quick to condemn most forms of nontherapeutic drug use, even if it plays a central role in a culture's spiritual life and collective sense of identity. As Foucault (1965, 1973, 1977, 1978) revealed in multiple fora, much of this censure has gone along iron-handed (but also velvet-gloved) with modernity's dual project of colonizing, regulating, and often criminalizing various states of mind or actions involving human bodies, all resulting in further intrusions of the state. The twentieth-century institutions charged with illicit drug control and those pushing entrepreneurial spirit and ingenuity to new heights in propagating them have been engaged in an escalating war of mutual construction that threatens to entangle all the world's peoples. Among the hundreds of regional conflicts that have flared across the globe since the end of World War II, many have had drug connections—either as causes or consequences. One only has to look to post–Cold War Afghanistan (see chapter 4) or the several-sided free-for-all in Colombia to see the hands of opium and coca largely directing the scripts at this point. It is also in this context that the concept of moral geography seems a useful tool in locating indigenous people on this larger map of both disintegrating and expanding states and nations. The relentless commodification of drugs provides the map's backdrop and their regimes of production and consumption its coordinates.

The notion of indigenous moral geography here parallels and in places intersects with the concept of moral economy as developed by E. P. Thompson (1963) in his epic study, *The Making of the English Working Class*, and in its adaptation by James C. Scott (1976, 1985) for his work on Southeast Asian peasantries. In this tradition, moral economy refers to the responses made by traditional communities and their individual members to threatened or actual disruption of their customary way of life by dominant classes and polities. These responses extend from full-scale *jacqueries* (or peasant uprisings) to lesser and more localized riots and revolts to low intensity but endemic disorder that has earned the term *everyday forms of resistance*.

Space here does not permit more than a few examples of these articulations. First, the question of spatial scale is central. From individual bodies and household domains to communities and locales and on up through regions, nation-states, and realms to the global, the scale at which drugs are collected or produced, consumed or exchanged, enframes identity issues and provides a structure for moral geographies. Of course, the human body is always the primary site of drug use and the final destination of its exchange. In some societies, what it means to be fully human, especially an adult male member of the group, is regular use of complex combinations of drugs. As already discussed, La Barre (1970) identifies a pan–North Asian–New World tradition of great antiquity and extent with shamanistic drug knowledge and use at its core. The clearest survivals of this tradition occur among egalitarian cultures in Amazonia wherein individuals drink a gallon or two of manioc beer, ingest several ounces of powdered coca leaves, and smoke many rolled to-bacco sticks during the course of a day. During the evening they may also regularly inhale powdered plant hallucinogens, and every fortnight or so they might drink in-fusions of extremely strong hallucinogenic preparations with a shaman's assistance. The spatial context of this nocturnal use is usually the communal dwelling. For adult men at least, one's individual, as well as cultural, identity is centrally constructed by these practices. Dominant cultures' suppression of these practices—whether by im-perial polities in pre-Columbian times or by European colonizers since their con-quest of Siberia and the New World—has meant modifications and transformations at the individual and household scales.

At the level of communities and locales, the articulations are often brought into strong relief in the face of outsiders' interest or outright suppression. The Mazatec community of Hauatla, Oaxaca, the famous location of the 1930's "rediscovery" of psilocybin mushroom use in Mexico, became a countercultural pilgrimage site by the 1960s (Feinberg 2003; Wasson 1972). This particular site and situation is one of the better-known destinations in the expanding global geography of drug tourism. Many lesser publicized but well-visited locations, especially in Asia and Latin America, have been subjected to similar disruptions and commodifications of their traditional drug practices. In the late 1990s, Dominica's and St. Vincent's remnant Carib communities were caught up in the U.S.-directed marijuana eradication of-fensive on those islands. It was made even more volatile by the banana trade war at that time. Increasingly, indigenous communities and locales in many parts of the world have been visited by similarly unwanted attention and forced to respond col-lectively.

At more expansive scales—the regional, national, and global—issues of drug production and use have become articulated in webs of significance and conse-quence that largely remove them from effective indigenous agency. Elsewhere I have argued that the plantation production of drug commodities played a central role in the making of the modern world (Mathewson 1991). Starting with sugar—which the anthropologist Sidney Mintz (1985) has aptly termed a "drug food"—modern slavery, plantations, and important elements of capitalism itself were ini-tiated in the Arab Near East a millennium ago. With sugar as the model, tobacco, coffee, tea, and cacao followed in patterns of widespread plantation production and global consumption (Courtwright 2001). Tobacco and cacao in particular were torn from the fabric of New World indigenous cultures and desacralized and commodi-fied. In the past century, much the same has happened with coca—although its pro-duction on clandestine plantations, mostly in Colombia so far, remains highly prob-lematic. The summary execution by FARC (Fuerzas Armadas Revolucionarios de Colombia) guerillas of three North American Amerind activists in Colombia in 1998 seemed to be linked to their presence in a zone of plantation-style coca pro-duction. Even if this were not so, there are many other examples of indigenous peo-ples being caught in the crossfires of the politics of drug wars waged at regional and national levels.

The chapters in this volume offer an important first step toward a more com-prehensive geography of indigenous peoples' relations with drugs. Beyond this, mapping at many scales and modes needs to be done, whether the straightforward cartographies of diffusions and distributions or the more representational terrains of moral geographies and power/knowledge domains. It is an immense, compelling, and critically important subject that somehow until now has largely escaped collation. Speaking for the other editors and contributors, I hope that this volume will lead to other collections, especially to detailed empirical studies of specific cases, along with new efforts at theorizing what must remain one of the last great untheorized topics of its dimensions and implications. Let the mapping begin.

References

Balick, M. J., and P. A. Cox. 1996. *Plants, People, and Culture: The Science of Ethnobotany.* New York: Scientific American Library.

Blue, G. 2000. Opium for China: The British Connection. In Timothy Brook and Bob Tadashi Wakabayashi, eds., *Opium Regimes. China, Britain, and Japan, 1839–1952.* Berkeley: University of California Press, pp. 31–54.

Bodley, J. H. 1994. *Cultural Anthropology: Tribes, States, and the Global System.* Mountain View, CA: Mayfield.

Clay, J. W. 1993. Looking Back to Go Forward: Predicting and Preventing Human Rights Violations. In Marc S. Miller, ed., *State of the Peoples: A Global Human Rights Report on Societies in Danger.* Boston: Beacon, pp. 64–71.

Courtwright, D. T. 2001. *Forces of Habit: Drugs and the Making of the Modern World.* Cambridge, MA: Harvard University Press.

Davis, W. 1985. Hallucinogenic Plants and Their Use in Traditional Societies—An Overview. *Cultural Survival Quarterly* 9(4): 2–5.

Feinberg, B. 2003. *The Devil's Book of Culture: History, Mushrooms, and Caves in Southern Mexico.* Austin: University of Texas Press.

Foucault, M. 1965. *Madness & Civilization: A History of Insanity in the Age of Reason.* New York: Random House.

———. 1973. *The Birth of the Clinic: An Archaeology of Medical Perception.* New York: Pantheon.

———. 1977. *Discipline & Punish: The Birth of the Prison.* New York: Random House.

———. 1978. *The History of Sexuality. Vol. I: An Introduction.* New York: Random House.

La Barre, W. 1964. The Narcotic Complex of the New World. *Diogenes* 48: 125–138.

———. 1970. Old and New World Narcotics: A Statistical Question and an Ethnological Reply. *Economic Botany* 24: 73–80.

———. 1980. *Culture in Context: Selected Writings of Weston La Barre.* Durham, NC: Duke University Press.

Lewin, L. 1931. *Phantastica: Narcotic and Stimulating Drugs—Their Use and Abuse.* New York: E. P. Dutton.

Mathewson, K. 1991. Plantations and Dependencies: Notes on the "Moral Geography" of Global Stimulant Production. In Charles V. Blatz, ed., *Ethics and Agriculture: An Anthology on Current Issues in World Context.* Moscow: University of Idaho Press, pp. 559–567.

McIntosh, I. 2000. Are There Indigenous Peoples in Asia? *Cultural Survival Quarterly*, Fall, pp. 4–7.

McKenna, T. 1992. *The Food of the Gods: The Search for the Original Tree of Knowledge: A Radical History of Plants, Drugs, and Human Evolution.* New York: Bantam.

Minahan, J. 1996. *Nations Without States: A Historical Dictionary of Contemporary National Movements*. Westport, CT: Greenwood.

Mintz, S. W. 1985. *Sweetness and Power: The Place of Sugar in Modern History*. New York: Viking.

Nietschmann, B. Q. 1988. Third World Colonial Expansion: Indonesia, Disguised Invasion of Indigenous Nations. In John H Bodley, ed., *Tribal Peoples and Development Issues: A Global Overview*. Mountain View, CA: Mayfield, pp. 191–207.

Schultes, R. 1963. Hallucinogen Plants of the New World. *Harvard Review* 1: 18–32.

Scott, J. C. 1976. *The Moral Economy of the Peasant: Rebellion and Subsistence in Southeast Asia*. New Haven, CT: Yale University Press.

———. 1985. *Weapons of the Weak: Everyday Forms of Peasant Resistance*. New Haven, CT: Yale University Press.

Stevens, S. 1997. Introduction. In Stan Stevens, ed., *Conservation Through Cultural Survival: Indigenous Peoples and Protected Areas*. Washington, DC: Island Press, pp. 1–11.

Thompson, E. P. 1963. *The Making of the English Working Class*. New York: Random House.

Wasson, R. G. 1972. The Divine Mushroom of Immortality. In Peter T. Furst, ed., *Flesh of the Gods: The Ritual Use of Hallucinogens*. London: George Allen & Unwin., pp. 185–200.

Weil, A., and W. Rosen. 1993. *From Chocolate to Morphine*. New York: Houghton Mifflin.

2

The Stimulus of Prohibition
A Critical History of the
Global Narcotics Trade

Alfred W. McCoy

The current war on drugs being waged by the United States and United Nations rests upon a fundamental misunderstanding of the global narcotics traffic. In 1998, for example, the White House issued a National Drug Control Strategy, proclaiming a 10-year program "to reduce illegal drug use and availability 50 percent by the year 2007," thereby achieving "the lowest recorded drug-use rate in American history." To this end, the U.S. program plans to reduce foreign drug cultivation, shipments from source countries like Colombia, and smuggling in key transit zones. Although this strategy promises a balanced attack on both supply and demand, its ultimate success hinges upon the complete eradication of the international supply of illicit drugs. "Eliminating the cultivation of illicit coca and opium," the document says in a revealing passage, "is the best approach to combating cocaine and heroin availability in the U.S." (U.S. Office of National Drug Control Policy 1998: 1, 23, 28).

Similarly, in 1997 the new head of the United Nations Drug Control Program, Dr. Pino Arlacchi, announced a 10-year program to eradicate all illicit opium and coca cultivation, starting in Afghanistan. Three years later, in the United Nation's *World Drug Report 2000*, he defended prohibition's feasibility by citing China as a case where "comprehensive narcotics control strategies . . . succeeded in eradicating opium between 1949 and 1954"—ignoring the communist coercion that allowed such success. Arlacchi also called for an "end to the psychology of despair" that questions drug prohibition, and insisted that this policy can indeed produce "the eradication of coca and opium poppy production." Turning the page, however, the reader will find a chart showing a sharp rise in world opium production from 500 tons in 1981 to 6,000 tons in 2000—a juxtaposition that seems to challenge Arlacchi's faith in prohibition (Bonner 1997; Wren 1998a, 1998b; United Nations

2000d, 1–2, 24). Examined closely, the United States and United Nations are pursuing a drug control strategy whose success requires not just the reduction but also the total eradication of illicit narcotics cultivation from the face of the globe.

Like the White House, the United Nations Drug Control Program (UNDCP) remains deeply, almost theologically committed to the untested proposition that the prohibition of cultivation is an effective response to the problem of illicit drugs. The Vatican does not debate God's existence in St. Peter's Basilica, nor does the UNDCP entertain evidence of prohibition's failure in its modernist Vienna headquarters. In 1997, for example, the UNDCP drew upon distinguished scholars, its own staff of 300, and thousands of official reports to compile the *World Drug Report*, which avoided two key questions: Has prohibition reduced the production and consumption of illicit drugs since the United Nations adopted its Single Convention on Narcotic Drugs in 1961? If supply has not declined, what has caused the increase in global drug trafficking since the early 1970s when the United States and the United Nations launched an aggressive prohibition effort?

Exploring these questions produces data and insights that challenge the reigning prohibition orthodoxy. In the half century since they launched their worldwide drug prohibition, the United States and United Nations have developed an almost mystical belief in their immaculate intervention in the illicit market. At the most elemental level, however, prohibition is the necessary precondition for the global traffic, creating both highland drug lords and transnational syndicates that control this vast commerce. Prohibition, moreover, forces syndicates to evade interdiction by constantly shifting smuggling routes, encouraging a proliferation of trafficking and consumption. Nor are states benign agents of prohibition. With their vast profits, drug syndicates can corrupt police and compromise governments, transforming enforcement into protection.

When we probe these documents for unexamined assumptions, the U.S. and United Nations prohibition effort seems, at its conceptual core, to assume inelasticity in international narcotics supply and thus to anticipate a simple, causal connection between repression and results. But in the open world after the Cold War, supply has proved surprisingly elastic. In this new world order, repression in one source region, instead of reducing availability, may instead stimulate production of narcotics in another, contributing thereby to an increase in global supply. The demand for drugs of addiction is, by its very nature, relatively inelastic; that is, if the price rises, addicted consumers cut other consumption or try to increase income to maintain their intake. But supply, by contrast, seems elastic; that is, if suppression reduces supply from one area, the global price rises (because of inelastic demand), spurring traders and growers to sell off stocks, old growers to plant more, and new producers or areas to enter production—the latter two responses coming, of course, after a delay of one agricultural season. In effect, for over 50 years the United Nations and United States have been pursuing a supply-control solution to the drug problem in defiance of the basic dynamics of global drug supply.

If recent history is any guide, narcotics production in Asia and the Andes may soon increase to levels that will defeat this war on drugs. Whatever suppression strategy the United States and United Nations might adopt, present trends in narcotics production and consumption indicate that world supply is likely to expand rapidly into the foreseeable future, compromising the aggressive prohibition that both have pursued for the past 30 years.

Since the early 1970s, narcotics production has, in fact, risen relentlessly in Southeast Asia, Central Asia, and Latin America. Despite four U.S. drug wars waged at a cost of nearly $150 billion, the world's illicit opium supply grew fivefold from 1,200 tons in 1971 to 6,100 tons in 1999 (1998: 11; U.S. Department of State 1997: 24–25; United Nations 1998b: ii, 2000a: 49). Similarly, after 15 years of U.S. bilateral eradication in the Andes, coca leaf production doubled to 600,000 tons in 1999 (U.S. Department of State 2000: 55–56). Can the White House really expect narcotics use in the United States to drop 50 percent by 2007 if world supply, following its current trajectory, doubles by that same date?

Driven by these growing supplies of cheap, pure heroin, opiate use is rising in established markets (western Europe and the United States) and spreading rapidly into new markets (China, India, Russia, and eastern Europe). By 2002, illicit drug abuse, largely heroin and amphetamines, was spreading like a pandemic across Asia, producing a record number of drug users—7 million in China, 4 million in Pakistan, 3 million in Iran, and 2 million in Thailand (Reid and Costigan 2002: 11, 103, 162, 172, 215). In the three decades since the U.S. drug war started in 1972, the estimated number of heroin users in the United States has increased over tenfold, from 68,000 to 980,000 (Epstein 1977: 173–177; U.S. General Accounting Office 1996: 2–7; Nieves 2001). More recently, British Columbia needed just a decade to achieve a comparable increase, as shown by a tenfold rise in its heroin overdose deaths during the 1990s (Verhovek 2000). Even if this drug war could somehow reduce drug abuse by eradicating all natural narcotics (opium and coca), criminal syndicates could easily expand the traffic in synthetic drugs that is currently sweeping much of the globe.

The reasons for this dismal prognosis are largely historical. Looking back over opium's modern history, we can discern two successive policy regimes toward narcotics—free trade in the nineteenth century and prohibition in the twentieth. For two centuries, narcotics traffic has operated through an extraordinary political economy shaped by the interaction of states and empires within changing global systems. In the nineteenth century, European powers deployed coercion, market and military, both to promote and to prohibit opium in Asia—promoting opium's production for trade and its consumption for colonial revenues, but prohibiting any cultivation that weakened their monopolies. At this high tide of empire, free trade in opium encouraged a steady increase in world production, which peaked at 41,000 tons in 1906. By then, China's own opium harvest of 35,000 tons was comparable to Colombia's coffee crop of 55,000 tons, giving opium a political economy similar to other stimulants such as tobacco, coffee, and tea (International Opium Commission 1909: 44–66, 356; U.S. Department of Commerce 1916: 713).

In a word, opium had become a commodity—not merely a trade good but also a building block of modern material life. As the anthropologist Sidney Mintz (1985: 214) argued in his classic work, *Sweetness and Power*, "The first sweetened cup of hot tea to be drunk by an English worker was a significant historical event because it prefigured the transformation of an entire society, a total remaking of its economic and social basis." To this insight we might add that, from the late eighteenth century onward, tea and opium became integral to an expanding world trade—embedding their production in the highland economies of Asia and their consumption in the urban cultures of Asia and the West. In short, by the time drug prohibition began, opium had already achieved the economic scale and social ramifications needed to resist suppression.

In the twentieth century, the world powers, ignoring opium's character as a commodity, moved resolutely to prohibit all narcotics use. When the prohibition movement gained momentum in the late nineteenth century, most societies around the globe still used drugs legally for medicine and recreation—kava in Melanesia, betel in Southeast Asia, opium in Asia, coca in the Andes, khat in East Africa, alcohol in Europe, and tobacco almost everywhere. With the rise of the temperance movement in the late nineteenth century, Christian moralism and Social Darwinism merged to stigmatize all drug use. Between 1909 and 2000, the international community went through several cycles of negotiation, diplomatic convention, and domestic legislation to create a prohibition regime of ever-widening and deepening powers, simultaneously spanning the globe and penetrating the human body.

Under the Anglo-Chinese treaty of 1907, Britain phased out India's opium exports to China; Peking, in turn, began domestic poppy eradication. Between 1906 and 1908, the United States outlawed all opium use in its Philippine colony and then, a year later, launched global drug diplomacy by convening the International Opium Convention at Shanghai. Under the Hague Opium Convention of 1912 and a parallel League of Nations convention in 1925, the great powers signed treaties that banned the nonmedical trade in narcotics and encouraged signatories to pass parallel domestic legislation. In the decades following World War I, this global prohibition campaign produced a sharp decline in the legal opium trade, but it also created an illicit market in prohibited drugs that fueled the growth of criminal syndicates in Europe, America, and Asia.

After World War II, the United Nations inherited the League's drug control efforts and negotiated a succession of conventions that expanded enforcement and raised the number of prohibited drugs from just 17 in 1931 to 245 by 1995. The 1961 Single Convention on Narcotic Drugs created a "streamlined control machinery" to restrict any production above "the amount needed for medical and scientific purposes." Over the next 40 years, the United Nations expanded this prohibition effort with conventions that banned psychotropic drugs (1971), imposed strict limits on opium production (1972), promoted police cooperation against drug smuggling and money laundering (1988), and created mechanisms to fight transnational organized crime (2000). Most recently, after a Special Session of the United Nations General Assembly in June 1998, attended by 185 states, the United Nations adopted the Convention Against Transnational Organized Crime to launch an assault on "illegal drugs and its associated threats to human security" by allowing states "legal force to deprive drug traffickers of ill-gotten financial gains and freedom of movement." Through these conventions, the international community has created an arsenal of coercive powers to extirpate every aspect of illegal drugs, from cultivation to traffic and consumption (United Nations 1997: 162–163; 2000d: 5, 13–14, 143–148).

The United States has launched a parallel domestic prohibition, passing the Harrison Act in 1914 to restrict opium use and the Volstead Act in 1920 to prohibit alcohol. After the Treasury Department's prohibition unit collapsed from corruption and alcohol prohibition was repealed in 1933, the United States continued the campaign against illicit drugs through the Federal Bureau of Narcotics, the first of several agencies that evolved into the Drug Enforcement Administration (Drug Enforcement Administration). In the early 1970s, President Richard Nixon declared a "war on drugs," expanding U.S. prohibition beyond its borders through bilateral operations in the Asian opium zone. A decade later, President Ronald Reagan redirected the U.S. drug war toward domestic enforcement and coca eradication in the Andes, a policy followed by all his successors. Between 1981 and 1994, funds for supply-side controls—international interdiction and domestic enforcement—represented 80 percent of America's antidrug effort, leaving little for treatment or education (United Nations 1997, 331). In 2000, President William Clinton expanded the drug war with his $1.3 billion Plan Colombia—an emphasis on enforcement further exaggerated by his successor George W. Bush, who promised, in February 2002, to cut drug abuse by 25 percent through aggressive law enforcement (A. Lewis 1996; Wren 1996; Bonner 1997; Schemo and Golden 1998; *New York Times* 1996, 2001, February 27, May 9; Marquis 2002a). At the start of the twenty-first century, the United States was fighting the drug war at home by creating the world's largest prison population and abroad by defoliating mountain farms in Asia and the Andes.

Our current prohibition policy is thus the culmination of an ambitious, century-long experiment in social control that, by the end of the twentieth century, had forged a formidable prohibition regime (Nadelmann 1990). Using a nineteenth-century concept of coercive social reform, the world's powers launched a global program in the early twentieth century whose methods have survived, largely unchanged and unexamined, into the twenty-first. This succession of policy regimes, from free trade to prohibition, has spawned a global traffic that may well survive any attempt at suppression—short of near-perfect coercion. By trying to crush global market forces with the raw power of paramilitary coercion, this prohibition policy has produced a concatenation of unwanted, even counterproductive outcomes—rising drug production, increased consumption, powerful crime syndicates, police corruption, and political collusion.

In trying to eradicate a commodity whose deep economic roots gave it an exceptional resilience, the prohibition regime, from its start in the 1920s, drove opium into an illicit market that soon adapted to suppression—transferring its trade from colonial merchants to criminal syndicates, and shifting cultivation from lowland peasants to hill-tribe farmers in the remote reaches of Asia and the Andes. After World War II, Asia's opium cultivation migrated from the plains of northern India and plateaus of central China to the mountain margins of Southwest Asia, Southeast Asia, and Mexico. In this slow shift, highland minorities on two continents were drawn into the global economy through both production of illicit commodities and, with equal force, later attempts at their suppression. In the decades after World War II, drug prohibition fostered a global illicit economy that would fund criminal syndicates, highland warlords, ethnic liberation movements, terrorist networks, and covert operations. Failing to understand the character of these commodities, the international community has attempted suppression with a range of ineffective, ultimately counterproductive policies that include arresting consumers, pursuing dealers, and harassing growers.

All these measures derive from a law enforcement model that assumes inelasticities in the illicit drug industry and thus an axiomatic correlation between repression and results. When states have proven capable of perfect coercion, as in colonial Asia or Communist China, determined suppression can have a decisive, dramatic impact upon the supply of illicit drugs. Indeed, for most of the twentieth century, colonial and communist states used coercive mechanisms that made prohibition effective, at least within their limited boundaries.

By the end of the twentieth century, however, a waning of these coercive capacities—colonial, national, and communist—opened Asia, and perhaps the entire globe, to unbridled economic and social forces for the first time in two centuries. In the last half of the twentieth century, there have been two broad countervailing trends that have influenced the capacity to control illicit narcotics—declining coercive capacities within individual states and a rising system of international sanctions. Whereas multilateral trade agencies have loosened restraints, internal and international, on the free movement of goods, capital, and skilled labor, the United States and United Nations have been struggling to replace the fading coercive powers of individual states with a global prohibition regime of treaties, multilateral agencies, and international cooperation. As the United Nations noted in its 1997 *World Drug Report*, the world is facing "two seemingly contradictory aims, namely, trade liberalization and the effective control of illicit drug traffic" (United Nations 1997: 25). Moreover, the transition beyond the last of these coercive political orders, communism, has sparked a recrudescence of primordial political forces—religion, ethnicity, and regionalism—that has further weakened states and stimulated trafficking across much of the Eurasian landmass. At this historical juncture, the United States and United Nations have intensified their supply-side prohibition, focusing on the growers, traders, and smugglers of illicit narcotics.

More broadly, in a resilient global drug market, repression has proven counterproductive—not simply failing to suppress the global opium traffic but actually stimulating production. Effective repression requires both elastic demand (i.e., rising prices reduce consumption) and inelastic supply (i.e., rising prices do not increase supply). But in the real world of illicit drug trafficking, supply is surprisingly elastic, responding quickly to price stimulus. In an era of global markets, this policy also assumes closed, localized markets. That is, the prohibition regime operates on the supposition that, when the force of law and police are applied, the targeted criminal behavior or illicit commodity is squeezed and then crushed in the grip of repression. These dynamics work, for example, when local police attack drug distribution within the spatial confines of an urban neighborhood—arresting dealers, seizing drugs, and securing strategic locations. But when the same model is applied to the international heroin trade, the effort often fails because there are no effective limits to either supply or demand. As the vice jaws of coercion tighten, supply and demand slip sideways into a spatial infinity. Since opium can be grown in any temperate or highland area, crop suppression simply shifts cultivation elsewhere within the vastness of the Eurasian landmass or to other continents, such as South America. And since the human brain's chemistry makes all humanity potential addicts, repression merely forces traffickers to seek new markets in another neighborhood, nation, or continent. With such flexible market constraints, the blunt baton of repression has become the wand of stimulus, pushing consumption and production into ever-widening spheres and thereby compounding the global drug problem.

If we survey the wreckage of the recent past, it seems as if prohibition has not simply failed to curb the illicit traffic but has actually contributed to an incessant increase in global drug supply. In each of America's drug wars, from Anatolia in the 1970s to the Andes in the 1990s, prohibition has produced unintended outcomes, transforming localized suppression into global stimulus. As in all agricultural markets, legal or illegal, a shortfall in supply without any reduction in demand raises the price, encouraging increased production elsewhere around the globe. In the 1990s, United Nations researchers observed this economic effect operating at the micro level among opium growers in Afghanistan and Laos (United Nations 1998d, 1999b: 12, 22). Even semiliterate hill farmers, subsisting from small plots of opium in these remote highlands, adjusted their planting every season in response to market stimuli—whether from drought, defoliation, political disruption, or rising demand; whether from nearby districts, neighboring nations, or far-off continents. As long as demand and prices remain at current levels in wealthy nations, traders will enter almost any potential production area with wads of currency to elicit supply that can meet that demand. Over the past 30 years, the U.S. war on drugs, in alliance with the United Nations, has simply served to push production, processing, and smuggling of illicit drugs back and forth across the globe's three critical trafficking regions—between Turkey and Laos in the Asian opium zone, from Bolivia to Colombia in the Andes coca belt, and from southern Florida to northern Mexico along the U.S. border. At each turn in these many shifts, consumption, production, and corruption have ratcheted upward. In sum, we can speak, with a certain authority, of a stimulus of prohibition.

Prohibition has contributed to the growth of drug trafficking as one of the world's largest industries. In the late 1990s, the United Nations reported that the global traffic in illicit drugs is a $400 billion industry with 180 million users (4.2 percent of the world's adults) and 8 percent of world trade—larger than the trade in textiles, steel, or automobiles. Among these 180 million consumers, some 13.5 million used opiates, 14 million took cocaine, 29 million abused amphetamines, and the rest consumed either marijuana or synthetics. Compounding the health implications of illicit drug use, by 1996 an estimated 5 to 10 percent of all HIV infections was being spread by intravenous drug use (Wren 1997b; United Nations 1997: 31, 32, 124; 2000d: 70).

Freed from formal regulation by prohibition, this vast illicit enterprise pays informal taxes to the police, customs officials, the military, and politicians across the globe, compromising the integrity of states in both the First World and the Third. With its extraordinary profits, the drug traffic has proven enormously corrupting of the police in cities as diverse as Sydney, Bangkok, Hong Kong, Manila, New York, Marseilles, and Istanbul. In most cases, corruption is limited to individual officers or police squads, but unless checked, it can metastasize, transforming enforcement into protection. In extreme cases—New York in the 1960s, Hong Kong in the 1970s, Sydney in the 1980s, and Mexico in the 1990s—criminal syndicates and corrupt police officers operate in symbiosis, with the police protecting traffickers from investigation and syndicates providing police with suspects from rival groups to sustain an aura of effective enforcement. By the late 1980s, for example, systemic corruption in Mexico's federal police officers allowed traffickers "protection and warning information" while giving the police "credit, praise, and promotions" (Lupsha 1992: 182).

Whereas police corruption often appears in cities with high drug consumption, it does not usually ramify beyond the locality or region. By contrast, in zones of production and processing the illicit traffic can, through its macroeconomic weight and strategic influence, transform the national government into a "narco-state." During the 1990s, drug syndicates moved from the social and geographical margins of key source countries—Colombia, Burma, Afghanistan, and Pakistan—to compromise law enforcement, neutralize national agencies, and win regional power for rebels or warlords. By 1988, Pakistan's heroin industry was grossing an estimated $8 billion annually, half the size of the legal economy; military intelligence directed the traffic; and top dealers determined parliamentary elections (Griffin 2001: 145). Similarly, by 1994, Mexico's cocaine cartels were paying bribes totaling $460 million, more than the attorney general's budget, and were grossing $30 billion, four times the value of the country's oil exports (Andreas 2000: 60–62). Clearly, both states had gone beyond simple police corruption. Drugs had achieved the multifaceted mix of economic and institutional influence that defines a narco-state.

Complicating these attempts at narcotics control, state security services have often allied with highland warlords and transnational criminals, bartering protection for their clandestine services. At the Cold War's start in the late 1940s, the Iron Curtain fell along an Asian opium zone from Turkey to Thailand, drawing the United States Central Intelligence Agency (CIA) into these remote, rugged borderlands to wage covert wars that became inadvertent catalysts for the region's drug traffic. During each of these decade-long operations—Burma in the 1950s, Laos in the 1960s, and Afghanistan in the 1980s—Asia's tribal warlords used the agency's protection to become well-armed drug lords, a transformation that CIA operatives generally ignored. In the aftermath of these secret wars, their battlegrounds became covert war wastelands where only opium seemed to flower, creating regions and whole nations with a lasting dependence on the global drug traffic. The peculiar character of covert warfare has denied its battlefields the usual forms of postwar reconstruction. Since these secret wars were fought outside conventional diplomacy, their resolution remained beyond the realm of international intercourse, forcing these societies to expand opium production as a substitute for postwar reconstruction aid. After CIA intervention in the 1950s, Burma's opium production rose from 18 tons in 1958 to 600 tons in 1970. During the CIA's covert war of the 1980s, Afghanistan's harvest increased from an estimated 100 tons in 1971 to 2,000 tons in 1991 (U.S. Cabinet Committee of International Narcotics Control 1972: 10–11, 47; U.S. Department of State 1984: 4; Chao 1987: 57; *Geopolitical Drug Dispatch* January 1992: 1, 3). A decade after the Cold War's end, the CIA's three main covert battlegrounds—Afghanistan, Burma, and Laos—were, in that order, the world's three leading opium producers. During the Cold War, a steady increase in illicit opium and coca cultivation thus sprang from a confluence of global forces: an irrepressible market in illicit narcotics, covert alliances with drug lords, and the unintended stimulus of drug prohibition.

During the 1990s, the collapse of the Iron Curtain and spread of drug consumption knitted the globe together in a cat's cradle of trafficking routes and criminal connections. Both cocaine and heroin are processed near their highland cultivation zones, requiring long-distance smuggling to markets that makes shipments vulnerable to seizure. Even so, only 10 to 15 percent of illicit heroin is seized worldwide. By contrast, amphetamines are usually manufactured close to markets, rendering its traffic impervious to suppression and making it a likely winner in any future drug war (United Nations 1997: 25). Illicit drugs produce extraordinary profits for corruption and criminality. In the mid-1990s, the price for a kilogram of heroin rose from $2,870 wholesale in Pakistan to $290,000 when retailed on the streets of America. The cost of a kilogram of cocaine was $1,500 wholesale in Bolivia and $110,000 if sold as cocaine powder in the United States. Freed from the costs and risks of long-distance smuggling, the manufacturer's profit on a kilogram of amphetamines was, in the late 1990s, $30,000—twice that for cocaine (United Nations 1997: 25, 126). According to a 1997 United Nations report, "highly centralized," transnational crime groups control most of the global drug trade. With some 3.3 million members worldwide, criminal syndicates active in the global traffic include Japanese *yakuza* clans, with up to 10,000 members each; Chinese triads, with a total membership of 170,000 divided into tight hierarchies; and Colombian drug cartels, with their distinctive vertical integration (United Nations 1997: 132).

In its broad sweep from past to future, this analysis will necessarily focus on just two narcotics until we reach the 1990s, when a third class of illicit drugs intrudes. Among the world's many natural drugs—alcohol, tobacco, marijuana, betel, kava, khat, and peyote—only opium and coca have been, alternatively, commodified and then prohibited. Significantly, the contradictory market dynamics of prohibition that first appeared in Asia's opium highlands over the span of a century have, in the last two decades, been repeated in coca fields along the Andes. In the future, these patterns may recur with the rising global traffic in amphetamines.

Reflecting Asia's venerable commercial history, opium, an extract from the poppy plant (*Papaver somniferum*), has been cultivated and traded along a mountain rim reaching 5,000 miles across Asia for over a millennium—first as a legal drug and then, in the twentieth century, as an illicit narcotic. Opium appears in ancient Assyrian, Egyptian, Greek, and Roman pharmacopoeia dating back to the Bronze Age (Merlin 1984: 96, 153–157, 217, 256, 273–277). In 1805, E. Merck & Company of Darmstadt, Germany, extracted morphine from raw opium, and in 1898 the Bayer Company of Elberfeld, Germany, coined the trade name Heroin for the legal marketing of diacetylmorphine, a compound of morphine and the common chemical acetic anhydride (United Nations 1953: 3–4, 6). In 1996, over 96 percent of the world's 280,000 hectares of illicit opium was still found in an Asian opium zone concentrated around the Golden Triangle (Burma, Thailand, and Laos) and the Golden Crescent (Afghanistan, Pakistan, and Iran). This sprawling zone produced 5,000 tons of raw opium of which one-third was consumed locally and the rest transformed into some 300 tons of illicit heroin for the international traffic (United Nations 1997: 18; U.S. Department of State 1999: 22–23).

The coca bush also has a venerable history of domestication in pre-Columbian South America. But the narcotic properties of its leaf were little known beyond the Andes until its listing in Lamarck's 1786 botanical encyclopedia as *Erythroxylon coca*. In contrast to opium's three centuries as a global commodity, coca's commercial extract, cocaine, has been traded for little more than a century—first as a legal pharmaceutical in the late nineteenth century and, since the early 1980s, as an illicit narcotic (Thornton 1983: 36–37). In 1996, over 98 percent of the world's 220,000 hectares of coca was still concentrated in the Andes (Colombia, Peru, and Bolivia) where a harvest of 300,000 tons of coca leaf yielded 1,000 tons of illicit cocaine (United Nations 1997: 18). In effect, the patterns set in the Asian opium trade, both its legal and illicit phases, have been repeated, years or even decades later, in the Andes coca zone.

Like heroin and cocaine, synthetic stimulants were a creation of the modern pharmaceutical industry. Amphetamine was first synthesized in 1887, Ecstasy (MDMA) in 1914, and methamphetamine in 1919 (United Nations 1997: 39). As illicit amphetamine abuse spread in the 1960s, the United Nations enacted its 1971 Convention on Psychotropic Substances, extending the prohibition of natural drugs to synthetics. Since the mid-1980s, the illicit manufacture of synthetic drugs, largely amphetamine-type substances, has produced what the United Nations called "a wave of synthetic abuse." During the 1990s, worldwide seizures, an apt index of abuse, increased at the rapid rate of 18 percent per annum, and the use of synthetics surpassed both heroin and cocaine. Like cocaine in the 1980s, amphetamines became "the key growth sector in the global drug market" during the 1990s, with 41 percent of its seizures in East and Southeast Asia, 38 percent in western Europe, and 16 percent in North America (United Nations 1997: 19, 23, 43, 129; 2000d: 35, 51).

Predicting the shape of the future from the confusion of the present remains an uncertain enterprise. With the end of Cold War, it seems possible that a peculiar complex of historical factors may continue to drive an explosive increase in Asia's opium cultivation and amphetamine production. During the Cold War, much of Asia's prime opium land, markets, and smuggling routes were closed to global forces under Communist rule in China and the Soviet Union. With the collapse of the Iron Curtain, market opportunity and postsocialist poverty have combined in ways that are creating vast new sources of supply and demand for Asia's illicit opium and amphetamines.

If the rapid increase in the global drug supply of the past 30 years persists into the twenty-first century, it may challenge the underlying rationality of prohibition orthodoxy and force an reexamination of the illicit drug problem. Through an analytical history of the Asian opium trade and then a comparison with the Andes coca zone, let us see whether the shape of the future can be found in the past.

Free Trade in Opium

Surveying the history of opium in Asia over the last millennium, we can discern three distinct phases shaped by both the scale and the quality of its commerce.

From its origins in the eastern Mediterranean, opium spread through long-distance trade to China by the eighth century, eventually creating by the nineteen century an Asian opium zone that extended for over 5,000 miles across the continent's mountain spine.

Then, in the sixteenth century, India's Mughal empire developed a modest commerce in opium as a recreational drug, though its use was still largely limited to the medicinal. Starting in the late seventeenth century, however, European shipments of smoking opium between India and China created one of the world's most lucrative trade triangles, transforming the drug from folk medication into a global commodity. Moreover, in the late nineteenth century, mass opium consumption grew rapidly in the West, amplified by the medical use of morphine and the later popularization of heroin after its commercial introduction in 1898.

Finally, in the early twentieth century, the major European powers prohibited narcotic drugs—a social experiment whose scale and costs are still not fully appreciated. During the interwar period from 1925 to 1941, the United States and the League of Nations led a global campaign that sharply reduced legal opiate cultivation and processing in both Asia and Europe. In this void between falling supply and constant demand, criminal syndicates quickly emerged to take control of the illicit drug traffic in both China and the West. Starting in the early 1950s, Asia's opium production recovered steadily, climbing to 1,200 tons over the next 20 years. Driven by rising demand and the changing geopolitics of the Cold War, Asian opium production soon reached 3,700 tons by 1989 (U.S. Cabinet Committee of International Narcotics Control 1972: 10–11; U.S. Department of State 1997: 24–25). Most recently, after the collapse of the Soviet bloc's repressive regimes and a parallel decline of dictatorships in the Americas, Asia's harvest soared to 6,100 tons in 1999, fueling a global proliferation of heroin abuse.

Within this larger history, there are two critical phases in opium's modern history—an expanding free trade in drugs from the late eighteenth to the late nineteenth century and then, during the twentieth, an aggressive attempt at prohibition. Since the juxtaposition of these policy regimes seems to be the source of the current growth in both supply and demand, each merits a closer study.

When European trading companies reached Asia in the sixteenth century, opium was just emerging as a significant commodity within intra-Asian trade. During this period, residents of Persia and India began eating and drinking opium mixtures as a recreational euphoric. Indeed, under the reign of Akbar (1556–1605), the great Mughal state of north India relied upon opium production as a significant source of revenue. Although cultivation covered the whole empire, it was concentrated in two main areas—upriver from Calcutta along the Ganges Valley for Bengal opium and upcountry from Bombay in the west for Malwa opium (Owen 1934: 5–6).

The rise of Europe's mercantile empires after the seventeenth century slowly transformed Asia's opium trade, amplifying its scale and changing its dominant use to recreational—adding a new dimension to a drug whose use had been, for several millennia, largely medicinal. Since opium combined the inelastic demand of a basic foodstuff like rice with the high margins of luxuries like cloves or pepper, it was the epoch's ideal trade good. Over the next two centuries, Asia's commercial history revolved in large measure around the marriage of India's rising opium production to

China's limitless consumption. European empires and their trading companies mediated and profited from their role as brokers in this vast trade.

In the 1640s, the Dutch East India Company (VOC) entered the India-China opium trade, stimulating both supply and demand. As Dutch colonials negotiated monopoly marketing rights for Java's populous districts, their Company's opium imports from India rose sharply from 617 kilograms in 1660 to 73 metric tons only 25 years later. Buying opium cheap in India and selling dear in Java allowed the Company a 400 percent profit on its 1679 shipments. By the end of the century, the Dutch dominated the India-China opium trade, while continuing substantial shipments of Indian opium—for example, 87 tones in 1699—for distribution in Java and the Indies. Opium was no longer a luxury or folk medicine, and its trade was starting to achieve the scale that would, over the next two centuries, make it a major commodity (Prakash 1988: 145–157; van Ours 1995: 261–279; Richards 1981: 59–62).

In the late eighteenth century, opium's commodification accelerated. Under the doctrine of mercantilism, successful European colonial ventures in Asia somehow involved the commercialization of drugs—whether caffeine, nicotine, or opiates. Starting in the late eighteenth century, European trade transformed these drugs from luxury goods into commodities of mass consumption, making them integral to the economies and lifestyles of both Asian and Atlantic nations. The Dutch controlled Java's coffee exports, the Spanish established their tobacco monopoly in the Philippines, and the British dominated the Bengal opium trade. Through mercantilism's fusion of political and economic power, the British East India Company raised exports of Indian opium to China from 13 tons in 1729 to 2,558 tons in 1839. Compounding the trade's profitability, China prohibited the drug from 1729 to 1858, thus conceding European merchants a de facto monopoly (Greenberg 1951: 221; Owen 1934: 51–52, 113–145; Rowntree 1905: 284–286).

The modern era in Asia's opium trade began in 1773 when Warren Hastings, the governor-general of Bengal, established a colonial monopoly that made the drug India's leading export. Over the next 130 years, Britain actively promoted opium exports to China, defying Chinese drug laws and fighting two wars, in 1840 and 1858, to open the Middle Kingdom's opium market for European merchants. Under new procedures introduced in 1797, the East India Company and the colonial state that succeeded it controlled opium from cultivation through processing to export. Bengal's opium country stretched for 500 miles across the Ganges River Valley, with over a million registered farmers growing poppy plants exclusively for the Company (Strachey 1903: 133–142).

For its first quarter century, this system ensured prosperity for British India and a stable opium supply for China. Opium remained a staple of colonial finances, providing from 6 to 15 percent of British India's tax revenues during the nineteenth century (Owen 1934: vii; Richards 1981: 66). More important, these opium exports were an essential component of a lucrative India-China-Britain triangular trade central to London's commercial empire. Trade figures for the 1820s, for example, show that this triangular exchange was large and well balanced: first, £22 million in Indian opium and cotton to China; next, £20 million in Chinese tea to Britain; and then £24 million in British textiles and machinery back to India. In managing this trade, the East India Company prized stability above profit and for over 20 years held India's opium exports at 4,000 chests (with 140 pounds of opium each)—just enough to finance its purchase of China's tea crop (Chung 1987: 114–130; Richards 1981: 67–69).

The system's remarkable success was the cause of its downfall. Profits attracted competitors, and the company's refusal to raise Bengal's opium exports beyond the annual quota of 4,000 chests left a vast unmet demand for drugs in China. As demand drove the price per chest upward from 115 rupees in 1799 to 2,428 rupees just 15 years later, the East India Company's monopoly on Bengal opium faced strong competition from Turkey and areas of western India outside British control.

The company's most daring rivals were the Americans. Barred from bidding at the Calcutta auctions, Yankee traders loaded their first cargoes of Turkish opium at Smyrna in 1805 and sailed them around the tip of Africa to China. Within a decade, opium made up 30 percent of all U.S. cargoes reaching China (Stelle 1940: 427–442). Although the Americans increased their shipments from 102 chests in 1805 to 1,428 in 1830, their largest cargoes were still just a quarter of the 5,672 chests the British brought from Bengal (Greenberg 1951: 221). Determined to defend their monopoly, in 1831 the company's directors decided to promote unlimited production in Bengal, thereby producing opium "at a price which would make competition unprofitable." Within the decade, 15 new opium districts opened inside India, doubling cultivation to 176,000 acres (Owen 1934: 105–108; Richards 1981: 65).

When the East India Company lost its charter in 1834, the informal regulation of the China opium trade collapsed, allowing merchant captains free reign and launching a fleet of new opium clippers (Lubbock 1914: 382–383). Among the 95 clippers in the Calcutta-to-Canton fleet, Calcutta's Cowasjee family owned six; the Americans of Russell & Co. had eight; and the British giants, Dent and Jardine, operated 27 (Stackpole 1954: 34–43; Owen 1934: 183–193; Lubbock 1914: 382–384). India's export boom flooded the China coast with illicit opium, rending the fragile political fabric that had veiled the smuggling trade for decades. As the company's grip weakened, China's opium imports increased tenfold—from 270 tons in 1820 to 2,555 tons 20 years later (Owen 1934: 113–145; Greenberg 1951: 221). Opium addiction spread rapidly, involving some 3 million Chinese by the 1830s and provoking anguish among the British clergy (Thelwall 1839: 13).

After Britain won the Second Opium War and forced China to legalize the drug in 1858, opium became a major global commodity, traded on the scale of stimulants such as coffee and tea. In the aftermath of China's legalization, smugglers became registered importers, plodding steamships displaced fast clippers, and state monopolies replaced private traders. As addiction spread throughout China, imports of Indian opium rose from 4,800 tons in 1859 to 6,700 tons 20 years later. After peaking in 1880, Indian imports declined slowly for the rest of the century as cheaper, China-grown opium began to supplant the high-grade Bengal brands (Rowntree 1905: 286–287).

To reduce the specie drain of escalating European imports, China legalized opium in 1858 and encouraged local cultivation, which spread rapidly in the country's southwest, particularly in Szechwan and Yunnan provinces (Adshead 1966:

98–99). In 1881, the British consul at Yichang estimated the total opium production in the southwest at 13,525 tons, a figure that at first seemed incredible (Owen 1934: 266–267). Twenty-five years later, however, official statistics showed that Szechwan and Yunnan were in fact producing 19,100 tons, equivalent to 54 percent of China's total harvest (International Opium Commission 1909: 56–57). At its peak in 1906, China harvested 35,000 tons of opium and imported 4,000 more to supply 13.5 million addicts, or 27 percent of its adult males—a level of mass addiction unequaled by any other nation. At 35,000 tons, China's annual opium harvest was similar in size to Japan's tea trade (31,000 tons), Brazil's cocoa crop (39,000 tons), and Colombia's coffee production (55,000 tons). Elsewhere along the Asian zone, opium, much of it destined for markets in China and Southeast Asia, became Iran's leading export by 1890 and provided farmers three times the income they could earn from staple food crops (International Opium Commission 1909: 44–66, 356; U.S. Department of Commerce 1916: 713; Rey 1963: 44–46; Issawi 1972: 238–240). By the time Britain formally abandoned its advocacy of the drug trade in 1907, opium had become a global commodity.

The Southeast Asian opium trade was another creation of European colonialism. During the nineteenth century, licensed opium dens became a unique Southeast Asian institution, sustaining mass addiction and generating substantial revenues. In 1905–1906, for example, opium sales provided 16 percent of all taxes for the Netherlands Indies, 20 percent for Siam, and 53 percent for British Malaya (International Opium Commission 1909: 359–365). In 1930, Southeast Asia had 6,441 government opium dens, serving in that year 272 tons of opium to 542,100 registered smokers. Opium use, legal and illicit, was found throughout the region, but its spread was uneven. There were no legal dens in the Philippines after the United States banned opium in 1908. By contrast, French Indochina had 3,500 licensed "opium divans," or 1 for every 1,500 adult males, and was home to 125,200 opium smokers, or 23 percent of the region's addicts. Southeast Asia's only independent state, the Kingdom of Siam, earned 14 percent of its tax revenues by selling 84 tons of opium through 972 licensed dens to 164,300 opium smokers, the largest addict population in Southeast Asia (League of Nations 1937: 72–75). In no other region of the world did so many governments promote mass drug abuse with such unanimity of means and moral certitude.

Although Southeast Asian states promoted opium consumption, they used their coercive powers to suppress both cultivation and smuggling. During the nineteenth century, the rapid growth of the India-China opium trade had sparked an eruption of maritime piracy and mountain banditry. As the volume of opium sailing on the Calcutta-to-Canton route started rising after 1800, pirate fleets appeared at the entrances, the vulnerable choke points, to the uncharted vastness of the South China Sea. Malay chiefs at its southern entrance off Borneo and Chinese villagers in its northern waters near Hainan launched pirate fleets to prey upon the unarmed British and Indian merchantmen (Pringle 1970: 46–96; Murray 1987, 1995: 209–212). By the 1860s, the British navy had swept piracy from these sea-lanes to create a secure maritime zone that stretched from the Suez Canal, through the Straits of Malacca, all the way to Shanghai.

But further north in the mountains that arched from Central Asia to southern

China, highland bandits and smugglers eluded colonial controls, undercutting Southeast Asia's state monopolies. To maximize revenue, the region's monopolies imported low-cost Indian opium and then marked it up severalfold for sale to consumers—creating both wide profit margins and a strong demand for cheaper smuggled drugs. Since local cultivation would mask contraband, mainland states along China's border tried to suppress tribal cultivation and intercept smugglers' caravans along their frontiers. In this attempt to seal their borders with China, French and Thai officials found themselves at war with the hardy Muslim traders from its southwestern province, Yunnan. With their strings of highland horses and formidable paramilitary skills, the Muslims, known as Panthays or Haw, became the logistic link between the poppy fields of southern China and the illicit opium dens of urban Southeast Asia (Yegar 1966: 80–82; Forbes 1987: 1–47, 1988: 91–95). After 1900, Siam and Indochina found that this overland smuggling reduced their opium revenues significantly. French officials formed "a special surveillance corps covering a wide area" along the China-Vietnam border and attacked 17 armed caravans with 15.5 tons of opium, equivalent to 22 percent of government sales (League of Nations 1930: 29–30). Similarly, the Dutch opium monopoly on Java, a model of colonial efficiency, promoted a rigorous suppression of seaborne smuggling (Rush 1990: 65–82).

Despite its mass consumption, Southeast Asia remained a minor opium producer in the decades before World War II. Even at its peak in the 1920s, Southeast Asia's 60-ton harvest was dwarfed by the 6,380 tons produced across the border in China (League of Nations 1923, 1930). In 1936, for example, the Shan States of Burma harvested only 8 tons of raw opium, whereas Laos and northern Vietnam together produced 7.5 tons in 1940 (League of Nations 1940: 42; Circular no. 875-SAE 1942: 115). Reflecting the coercive capacities of its colonial states, Southeast Asia did not develop widespread poppy cultivation until the late 1950s, more than 80 years after China.

Like sugar before it, opium's growth as a commodity penetrated far more deeply into modern societies than trade statistics and tax revenues, changing diet and culture. In the late eighteenth and early nineteenth centuries, southeastern China suffered an acute caloric crisis, and opium's quality as an appetite suppressant may have made its mass consumption viable or even economically rational in times of extreme hardship. Similarly, the spread of mass addiction in the Western industrial nations in the late nineteenth century was part of a new diet sustained by a global trade in proteins and stimulants. After several centuries of constant dietary habits, English consumption of sugar jumped fourfold from 1850 to 1900 while tea increased threefold in the same period (Hobsbawm 1968: 15, 55–56, 119, 311). Similarly, in the United States, coffee consumption rose nearly threefold between 1865 and 1902, while sugar use jumped fourfold (U.S. Department of Commerce and Labor 1911: 536–537, 540). In sum, the simple eighteenth-century diet of milled grains had given way to one spiced with large quantities of protein (eggs and beef), glucose (sugar), and stimulants (coffee and tea). If such an energized diet could be used to stimulate the body during a long working day, then narcotics could relax it in the short hours of rest. In parallel with the growth of sugar and coffee, American consumption of opium—driven by the legal marketing of narcotics as patent medicines—rose over fourfold from the 1840s to the 1890s, and the number of addicts peaked at 313,000 in 1896 (Musto 1973: 5; Courtwright 1982: 9–28). In the United Kingdom, sales of patent medicines, most of them opium-based, increased almost sevenfold between 1850 and 1905 (Parssinen 1983: 32–33). Significantly, the annual English consumption of opium per 1,000 population increased sevenfold, from 1.3 pounds in 1827 to over 10 pounds a half century later (Berridge and Edwards 1987: 21–35, 274).

The Prohibition Regime

The global movement for prohibition of narcotics began in the 1870s when the Protestant churches of England and America, reviving the tactics of their earlier antislavery campaign, launched a moral crusade against the opium trade. For the first time in the modern era, the antiopium movement, in alliance with the larger temperance crusade, won passage of laws that applied the full force of modern policing and penology to limit the individual's control over his or her body. Through a parallel diplomacy between 1907 and 1925, Western powers imposed global restrictions on recreational drug use that soon effected a major decline in legal opium production. Significantly, the success of this early prohibition of drug use came at the height of the imperial age, when Asia's colonial regimes had extraordinary coercive powers, allowing them to control narcotics production almost at will.

Although similar to earlier international efforts against piracy and slavery, this narcotics prohibition regime fused diplomacy with domestic laws to extend the bounds of coercion (Nadelmann 1990: 484–513). Through diplomatic accords that spanned the globe and domestic laws that invaded the human body, drug prohibition became a bold experiment in the use of coercion for social control. These laws and treaties thus amount to something of a social revolution in the relation between law and individual liberties.

The early antiopium movement was a loose alliance between British Protestants, China missionaries, and Chinese imperial officials. With a generous endowment from a British Quaker, the Anglo-Oriental Society for the Suppression of the Opium Trade formed in 1874 and soon attracted the patronage of a Catholic cardinal and the archbishop of Canterbury (Owen 1934: 261–263). For 30 years, moral crusaders fought a relentless campaign that culminated in 1906 when the British Parliament passed a motion to end India's opium trade. Under the terms of the Anglo-Chinese opium treaty of 1907, Britain reduced its shipments of Indian opium, and China struggled to suppress smoking in the coastal cities and eradicate cultivation in inland provinces such as Szechwan. After the revolution of 1911 against the Manchu dynasty, however, the succeeding Republican government proved corrupt and opium suppression faltered (Dunn 1920: 118–130).

While Britain engaged in bilateral negotiations with China, the United States sought a parallel solution through global drug diplomacy. After purchasing the Philippine Islands from Spain in 1899, the United States discovered that it had acquired, along with 7,000 islands and 6 million Filipinos, a state opium monopoly similar to those elsewhere in Southeast Asia. In 1902, for example, Manila's 190 licensed dens sold 130 tons of opium, largely to overseas Chinese smokers (International Opium Commission 1909: 21–26). In 1903, the colonial regime appointed the Episcopal missionary Bishop Charles Brent to an investigative opium commission that recommended prohibition (Musto 1973: 25–28). Five years later, the United States colonial regime outlawed all opium smoking in the Philippines—an event that marks the start of America's century-long campaign of drug prohibition. Although opium smuggled from China met much of the illicit demand, drug abuse in the Philippine Islands soon declined to levels far below other Southeast Asian colonies (International Opium Commission 1909: 22–26).

Whatever its actual impact might have been, the Philippine ban won fame for Bishop Brent and launched America's attempt at drug diplomacy. Aware that opium smuggled from China was sabotaging the Philippine prohibition, the bishop wrote to President Theodore Roosevelt, urging an international conference to assist the struggle against the drug trade. With Bishop Brent in the chair, delegations from 13 countries—including Britain, France, Persia, Siam, and China—met at Shanghai for a month in 1909 (Lowes 1966: 102–111; Musto 1973: 28–37). In unanimous, nonbinding resolutions, the Shanghai commission defended the colonial interest by advising "the gradual suppression . . . of opium," the drug its members did sell, and urging "drastic measures" against the "grave danger" of morphine, the drug its members did not sell. Thus, the commission left a mingled legacy, defending Asia's colonial opium trade while simultaneously launching a global antinarcotics diplomacy (International Opium Commission 1909: 79–84; Courtwright 1982: 29–30). Simultaneously, the US delegate Hamilton Wright, a physician and moral crusader, successfully lobbied the US Congress for passage of the Smoking Opium Exclusion Act that banned all imports of non-medicinal opium (Courtwright 1982: 29–30, 82).

Two years later, the United States convened a second round of drug diplomacy through the International Conference on Opium at The Hague. With the support of President William Howard Taft, who knew Bishop Brent from their colonial service in Manila, the bishop again chaired the conference and maintained its moral momentum against the colonial interest. To give substance to sentiments articulated at Shanghai, these sessions drafted the International Opium Convention of 1912, restricting opium to medical use and closing recreational opium dens. As a party to these proceedings, the United States Congress enacted the Harrison Narcotics Act in 1914—a modest compromise measure that regulated, but did not prohibit, drug use by requiring a doctor's prescription to purchase narcotics. However, the United States Internal Revenue Bureau soon sought indictments against so-called dope doctors for conspiracy to violate the Harrison Act and, in 1919, won a Supreme Court decision supporting its strict interpretation—transforming regulation into prohibition. As exemplified by this legislation, America's first decades of drug prohibition were focused on reducing demand—a striking contrast to its later strategy of supply-side suppression (Taylor 1969: 120, 129–131; Musto 1973: 49–63; Courtwright 1982: 103–107).

Before the Hague convention could take effect, World War I intervened, delaying further drug diplomacy. After assuming responsibility for the Hague convention, the League of Nations convened a conference at Geneva in 1925 that approved a second International Opium Convention, creating a system for registering legal narcotics shipments. Six years later, the League's 1931 Convention for Limiting the Manufacture of Narcotic Drugs replaced voluntary registration with compulsory bans on manufacture beyond medical needs. Under the League's leadership, drug controls moved slowly from voluntary national laws toward mandatory controls over the production and sale of narcotics (Kusevic 1977: 34–53; Renborg 1944: 20–26; United Nations 1997: 162–163). Restrained by the colonial lobby, this cautious diplomacy produced international treaties that gradually restricted the right of governments to trade in narcotics. Although none of Southeast Asia's states abolished their monopolies, all made gestures that reduced the region's total opium sales by 65 percent in the 15 years after World War I. The Netherlands Indies, for example, cut its consumption by 88 percent, from 127 tons to only 15 tons (League of Nations 1923: 4; 1935: 70–71). Multilateral controls thus reversed the century-long climb in drug abuse—reducing world opium production from 41,600 tons in 1907 to an estimated 16,000 tons in 1934. Similarly, legal heroin production dropped from 20,000 pounds in 1926 to only 2,200 in 1931. (International Opium Commission 1909: 355–365; League of Nations 1937: 46–47; United Nations, Department of Social Affairs 1953: 3–4, 6–7). Relying on reports from member states, the League reported world production at 7,653 tons for 1934, with 6,378 of that total coming from China. That same year, the United States Treasury Department attaché in China reported an illicit traffic of 28,000 tons. The adjusted world figure of 16,000 tons cited above is a rough compromise between these two figures for China's production. (See M. R. Nicholson, United States Treasury Attaché, Shanghai, "Survey of Narcotic Situation in China and the Far East," written to the commissioner of customs in Washington, DC, on July 12, 1934. I am indebted to Alan Block for calling my attention to the Nicholson reports.)

Despite these impressive successes, the high profits inherent in the opiates traffic encouraged the emergence of criminal syndicates—a market response that limited state control of the drug trade (Block 1989: 315–337). As the illicit trade grew into global traffic from Asia to America, smugglers increasingly ignored the odorous, bulky opium and concentrated on its compact derivative, heroin. First manufactured commercially by Germany's Bayer pharmaceutical corporation in 1898, heroin had attributes that would make it an ideal criminal commodity—high value for weight, compact, odorless, and highly addictive.

Narcotics prohibition did not eradicate the trade but simply drove it into an illicit economy controlled, over time, by upland drug lords and urban crime syndicates. From the outset, each state action thus produced an equal and opposite criminal reaction. In the decade following the League's opium ban in 1925, Shanghai emerged as a major center for illicit heroin, supplying a substantial but unquantifiable share of the U.S. market. In 1931, the League of Nations imposed restrictions on the manufacture of heroin in Europe, and just 3 years later the United States Treasury attaché in Shanghai noted a "sudden shift of the traffic in narcotics from Europe to the Orient" (Nicholson 1934: 18–26). Similarly, in Southeast Asia, the League's efforts reduced legal opium sales but could not eradicate a mass demand cultivated by three centuries of colonial rule. As soon as governments slashed imports or closed opium dens, traffickers emerged to service the unmet demand. With 50 percent of the region's smokers and 70 percent of its dens, Bangkok and Saigon were Southeast Asia's premier opium markets, offering high profits that drew the smugglers' caravans southward from the opium hills of southern China (League of Nations 1937: 72–75).

Cold War Expansion

The half century of global conflict from the start of World War II through the end of the Cold War transformed the character of the global opium trade. In an age when war gave the major powers unequaled coercive capacities, the prohibition regime finally eradicated the remnants of legal opium trading. But the Cold War also brought covert operations that encouraged alliances with criminal syndicates at the interstices of global confrontation. In the last half of the twentieth century, the multilateral attempt at prohibition was slowed by informal state protection for traffickers who were deemed useful to their security services. During the 40 years of the Cold War, therefore, international narcotics control was the sum of a subtle and little understood interaction between prohibition and protection. These contradictory forces, prohibition and protection, shaped the heroin trade for 4 decades after World War II.

During World War II, restrictions on shipping and strict port security produced a marked hiatus in global opium trafficking. With only limited supplies of low-grade heroin from Mexico, the addict population in the United States plummeted in just 4 years to a historic low of some 20,000 heroin users by the end of the war (McCoy 1991: 18, 41–44).

In the 40 years of Cold War that followed, Asia's opium trade became concentrated in three distinct regions—Turkey, Southwest Asia, and Southeast Asia's Golden Triangle—making its recent history a fusion of global trends and local politics. In Turkey's main opium district, the Anatolian plateau, farmers delivered legal quotas to a national marketing organization. They then sold illegal surpluses to smugglers, fueling a traffic that moved east to Iran's opium dens and west to Marseilles's heroin laboratories. In Southwest Asia, the poppy fields of Afghanistan and western Pakistan supplied regional markets, particularly Iran's almost limitless demand for smoking opium. In Southeast Asia, the opium-producing highlands of Burma, Thailand, and Laos—known as the Golden Triangle for the shape its poppy districts traced on the map—produced smoking opium in the 1950s for Saigon, Bangkok, and Hong Kong and then, in the 1970s, processed heroin for America, Australia, and Europe. Apart from supplying illicit demand, the drug traffic, in concert with covert warfare along this mountain rim of Asia, integrated highland tribes, peasants, and minorities into both global trade and geopolitical conflict.

During the Cold War, the interaction of prohibition and protection defined the global drug trade. Above all, the Communist victory in China soon eliminated the world's largest producer and consumer of opium. After taking power in 1949, the Communist regime launched an antiopium campaign, focused primarily on users, that culminated in 1952 with the identification of 369,000 traffickers—quickly followed by 82,000 arrests, 35,000 prison sentences, and 880 public executions. Then, through mass mobilization and compulsory treatment, users quickly abandoned the habit, making China drug free by the mid-1950s (Zhou 1999: 97–111). More broadly, communism's victory in China extended authoritarian rule over much of the Eurasian landmass, closing this vast region to illicit opium production and creating a barrier that diverted the traffic to new smuggling routes. Although Asia's opium zone thus contracted geographically, geopolitics, combined with illicit market forces, stimulated a steady increase in production within the remaining area, which now stretched from Turkey to Laos.

In one of history's accidents, the Iron Curtain came down during the late 1940s along the Asian opium zone, creating a conjuncture between covert warfare and opium trafficking. Along this 5,000 mile southern frontier of China and the Soviet Union, history and geography converged to form two flash points of Cold War confrontation—Afghanistan in the west and Southeast Asia's Golden Triangle in the east. With historic trade routes deflected east and west by the soaring massif of the Himalayas and Hindu Kush, 2,000 miles long and 5 miles high, both regions had long been crossroads for caravans traveling south from China and Central Asia. Through these circuits of commerce moved arms, opium, and Islam—sustaining rugged highland tribes in traditions of trading, raiding, and resistance to lowland empires. Along the trade routes through northern Afghanistan to Kabul, "the organized raiding of caravans regularly satisfied the appetites of local elites" (Allan 1991: 71). Similarly, caravan routes radiating from the Yunnan plateau in southwestern China drew hill tribes from Assam to Tonkin into raiding, trading, and opium cultivation (1–47; Leach 1964: 21, 28, 30, 59-60, 95, 187–188: Yegar 1966: 80–82; Forbes 1987).

In the late nineteenth century, as states established frontiers along mountain spines that arched from Central Asia to southern China, highland bandits, smugglers, and martial tribes resisted colonial controls. To tame the warlike Pashtun tribes and block Russia's advance toward the Indian Ocean, British India sent 42 expeditions into its northwest frontier until it abandoned this futile effort in 1892 and negotiated a boundary with the emir of Afghanistan. As Asia's empires demarcated such fixed frontiers, surveyors followed European hydrological principles in tracing these metaphysical lines we call borders—powerful but insubstantial, precise but invisible. International borders thus marched through straits, up rivers, and between watersheds, leaving highland tribes and minorities from Turkey to Vietnam straddling these new lines—insubstantial yet so formidable that even powerful armies were loath to cross. In rugged highland terrain that restrained central control, minorities could use superior physical conditioning, political support, and local knowledge to keep lowland troops at bay. Geography and geopolitics thus merged to make these mountain frontiers sanctuaries for smuggling, drug production, ethnic revolt, and in later years, covert operations.

For 40 years, the CIA fought covert wars in and around these two flash points at the antipodes of the Asian massif—in Burma in the 1950s, Laos in the 1960s, and Afghanistan in the 1980s. As the CIA allied with highland warlords to mobilize tribal armies, these local allies used the agency's arms and protection to become major drug lords. From a narrow Cold War perspective, such informal tolerance of drug dealing often amplified the agency's operational effectiveness. Viewed from the mission-oriented perspective of a CIA operative, the opium trade relieved the agency of the prohibitive cost of welfare for tribes with dependents numbering in the hundreds of thousands. Of equal importance, control over this critical income allowed the CIA's chosen warlord to command tribes, clans, and villages in bloody paramilitary campaigns that ground on for years with heavy casualties. Since ruthless drug lords made effective anticommunist allies and opium amplified their power, CIA agents, operating alone half a world away from home, tolerated trafficking by their covert-action allies. And, as the opium moved down country to laboratories and urban markets, the CIA also found allies among crime syndicates who controlled this traffic (McCoy 1991: 53–63, 184–189). In the context of the Cold War, there was, moreover, a certain sympathy, even a symbiosis, between security agencies and criminal syndicates that shared an ability to conduct complex operations in a covert netherworld beyond civil society. As our knowledge of the Cold War grows, the list of drug traffickers who served the CIA has lengthened to include Corsican criminals, Nationalist Chinese irregulars, Lao generals, Afghan guerrillas, Haitian colonels, Panamanian generals, Honduran smugglers, and Nicaraguan Contra commanders.

Looking back on CIA covert wars that became enmeshed in narcotics trafficking, there is a striking contrast between short-term gains in paramilitary capacity and their troubling, long-term political costs. During each operation and its aftermath, there was a sharp rise in both opium production and opiate exports to international markets, including Europe and America. While covert warfare continued, tribal warlords used CIA arms, logistics, and political protection to become major drug lords, expanding local opium production and shipping heroin to international markets. Instead of stopping this drug dealing, the agency tolerated it and, when necessary, blocked investigations, making these covert war zones enforcement-free areas, where drug trafficking could expand without restraint (McCoy 1991: 385–386, 453–460, 484). Once the operation was over, its legacy persisted in steadily rising narcotics production. American agents may have departed, but the economic dependence, market linkages, and warlord power remained to make these regions major drug suppliers for decades to come. During the 40 years of the Cold War in Asia, the CIA's covert war zones were thus transformed from minor opium growers into the world's leading heroin producers. After CIA intervention in the 1950s, Burma's opium production, stable for decades with harvests of only 8 tons in 1938 and 18 tons in 1958, surged to an estimated 400 to 600 tons by 1970 (League of Nations 1937: 9, 46–47; U.S. Cabinet Committee of International Narcotics Control 1972: 10–11; Chao 1987: 57). Similarly, after growing slowly from 75 tons in 1932 to only 100 tons in 1971, Afghanistan's opium output surged tenfold during the CIA's covert war of the 1980s to 2000 tons by 1991 (U.S. Cabinet Committee of International Narcotics Control 1972: A7; U.S. Department of State 1984: 4, 1998: 23; Rupert and Coll 1990; *Geopolitical Drug Dispatch* January 1992: 1, 3; Reid and Costigan 2002: 20).

As the United Nation's prohibition regime reached around the globe after World War II, Southeast Asian states were finally forced to abolish their opium monopolies. After the legal opium trade was finally outlawed by 1961, the United Nations then turned to eradication of illegal poppy cultivation while the United States focused on the pursuit of international traffickers. Since Asia's opium zone coincided with a major frontier of anticommunist containment, the continent's southern rim became a covert battleground, periodically erupting in bloody, protracted warfare and providing de facto political protection for drug dealers in key source regions—blunting the U.S. and United Nations emphasis on narcotics suppression. In the first decades after World War II, Asia's opium zone functioned within localized trading spheres in the continent's southeast and southwest. Over time, however, covert warfare operations and rising worldwide opium demand, in an elusive combination, drew these disparate regions into the international drug traffic and integrated this southern rim of Asia into a coherent narcotics production zone.

In the first decades after World War II, Southeast Asia's highlands experienced a fundamental transformation that produced the present Golden Triangle—a rugged region of 100,000 square miles that sprawls across the northern reaches of Burma, Thailand, and Laos. After mainland Southeast Asian states, under United Nations pressure, finally abolished their opium monopolies between 1950 and 1961, their security services allowed favored paramilitary groups to control the now illicit traffic.

Seeking a second front against Communist China during the Korean War, President Harry Truman ordered the CIA to invade southwestern China by arming 14,000 Nationalist Chinese troops who had recently fled the Communist advance into Burma. After their incursions were repulsed in 1950–1951, the Nationalist troops occupied Burma's northeast for another decade, turning to opium to finance their operations. By forcing local hill tribes to produce the drug, these Nationalist irregulars, loyal to General Chiang Kai-shek's exile regime on Taiwan, presided over a massive increase of poppy cultivation on the Shan Plateau—from some 18 tons in 1958 to an estimated 400 to 600 tons in 1970 (Chao 1987: 57; U.S. Cabinet Committee of International Narcotics Control 1972: 10–11).

Clandestine warfare in nearby Indochina followed a similar pattern. After French Indochina's civil authorities abolished the opium monopoly in 1950, French military intelligence, the SDECE, used the drug trade to finance its covert operations against the Communist forces. This transfer of opium funds from the colonial Finance Ministry to the *caisse noire* of covert operations foreshadowed a basic shift in the political economy of opium during the Cold War. Despite the rapid increase in cultivation, the region's opium traffic remained self-contained until 1970, supplying opium for urban smokers in nearby cities such as Bangkok, Saigon, and Hong Kong (McCoy 1991: 131–146).

In Laos during the 1960s, the CIA, following the French pattern of covert operations, battled local communists with a 30,000-strong secret army of Hmong tribesmen—tough highlanders whose only cash crop was opium. Divided into tribes and clans, the Hmong were the most isolated of Laos's ethnic groups—building their clusters of plank houses on peaks and ridges at 3,000 to 5,000 feet elevation. After the Vietnam War started in 1965, a seesaw battle raged back and forth across a narrow 200-mile span of rugged mountains in northern Laos—from the capital at Vientiane, across the Plain of Jars, to North Vietnam's border. Even though the outcome would determine the fate of the royalist government in Vientiane, the lowland conscripts of the Royal Lao army often failed to fight, shifting the burden to the

CIA's Hmong soldiers. From a secret base at Long Tieng just north of Vientiane, the CIA operated a shuttle service of helicopters and light aircraft to over 200 airstrips across northern Laos, making these scattered Hmong villages the mass base for its secret army.

Throughout this decade of secret war (1964–1974), the CIA's relationship with its Hmong commander, General Vang Pao, was the key to this covert operation. By allowing Vang Pao authority over all flights into these villages, the CIA gave him control over the economy of every Hmong household—power that he used to knit disparate, diffuse clans into an armed people. For nearly a century before this war, the Hmong economy had depended upon rice cultivation for subsistence and opium for cash. As the fighting withdrew Hmong males from the villages, the slash-and-burn rice fields soon lost their fertility and families grew dependent upon United States air drops of rice—shipments that General Vang Pao controlled. As fighting denied itinerant Chinese opium traders access to these hills, the secret army used the CIA's Air America to transport the crop from village air strips to regional markets. Though long a source of cash for the Hmong, opium's importance increased during the war since poppy fields remained fertile for up to 10 years—compensating, in part, for the loss of male labor to combat and casualties. By tolerating Hmong involvement in the opium trade, the CIA increased the power of its chosen client, Vang Pao, and reduced the cost of sustaining his thousands of tribal followers. When the agency's covert allies opened a cluster of heroin laboratories in the Burma-Thai-Lao border area in 1970, the United States mission in Laos failed to act even though their output was directed, first, at American forces fighting in South Vietnam and, later, at illicit markets in the United States (McCoy 1991: 254–259, 305–343).

In Southwest Asia, the region's opium traffic followed a similar pattern, with most production absorbed in regional markets and only limited amounts available for export to the West. Despite an imperfect ban on consumption between 1955 and 1969, Iran's cities remained the world's largest consumer of opium and absorbed much of the surplus from neighboring nations—Turkey, Pakistan, and Afghanistan (U.S. CIA 1972:1–2). Although the Turkish Marketing Organization was a legal pharmaceutical producer, Anatolian farmers exceeded their official opium quotas and exported the illicit surplus to two markets—east into Iran for smoking opium and west to Marseilles, where criminal laboratories produced 80 percent of America's heroin.

In these transitional decades between the international convention and the full prohibition regime, Asia's opium production was low, markets were largely regional, and heroin production was, until 1970, insignificant. In the 1970s, however, President Nixon's drug war would produce a radical transformation in Asia's drug trade, inadvertently integrating it more fully into the international traffic.

Bilateral Suppression in the 1970s

In 1971, United States narcotics suppression moved beyond its borders when President Richard Nixon announced that the drug problem was a "national emergency" and declared the first in a succession of American drug wars that have continued to the present. In his first battle, Nixon attacked Turkish opium production, then the second highest in Southwest Asia and the source of an estimated 80 percent of America's heroin supply. With $35 million in U.S. aid to fund alternative crops, Turkey, a close U.S. military ally, announced a ban on legal opium cultivation after the 1973 harvest, depriving some 100,000 registered farmers of the right to grow an important cash crop. After effecting the eradication of Turkey's opium crop, the Nixon White House then forced French authorities to close Marseilles's clandestine heroin laboratories. In the words of the DEA's administrator of that day, "the whole pipeline was drying up." In the next battle, the Nixon White House shifted its attack to Southeast Asia, focusing on Bangkok's exports. To prevent Southeast Asia from filling the void in the United States' supply, the Nixon White House sent a team of Drug Enforcement Administration agents to Bangkok, where they soon cut the flow of Golden Triangle heroin toward the United States (U.S. Congress 1975a: 45–47, 57–59).

By the mid-1970s, the street price of heroin in New York had tripled and purity dropped by half—both strong indicators of a serious shortage. Nixon had won a total victory in the first of America's four drug wars (Cusack 1974: 3–7; U.S. Congress 1975a: 1–7, 38–71).

In his success, Nixon defined the character of subsequent drug wars by applying the full coercive resources of the United States government to eradicate narcotics production at its source. After heavy diplomatic and military pressure on allies to join his assault on cultivation and refining, Nixon then dispatched agents to track down traffickers who had survived this broadbrush suppression. Simultaneously, Nixon's Republican rival, Governor Nelson Rockefeller, won the passage of harsh laws in New York, requiring mandatory minimum sentences of 15 years to life for possession of just 2 ounces of heroin or cocaine (Labrousse and Laniel 2001: 168).

In sum, Nixon's drug war provided an impressive and unparalleled demonstration of the coercive capacities of the world's paramount power. Yet compared to the repressive resources of earlier colonial or communist regimes, Nixon's instruments were feeble and his range finite, producing an imperfect coercion with unpredictable consequences. Under such circumstances, the little-understood dynamics of the illicit drug market soon turned his victory into defeat.

Why this unexpected outcome? Although Turkey was the source for some 80 percent of U.S. heroin supply, it produced only 7 percent of the raw poppy in Asia's opium zone (U.S. Cabinet Committee of International Narcotics Control 1972: 10–11). With global demand constant and supply now reduced, the illicit world price rose, stimulating opium production elsewhere along the continent's vast southern rim, particularly in Southeast Asia. When President Nixon brought the blunt baton of law enforcement down upon a global commodity, his drug war stimulated both opium production and heroin consumption. From this predictable but unrecognized market logic, every short-term victory, every successful eradication or crop substitution, would become a market stimulus that would inflict a succession of defeats on America's drug wars.

Nixon's modest eradication in Turkey unleashed market forces that would ultimately expand the drug trade on five continents—including, higher heroin output in Southeast Asia, mass addiction in Europe and Australia, a booming amphetamine manufacture and cannabis cultivation in the United States, and rising coca production in South America. Responding to the stimulus of Turkish eradication, the Chinese syndicates of Southeast Asia began exporting heroin to America. Rising from insignificant levels in the late 1960s, Southeast Asian heroin captured 29 percent of New York's street supply by 1972. In Chicago, Southeast Asia's share jumped from 6 percent of all samples seized in 1972 to 48 percent in 1973 (U.S. Drug Enforcement Administration 1972–1975). By 1973, Southeast Asia's share of the U.S. heroin market had more than doubled, to 30 percent (U.S. Congress 1975c: 91).

Concerned about rising seizures of Southeast Asian heroin, the Nixon administration dispatched a firebreak team of 30 DEA agents to Bangkok in 1973–1974 to cut the flow. Armed with a financial war chest of $12 million in narcotics assistance funds, the Bangkok Drug Enforcement Administration team began intercepting shipments of American-bound heroin—creating a de facto customs barrier that discouraged further exports to America (U.S. Congress 1975b: 38–40) Complementing the immediate United States interdiction effort, in 1971 the newly established United Nations Fund for Drug Abuse Control launched an experimental crop-substitution program in Thailand, seeking to eradicate opium over the long term by encouraging hill farmers to plant fruit trees, coffee, beans, and flowers (McCoy 1980: 361–362; United Nations 2000d: 148). By late 1975, Southeast Asia's share of the U.S. market had dropped back down to only 8 percent, leaving a void that was partially filled by Mexico's rising production.

Again, the White House responded with paramilitary repression. Under pressure from Washington, Mexico launched Operation Condor in 1975—an aggressive aerial eradication that cut the heroin flow into the United States from 6.5 tons in 1975 to just 3 tons in 1977 and reduced Mexico's share of the U.S. supply from 67 percent in 1976 to 25 percent in 1980. This operation also devastated Mexico's marijuana farms, cutting their share of the U.S. supply from 75 percent to only 4 percent. Though hailed as a victory, this disruption simply shifted cannabis production south to Colombia, fostering that country's first criminal linkages to the United States (U.S. Drug Enforcement Administration 1972, 1975; U.S. General Accounting Office 1988: 8, 15; Andreas 2000: 41). As supplies of low-potency Mexican marijuana waned in the late 1970s, entrepreneurs developed domestic cultivation in northern California, creating a market for marijuana with five times the potency (Skolnick 1990: 86).

Since the Drug Enforcement Administration had neither eradicated opium cultivation in Burma nor closed the heroin refineries in Thailand, its seizures erected a de facto custom's barrier that deflected exports from the United States to Europe and Australia—continents that had been heroin free for decades (Wicinski 1981: 14–15). Total European seizures of Southeast Asian No. 3 heroin jumped from 22 pounds in 1972 to 873 in 1978 (Antonelli 1975: 32; Cusack 1976: 34–35, 1979: 20–21). In West Germany, deaths from heroin overdoses increased from 9 in 1969 to 623 a decade later (Wicinski 1981: 15–16). By 1976, European seizures of 1,177 pounds of heroin, almost all from Southeast Asia, were higher than the U.S. total—

indicating that Europe's drug problem had, in only 5 years, begun to rival America's (Falco 1979: 2–3). Similarly, in Australia narcotics arrests in New South Wales increased fivefold, from 173 in 1972 to 909 5 years later, and overdose deaths were up threefold, from 14 in 1974 to 49 in 1976 (N.S.W. Parliament 1978: 125, 28, 129–133).

Inside the United States, the illicit drug market responded to the decline in imported narcotics by substituting domestic synthetics. As Asian heroin imports dropped in the mid-1970s, organized crime syndicates saw an opportunity, and illicit amphetamine laboratories soon dotted the northeastern United States, with a significant cluster that made Philadelphia the "speed capital of the world" (Jenkins 1992: 312–316; U.S. Congress 1980).

Despite some initial success, America's drug war had thus produced a paradoxical strengthening of the global narcotics traffic. By the late 1970s, the simplex of the Turkey-Marseilles-New York heroin pipeline had been replaced by a complex of international smuggling routes that tied the disparate zones of First World consumption to Third World drug production. With production and consumption now dispersed around the globe, the international traffic was far more resistant to suppression than ever before.

Operating on a nineteenth-century model of localized vice suppression, the United States had applied the coercive apparatus of arrest, seizure, and eradication without considering the complex market dynamics of the illicit drug trade. With global demand constant, a sudden reduction of supply in one sector simply raised illicit prices, which in turn stimulated increased cultivation elsewhere across the vastness of the Asian opium zone. In essence, the five U.S. drug wars of the past 30 years extended local law enforcement practice into the international arena in ways that would contribute to an increase in world opium supply from 1,200 tons in 1970 to 3,700 tons in 1989.

Conventional literary metaphors seem too flat, too linear, to convey the extraordinary, even explosive volatility of the global drug market. In his restless pursuit of drug dealers across the arc of Asia, Nixon seems rather like Mickey Mouse in the animated Disney film *Fantasia*—a sorcerer's apprentice, frantic to stem rising waters by attacking the bucket-carrying brooms with an ax, only to have the chips resurrected as full-grown brooms and the flood turn into a torrent.

Although Nixon's drug war thus stimulated the global market, its impact on domestic demand was more ambiguous. In the late 1970s, every indicator pointed to a marked decline in the U.S. heroin supply. The estimated number of heroin addicts plummeted. Heroin purity declined markedly in New York City, reaching a low of 3 percent (Cusak 1974: 3–7).

Why the decline? I cannot answer with any certainty. Perhaps Nixon's drug war may have actually succeeded in disrupting the flow of drugs from Asia into the United States. Mexico soon captured nearly 90 percent of the remaining U.S. heroin market, but massive eradication and consequently erratic shipments of crude No. 3 heroin somehow failed to satisfy American demand for the pure, powdery No. 4 (U.S. General Accounting Office 1988: 8, 15). Looking at these changes, we could conclude that Nixon's drug war had worked. Examining other evidence, however, we could attribute this decline to President Jimmy Carter's foreign policy, particularly his ban on major CIA covert operations from 1976 to 1978, which may have removed the protection that drug lords seem to require. Similarly, the Carter administration abandoned the supply-side drug war in favor of treatment, a demand-side intervention—possibly stilling, momentarily, the stimulus of prohibition. Given the complexities of the global drug trade, we cannot decide this issue with any certainty. Nonetheless, changes in the global traffic indicate that prohibition and protection were, on balance, significant factors in both the decline of the heroin supply in the 1970s and its subsequent increase during the 1980s.

This first drug war thus proved to be a revealing experimental demonstration, largely ignored, of the contradictory market response to repression that would be repeated over the next quarter century. The illicit drug market had quickly transformed suppression into stimulus—producing a shift to synthetics, increased narcotics production elsewhere, and an expansion of trafficking into new markets. Over the next 25 years, each attempt at suppression would, through this same market dynamic, compound the problem.

Thus, by the late 1970s, a confluence of political and economic forces were in place for a rapid increase in illicit supply during the next decade—a dynamic illicit drug market, covert warfare operations in the drug zones, the stimulus of source-country suppression, and rising global demand. In the drug wars that followed, every victory would become a defeat.

Rising Harvests of the 1980s

Whatever the cause of the opiates decline in the 1970s, imperfect coercion and covert protection led to an increase in the United States and European heroin problem during the 1980s. In this twilight of the Cold War, highland drug lords became independent entrepreneurs, powerful enough to shape the direction of Western drug markets, by sending vast shipments of Asian heroin to Europe and an unchecked flood of cocaine to America. This decade also witnessed massive increases in illicit production around the globe—with rising coca cultivation in the Andes, a surge in opium production in Southwest Asia, and a heroin boom in the Golden Triangle. In the view of the United Nations, global narcotics production "skyrocketed" during this decade, with world opium output rising tenfold, from 500 to 5,000 tons, and the coca leaf harvest tripling, from 100,000 to 300,000 tons (United Nations 2000d: 24, 150). Stimulated by the disruption of the Asian opium trade in the 1970s, a rising traffic in heroin, marijuana, and cocaine between Latin America and the United States fostered a political economy that by the 1980s quickly replicated Asia's long-established patterns.

Responding to this sudden flood of drugs from the south, the United States extended its drug war into the Andes during the 1980s, repeating the failed repression seen earlier in the Asian opium zone. President Ronald Reagan revived Nixon's drug war, directing it away from Asian heroin to focus on Latin American cocaine through a mix of repression and regional diplomacy.

During the 1980s, a changing mix of prohibition and protection allowed an unprecedented expansion in Asia's opium zone. After the United States withdrawal from the Southeast Asian mainland in 1975, warlords who had depended upon foreign patrons, like the Nationalist Chinese militia and the Lao military, faded while drug lords with deeper local roots emerged. Although CIA covert operations in Burma had ended, their legacy persisted through former assets active in the traffic and the chaos in the country's northeastern borderlands. Whereas Thai protection for drug syndicates gradually diminished, Rangoon allied openly with ethnic warlords in ways that allowed rapid growth in opium production. By the mid-1980s, a rising warlord, General Khun Sa, had seized control of the Burma-Thai border from the Nationalist Chinese militia. After imposing his leadership over the factionalized Shan ethnic rebels, the general used his control over this strategic territory to encourage a rapid increase in Burma's opium production, from 550 tons in 1981 to 2,430 in 1989 (U.S. Department of State 1984: 101, 1990: 271–279, 286, 1998: 23). As Burma's exports soared, Southeast Asia's share of New York City's heroin supply jumped from 5 to 80 percent between 1984 and 1990 (Erlanger 1990).

In 1989–1990, this flood of Southeast Asian heroin lowered the wholesale price of so-called China white in New York City from $100,000 a kilogram to only $60,000, undercutting the cocaine market and creating a new clientele for heroin. Crack addicts who were seeking an easier withdrawal were reportedly using heroin in large quantities, as were those mixing the two drugs for a more prolonged euphoria. City narcotics police reported that heroin-related arrests jumped from 1 percent to 19 percent of their total (Associated Press 1989).

This flood of Burmese heroin brought lower prices and higher purity in the American drug market. Between the mid-1980s and mid-1990s, annual heroin consumption in the United States rose from 5 to some 10–15 metric tons, sustaining an expanded population of 600,000 hard-core addicts. As Burmese heroin, known on the street as China white, landed in unprecedented quantities and Colombia's coca cartels began exporting heroin, the retail price in New York City dropped from $1.81 per milligram in 1988 to just $0.37 in 1994. Simultaneously, the national average for heroin content in street deals rose from just 7 to 40 percent, reaching 63 percent in New York City and even higher elsewhere. On the streets, unknown entrepreneurs—negotiating the variables of price, purity, supply, and market—dealt with this surge in supply by raising purity and changing the drug's demographics (U.S. Drug Enforcement Administration 1996; U.S. General Accounting Office 1996: 2–7).

Commodity transformed culture, creating New York's "heroin chic" of the 1990s. The new, pure heroin could be snorted or smoked, cutting the link between intravenous injection and HIV infection. Once stigmatized in the 1960s as a ghetto drug—the mark of the socially marginal—American youth culture of the 1990s reinvented this cheaper, "safe" heroin as a badge of alienated authenticity. In May 1996, *Rolling Stone* magazine ran a feature entitled "Rock & Roll Heroin," which listed dozens of mega-stars with major habits (Colapinto 1996: 15–20, 58, 60). Two months later, the glossy lifestyle magazine *Allure* reported that the fashion industry's "baffling concept of heroin chic" was a reality snapshot—top models were regular users (Konisberg 1996: 90–95). After drug-look photographer Davide Sorrenti died of a heroin overdose, President Bill Clinton called a press conference in May 1997 to attack the fashion industry's self-indulgence (Spindler 1997; Wren 1997a).

This extraordinary growth in Burma's harvest was in some measure a market response to the success of the United Nations opium eradication program in neighboring Thailand. After Nixon declared his drug war in 1972, the United States pursued major antinarcotics programs in both Thailand and Burma. But there was a difference. Whereas the DEA worked closely with the Thai police in Bangkok and on the border, Washington had to buy its way into Burma. Between 1974 and 1978, Rangoon accepted 18 helicopters under the U.S. narcotics assistance program and cooperated with the Thai police in sweeps against smugglers along their common border. In the mid-1980s, moreover, the Drug Enforcement Administration worked with the Burmese to spray some 60,000 acres of Shan State forest with the lethal 2,4-D defoliant. After testing in Burma in 1984, the United States launched an eradication program in November 1985 with three of the new turbo Thrush-65 fixed-wing aircraft, whose "improved spray boom represents a significant technological improvement." Despite these displays of cooperation, Rangoon diverted U.S. resources to counterinsurgency and protected favored drug lords like Khun Sa and Lo Hsing-han. By the time the United States suspended its drug program in 1988 to protest the massacre of prodemocracy demonstrators in Rangoon, everyone in the United States mission, except the DEA, regarded it as an expendable failure (M. Smith 1991: 314; Lintner 1991: 22–23; U.S. Congress 1986: 577).

By contrast, Thailand, in close cooperation with the United States and the United Nations, attacked the foundations of the traffic, forcing a steady decline in its illicit opium output from 145 tons in 1970 to only 24 tons in 1992—virtually eliminating poppy cultivation in most tribal villages. By the late 1980s, Thailand, with some 200,000 heroin addicts, had become a net heroin consumer, and the drug war there, from a U.S. perspective, was virtually won. Within the inexorable logic of global traffic, however, victory on one drug battlefield soon brought defeat on another. Since demand, in this case, had remained constant, reduced output in Thailand raised prices so that supply responded with rising opium harvests in Burma. During the 1980s, the steady eradication of opium farming in Thailand drove the traffickers across the border, where their drug purchases created new supply areas that contributed to the dramatic fivefold increase in Burma's harvest. As smoking opium disappeared from northern Thai hill tribe, local addicts began injecting Burmese heroin, sharing needles in ways that led to a virulent AIDS epidemic in the late 1980s. In the first 9 months of 1988, the HIV rate among intravenous drug users in Bangkok increased from less than 1 percent to 40 percent. By 1990, an estimated 800,000 Thais were infected (Muecke 1990: 2–27; U.S. Department of State 1998: 23; Vienne 1998: 66–72).

A somewhat different array of global forces drove an equally explosive increase in Southwest Asia's heroin output during the 1980s. Reporting from Tehran in 1974, Ambassador Richard Helms ([1974] 1992), the former CIA director, had insisted, accurately enough, that there was little heroin production in this region—only a localized opium trade. In 1972, for example, Iran's traffickers imported an estimated 195 tons of opium—largely from Turkey and Afghanistan—since its own harvest of 217 tons was insufficient for the country's 400,000 users (Chouvy 2001: 79).

During the early 1980s, however, Afghan-Pakistan borderlands became a covert war zone and, almost simultaneously, the world's leading heroin producer. In 1980, "nobody knew what heroin was," recalled the Pakistan's customs supervisor at Peshawar, Jehangir Khan, including his own inspectors (Stevens 1983). As a network of heroin laboratories opened along the Afghan-Pakistan border in 1979–1980, Pakistan's opium production soared to a momentary peak of 800 tons, far above its 1971 harvest of some 90 tons. Just across the border in neighboring Afghanistan, opium production also rose sharply, from 250 tons in 1982 to 750 tons just 6 years later. Although this region had zero heroin production in the mid-1970s, by 1981 Pakistan had become the world's largest heroin producer, supplying 60 percent of the U.S. market and 80 percent of the European (Falco 1979: 2–3; U.S. Cabinet Committee of International Control 1972: A7, A14, A17; U.S. Department of State 1984: 4, 1986: 480; W. F. Smith 1982: 2–3).

Inside Pakistan the consequences were even more striking. From zero heroin addicts in 1979, Pakistan, according to official figures, had 5,000 addicts in 1980 and 1.2 million in 1985—one the highest rates of heroin addiction in the world. In 1998, the United Nations reported that 1.7 percent of Pakistan's adults were opiates users, about three times the rate for Thailand and the United States (Pakistan Narcotics Control Board 1986: iii, ix, 23, 308; Hussain 1989: 17; United Nations 2000d: 162–165).

How did Pakistan become the world's leading heroin producer? After the Soviet Union invaded Afghanistan in 1979, the White House assigned the CIA to support the Afghan resistance. Once again, the agency found itself fighting a covert war in the Asian opium zone, this time from Pakistani tribal territory adjacent to Afghanistan known as the North West Frontier Province. "In the tribal area," the State Department reported in 1986, "there is no police force. There are no courts. There is no taxation. No weapon is illegal. . . . Hashish and opium are often on display." With some 300 trails and passes leading into Afghanistan and, in the CIA's words, "the largest expanse of territory in the world without any government presence," this remote region was an ideal base for the agency's secret war against Soviet expansion and an ideal zone for illicit heroin production (U.S. CIA [1983] 1995).

Following the pattern of past covert wars in Burma and Laos, the CIA conducted its Afghan operation through a single local commander—making its own success synonymous with his power and leaving the agency little leverage when its chosen warlord decided to become a drug lord. During the 1980s, the CIA, working through Pakistan's Inter-Service Intelligence (ISI), spent over $2 billion to arm, supply, and train the Afghan resistance. As the chief of the CIA's South Asia Division, Charles Cogan, later explained, "the dominant operational role on the front lines belonged to Pakistan's ISI . . . which insisted on control." On the American side, it was "the CIA's war." Since the agency had only 50 operatives, compared to thousands of ISI officers, numbers alone put Pakistan in control (Cogan 1993: 76, 79). Instead of forming a broad coalition of resistance leaders, ISI offered the CIA an alliance with its own Afghan client, Gulbuddin Hekmatyar, the leader of the fundamentalist Hezb-i-Islami group who was already notorious for throwing acid in the faces of unveiled women in Kabul during the 1960s. The CIA, with little intelligence and fewer alternatives, accepted the offer and, over the next decade, gave more than half its covert aid to Hekmatyar's extremist Muslim faction. After the CIA built his Hezbi-i Islami into the largest Afghan guerrilla force, Hekmatyar would prove himself brutal, fanatical, and militarily incompetent—so problematic, in fact, that the CIA itself eventually attempted in May 2002 to assassinate him (Lifschultz 1989: 49–54; Rohde 2001; Dao 2002a). Not only did he command the largest resistance army, but Hekmatyar would also use it to become one of Afghanistan's leading drug lords.

At the start of the fighting in 1979, a confluence of factors, global and regional, complemented the covert war to stimulate opium production inside Pakistan's North West Frontier Province—notably, a prolonged drought in Southeast Asia's Golden Triangle; Pakistan's decree in February, banning both opium cultivation or consumption; and Iran's prohibition on opium farming in April. With rising stocks of surplus opium and traditional trafficking routes across Afghanistan cut, the Afridi and Shinwari tribes of Pakistan's northwest turned to heroin production for local and foreign markets (Abou Zahab 2001: 143–145).

During this decade of covert warfare, Afghanistan's opium production rose nearly tenfold, from an estimated 250 tons in 1982 to 750 tons in 1988 and 2,000 tons by 1991 (U.S. Department of State 1984: 4, 1998: 23; Rupert and Coll 1990; *Geopolitical Drug Dispatch* January 1992: 1, 3). As the State Department noted in a 1986 report, opium "is an ideal crop in a wartorn country since it requires little capital investment, is fast growing and is easily transported and traded." Afghanistan's climate was ideal for the crop, with yields two to three times higher than those in Southeast Asia. Moreover, smuggling, the State Department noted, "is a traditional way of business among various tribal groups" who carry the opium through mountains "laced with innumerable smugglers' trails" to laboratories in Pakistan's North West Frontier Province (U.S. Department of State 1986: 480–481.) Two years later, the State Department reported that opium has been "a common source of income for tribal Afghans for centuries" and is "elaborately woven into tribal habits and mores." Though the crop was common in many tribal areas, Afghanistan had three main opium regions—Nangarhar in the east, "which is by far the largest producer"; Helmand in the south; and Badakhshan in the north. With the war generating 5 million refugees and disrupting food production, farmers had turned to opium "in desperation" since it allowed "high profits," which covered rising food shortages. Moreover, said the State Department, "resistance elements engage in opium production and trafficking . . . to provide staples for population under their control and to fund weapons purchases" (U.S. Department of State 1988: 177–178.)

As the mujaheddin guerrillas gained control over liberated zones inside Afghanistan, they collected tax payments from peasants in opium. During most of the war, for example, the local commander Mullah Nasim Akhundzada controlled the irrigated lands of the fertile Helmand Valley, once the breadbasket of Afghanistan, and decreed that half of all peasant holdings would be planted in opium. In early 1986, *New York Times* correspondent Arthur Bonner spent a month traveling in Helmand, where he found extensive poppy fields in every village and town. "We must grow and sell opium to fight our holy war against the Russian non-believers," explained Mohammed Rasul, the commander's elder brother (A. Bonner 1986).

Caravans carrying CIA arms to the Afghan resistance often returned to Pakistan loaded with opium—sometimes, in the words of the *New York Times*, "with the assent of Pakistani or American intelligence officers" (Golden 2001). Once the mujaheddin brought the opium across the border, they sold it to Pakistani heroin refiners, operating under the protection of General Fazle Haq, an ISI officer who also served as governor of the North West Frontier Province. By 1988, there were an estimated 100 to 200 heroin refineries in the Province's Khyber district alone (Evans 1989: 26). Further south, in the Koh-i-Soltan district of Baluchistan Province, Hekmatyar himself controlled six refineries that processed much of the opium harvest from the Helmand Valley into heroin (Rubin 1990: 18–19). From these borderlands, trucks of the Pakistan army's National Logistic Cell, arriving from Karachi with crates of CIA arms, carried the heroin to ports and airports for export to world markets (Lifschultz 1988: 495–496). As Pakistan's heroin output rose, the regime of General Zia ul Haq (1977–1988), particularly his powerful ISI, was soon tainted by the traffic. To cite only one example, the son of ISI's director, Akhtar Abdul Rahman, soon became one of the richest men in Pakistan (Abou Zahab 2000: 143–145).

In May 1990, as this covert operation was ending, the *Washington Post* reported that Gulbuddin Hekmatyar, the CIA's favored Afghan asset, was also the rebels' leading heroin trafficker. Significantly, the *Post* claimed that U.S. officials had refused for many years to investigate charges of heroin dealing by Hekmatyar and Pakistan's ISI largely "because U.S. narcotics policy in Afghanistan has been subordinated to the war against Soviet influence there" (Rupert and Coll 1990). In 1995, the former CIA director for the Afghan operation, Charles Cogan, spoke frankly about his agency's choices. "Our main mission was to do as much damage as possible to the Soviets," he told Australian television. "We didn't really have the resources or the time to devote to an investigation of the drug trade. I don't think that we need to apologize for this. Every situation has its fallout. . . . There was fallout in term of drugs, yes. But the main objective was accomplished. The Soviets left Afghanistan" (Aspire Films 1994).

Declaring War on Cocaine

During the 1980s, the stimulus of suppression, first seen in Asia, recurred as the United States extended its drug war into the Andes. Nixon's success in cutting shipments of Asian heroin to the United States seems to have stimulated the production of substitutes in the Americas—amphetamines in Philadelphia, black-tar heroin in Mexico, and cocaine in the Andes (U.S. General Accounting Office 1988: 8–15). Most important, a surge in cocaine demand in the United States raised Peru's coca cultivation from 15,000 tons in 1970 to 191,000 tons in 1987 and Bolivia's from 4,800 tons in 1963 to 79,000 tons in 1987. After being processed into paste, the coca base was flown north to Colombia for processing into fine cocaine powder and then smuggled across the Caribbean into the United States, usually on light aircraft. Indicative of the rapid rise in Colombia's processing industry, the number of labs seized rose from 275 in 1984 to 725 a year later (U.S. Congress 1986: 579; U.S. Department of State 1988: 16, 69–78, 104–110, 1991: 80–87, 114–122; Morales 1989: 47; Ardila 1990: 2). By the late 1980s, cocaine was growing into a major commodity that was integrated, albeit invisibly, into legitimate inter-American economic relations.

Ignoring the lessons from Nixon's drug war in Asia, the White House pursued a parallel policy in Latin America with dismal results. During the 1980s, President Ronald Reagan revived Nixon's drug war, redirecting its focus away from the Asian heroin traffic to counter the cocaine flow from Latin America. To Nixon's arsenal of bilateral negotiations and DEA enforcement, Reagan added both regional diplomacy and intensified domestic enforcement. In 1982, Reagan declared a "war on drugs" in Latin America and, 2 years later, reinforced this unilateral declaration when the Andean nations issued the Quito Declaration against narcotics in August 1984. Building upon this diplomatic momentum, President Reagan issued National Security Decision Directive No. 221 in April 1986, stating that drug traffic was a threat to the security of the American continent, thereby legitimizing an extension of the drug war beyond U.S. borders to Latin America (Aureano 2001: 24–25, 27).

Under President Reagan's renewed drug war, funding doubled, and much of this expanded effort was focused on sealing America's southeastern borders from trans-Caribbean drug flights. Although cocaine seizures soared from 2 tons in 1981 to 100 tons in 1989, this enforcement cordon around Florida simply deflected smuggling westward into northern Mexico, forging an alliance between Colombian and Mexican cartels. As the volume of cocaine crossing the border into the United States surged, Mexico's smuggling cartels increased their total bribes from $3 million in 1983 to $460 million a decade later—more than the budget of the Mexican attorney general's office. By the time President Carlos Salinas de Gotari finished his 6-year term in 1994, Mexico's cartels had gross revenues of $30 billion, far more than the $7 billion the country earned in oil exports, and had penetrated the federal government, making the country a narco-state. Under the Salinas Gotari government, the attorney general was allied with the drug cartels, his top antidrug prosecutor sold border commands to officers for as much as $1 million, and the police protected favored cartels by attacking their competitors. In 1994, the senior adviser to the attorney general resigned in protest, charging that cocaine cartels were "driving forces, pillars even, of our economic growth" (Andreas 2000: 42–45, 60–64). During Latin America's cocaine boom of the 1980s, narcopolitics dominated three governments—Bolivia's Garcia Meza (1980–1981), Panama's Noriega (1983–1989), and Paraguay's Stroessner (1954–1989)—but all three faded under U.S. pressure, leaving Mexico and Colombia to become the region's sole narco-states (Aureano 2001: 17–18).

The Reagan administration's parallel eradication efforts in Bolivia simply shifted coca cultivation northward along the Andes to new areas, more than compensating for any lost acreage. In 1986, the State Department's turbo Thrush-65 defoliation program eliminated cannabis cultivation in Colombia, source for 60 to 80 percent of American demand. The fumigation simply forced cannabis north into Belize and Jamaica, while inadvertently freeing labor and capital inside Colombia for a later shift into coca (see chapter 6 in this volume; U.S. Department of State 1991: 95). Under a bilateral agreement with Bolivia in 1987, U.S. suppression drove coca cultivation from the central Chapare region eastward toward Brazil and then north into Peru and Colombia (U.S. Department of State 1993: 91). Between 1987 and 1990, for example, early eradication programs in Bolivia sliced just 2,000 tons off its 79,000 ton output, while Colombia's harvest rose 50 percent, to 32,000 tons—producing a net gain in total coca production (U.S. Department of State 2000: 55–56). After 15 years of aggressive suppression in the Andes, the total coca leaf production doubled, from 291,000 tons in 1987 to 613,000 in 1999 (U.S. Department of State 2000: 56).

The impact of Reagan's policy was felt most directly in Colombia. Although marijuana exports had surged in the 1970s, criminality was still contained and few could have foreseen the catalytic effect of cocaine in drawing together diverse social forces for Colombia's drug violence in the 1980s. After the industrial base of northern Antioquia Department collapsed in the 1960s, mass migration eventually sent some 2 million people to America, laying the foundation for future criminal diaspora. As a cartel based in the provincial capital Medellin started shipping cocaine north in the late 1970s, it was the "genius" of Pablo Escobar to amplify its profits by controlling street-level distribution in cities across America via contacts within this Antioquia diaspora. When the United States pressed Colombia for action against the Medellin cartel, Escobar and his allies responded with a spectacularly violent attack on the state (Labrousse 1991: 195–199).

Domestic suppression produced equally dismal results. Under the imprimatur of this drug war, mandatory minimum jail sentences, first used in New York in 1973, proliferated at federal and state levels, denying judges any discretion and creating a doomsday machine for a relentlessly rising prison population (Martin 1990: 135–136). During Reagan's two terms, annual drug arrests inside the United States doubled from 569,000 in 1977 to 1,155,000 in 1988 (Martin 1990: 118). Driven by rising drug arrests, the prison population doubled, from 369,930 in 1981 to 627,402 in 1988. After remaining constant at 100 prisoners per 100,000 population for over half a century, the incarceration rate started soaring, from 138 in 1980 to 426 prisoners in 1989, and kept on rising with no end in sight (U.S. Department of Justice 1989: 1, 1991: 604; Nadelmann 1988: 99). There was, moreover, a striking racial disparity in this repression. Under the Anti-Drug Abuse Acts of 1986 and 1988, suspects convicted of possession of just 5 grams of crack cocaine worth $125 faced the same mandatory five-year sentence as those having 500 grams of cocaine powder worth $50,000. Since white users tended toward powder and black toward crack, by the end of the Reagan-Bush era in 1993, blacks, though only 12 percent of the population, were 44 percent of those in prison. In 1990, a Washington, DC research group reported that "almost one in four (23 percent) Black men in the age group 20-29 years of age is either in prison, jail, probation or parole" (Brown 1990: 84, 86, fn 2, 3; Fitzgerald 1990; Laniel 2001: 212–219).

The results of this repression were, moreover, decidedly mixed. Although casual marijuana smokers dropped from 29 million in 1985 to 21 million in 1988, regular cocaine users rose from 647,000 to 862,000. As cocaine flooded in from Colombia, the price per kilogram dropped from $50,000 in 1979 to just $10,000 a decade later—slashing the street price, sustaining hard-core addiction, and fueling a murderous competition for market share. In major urban drug markets across America, cocaine-related murders produced a sudden surge in the homicide rate (Martin 1990: 125–126, 131).

Reagan's successor, George H. W. Bush, expanded the drug war but shifted its focus toward domestic suppression and border interdiction. In his famous September 1989 address to the nation, President Bush held up a bag of crack cocaine, supposedly seized in a drug bust in front of the White House, and urged more money for the drug war. Simultaneously, his drug policy chief, William J. Bennett, released the National Drug Control Strategy, calling for an "unprecedented" expansion of police, courts, and prison to win the war on drugs (Skolnick 1990: 75–76). By the time Bush left office in 1993, the incarceration rate had risen further, to 519 prisoners per 100,000 population, and the prison population had grown substantially, from 900,000 in 1988 to 1.3 million in 1992 (Mauer 1991: 2; U.S. Department of Justice 2000; Laniel 2001: 212–213).

Asian Drug Proliferation in the 1990s

The 1990s witnessed an explosive growth in global drug trafficking, with narcotics production doubling in Asia and the Andes while synthetics spread around the world. As indicated by statistics on drug seizures, there was by the end of the decade considerable regional specialization—cocaine was dominant in North America (42 percent of total seizures), opiates in the whole of Asia (73 percent), and amphetamines in East and Southeast Asia (90 percent). By the late 1990s, there were 180 million people, or 4.2 percent of the world's adult population, using illicit drugs worldwide, including 13.5 million for opiates, 14 million for cocaine, and 29 million for amphetamines. Though Asia still produced over 90 percent of the world's heroin, over half the amphetamine users worldwide were now found in East and Southeast Asia, notably in Taiwan, Thailand, and the Philippines (United Nations 2000d: 56–61, 70, 74).

With the end of the Cold War, a new world order and its economic globalization transformed the dynamics of the illicit drug trade. For 40 years, the Cold War had imposed a bipolar division across Asia that led rival superpowers to defend the territorial integrity of their respective clients. The end of this global division brought a recrudescence of the primordial politics—religion, regionalism, race, and ethnicity—that weakened, in some cases shattered, the capacities of key states in Asia's opium zone. The collapse of the Iron Curtain destroyed the global template that had shaped the world's opiate traffic for 40 years—allowing a rapid expansion of opium trafficking in and through former Soviet Central Asia, creating new criminal syndicates, and opening smuggling routes that now cross China, Russia, and eastern Europe. Complicating any attempt at crop reduction, the world's leading heroin producers, Burma and Afghanistan, became outlaw states—diplomatically isolated, detached from the legitimate world economy, and economically dependent upon the illicit opium trade. Driven by these complex forces, heroin recovered its historic preeminence as the leading illicit narcotic and became in the 1990s something of a world drug. Expansion of opium cultivation in Burma, Central Asia, and the Americas fueled a sudden proliferation of heroin abuse around the globe— a phenomenon that allows us to speak, without hyperbole, of the "globalization" of heroin.

In the aftermath of the Cold War, Burma defied the world order by harnessing the country's drug trade to the twin tasks of national security and development. During the 1990s, Rangoon's military regime forged alliances with leading drug lords, stabilizing the traffic but stigmatizing the state. By attacking ethnic rebels but protecting allied drug lords, Rangoon's military regime created an effective synergy between increased borderland control and an expanding heroin traffic. After 1990, Burma, needing hard currency to buy the arms for these military operations, changed its tax and exchange regulations in ways that channeled illicit income from gems and drugs into its legitimate economy. In a review of trade figures for 1995–1996, the Centre Français du Commerce Extérieur in Paris identified $400 million in unexplained inflows and $200 million in defense imports that were probably financed by some $700 million earned from heroin exports (Lintner 1992: 24, 1997: 18–19).

Rangoon's strategy proved effective, particularly against General Khun Sa, who had long been protected by patrons in the Thai and Burmese military. During the 1980s, Khun Sa had become Burma's dominant drug lord, using his exceptional power to expand heroin exports to the United States (Erlanger 1990; Purdy 1995; U.S. General Accounting Office 1996: 2–7; U.S. Drug Enforcement Administration 1996). In the 1990s, however, Khun Sa's embrace of the Shan secessionist revolt forced Rangoon to launch a sustained offensive to regain control of these strategic borderlands.

In 1996, Khun Sa, caught in a pincer between two Burma army divisions and heavily armed Wa tribal militia, surrendered his army and retired to Rangoon for a new life as a legitimate financier. In the last years of this war, Khun Sa had been desperate for income to defend his enclave against Rangoon's relentless attacks but was unable, with caravan routes cut and international markets saturated, to expand opium production. So the heroin king, in his genius, introduced a new drug to service a local clientele. From his borderland laboratories and marketing networks, Khun Sa began mass marketing cut-price, low-purity methamphetamine tablets, called *yaba*, to poor Thai consumers, unleashing an epidemic of cheap stimulants that soon swept Southeast Asia. Between 1994 and 1998, Thai seizures of methamphetamine tablets surged from 5 million to 32 million tablets, a trend the United Nations called "alarming." Inside Thailand, an estimated 257,000 workers—truckers, taxi drivers, and factory hands—were by 1999 regular amphetamine users, surpassing for the first time the country's 214,000 heroin addicts (Suvichapouaree 1993; Lintner 1999; United Nations 2002: 61). Thus, the surrender of the world's most powerful drug lord, who once controlled half its heroin supply, had only a limited impact on the Golden Triangle's drug traffic. Diversification had made the traffic more resilient and rival drug lords of the United Wa State Army soon filled any void created by his fall.

In the eastern Shan States, the United Wa State Army (UWSA) and two allied Chinese warlords soon replaced Khun Sa as the region's dominant drug traffickers. After breaking with the Burmese Communist Party in 1989, the UWSA and its 15,000 troops allied with Rangoon's powerful intelligence chief, General Khin Nyunt. Under his protection, the Wa armies seized strategic territory along the Thai border, where by mid-2000 they were operating some 60 methamphetamine laboratories. Western narcotics agents estimated that the family of the UWSA commander Pao Yuchang grossed $240 million annually from his drug operations. Similarly, the Wa ally and Chinese warlord Wei Hseuh-kang—a former KMT-CIA operative who had served as Khun Sa's treasurer from 1976 to 1983—ran a heroin-amphetamine complex at Mong Yawn, a newly built city of 30,000 in the jungles near the Thai border with paved roads, dams, clinics, and schools. Further north, in Special Region 4 along the China border, the Chinese warlord Lin Minxian, a former Red Guard, operated heroin and methamphetamine laboratories to service markets across China and Southeast Asia (Lintner 1993a, 1993c, 1994, 1999; Tasker 2000; Tasker and Lintner 2001a; *Geopolitical Drug Dispatch* January 1996b: 3).

Under the Wa, Burma's borderlands made a decisive shift from opium to amphetamines. In 1998–1999, the Wa command reportedly did an informal market study warning that opium had short-term risks of overproduction in Afghanistan and long-term costs such as interdiction, payments to the SLORC, and the loss of political respectability. But the study also found that amphetamines had brilliant market prospects—notably, short supply routes to prosperous Asian markets, differentiated products (cut-price speed for laborers; Ecstasy for middle-class youths), and little international pressure (Fegan 2002). Not surprisingly, the Wa drug lords, like any businessmen, have weighed risks and reward. In the late 1990s, the UWSA, at Rangoon's behest, began working with the U.N. Drug Control Program to replace opium with alternative crops in the Wa hills—a tenuous cooperation facilitated by the simultaneous shift into amphetamine manufacture. Since a methamphetamine tablet manufactured for just 8 cents in the Shan States could be sold in Bangkok for $3, the profits from synthetics surpassed opiates—an economic reality that encouraged the Wa's shift from heroin. With their massive profits from drug operations, the Wa also began investing in the legitimate economy by taking control of Yangoon Airways, a major Rangoon bank, and a leading Burmese telecommunications company. But future prospects of the Wa were no more certain than those for any of their predecessors. By early 2002, infighting within Rangoon's military regime, between the Wa's patron Khin Nyunt and their enemy army chief Maung Aye, led to increased army seizures of Wa drug shipments and created the potential for a future war (Lintner 1993b; Gearing 1999; *Geopolitical Drug Dispatch* January 2000: 7; U.S. Department of State 2000: 291; Tasker and Linter 2001b; Zaw 2001; Reid and Costigan 2002: 142).

By mid-2000, Burma's warlords were exporting some 600 million methamphetamine tablets, worth $2.8 billion annually, to Thailand (Tasker 2000). Two years later, Burma had become, in the words of the U.S. Department of State (2002: Southeast Asia), "the primary source of amphetamine-type stimulants in Asia," with production of 800 million tablets annually. As these tablets flooded across the border almost unchecked, synthetics accounted for 75 percent of drug use among Thailand's swelling population of 2 to 3 million drug users (Reid and Costigan 2002: 210–211).

Supplied by Chinese networks in Hong Kong and the Netherlands, Indonesia and the Philippines also developed major amphetamine markets. Starting in the late 1980s, methamphetamine hydrochloride, known locally as *shabu*, spread like a pandemic through Philippine slums, with 1.5 million users by 1998. By the late 1990s, the Philippines had its own labs and introduced the drug into Indonesia, where use spread rapidly among the country's 1.3 to 2.0 million drug users (*Geopolitical Drug Dispatch* August 1998: 6–7; Burgos 1998; Associated Press 1999; Reid and Costigan 2002: 91, 172–173). If the past is any guide, the future success of opium eradication in the Golden Triangle may both stimulate amphetamine production in Southeast Asia and poppy cultivation elsewhere in Asia or in the Andes.

After Khun Sa's surrender in 1996, most surviving warlords accepted an alliance with the Rangoon junta as the price of survival. Indeed, the U.S. State Department reported that the Burmese government had "given the trafficking armies free hand to continue their trade" and noted that "the return of narcotics profits . . . is a significant factor in the overall Burmese economy." Under Rangoon's military regime, Burma remained, until 1998, the world's largest opium producer, with production steady around 2,500 tons per annum, according to U.S. estimates (U.S. Department of State 1998: 23, 266). Reacting to these reports, Secretary of State Madeleine Albright denounced Burma's military regime in 1997 as "drug traffickers and thugs" (Erlanger 1997). Burma had, in the eyes of the West, become an outlaw state.

In response to international criticism, Rangoon announced in 1999 a 15-year program for eradication of all narcotics and pressed minorities for opium-free pledges with firm eradication deadlines. In November 2000, Rangoon broke up the Mon Ko Defense Army and began a crackdown on other militia, such as the government's own Ka Kwe Ye, that had been allowed to cultivate opium in the Lashio area. After warlords like Peng Jiasheng missed their opium-free target date for their territory along the Chinese border, Burma's army mounted joint operations with China's military in September 2001, destroying heroin and methamphetamine laboratories throughout the Kokang Chinese Special Region. The regime's First Secretary Khin Nyunt reinforced these raids by threatening the Kokang warlords with "all necessary measures" if they did not quit the drug traffic by 2002. But Rangoon remained more circumspect towards the Wa and their "formidable military force," conceding the autonomy of their Southern Military Region along the Thai border and allowing them a distant opium-free date of 2005. To reduce intensive poppy planting in their tribal highlands near China, Rangoon has supported the United Nations Drug Control Program's Wa Alternative Development Project, a 5-year, $12 million program to introduce alternative crops such as buckwheat (U.S. Department of State 2002: Southeast Asia). In May 2002, as Burma's economy continued to collapse, the military regime freed its chief critic, Aung San Suu Kyi, and its spokesman promised to work for the "total eradication of narcotic drugs which are threatening mankind" (Mydans 2002).

Through this complex of pressures, compounded by protracted bad weather, Burma's opium output fell fast, from a peak of 2,560 tons in 1996 to only 1,090 tons 3 years later. The events that accompanied and encouraged this shift illustrate the complex dynamics of an interwoven, international drug market. The surrender of Khun Sa and the decision of his successors, the Wa warlords, to shift into amphetamines reduced demand for opium inside Burma, stimulating production in neighboring Laos (U.S. Department of State 2000: 55). As Burma's harvest failed to meet global demand, farm prices in neighboring Laos rose sharply, from $82 per kilogram in 1993 to $263 in 1996—producing a parallel increase in poppy areas, from

19,650 hectares in 1994 to 28,150 just 3 years later. Since Khun Sa's 1996 surrender disrupted Burmese heroin refining, there was, in the United Nation's words, "a void in the region" that encouraged "the emergence of heroin production in Laos." Then, the global drug market intruded. Over the next 2 years, the United Nations reported, "the rising share of high-quality Latin American heroin . . . on the US market" reduced demand for Laos's opium, plunging its farm price to only $65 per kilogram in 1998 and reducing its poppy area to 21,800 hectares a year later. Although Burma's decline had stimulated production in nearby Laos, the net result of these regional and global shifts was a sharp drop in Southeast Asia's opium production, from 2,790 tons in 1996 to 1,240 tons 3 years later (United Nations 1999b: 12, 22; U.S. Department of State 2000: 53, 55).

At the close of the twentieth century, Southeast Asia's drug trade was in the midst of a major transition. After 40 years as the world's leading source of illicit opiates, rising pressures for reform, both local and international, were beginning to overcome the power of drug lords and allow a serious attempt at opium eradication. After launching an antinarcotics program in 1969, Thailand had cut the country's opium production to only 6 tons in 2001, enough for just 10 percent of its total consumption (U.S. Department of State 2002: Southeast Asia). Since taking power in 1975, Laos's Communist Party had been unconcerned by the country's status as a leading opium producer and had let farmers plant poppies undisturbed, with harvests steady at 180 tons in 1993 and 200 tons in 2001. But in 1999, the socialist regime was "alarmed" by United Nations reports of rising drug abuse—with 2.1 percent of all Laotian adults taking opium, the world's second highest rate; and 17 percent of Vientiane teenagers using amphetamines. In response, the government announced a program for complete opium eradication by 2006 (United Nations 2000d: 162–165; Reid and Costigan 2002: 118–121; U.S. Department of State 2002: Southeast Asia). Burma still had 300,000 hill tribe farmers employed in opium production, but rising drug addiction, estimated at 500,000 heroin users, and spreading HIV infection created strong internal pressure for eradication. Since most of Burma's intravenous users shared needles, often in tea shop shooting galleries, 63 percent were HIV positive, producing "one of the most severe HIV epidemics in Asia" (Reid and Costigan 2002: 140–148). Despite recent declines, Southeast Asia still produced an ample surplus of heroin to service international markets for the short term. Even with its high addiction, Laos consumed only 70 of the 167 tons of opium produced in 2000, and Burma used only 10 percent of its heroin output (United Nations 1998a: 1–2; Reid and Costigan 2002: 118–119). And even if Laos does eradicate opium by 2006 and Burma by 2014, the region's mobile methamphetamine labs might still survive to supply Southeast Asia's booming demand for synthetic drugs.

In Central Asia, the end of the Cold War produced an unprecedented expansion of heroin production. The United States-Soviet disengagement from Afghanistan after 1989 and the simultaneous breakup of the Soviet Union combined to produce dramatic changes in Southwest Asia's drug traffic. As Afghanistan's opium production, in United Nations estimates, climbed relentlessly toward a record harvest of 4,600 tons in 1999, this war-ravaged land became history's first opium monocrop, with much of its land, capital, and labor dedicated to producing 75 percent of the world's heroin supply. Its rising heroin exports financed a bloody civil war and fueled an eruption of ethnic insurgency across a 3,000-mile swath from Central Asia to the Balkans. During the tumult of the 1990s, many of ethnic rebels who roiled this region—in Uzbekistan, Chechnya, Georgia, Turkey, Kosovo, and Bosnia —armed themselves by participating in the westward flow of Afghan heroin toward Europe.

Whereas Latin America's cocaine boom of the 1980s had created a succession of narco-states, Central Asia's rising heroin traffic of the 1990s pushed many of the region's newly independent nations even further toward disorder by fostering "grey areas" where, in the words of one analyst, "the nation state has disappeared for good and where real power is exercised by coalitions between guerrillas or militias and drug traffickers." Despite its potential for opium cultivation, Central Asia instead became by 2000 the key transit area for 85 percent of Afghanistan's heroin exports. By 1998, for example, Kyrgyzstan had 4 million people employed in drug trafficking, and within 2 years the country was exporting more heroin than Burma. Rather than responding forthrightly to the threat of instability posed by the drug traffic, Central Asian governments like the Karimov regime in Uzbekistan have used the drug war as a pretext for repression, just as Russia has played upon it to regain lost regional influence in Central Asia (Makarenko 2001: 88–89, 92, 109–110).

The torrent of heroin during the 1980s transformed Pakistan into a narco-state—with drug money dominating politics and heroin profits making military intelligence independent of central control. In a 1993 report, the CIA concluded that "heroin is becoming the life blood of Pakistan's economy and political system" (Griffin 2001: 150). After General Zia's death in a 1988 air crash ended military rule, this flood of drug money corroded Pakistan's restored democracy, both creating and destroying governments (Block 2001). In the 1988 parliamentary elections, a number of drug traffickers won seats under the banner of Benazir Bhutto's Pakistan People's Party and her first cabinet included several of the most notorious, notably Minister of Tribal Affairs Malik Waris Khan Afridi. In response to U.S. pressure, however, Prime Minister Bhutto cracked down on the drug traffic, arresting North West Frontier Governor Fazle Haq, notorious for his complicity in the traffic. After she lost power in a no-confidence motion in November 1989, Bhutto charged that drug traffickers had spent 194 million rupees to buy members' votes. The succeeding government of Prime Minister Nawaz Sharif (1990–1993) had similar ties to the traffic (Abou Zahab 2000: 147–153; Emdad-ul Haq 2000: 213; Rashid 2000: 121–122). To cite the most notorious example, Haji Ayub Afridi, chief opium broker for the Afghan resistance, emerged from the shadows of the covert war to win a parliamentary seat in 1990. From his fabulous, 15-acre palace at Landi Kotal near the Afghan border, Afridi became a power broker, first backing Sharif for prime minister and then allying with Bhutto to oust him in 1993 (Labrousse 2001: 68–69; Shahzad 2001).

In a parallel trend, Pakistan's Inter-Service Intelligence (ISI), with vast profits from both its CIA alliance and the heroin traffic, grew dangerously independent within the military and won the autonomy to continue covert wars inside Afghanistan and Kashmir in alliance with militant Muslim parties (Labrousse 2001: 66). In

1988, a special committee headed by a Pakistani air marshal warned Prime Minister Bhutto that the ISI was becoming "a de facto government," and she responded by dismissing ISI chief Hamid Gul. As CIA covert funds slowed in 1991–1992, the army Chief of Staff Aslam Beg and ISI's new head, Asad Duranni, informed her successor, Nawaz Sharif, that they compensated by financing their covert operations with drug money. When Bhutto's second government later objected to ISI's massive support for the Taliban, the military, she claims, pushed her from power in November 1996. Though Nawaz Sharif, who again succeeded her, was consequently careful to back the Taliban, he, too, lost power, in October 1999, in part because he displeased the ISI by wavering in his support of the Taliban when pressured by Washington. Even after the attack on the World Trade Center in September 2001, the ISI's head, General Mehmood Ahmed, urged the Taliban's head to resist American demands for the surrender of Osama bin Laden. When the United States began bombing Afghanistan a few weeks later, Prime Minister Pervez Musharraf fired General Ahmed and began the long, difficult process of curbing ISI's entrenched power as a state within a state (Abou Zahab 2000: 149–153; Emdad-ul Haq 2000: 213; Burke 2001; Frantz 2001b; Griffin 2001: 149; French 2002b).

Heroin's influence was not limited to the political elite. Along Pakistan's borderlands, the political economy of Baluchistan, adjacent to Afghanistan, was transformed by the heroin exports of the 1980s. Leading tribal traffickers soon dominated provincial politics. In April 1991, for example, a member of the provincial assembly, Mohammad Asim Kurd, was caught with 500 kilograms of heroin in his official car; he evaded arrest by seeking refuge in the provincial offices. Two years later, six delegates in the provincial assembly and three provincial ministers were "directly implicated in the traffic" (Abou Zahab 2001: 153).

With heroin ravaging its urban poor and narco-politics corrupting its political elite, Pakistan steadily cut its own opium harvest, from a momentary peak of 800 tons in 1989, and an average of 100 to 200 tons during the early 1990s, to just 2 tons in 1999—a radical reduction that may have stimulated production in neighboring Afghanistan. Under police and political pressure, heroin labs also disappeared from Pakistan between 1997 and 1999. By attacking the drug trade, Pakistan was restraining autonomy in the North West Frontier Province and curbing the ISI's formidable independence (Rashid 2000: 121–122; Burke 2001; Griffin 2001: 149; Jehl 2002). In an impressive display of global power, the United States had informally tolerated Pakistan's traffic when it supported the CIA's covert Afghan war in the 1980s; but then, in a reversal of policy, it pressed Pakistan for suppression in the 1990s when security imperatives no longer interfered with the drug war. In addition to its diplomatic pressure, the United States financed Pakistan's Anti-Narcotics Force in 1995 and supported passage of the harsh Control of Narcotics Substances Act in 1997, providing Pakistan with the means to eradicate its own opium production. To symbolize the success of this bilateral effort, in February 1999 Pakistan burned 400 kilograms of heroin and opium in a spectacular bonfire at Peshawar. However, the Afridi tribal traffickers simply moved their heroin labs 100 kilometers west across the border into Afghanistan, where they operated around Jalalabad under Taliban protection (Abou Zahab 2001: 155–158).

In marked contrast to Pakistan, Afghanistan became an outlaw state and opium its main cash crop. After the covert war had raised Afghanistan's opium crop ten-fold during the 1980s, the subsequent decade of civil conflict doubled its opium production, making it the world's top producer. During the 1990s, Afghanistan's rising harvest funded all sides in a devastating civil war among rival mujaheddin factions. The damage from these two wars, covert and civil, rendered Afghanistan, in effect, doubly dependent upon opium. For most of the twentieth century, the narcotics traffic, concealed in interstices within and among societies, had been shaped by larger political forces; but in the 1990s the opium so dominated Afghanistan's economy that it could emerge from the margins to shape the course of a nation's history. This extraordinary chapter in opium's modern history thus commands our attention, partly because of its sheer scale but, more important, because the relentless rise of Afghanistan's output reveals much about the dynamics of the global drug trade.

As Afghanistan's covert war wound down between 1989 and 1992, the Western alliance failed to sponsor a settlement or finance reconstruction, effectively abandoning a nation ravaged by years of brutal warfare. After investing $2 billion in Afghanistan's destruction, Washington refused to invest any diplomatic or financial capital in its reconstruction—leaving the country devastated, with 1.5 million dead, 3 million refugees, a ravaged economy, no functioning central government, and well-armed warlords primed to fight for power. International aid for refugees and famine relief plunged from $87 million in 1981 at the height of the covert war to only $13 million in 2000, even though the country was suffering a devastating drought. In the early 1990s, the good offices of special U.S. ambassador Peter Tomsen failed "to put together a polity in the ghost town Kabul had become"—a failure that CIA veterans like Charles Cogan applauded since such involvement might "lead to a dangerous overextension of American forces" (Cogan 1993: 82; Weiner 2001c). A decade later, the *New York Times* (2002, March 27) would condemn this decision to abandon Afghanistan as "a catastrophic mistake," but at the time few outside the agency noticed. Without any means to resolve the past or plan the future, Afghan rebels, armed with opium profits, plunged into a bitter civil war.

After the Soviet army withdrew in February 1989, the southern Pashtun mujaheddin armies, distracted by struggles over booty and opium, failed to mobilize effectively and crawled toward the capital in fitful offensives. For the next 2 years, both superpowers funded a proxy war between the Marxist Najibullah regime in Kabul and the mujaheddin guerrillas in the southeast. Though the Soviets had withdrawn their troops, the CIA felt that it had a "moral duty to arm the Mujaheddin" for a final assault on Kabul and raised its covert aid to $350 million in 1989, even though the "dominant fundamentalist strain in the movement . . . seemed to be turning increasingly against the United States" (Cogan 1993: 76, 81–82). During this period, the de facto commander of this covert war was ISI's chief, Lieutenant General Hamid Gul, an Islamic fundamentalist who may have encouraged the more militant tendencies among the Pashtun mujaheddin (Frantz 2001b). After months of desultory fighting, rival rebel armies—Tajik and Uzbek commanders from the north and Hekmaytar's Pashtuns from the south—seized Kabul from the Soviet client regime in April 1992. Fighting broke out almost immediately within the ranks of the resistance, culminating in three destructive battles for control of the capital in September 1992, January 1993, and May 1993 (Gargan 1982; Luhan 1991; Reuters 1991; Cogan 1993: 78).

During the civil war's first phase in 1992–1994, ruthless local warlords emerged to combine arms and opium in a brutal struggle for local power—almost as if Afghanistan's soil had been sown with dragons' teeth. Determined to install its Pashtun allies in Kabul, Islamabad, working through the ISI, backed its clients with arms and finance, serving in effect as a catalyst for the bloody factional fighting. The nominal prime minister of this fractious coalition, the ISI's ally Hekmatyar, was determined to dominate and spent 2 years shelling and rocketing Kabul in fighting that left the city ruined and some 50,000 dead (Weiner 2001d; Filkins 2002b). When Hekmatyar failed to take power, Pakistan then backed the formation of a new Pashtun force, the Taliban. With arms from the ISI and fanatical recruits from Pakistan's militant madrasahs (Muslim fundamentalist schools), the Taliban launched a campaign to capture Kabul in 1995 from its mass base around the southern city of Kandahar.

During this protracted civil war, rival factions used opium to finance the fighting. From satellite photography controlled by the CIA, the U.S. State Department estimated, quite conservatively, that Afghan opium production had doubled during the anti-Soviet resistance, from 250 tons in 1982 to 570 tons in 1991, and then doubled again during the civil war, from 685 tons in 1993 to 1,670 tons in 1999 (U.S. Department of State 1997: 25, 2000: Afghanistan: para. III–IV). From its more accurate field data, the United Nations found both a sharper increase and much larger harvests. In 1991, a United Nations report claimed that Afghanistan's opium crop was already 2,000 tons, and its antidrug officials privately predicted a 1992 harvest of some 4,000 tons—large enough to double the world's illicit supply (Labrousse and Laniel 2001: 44–46; U.S. Department of State 1991: 22; *Geopolitical Drug Dispatch* January 1992: 1, 3). Although unseasonable rainfall destroyed much of that harvest, in 1994 the first of the United Nation's careful field surveys of thousands of Afghan villages reported the crop at 3,300 tons (*Geopolitical Drug Dispatch* January 1992: 1, 3; August 1994: 5).

If we combine U.S. satellite estimates and United Nations field surveys, Afghanistan's opium harvest grew tenfold during the covert war of the 1980s, from 250 to 2,000 tons, and then doubled during the civil war of 1990s, from 2,000 to 4,600 tons (United Nations 2000b: 15; U.S. Department of State 2000: 56). Through this twentyfold increase during 2 decades of warfare, Afghanistan was transformed from a diverse agricultural system—with herding, orchards, and 62 field crops—into the world's first opium monocrop. With much of its arable land, labor, water, and capital devoted to opium, the drug trade became the dominant economic force shaping the nation's destiny. The superpower withdrawal from Afghanistan left behind chaos, which encouraged a rapid growth in opium production. By 1992, when Russia and the United States ended military aid to their respective clients, 14 years of warfare had left—in a population of some 23 million—1.5 million dead, 4.5 million refugees, 10–20 million landmines, and a ruined economy (Allan 1987: 200–202; Rashid 2000: vii, 126–127; Chivers 2001a; Virtual Information Center 2001). One-third of the country's population was displaced, and rural subsistence economies had been "deliberately destroyed" (Good-hand 2000: 266).

Lying at the northern reach of the monsoon, where rain clouds are already squeezed dry, Afghanistan is an arid land with a delicate ecology that could not recover unaided from such unprecedented devastation. Outside of irrigated areas like the Helmand Valley, the country's semiarid highlands have a fragile ecosystem that was already straining to carry their heavy populations when war first came in 1979. To supplement field crops such as the traditional staple wheat, tribesmen in these uplands practiced transhumance, the nomadic shifting of flocks to summer pasture. Every spring, tribes in the densely populated eastern provinces moved their flocks hundreds of miles west to summer pastures in the sprawling central uplands (U.S. Library of Congress 1986; Balland 1988: 265–270). Most important, these highlanders planted perennial tree crops, fruit and nuts, that took many years to root and bear. In these dry mountains, where irrigation relies on snow melt and droughts are regular, Afghan villages have long relied on tree crops—walnut, pistachio, and mulberry—since they root deep, resist drought, and serve as famine relief in dry years. In the Hindu Kush uplands, such as the Nuristan Valley in Afghanistan's northeast, "anarchic" societies had long favored tree crops because they are immune to burning by "local enemies." In that region's traditional warfare, "the wealth and permanence of the community lay in the trees." One walnut tree, for example, could sustain an adult for a full year (Allan 1974: 117–118, 1985a: 17). Further west, in the Shamali Plain surrounding Kabul, mulberry trees, drawing water deep beneath the ground, served as an "indigenous famine relief program" from the "omnipresent fear" of drought. Historically, these orchards gave villagers the "leisure time . . . to hone their skills in punitive warfare"—which, significantly, always spared these trees to avoid the certainty of deadly retaliation in kind. In the early 1970s, a survey of this valley's 410 villages found that 91 percent grew wheat and 72 percent tended mulberry trees (Allan 1978: 63–65, 92–94, 222). On the eve of war in the mid-1970s, many areas of northern Afghanistan, like the Shamali Plain, still cultivated orchard crops but now used them for both subsistence and export to Pakistan on modern roads (Allan 1985b: 246–251). Even so, these highlands were incapable of anything approaching ecological equilibrium. Instead, they produced a volatile history of "trading, caravan and slave raiding, conquest, starvation, and subsequent death, and continual migration to the plains" (Allan 1991: 68–70).

In sum, when war started in 1979, the highland societies of central and northeastern Afghanistan were struggling to survive through a fragile, inherently unstable balance of annual field crops, orchards, and herding. Burdened by recent population growth, the country's ecosystem was already showing resource strain, evident when the severe droughts of the early 1970s brought starvation. During the covert war of the 1980s, the Soviet army's modern firepower ravaged the herds and destroyed orchards that would have survived the traditional warfare of centuries past, crippling this unstable human ecology's capacity for recovery. In the decade of civil war that followed, collateral damage and calculated destruction continued to ravage the country's herds and orchards. Along their ragged battlefront with the

Northern Alliance, the Taliban's harsh pacification perpetuated the devastation of the Soviet war, increasing the society's dependence on opium. In 1999, for example, Taliban militia, with an unerring instinct for their society's economic jugular, attacked their enemy's mass base by cutting down mulberry and walnut trees across a swath of ethnic Tajik areas on the Shamali Plain north of Kabul (Bearak 2001b).

As these strands of postwar devastation wove themselves into a Gordian knot of social, economic, and ecological suffering, opium became the Alexandrine solution. With the return of some 3 million Afghan refugees to a war-ravaged land after 1989, opium solved several daunting social problems. In 1972, 7 years before the war began, a U.S. cabinet committee had reported that Afghan farmers made $300–$360 per hectare from opium, twice the average of $175 for fruit. "There is no substitute crop—except for hashish," the White House reported, "that can . . . provide anywhere near an equal income" (U.S. Cabinet Committee of International Control 1972: A18). Without any aid to rebuild their ravaged herds and orchards after the war of the 1980s, farmers now turned to opium, a reliable annual crop whose demands were already well known. "I fought in the Jihad for ten years," one Afghan farmer told a foreign correspondent. "In 1991, I returned to my village to farm. I planted 5 percent of my land with this filth (opium). This year, my family has returned from Pakistan to join me, and so I had to plant 25 percent this year." As the country plunged into civil war after 1992, Afghanistan did not have a recognized government to negotiate either foreign aid or trade agreements, so its farmers instead increased their plantings of a cash crop with ready markets and an informal *laissez-passer* at every customs barrier. Indeed, in late 1991 the United Nations reported that the Afghan guerrillas, anticipating a cut in CIA support, were already planting a greatly expanded opium crop as an alternative source of finance (*Geopolitical Drug Dispatch* August 1992: 1). In Nangarhar Province, a key battleground in the anti-Soviet struggle, villages were devastated and depopulated by 1989; but within 5 years, opium revived the local economy, with harvests of 1,500 tons annually and additional employment from the start of large-scale heroin production (Griffin 2001: 146–147).

Opium also generated a major demand for labor at a time of high postwar unemployment. Whereas the traditional staple, wheat, required only 41 work days per hectare, opium needed 350 days. If we multiply 350 days by the 91,000 hectares harvested in 1999, we see that opium offered seasonal employment of 30 days for over a million Afghans, or about a quarter of the potential labor force (United Nations 1999a: 2, 2000b: 23; Bearak 2001a; Chivers 2001b). In a society with unemployment that reached 70 percent in Kabul by early 2000, 25 percent of the total *available* work force would mean a much larger, albeit unquantifiable share, of *actual* employment (Bearak 2000; Chivers 2001b). By 1999, opium may have provided over half the employment in Afghanistan. In a devastated economy, moreover, opium merchants could accumulate capital rapidly to provide poor farmers with crop advances equivalent to over half their annual income—credit critical to the survival of many poor villagers. Although the 91,000 hectares planted in 1999 represented only 1.1 percent of Afghanistan's arable land, the economics of opium were so favorable that this limited area absorbed a disproportionate share of essential resources—a quarter of the country's available labor, much of its merchant capital, and a considerable share of its water (United Nations 2000d: 7).

In such a lawless, isolated nation, opium had other advantages over conventional crops — notably, in the words of the United Nations, "credit access, storeability, increasing value over time, permanent marketability, and easy transportability" (United Nations 1997: i, 11; 2000c). In an arid ecosystem with chronic water shortage and periodic drought, opium has the advantage of using less than half the water needed for food crops such as wheat (Weiner 2001e; Waldman 2002c). Later United Nations studies, done in the late 1990s, found that 20 years of fighting had destroyed the infrastructure for nonfarm income, forcing "the great majority of households" to rely on a weak agriculture that in many districts could only feed the population 5 to 10 months out of the year. In such a "highly volatile socioeconomic, political, and legal environment," opium cultivation "represents a low risk strategy for an increasing number of households across Afghanistan" (United Nations 1999d).

In 1996, after 4 years of civil war among rival resistance factions, the victory of the militant Taliban movement introduced new forces for a further expansion of opium. After capturing Kabul in September, the Taliban drove the Uzbek and Tajik factions into the country's northeast, where they formed the Northern Alliance and clung to some 10 percent of Afghanistan's territory (Burns and LeVine 1996). Over the next 3 years, a seesaw battle for the Shamali Plain north of Kabul raged until the Taliban finally won control in 1999 by destroying the orchards and irrigation in a prime food-producing region, generating over 100,000 refugees and increasing the country's dependence on opium (Revkin 2001; Landler 2002; Waldman 2002b). Once in power, the Taliban made opium its largest source of tax revenues. By 1997, the Taliban were collecting a 20 percent tax from the national opium harvest valued, in United Nations estimates, at about $100 million. To raise revenues estimated variously at $20 to $100 million, the Taliban collected a 5 to 10 percent tax in kind on all opium harvested, which they then sold to heroin laboratories; a flat tax of $70 per kilogram on heroin refiners; and a transport tax of $250 on every kilogram exported (Rashid 2000: 119; Association d'Études Geopolitiques des Drogues 2001b: 1; Labrousse and Laniel 2001: 63–64). The head of the regime's antidrug operations, Abdul Rashid, enforced a rigid ban on hashish "because it is consumed by Afghans, Muslims." He explained, "Opium is permissible because it is consumed by kafirs [unbelievers] and not by Muslims or Afghans." A Taliban governor, Mohammed Hassan, added, "Drugs are evil and we would like to substitute poppies with another cash crop, but it's not possible at the moment because we do not have international recognition." Giving weight to his words, opium production in the Taliban heartland of Kandahar Province jumped from 79 tons in 1995 to 120 in 1996 (Rashid 2000: 118–119).

More broadly, the Taliban's policies provided stimulus, both direct and indirect, for a nationwide expansion of opium cultivation. Farmers saw the regime's agricultural tax, called ushr, "as implicit support for the cultivation of the opium poppy" (United Nations, 1999d). Significantly, the regime's ban on the employment and education of women created a vast pool of low-cost labor to sustain an accelerated expansion of opium production. With the "low opportunity cost associated with women's labor," opium, an extraordinarily labor-intensive crop, became "a more attractive option for the household." In northern and eastern Afghanistan, women of all ages played "a fundamental role in the cultivation of the opium poppy"—planting, weeding, harvesting, cooking for laborers, and processing byproducts such as oil (United Nations 2000c). The Taliban not only taxed and encouraged opium cultivation but also protected and promoted exports to international markets (Rashid 2000: 118–119).

In retrospect, however, the Taliban's most important contribution to the illicit traffic was its support for the introduction of large-scale heroin refining. As Pakistan eradicated poppy cultivation and closed heroin refineries during the mid-1990s, heroin production moved westward across the border from Peshawar, Pakistan, to Jalalabad, capital of Afghanistan's opium-rich Nangarhar Province. There the Taliban tolerated hundreds of heroin labs clustered around the city in exchange for a modest production tax of $70 per kilogram of heroin.

During its first years in power, the Taliban's leader, Mullah Omar, made periodic offers to both the United Nations and the United States to swap an opium eradication for international recognition. After capturing Kabul in September 1996, the Taliban made its first such overture. Only days after the DEA released a report in November saying that the "Taliban had reached a de facto agreement with the cultivators," the regime's foreign minister, Mullah Mohammed Ghaus, sent the United Nations Drug Control Program (UNDCP) a note offering "necessary measures to suppress the traffic"—a commitment, the regime later hinted, that was contingent upon diplomatic recognition (Griffin 2001: 155). Though the negotiations were inconclusive, these overtures allowed the United Nations access to Afghanistan for a more ambitious eradication effort. In 1997, the new head of the UNDCP, Dr. Pino Arlacchi, launched a program for the total eradication of opium in Afghanistan, then the world's second-largest producer, with modest plans for crop substitution and construction of a few factories (R. Bonner 1997). Although the Taliban promised a one-third reduction in cultivation, donors were unconvinced and provided only half the $16.4 million that the United Nations had requested. The United States, for example, contributed only $3.2 million over 5 years from a drug war budget that climbed beyond $19 billion by 2000. In a series of heavily publicized raids in February 1999, the Taliban destroyed 34 heroin laboratories in eastern Nangarhar Province. But observers reported that the raids hit a negligible share of the 200 "kitchens" that were operating in the area. Although this clearly was not the Taliban's intention, the raids revealed a boom in heroin processing that was spreading into the Helmand Valley and the northeastern borderlands (Golden 2001; Rashid 2000: 123–124; *Geopolitical Drug Dispatch* April 1999: 5–6). In May 1999, Kabul's Anti-Narcotics Department finally announced a modest eradication effort in three districts of Kandahar. But observers felt that the 325 hectares actually destroyed were an insignificant loss in a region with 5,602 hectares of poppy (*Geopolitical Drug Dispatch* April 1999:5–6, June 1999: 6, September 1999: 7–8; United Nations 2000a: para. 370–371, 49).

Instead of eradication, the United Nation's annual opium surveys showed that Taliban rule had doubled Afghanistan's opium production, from 2,250 tons in 1996 to 4,600 tons in 1999—the latter figure equivalent to 75 percent of worldwide illicit production. In 1999, the United Nation's International Narcotics Control Board (INCB) reported that the poppy "continued to spread" to new areas under the control of the Taliban regime, which then ruled 96.4 percent of the country's opium districts. In some areas of Nangarhar Province, a bastion of the Taliban, farmers tore up food crops to plant opium on over 60 percent of all available land. Consequently, the United Nations noted that the regime's commitment to opium eradication "remains questionable, as it continues to collect taxes on the opium poppy crop that is harvested and the heroin that is manufactured." In much less diplomatic language, the U.S. State Department's 1999 report expressed strong pessimism about the country's drug control efforts, claiming that the Taliban collected a 10 percent tax on the opium harvest, "benefit directly from the whole opium business," and were "in active collusion with smugglers and criminal elements to manufacture and export heroin" (United Nations 1997: ii, 2000a: para. 370–371, 49; U.S. Department of State 1999: Afghanistan, para. I–II; Labrousse 2001: 62). By its de facto legalization of the opium traffic, Afghanistan, along with Burma, had become an outlaw state.

Although eradication proved ineffective, the United Nation's regional office did a series of field studies that represent, in sum, the most detailed research into the opium trade in over a century. In essence, these studies were trying to understand how such a damaged society, without any institutional support, could sustain all the complex requisites for commodity production—credit, labor supply, and marketing. Significantly, the United Nations was conducting its field surveys during the very years, 1994 to 1999, in which Afghanistan doubled its production to become an opium monocrop—documenting how the country mobilized its land, labor, and capital to overcome its enormous poverty and become the source of 75 percent of the world's heroin supply. More broadly, the United Nations corroborated, through these microlevel studies, the stimulus effect of crop eradication that had previously been evident only at the macro, or international, level.

In their early research, United Nations researchers found that poppy farming spread spontaneously across Afghanistan through market forces like those that had shaped the Asian opium zone throughout the twentieth century. A 1998 survey found that the Afghan opium trade was "not highly structured but a relatively free market," and cultivation thus spread through "the interdependent nature of labour markets and commercial trade between districts, combined with cross district ethnic and family links." Typically, a young male laborer, pressed by high prices and low income, became an itinerant harvester in older opium districts. Then, having learned how to cultivate the crop, he returned to his native village to plant opium on the family lands. At the next harvest, neighbors followed suit after witnessing the yield. Then came traders to offer credit and cash for subsequent harvests (United Nations 1998c: 3, 8–14).

Subsequent United Nations studies showed that opium had filled an economic void inside Afghanistan, helping to rebuild a shattered society with networks of credit, labor, and trade. Even though civil war still raged in many parts of the country, Afghan society conducted this commodity trade largely on trust, moving the opium harvest from seed to refined heroin without any violence. Since opium was nonperishable and its price was stable, farmers favored it over other crops as a source of savings and credit. In a survey of 108 opium-growing households in 1998, the United Nations found that 95 percent had taken loans in the past year. The 60 percent who borrowed from traders against their future opium crop sold an average of 18 kilograms at 43 percent below the harvest value. Similarly, landless farmers, with only their opium crop as collateral, borrowed an average of $709, or 53 percent of their annual household income, to purchase such necessities as food, clothing, and medicine. In 1998, a dramatic decline in opium yields forced debtors either to postpone payments or to purchase opium at four times the anticipated price to meet their scheduled repayments. Although extending the loan until the next harvest doubled or tripled the amount due, there were "very few defaulters among the existing informal credit arrangements"—even among the landless who had "the greatest opportunity to abscond" (United Nations, 1999c).

In a separate study, the United Nations found that opium, with labor demands nine times those for wheat, generated a heavy demand for itinerant harvesters. The irrigated Helmand Valley, source of half the country's opium production, drew seasonal workers from 5 surrounding provinces by offering workers a one-fifth share of the harvest, or an average daily wage of only $2.50—an apt index of the country's poverty. Since climatic and ecological differences between districts staggered the harvest, a majority of laborers harvested in two districts and a quarter worked in three. Almost 80 percent of harvesters cultivated poppies on their own small plots, supplementing their insufficient income by this seasonal labor. Despite the apparent randomness of a seasonal labor market, landlords picked harvesters with the skills to lance the poppy bulb for optimum yield in each phase of the 15- to 20-day harvest. Even within this casual labor market, trust also seemed to be an organizing principle. When the harvest looked poor and laborers knew their shares would be lower than expected, all regarded their agreement with the landowner as binding and none abandoned the crop (United Nations, 1999a: 2, 4, 9, 14–16, 21).

Following the opium from farm to market, another United Nations study interviewed 38 Afghan traders in mid-1998 to discover the dynamics of the farmgate narcotics traffic. In sum, the United Nations wanted to know if crop reduction would in fact stimulate demand and hamper the introduction of alternative crops. If the illicit opium trade is "localized and dominated by large traders who directly employ agents to purchase opium and coca at the farmgate," then this vertical integration would allow merchants to respond quickly to any crop reduction "with a concomitant increase in market prices." If, by contrast, the drug trade is "relatively free with numerous buyers and sellers operating independently," then harvest shortfalls "will not necessarily be transmitted to major traders through the price mechanism," allowing the United Nations time to introduce alternative crops. Although the United Nations found differences in Afghanistan's drug markets, their ongoing integration at regional and national levels made the country's opium trade responsive to the price stimulus of crop reduction (United Nations, 1998d). Although the United Nations study is useful, its conceptual frame ignored a key facet of the drug trade. Whereas it might be possible to cut opium supply without stimulating production locally, drugs are traded internationally and any cut in production will raise the price, stimulating production in another country or continent.

Specifically, the United Nations study discovered that the bulk of Afghanistan's opium trade was concentrated in two markedly different commercial centers—

Sangin bazaar in the south and Ghani Kel in the east. Lying at the heart of the irrigated Helmand Valley, source of half of Afghanistan's harvest, Sangin's free-market bazaar had some 200 traders who specialized in the export of smoking opium westward across the desert into Iran. By contrast, at the Ghani Kel bazaar in Nangarhar Province, producer of a quarter of the country's opium, the trade was centralized under 40 merchants who exported morphine and heroin eastward into Pakistan. Instead of a formal syndicate structure, the eastern trade operated through "vertical integration on the basis of tribe"—Baluchi tribes, who straddle the border, controlled smuggling, and various Pashtun tribes focused on cultivation and trading within Afghanistan. Recently, however, the Shinwari Pashtuns in the east, through their relations with Afridi Pashtuns across the border, had "developed a virtual monopoly on processing and final transportation of heroin into Pakistan" (United Nations 1998d).

The traders themselves, the United Nations found, were reputable members of their communities. In the south, the traders were educated, influential landholders who enjoyed local prestige (22 of 26 interviewed had gone on a haj to Mecca). Some were experienced merchants with 25 to 30 years' experience in the trade, but most were civil servants, professionals, or landholders who sold opium to survive the chaos of civil war. Although 60 percent handled less than 100 kilograms per annum, all had prospered. One trader's capital had grown from just $270 in 1994 to $9,000 only 4 years later. Although all traveled about this war-torn land with cash, traders were rarely victimized, and they in turn dealt with farmers on the basis of trust—with 60 percent offering cash advances collected in opium at the harvest. To maximize profits, a quarter of the traders followed the opium trail across the borders—with the price and profits rising from $82 per kilogram at the bazaar, $95 at the border, and $126 inside Pakistan. Even with direct exports, the United Nations estimated that only 8.5 percent of opium profits remained in Afghanistan —1 percent for farmers, 2.5 percent for local dealers, and 5 percent for the smugglers (United Nations 1998d; Rashid 2000:119). In sum, the illicit opium trade in Afghanistan, like the farming that produces the crop, was conducted in a civil culture with a tradition of trust that sustained the complex market relations needed to move this commodity from farmgate to international markets.

During the 1990s, Afghanistan's soaring opium harvest fueled an international smuggling trade that knitted Central Asia, Russia, and Europe into a vast illicit market of arms, drugs, and money laundering—drugs moving west from Afghanistan to Europe while guns and money flowed east. In this 3,000-mile journey toward Europe by truck, camel, air, and sea, narcotics swept westward with surprising speed across a dozen boundaries, almost immune to interdiction or interference. Yet wherever this invisible commerce touched ground for processing, packaging, or exchange, the illicit enterprise quickly ramified—encouraging drug production, official corruption, mass addiction, and HIV infection. Through the alchemy of capitalism, mafias formed, ethnic separatists armed, and a culture of criminality crystallized.

The northern routes toward Russia touched ground in Kyrgyzstan, where they have fostered a lethal mix of intravenous injection and HIV infection, with 32 to 49 percent of all addicts in Osh infected in October 2000 (Frantz 2000). From Kyrgyzstan's cities, some routes moved northeast to Siberian cities such as Irkutsk and Vladivostock or northwest en route to Russia and Europe (Association d'Études Geopolitiques des Drogues, November 2001b: 1–3). In April 2000, only 18 months after trafficking first reached into central Russia from Afghanistan, the city of Irkutsk, long free of both drugs and HIV, had registered 8,500 heroin addicts and 5,000 new HIV cases—with officials fearing that actual numbers for both could be 10 times that high. About the same time, in late 1998, these heroin routes reached Russia's far eastern port of Vladivostock, where Chechen, Tajik, and Azeri gangs controlled a traffic that soon engulfed the city in petty crime and fueled an illicit international trade in fish, timber, and stolen cars. In the first half of 1999, heroin use across Russia increased 4.5 times over 1998 (Tyler 2000; Wines 2000; Kattoulas 2002). Within a year, Russia's official number of HIV cases had tripled to 58,000 (Fisher 2001). In releasing the United Nation's annual review of AIDS in November 2001, its program director, Dr. Peter Piot, highlighted an "explosion" of HIV from eastern Europe to Central Asia, with 250,000 new infections, largely from injected drugs, raising the total to over a million (Altman 2001).

Across these vast distances with poor communications, ad hoc alliances within and among ethnic diasporas provided critical criminal linkages—-Kosovars scattered from Geneva to Macedonia, Turks from Berlin to Kazakhstan, Armenians from Moscow to Lebanon, Azerbaijanis from Sumgait to Kyrgyzstan, and Chechens from Baku to Kazakhstan. In the cities that serve as trading posts in this traffic— Osh, Tashkent, Samarkand, Baku, Tbilisi, Skopje, Pristina, and Tirana—extraordinary profits from drugs and guns have produced mafia gangs, criminal diasporas, tribal warlords, and rebel armies. Among these many ethnic syndicates, the Georgians, Azeris, and Chechens control drug distribution in Russia, and the Turks dominate the refining of Afghan opium into heroin for distribution in Europe (Makarenko 2001: 94).

In the grand hotels of Central Asia, the Caucasus, and the Balkans, mafias and narco-nationalists were a distinctive presence—muscular men with designer suits, high-powered weapons, and stolen Mercedes sedans. Cutting across the ethnic syndicates, Osama bin Laden's Al Qaeda organization, in the view of British Prime Minister Tony Blair and Saudi Crown Prince Abdullah, used its militant Muslim network to traffic in drugs from Afghanistan to Bosnia (Tyler 2001; Gordon 2002b). Already attenuated by postsocialist economic miasma and the strains of new nationhood, state control and civil society weakened before the power of these new narco-mafias with their superior firepower, wealth, and political influence.

During the 1990s, Afghan opium fed both regional and international markets, creating local smuggling routes and complex international connections. In 1998, the United Nations estimated that 40 percent of Afghanistan's harvest fed European markets, but the balance, fifty-eight percent, sustained addicts within the region—3 million in Iran, another 2 million in Pakistan, and lesser numbers in Tajikistan, Kyrgyzstan, and Kazakhstan (Rashid 2000: 122; Labrousse and Laniel 2001: 53; Virtual Information Center 2001). In Afghanistan, opium smuggling started at two points—Helmand Province in the south and Nangarhar Province in the east. With easy transport through the Khyber Pass, Nangarhar, source of a quarter of the country's harvest, sent its opium eastward to feed Pakistan's million-plus heroin addicts. From the fertile Helmand Valley, home to half of Afghanistan's opium harvest, armed convoys joined the daily traffic of 300 trucks moving west from Kandahar toward Iran and north into Central Asia, the main corridor in Afghanistan's $3 billion smuggling trade (Rashid 2000: 124).

Between 1990 and 1997, Iran's opium seizures along its Afghan border surged from 21 to 162 metric tons, forcing Tehran to close the border in 1998. In the violent shoot-outs that followed, Iran seized 5 tons of heroin in just a few weeks and, by the end of the year, over 16 tons of heroin and morphine base, much of the latter destined for heroin laboratories in Turkey (United Nations 1998d; Rashid 2000: 122, 124; Labrousse and Laniel 2001: 65). Over the past 20 years, some 2,700 Iranian police officers have been killed in clashes with drug smugglers, most along the Afghan border (MacFarquhar 2001). In 2000 alone, 142 Iranian personnel died in 1,532 armed confrontations. But not even this aggressive enforcement could stop smuggling by "fierce and rebellious" Baluchi tribes, who moved freely across the desert frontier into southern Iran (United Nations 2001b). Two years after closing the border, Iran's opium seizures had dropped 12 percent, to 179 metric tons, but heroin seizures were up 3 percent, to 6 tons—a shift indicative of improved processing inside Afghanistan. According to the United Nations, Iran's drug seizures of 254 tons in 2000 represented nearly 90 percent of the world's total. Fueled by this irrepressible flow, Iran's addict population soared beyond the official tally of 1.2 million to an estimated 3.3 million in 2001 (MacFarquhar 2001; Reid and Costigan 2002: 101, 103). By 1997, even the official figures showed that 1.4 percent of Iran's adults were opiate users—the world's second-highest rate of addiction after Pakistan (United Nations 1999b: 24). Although Iran could not seal its border, its efforts diverted much of the Europe-bound traffic northward to Herat and then into southwestern Turkmenistan (*Geopolitical Drug Dispatch* January 1997: 1–3, 5; February 1999: 5–6).

After Iran and Pakistan absorbed the bulk of Afghanistan's opium harvest, the rest, some 40 percent, began a complex westward journey that delivered 90 percent of Europe's heroin supply. One of the main flows started with the daily traffic of some 200 trucks, moving north from Jalalabad and Kabul toward the country's desolate northeastern corner, adjacent to Tajikistan, where the independent commanders of the Northern Alliance financed their rebel armies with heroin. By 1996, the heroin labs were opening along the northern border in Badakhshan under control of the Northern Alliance and in the provinces of Balkh and Faryab under the Uzbek warlord General Abdul Rashid Dostum (*Geopolitical Drug Dispatch* January 1997: 4; Rashid 2000: 124; Harris 2001). In the border province of Kunduz, the fundamentalist Hezb-i-Islami faction under Gulbuddin Hekmatyar operated several heroin laboratories until the Taliban captured the area in May 1997, forcing him to shift operations eastward to Badakhshan (*Geopolitical Drug Dispatch* July 1998: 1; Goodhand 2000: 272).

From these northern borderlands, the young Muslim warlord Juma Namangani, backed by Osama bin Laden, coordinated a loose trafficking syndicate that spanned Central Asia—flying opium from Nangarhar in eastern Afghanistan to labs in the northern city of Kunduz, operating heroin labs in Tajikistan, and "using its network of militants across the region as couriers" to Chechnya in the Caucasus (Griffin

2001: 150; Rashid 2002:133, 140, 154, 165–166). During the Tajik civil war of the mid-1990s, rival warlords had moved much of Afghanistan's opium north along the twisting 725-kilometer Khorog-Osh highway into the Ferghana Valley, where much of the traffic then turned west toward Turkey. At the end of this conflict, in 1997, the Uzbek Muslim militant Juma Namangani gathered rootless fighters into his Islamic Movement for Uzbekistan (IMU) and used them to dominate the drug routes through Tajikistan. By 2000, the IMU controlled an estimated 70 percent of the narcotics passing through Tajikistan to Kyrgyzstan (Makarenko 2001: 99–106). After Afghanistan's record harvest of 1999, the IMU used drug money to extend guerrilla operations into Uzbekistan and Kyrgyzstan. When his invasion of Kyrgyzstan with a force of 750 men was repulsed, Namangani fell back to northern Afghanistan as a base for incursions into southern Uzbekistan. In September 2000, the Paris daily *Le Monde* reported that this "young warlord whose brutality is legendary, seeks to control the prime drug transit routes in order to increase his market 'area,' and thereby his power" — a bid that ended with his death during the United States attack on Afghanistan in November 2001 (Shihab 2000; Association d'Études Geopolitiques des Drogues October 2001a: 1–2; Frantz 2001a; Myers and Dao 2001).

Through the plains and passes of northeastern Afghanistan, an array of rebel commanders sent heavily armed caravans across the border into Tajikistan, the first stage in a journey toward Central Asia, Russia, and Europe. In a vain attempt to stem this flow, Tajikistan's Federal Guards had 96 armed clashes with smugglers in 2000, suffering 12 casualties and seizing 3 tons of opium and heroin (Virtual Information Center 2001). From 1992–1997, the Tajik civil war expanded the country's role as a transit zone for Afghanistan's heroin as local warlords smuggled drugs to buy arms and then retained their drug connections after the peace settlement brought them into the government. By 1997 the United Nations estimated that one-third of Tajikistan's gross national product was generated by the transit traffic in drugs (Makarenko 2001: 90–91).

Across this vast swath of the Eurasian land mass—500 miles south to north and 3,000 miles west to east—an ever-changing web of smuggling routes traced recurring patterns within four distinct sectors between Central Asia and the Balkans. As morphine and heroin shipments left Afghanistan's laboratories, they moved west through Iran; northwest across Turkmenistan; or, more commonly, north across Tajikistan to Osh and Bishkek in Kyrgyzstan—crossing a maze of indefensible, illogical borders, the legacy of a Stalinist strategy for blocking ethnic secession. From the Osh drug market, ruled by the Kyrgyz warlord Bekmanat Osmonov in the mid-1990s, or lesser trade centers at Dushanbe and Bishkek, drug shipments then turned generally westward—by air to Moscow, overland across Turkmenistan, or more circuitously through Uzbekistan and Kazakhstan. Indicative of the traffic's scale, in September 1997 Turkmeni officials seized 502 kilograms of heroin in a truck carrying rice from Kandahar, Afghanistan, to Baku, Azerbaijan; in November, they intercepted 1.2 tons of the drug on a truck en route to Gaziantep, Turkey; and then, in the first 7 months of 1998, confiscated 41 tons of acetic anhydride, heroin's precursor chemical, from Iranian trucks bound for Afghanistan (*Geopolitical Drug Dispatch* February 1999: 5; May 1997: 3; Labrousse and Laniel 2001: 57–59).

Once across the Caspian Sea, these diffuse westerly routes merged as they entered the Caucasus, with its volatile mix of contested boundaries, ethnic insurgency, local mafias, and criminal clans. In this rugged isthmus between the Caspian and Black Seas, a volatile array of armed groups processed morphine and smuggled heroin with near impunity: the Kurdistan Workers Party (PKK), that manufactured heroin in Azerbaijan; local Azerbaijani mafia clans in Baku, Sumgait, and Nakhichevan; Armenian syndicates allied with the nationalist Dachnak Party; the Azeri Grey Wolves; Ossetian and Abkhazian separatists in Georgia; and Chechen nationalists to the north.

Whether directly across Iran or less directly through Turkmenistan and the Caucasus, most shipments of heroin and morphine base passed through Turkey, where 2.9 tons of Europe-bound heroin were seized in 1999, representing 30 percent of total world seizures (Labrousse and Laniel 2001: 142). In April 2002, Turkey's gendarmes seized a shipment of 7.5 tons of morphine base from Afghanistan, a record haul indicative of the enormous scale of Afghanistan's exports and Turkey's heroin industry (Frantz 2002). In a reprise of its role as a cultural crossroads, Turkey drew precursor chemicals from Europe and morphine from Afghanistan to become the transshipment point for an estimated 80 percent of the heroin seized in Europe (United Nations 2000d: 41).

Moving north from Turkey or around and across the Black Sea from the Caucasus, drug shipments, now almost entirely heroin, passed through the Balkans, where rival ethnic militias—Serb, Croat, Bosnian, and Kosovar—used drug profits to purchase arms and pay fighters. As Turkey became the site for refining Afghan opium into heroin for Europe, traffic along the so-called Balkan route soared. During the 1980s, an alliance between a new Italian syndicate, La Sacra Corona Unita, and rising Armenian crime groups made the Adriatic Sea a southern route between Turkey and Europe. After the abolition of Albania's security service, the Sigurimi, in July 1991, several thousand ex-agents used the Adriatic ports of Vlora and Durres as an entrepôt on this route for the smuggling of guns, drugs, prostitutes, and stolen cars. Steady Albanian migration to Europe, which intensified between 1992 and 1995 when 350,000 refugees fled Kosovo, created a criminal diaspora that dominated heroin distribution in Switzerland and Germany. In 1990, the Swiss Federal Police launched Operation Benjamin, which uncovered arms-heroin traffic with Kosovo and, 8 years later, reported that Albanians dominated heroin distribution in all cantons. While a Kosovar criminal diaspora based in Skopje, Pristina, and Tirana smuggled heroin across the Adriatic Sea, Albanian exiles in western Europe used drug profits to ship Czech and Swiss arms back to Kosovo for the separatist guerrillas of the Kosovo Liberation Army (KLA). In 1997–1998, these Kosovar drug syndicates armed and financed the KLA for a revolt against Belgrade's army (Chassagne and Gjeloshaj 2001: 162, 167–186).

After 1995, moreover, the drug traffic expanded along the northern route—from Turkey through Yugoslavia to Central Europe—making Belgrade a crime capital and providing a more direct route for Kosovar smugglers like Princ Dobroshi, one of Europe's leading traffickers, who used his heroin profits to purchase arms for the KLA until his capture in March 1999 (Chassagne and Gjeloshaj 2001: 169, 182–183; Association d'Études Geopolitiques des Drogues October 2001b: 2–4; Labrousse and Laniel 2001: 30, 150). Within Serbia and its satellite states, the notorious "Arkan" (Zeljko Raznatovic), one of several narco-nationalists backed by Belgrade state security, used drugs, contraband, and counterfeiting to finance his Scorpion gang, which terrorized Kosovo and murdered rival Kosovar drug dealers in the mid-1990s (*Geopolitical Drug Dispatch*, November 1991: 1, 3; June 1995: 1, 3; November 1996: 1, 3–4; May 1997: 1, 3–4; July 1998: 1, 3; February 1999: 5–6, June 1999: 6).

Even after the Kumanovo agreement of June 1999 had settled the Kosovo conflict, the United Nations administration of the province, preoccupied with mediating ethnic conflict, allowed a thriving heroin traffic along this northern route from Turkey (Chassagne and Gjeloshaj 2001: 185–186). The former commanders of the KLA, both local clans and aspiring national leaders, continued to dominate the transit traffic through the Balkans. In January 2000, the Army for the Liberation of the Albanian Population of Presevo, Medvedja, and Bujanovac (UCPMD) began battling Serbian police for control of a strategic smuggling corridor along the Serbia-Kosovo border—with much of the fighting around the town of Veliki Trnovac, a major heroin depot for local criminal clans. The most militant of these local commanders, Muhamed Xhemajli, had reportedly been a major drug dealer in Switzerland before joining the KLA in 1998 (Association d'Études Geopolitiques des Drogues October 2001b:2–4; Labrousse and Laniel 2001: 30, 150). In May 2001, Italian peacekeepers in KFOR seized a truckload of heavy weapons, including 52 rocket launchers and 5 SAM-7 ground-to-air missiles, near the Kosovo border believed destined for Albanian guerrillas inside southern Serbia. According to Croatian police sources, Albanian syndicates probably bartered heroin for these arms from Croatian criminals, many of them former officers (Association d'Études Geopolitiques des Drogues, May 2002: 1–3).

Although this traffic across Central Asia flourished for a decade, it all depended on high-volume heroin production in politically volatile Afghanistan. In July 2000, as a devastating drought entered its second year and mass starvation spread across Afghanistan, the Taliban's Mullah Omar ordered a sudden ban on all opium cultivation in an apparent bid for international recognition. With the drought reducing yields, the recently completed harvest was already down to 3,276 tons of opium from the 1999 record of 4,600 tons. But Afghan farmers hoarded up to 60 percent of their harvest, so the country still had massive stockpiles to cushion the blow (United Nations 2000b: iii, 14; Revkin 2001). Right after the ban, the local price for a kilogram of opium shot up from $110 to $500—allowing the Taliban, in the words of the U.S. State Department, to profit by "dumping opium stocks at prices higher than otherwise could have been achieved" (U.S. Department of State 2000: 460–461, 474–475, 2002: Southeast Asia; Bearak 2001a; Crossette 2001b).

Only 3 months after the ban, in an apparent bid to barter prohibition for recognition, the Taliban sent a delegation to United Nations headquarters in New York, where Deputy Foreign Minister Abdur Rahman Zahid denounced the Northern Alliance as a "band of thugs" who controlled the country's heroin traffic (Crossette 2000a). The United Nations could not overlook the regime's human rights violations, and the Northern Alliance retained Afghanistan's seat. Some months later, the Taliban's foreign affairs spokesman, Faiz Ahmed Faiz, expressed deep disappointment at the United Nation's cool reaction to their "epic task": "The response to this tremendous achievement was unexpected. They imposed more and more sanctions on us" (Harding 2001). Adopting a parallel position, the United States rewarded the Taliban with $43 million in additional humanitarian aid while supporting the United Nations sanctions. Announcing this aid in May 2001, Secretary of State Colin Powell referred to "the ban on poppy cultivation, a decision by the Taliban that we welcome," but he urged the regime to "act on a number of fundamental issues that separate us: their support for terrorism; their violation of internationally recognized human rights standards, especially their treatment of women and girls" (U.S. Department of State 2001).

Initially, United Nations and U.S. observers were skeptical, but firsthand observation showed that the regime, with its characteristic ruthlessness, had imposed a brutally effective ban (Crossette 2000b; U.S. Department of State 2000: 252). The CIA reported that opium production had dropped from 4,042 tons in 2000 to a potential harvest of only 81.6 tons in 2001 (Golden 2001). A United Nations survey of 10,030 villages found that the Taliban, by enforcing its ban with mass arrests, had cut the harvest to only 185 metric tons in 2001, a 94 percent reduction—virtually eradicating opium in two of the country's three main opium districts. In the southern provinces of Helmand and Kandahar, producers of over half the country's opium, the regime eradicated 100 percent of the 46,280 hectares of poppy planted the year before. In eastern Nangarhar Province, source of a quarter of the country's crop, opium dropped from 19,747 hectares in 2000 to only 218 hectares a year later—a 99 percent decline. But in northeastern Badakhashan Province, bastion of the opposition Northern Alliance, poppy planting more than doubled, to 6,342 hectares (United Nations 2000b: 21–23, 2001a: iii, 11, 15–17; Weiner, 2001a).

Indeed, after the Taliban's poppy ban, the warlords of the Northern Alliance raised Badakhshan's opium output from 40 to 150 metric tons, accounting for 83 percent of Afghanistan's harvest in 2001 (United Nations 2000b: 26; 2001a: ii–iii, 18). This sudden surge was the culmination of ongoing changes that made opium the mainstay of the provincial economy. Even before the covert war began in 1979, local farmers could supply only 50 percent of the province's food, making villagers dependent on long-distance cattle trading. After the civil war started in 1992, a combination of factors—easy credit from money lenders, strong demand from regional markets, and above all the dictates of local commanders—had encouraged a systematic shift from wheat and cattle to opium (Goodhand 2000: 268–269, 272–273).

"The bad side of the ban is that it's bringing their country . . . to economic ruin," said Steven Casteel, the DEA's intelligence chief, adding that the sudden switch to food crops without any transitional support would bring serious hardship (Crossette 2001c). Indeed, in March 2001, a farmer named Rashid in eastern Afghanistan told reporters, "All the young people have gone to Pakistan. Ninety percent of this area used to be cultivated with poppy. How much money can you make from wheat?" (Harding 2001). Another Afghani farmer, Zulman Khan, said that the switch from opium to wheat would cut his annual income from $10,000 to $400 (Associated Press 2000). Veteran observer Olivier Roy (2001) concluded that many poppy growers, most from the dominant Pashtun tribes, "resented being . . . commanded to cease growing opium poppies at a time of profound economic desperation." Villagers were cynical about the Taliban's motives, suspecting that Arab and Afghan traders close to the regime made bumper profits by cashing in surplus stocks at inflated prices (Waldman 2002a).

In banning opium, the Taliban had destroyed the country's only major industry. To an extent not generally appreciated, Afghanistan had for over two decades invested a growing share of its scarce resources in opium—capital, land, water, and labor. As its dependency on the drug trade ratcheted upward, opium became by the late 1990s the mainstay for many sectors of society, including the ruling Taliban, the opposition Northern Alliance, bazaar merchants, long-distance traders, small farmers, and landless laborers. Then, in 2000–2001 a drought devastated much of the countryside, increasing the economy's dependence upon opium (United Nations 2000b: 15–18; Weiner, 2001c). In 1997, the Taliban's opium eradication officer for Kandahar, Abdul Rashid, had warned that eradicating opium would alienate the growers, who were "an overwhelming majority of the population" (Chouvy 2001: 81). By the time the Taliban banned cultivation in July 2000, Afghanistan had, by design and default, become an opium monocrop dependent on the drug trade for most of its tax revenues, almost all export income, and much of its employment. In this context, the Taliban's opium eradication was slow economic suicide, which brought an already weakened society to the brink of collapse. When the U.S. bombing began in October 2001, the Taliban regime collapsed, in the word of a *New York Times* analyst, with a speed "so sudden and so unexpected that government officials and commentators on strategy . . . are finding it hard to explain" (Apple 2001). Although the U.S. bombing campaign did enormous psychological and physical damage, it may have played a catalytic, not a causal, role—accelerating an ongoing internal collapse that may have eventually swept the Taliban from power without foreign intervention. In effect, the Taliban's economic evisceration left its theocracy a hollow shell of military force that shattered with the first American bombs.

The outbreak of war with America in September 2001 ended the Taliban's opium ban. At the start of fall planting in early September, the Taliban had already rescinded its prohibition with an announcement over its Voice of Shariat radio. United Nations observers soon saw peasants preparing poppy fields in Nangarhar and Kandahar provinces, the regime's heartland. Only days after U.S. military operations began, local traders dumped their stockpiles on the market, sending opium prices down by 500 percent and filling any possible gaps in global supply. "All the ingredients for illicit cultivation are there," said the United Nations Drug Control Program's Islamabad representative, Bernard Frahi, "war, continuing poverty, and a breakdown in law and order. We could see a huge resumption in cultivation" (Ahmed 2001; Golden 2001; Hamill 2001; Harding 2001).

Although the Taliban formally reiterated its ban a few weeks later, the regime's loss of Kabul and some 80 percent of the countryside by mid-November rendered its dictates irrelevant. Within weeks, a drug control official in the new interim government for the three eastern provinces around Jalalabad, Shamshul Haq, reported an burst of poppy planting in Nangarhar: "Without a lot of help from the world community, they grow it not only in their fields but on the roofs and in their flowerpots." A farmer named Aubaidullah in Kherabad said his income from 1 hectare of land dropped from $13,000 from opium before the ban to only $100 for wheat. "A lot of people under the Taliban tried to plant corn or wheat," he explained, "and they had to leave the country because of their debts" (Reuters 2001; Weiner 2001e). In travels through the bleak, devastated villages of Nangarhar, one *New York Times* reporter found ruined orchards, farmers crippled by mines, and opium planting. Surveying a landscape of dead trees and dry fields, villagers living north of the Ghani Kel opium bazaar recalled sadly that there had once been "pomegranates, grapes, and sour orange trees," but now there was only devastation and opium. "I know the poppy is poison for everyone," said Timur Shah, a 27-year-old farmer in Nangra village. "But are you ready to tell me not to cultivate it? We will die from lack of bread and food" (Weiner 2001f). By late November, the country's main opium bazaars were back in business. At Ghani Kel in Nangarhar, 100 of the market's 300 stalls were selling opium stockpiled during the ban, and some 200 merchants at Sangin in Helmand were again trading opium for export, largely to Iranian smugglers who left in four-wheel drive vehicles for a race across the desert (Harris 2001; Waldman 2002c).

As the Taliban collapsed in mid-November, this dragons' teeth soil suddenly raised a new crop of warlords who used their drug money to arm fighters and seize territory. Under the covert warfare doctrine first developed in Laos during the 1960s, the United States had deployed massive air power and Special Forces as advisers to Afghan warlords—providing arms and money that reinvigorated local commanders after 4 tough years under the Taliban, which had driven many into retirement or exile. Across the country, brutal warlords suddenly reemerged to battle for territory, seize food shipments, and smuggle drugs. To capture Kabul and other key cities, the United States backed Northern Alliance leaders, who had long dominated the local drug trade; and in the southeast the CIA delivered money to Pashtun warlords active along the border as drug smugglers.

When the Taliban regime collapsed suddenly in mid-November, these corrupt and brutal warlords soon filled the political void by forming private armies and occupying cities across the country—conditions ideal for a resumption of heroin trafficking (Rubin 2002). In the northeast, the Taliban's defeat affirmed the authority of Northern Alliance commanders, who had long dominated drug smuggling into Tajikistan. On the frontier near Uzbekistan, for example, the brutal Uzbek warlord General Abdul Rashid Dostum, who had controlled the region's heroin complex before his ouster by the Taliban, regained control with CIA support, using his arms to drive ethnic Pashtuns out of the north and to battle a rival warlord for territory (Filkins 2002d, 2002f). In the northwest, the warlord Ismail Khan ruled Herat and its borderlands with an army of 50,000 troops and a tank corps that could ignore Kabul's toothless directives (Waldman 2002a). "The Northern Alliance has . . . taken no action against cultivation and trafficking in the area it controls" (U.S. Department of State 2002: Southwest Asia).

In the Pashtun-dominated southeast, former warlords long active in the heroin trade suddenly reappeared to seize local power. Under the new Eastern Shura government, for example, the Pashtun warlord Hazarat Ali used his opium profits to arm 6,000 militiamen and then install himself as security minister in Nangarhar's capital, Jalalabad. In the early 1990s, warlord Ali had gained notoriety as head of

Jalalabad's airport when weekly flights to India and the gulf states often carried cargoes of illicit opium. In December 2001, during critical U.S. air attacks on Taliban and Al Qaeda leaders hiding in the Tora Bora caves, Hazarat Ali commanded the key sector along the Pakistani border through which Arab terrorists escaped by paying his officers $5,000 a head. In this same region, the overall warlord, Abdul Qadir, again ruled Nangarhar Province, where as governor before the Taliban he had controlled the province's large opium harvest. In the early 1990s, he cut production in half in exchange for international aid but then allowed an unchecked expansion after the crop substitution funds were spent. Elsewhere in the Pashtun southeast, other commanders long active in the heroin trade quickly emerged to fight for local power with an extraordinary brutality (Gordon 2001; Harding 2001; Harris 2001; McNeil 2001; Onishi 2001a, 2001b; Schmemann 2001; Shahzad 2001; Weiner 2001a; Golden 2002). In February 2002, the warlord Padsha Khan Zadran, known for corruption and brutality during his rule 10 years before, attacked the fortress city at Gardez to oust a rival, shelling houses randomly and promising he would "kill them all, men, women, children, even the chickens," before his unpaid troops deserted en masse and his attack collapsed (Bearak 2002; Burns 2002b).

Further south, in Kandahar, Gul Agda Shirzai, the pre-Taliban governor of the province, returned to power at the head of 3,000 fighters after 7 years on the Pakistan border engaged in what the *New York Times* called, with wry wit, "getting rich through commerce of a sometimes murky nature." During his month-long drive to retake the province in November, he advanced on Kandahar with a mix of cunning (buying off commanders with bundles of Pakistani currency from a Toyota Land Cruiser) and cruelty (summarily executing foreign-born Taliban). After a bloody battle, he captured the city's airport with U.S. Special Forces and paraded joyfully among the corpses. When the Taliban tried to surrender their sacred city to a friendly warlord, Mullah Naquib Ullah, also closely allied with Prime Minister Karzai, Gul Agda seized Kandahar with U.S. backing in a bold move that forced the Taliban to flee unconditionally, winning him the post of regional governor over both Kandahar and Helmand. As Kandahar's governor from 1992–1994, Gul Agda was known as a "cruel leader" who let his men "beat and steal from people," and there was no sign that his current rule would improve on that record (Eckholm 2001; Onishia 2001a; Maas 2002). Only weeks after the Taliban's fall, all of Afghanistan's key opium-producing regions—Helmand, Nangarhar, and Badakhshan—were again under the control of powerful drug lords.

The new government made diplomatic bows toward opium eradication. During its founding at Bonn in December 2001, the Interim Authority asked for aid "to combat . . . cultivation and trafficking of illicit drugs and provide Afghan farmers with financial, material and technical resources for alternative crop production." A few days before the Tokyo donors' conference in January 2002, Prime Minister Karzai proclaimed a ban on all drug production (Filkins 2002a; Schmemann 2002; U.S. Department of State 2002: Southwest Asia). Although the conference produced generous aid commitments, it still left serious gaps in the country's reconstruction, which only opium can fiill. Donors promised just $4 billion of the $10 billion needed to rebuild the economy over the next 5 years. Moreover, donors had by late March committed only 5 percent of the $285 million that the United Nation's World Food Program needed to feed 5 to 9 million Afghans for the rest of the year. For normal agriculture to resume, Afghanistan will need 125,000 tons of seeds annually, new credit facilities, road reconstruction, law enforcement, and a viable government (Crossette 2002; French 2002a; Landler 2002).

Among these many requisites for reconstruction, donors have been most reluctant to fund the formation of an Afghan national army—the country's only means of checking the local warlords who control the drug trade. At current funding levels, the Afghan army will have only 12,000 troops by September 2003, half the minimum force needed for rudimentary order. Despite rhetoric about a "Marshall Plan" for Afghanistan, the Bush administration, ignoring State Department counsel, has confined the coalition's 5,000 international peacekeepers to Kabul and restricted the U.S. role to minimal training for a future Afghan army. Three months after taking office, Prime Minister Karzai's authority did not extend beyond the capital, making him appear, in the words of one reporter, "less a head of state than a mayor." Under such circumstances, the prime minister's aides estimated that it will take 5 years to build an army capable of checking the warlords, ample time for opium to proliferate. In the words of an anonymous British law enforcement officer, "The fight against terrorism takes priority. The fight against narcotics comes in second." In March 2002, the former U.S. ambassador to the United Nations, Richard C. Holbrooke, criticized the Pentagon's "strict limits" on international peacekeepers, warning that "the country is in extreme danger of falling back into the hands of warlords and drug lords and terrorists." Sharing these concerns, in May 2002 the House of Representatives demanded that the president submit a plan for rebuilding Afghanistan and combating opium within 45 days and approved, by a margin of 390 to 22, $1.3 billion to fund these initiatives (Dao 2002b; Golden 2002; Gordon 2002a; Filkins 2002d; *New York Times* March 24, 2002; Pear 2002; Schmitt 2002; Traub 2002).

Without waiting for donors to write checks or a weak government to dole out the aid, the country's informal credit networks had financed extensive poppy planting across all of southeastern Afghanistan. In February 2002, the United Nations estimated the country's opium area at 46,000 to 67,000 hectares and the spring harvest at 2,100 to 3,000 tons, whereas the British press, citing intelligence sources, projected a crop that would rival the 1999 record of 4,600 tons. Although the government's ban had closed the opium bazaar at Sangin, farmers in surrounding Helmand Province were cultivating the new poppy crop openly. To plant 1.5 acres of opium, one farmer near Sangin, Abdul Wahid, 35, had borrowed $700 from a local shopkeeper, Abdul Bari, who in turn had borrowed $1,166 from a powerful Kandahar merchant—a series of debts that can only be satisfied when farmer Wahid harvests his crop in June or July 2002 and delivers the agreed 20 pounds of opium to shopkeeper Bari. Everyone in this district was similarly implicated in the opium trade: The deputy mayor was a warlord with an opium shop, the education director planted 2 acres of poppy, and the elders of the district council all had opium farms. Even Helmand's provincial governor, a nephew of the famed mujaheddin drug lord Mullah Nasim Akhundaza, who ruled this valley in the 1980s, stated bluntly that any attempt at eradication without compensation would produce a revolt by rival warlords. As one of Sangin's opium merchants put it, "No one can stop the opium smuggling until we have jobs, factories, schools" (Golden 2002; Hopkins and Taylor 2002; Waldman 2002c).

As Afghan farmers began harvesting in April 2002, the European powers, faced with a surge of heroin, provided $50 million, later $80 million, for the Karzai government to pay farmers $1,250 a hectare for opium eradication. Since they could earn $8,000 for each hectare harvested, farmers in Nangarhar Province killed nine officials who tried to eradicate their crops and protested by blockading the main road to Pakistan for several days. When two of the province's warlords escorted Defense Minister Muhammad Fahim into Jalalabad's main square during these protests, a bomb exploded, killing 27 bystanders and wounding 60 more. Under Afghanistan's warlord rule, enforcement of the opium ban soon proved problematic, particularly in the heroin heartland of Nangarhar. Although angry at the West for imposing this poppy ban, the provincial governor, warlord Hajji Abdul Qadir, shut down the opium bazaar at Ghani Kel and seized, by his account, 2,000 kilograms of opium, which witnesses claimed was at least 10 times more. Within weeks, observers reported that warlords were stealing the crop eradication payments due farmers, and "miles of undisturbed poppy fields . . . their opium capsules swollen to the size of tennis balls" were ready for harvest. But Afghanistan supplied just 5 percent of America's heroin, and the White House attached a low priority to the problem, saying that Britain and Germany would have to "pay the price" to curb the country's heroin exports. In March, the U.S. Department of State (2002: Southwest Asia) reported, with a note of resignation, that "there is virtually no counternarcotics enforcement in Afghanistan" and predicted that "the drug trade will continue to flourish absent concerted enforcement efforts" (Burns 2002a; Filkins 2002a; 2002c; 2002e; Frantz 2002; Reuters 2002b; Torchia 2002; Zucchino and Tempest 2002). Once again, Afghanistan was in the grip of the warlords and a land of opium, arms, and endless warfare.

If some future Afghan government were to repeat the Taliban's successful opium ban, the elimination of the world's top opium producer might well unleash powerful economic forces for proliferation—particularly in the impoverished states of Central Asia. Under Soviet rule, Kyrgyzstan was one of the world's largest producers of medicinal opium, leaving behind a cadre of skilled farmers and processors (U.S. Department of State 2000: 412). In the years before the Taliban's prohibition, both opium cultivation and heroin refining were already proliferating beyond Afghanistan into former Soviet Central Asia. In its 1999 report, the United Nations expressed concern "about the rapid spread of illicit opium cultivation and the traffic in and abuse of drugs, especially heroin, in countries in central Asia (Kazakhstan, Kyrgyzstan, Tajikistan, and Uzbekistan) and the Caucasus (Armenia, Azerbaijan, and Georgia)." Moreover, the United Nations (2002a: 49) warned that "in view of the overall rise of criminal activities in Central Asia and the Caucasus, drug abuse and illicit drug trafficking, if left unchecked, would have devastating consequences for societies in those subregions." Similarly, the U.S. State Department claimed that "morphine and heroin pour across Afghanistan's difficult-to-police borders with Pakistan, Iran, and the Central Asian Republics of Tajikistan, Turkmenistan, and Uzbekistan . . . destabilizing the entire region" (U.S. Department of State 1999: Afghanistan, para. II.).

Instead of celebrating the Taliban's sudden opium ban, the head of the United Nations Drug Control Program, Pino Arlacchi, had reacted to their July 2000 prohibition with concern, not relief: "The prices of heroin and cocaine have been declining over 10 years. That trend will now be interrupted. Prices will increase without demand reduction, and there will be more powerful incentives to cultivators and traders" (Crossette 2001a). If the elimination of just 7 percent of the world's illicit opium in Turkey during the mid-1970s could stimulate drug trafficking on 5 continents, then the future disappearance of some 70 percent of world supply from Afghanistan might have profound, almost unimaginable consequences.

Whatever the future might bring, the decade of the 1990s produced dramatic changes in these Asian borderlands. For 40 years, the Iron Curtain had served as a massive antinarcotics barrier, preventing drug production inside the communist bloc and diverting smuggling around its frontiers. Since the opening of southern China for trade with Southeast Asia in the 1990s, Burmese drug shipments bound for Hong Kong have been trucked directly across China's southern provinces—leaving a trail of drug, gangs, and heroin addicts in their wake. In 1999, for example, Chinese police and customs seized 7.3 metric tons of heroin and 1.6 tons of "ice," an amphetamine-like stimulant (Specter 1995; Tyler 1995a, 1995b; Labrousse and Laniel 2001: 85). As the Soviet empire broke apart and new nations formed at its margins, drug syndicates and smuggling proliferated from Central Asia to eastern Europe, knitting a tight web of trafficking routes. Indicative, moreover, of the growing integration of the global drug market, these changes in Asia were soon felt in Latin America.

Latin America in the 1990s

During the 1990s, drug eradication in the Andes failed to reduce the region's coca production. Just as U.S. and UN crop eradication programs had once pushed opium cultivation back and forth across the Asian opium zone, so U.S. bilateral programs have simply shifted coca cultivation up and down the Andes. At the start of the decade, the United States launched aggressive coca eradication programs in Bolivia and Peru, source of 90 percent of the Andes coca crop. Ten years and several billion aid dollars later, coca production in Colombia had boomed to compensate for losses elsewhere, and the United States felt forced to launch a massive eradication program in the midst of a intractable civil war (U.S. Department of State 2000: 56). By the end of the decade, a slowing of cocaine imports probably had more to do with changing consumer tastes than efforts at interdiction. The cocaine craze of the 1980s had simply exhausted itself and consumption leveled off, leaving 3.3 million users in 1998, while heroin use gained steadily to reach 1.0 million users by 1999 (United Nations 2000d: 79, 121–122).

With the end the Cold War, the CIA focused on fighting drug lords in Latin America, applying the same clandestine tactics that had proved so corrupting of host societies for the past 40 years—an expediency exemplified by its alliance with Peru's notorious intelligence chief Vladimiro Montesinos. After his expulsion from the military in 1976 for selling secrets to the CIA, Montesinos had worked as a lawyer for drug lords, notably the lethal Rodriguez Lopez brothers, until his support for Alberto Fujimori in the 1990 presidential elections elevated him to command of Peru's security services (Association d'Études Geopolitiques des Drogues 2000: 1, 4; Krauss 2001a). When Montesinos subsequently emerged as the key power broker in the Fujimori government, the CIA placed its antidrug program under his control—thereby gaining high-level access that facilitated its interdiction programs. The agency's alliance also provided Montesinos with at least some of the support he needed to weave an extraordinary web of corruption—bribing the legislature, protecting local drug lords, and even compromising Drug Enforcement Administration operations (Krauss 2001b). To cite just one example, Montesinos's close ally in the drug war, General Nicolas Hermoza, chief of the Armed Forces from 1992 to 2000, has been accused of taking $14.5 million from drug smugglers (Weiner 2001b). By 1998–1999, U.S. officials—aware of his shipment of arms to Colombia's leftist FARC (Revolutionary Armed Forces of Columbia) guerillas and the sale of DEA intelligence to major traffickers—began to distance themselves. After Fujimori fled into exile in November 2000, his successor, President Alejandro Toledo, reported that Montesinos had engaged in "state-sponsored narcotics trafficking" that earned much of the $264 million he had stashed in foreign banks (DePalma 2001; Krauss, 2001a).

The U.S. program in Peru, despite all the corruption and compromises, still produced the desired short-term results. Through their alliance with the Fujimori government, U.S. agencies—Defense, DEA, and CIA—interdicted drug flights and defoliated Peru's coca crop, cutting its harvest from 222,000 tons in 1991 to only 69,000 tons in 1999. Similarly, Bolivia's coca harvest fell sharply, from 77,000 tons in 1990 to 22,800 tons in 1999 (U.S. Department of State 2000: 55–56.)

Yet these gains, in retrospect, may not have been worth their cost. To compensate for rapid eradication in Peru and Bolivia, Colombia cocaine processors expanded coca production inside their own country, eliminating a vulnerable supply line north along the Andes. With the perfect symmetry that nature exhibits in a leaf or a snowflake, Peru's cultivation dropped from 120,000 hectares to 38,000 during the 1990s, while Colombia's kept pace, almost to the acre, rising from 37,000 hectares to 122,000 (U.S. Department of State 2000: 53). Despite these massive eradication efforts, the Andes coca harvest still doubled, from 330,000 tons in 1991 to 613,000 by the end of the decade (U.S. Department of State 2000: 53). Observing the changes, the United Nations noted in its 1999 report on drugs that "the impressive achievements in reducing illicit coca bush cultivation in Bolivia and Peru in the past two years seem to have been offset by increased production . . . in Colombia" (Labrousse and Laniel 2001: 21).

This balanced shift of coca production northward to Colombia was by no means benign. In effect, U.S. eradication efforts drove coca out of areas with limited insurgency in Bolivia and Peru into Colombia's ongoing civil war. During the 1990s, the powerful cartels peaked and then collapsed, leaving the traffic to violent partisans in Colombia's spreading civil war. After the Medellin cartel's terror ended with Pablo Escobar's death in December 1993, the rival Cali cartel's quiet infiltration of the state peaked, with secret contributions responsible for election of President

Ernesto Samper and half the Congress. Within 2 years, however, Cali's leaders, too, were jailed and the traffic fragmented among dozens of smaller syndicates. In this vacuum, the leftist FARC guerillas, blood rivals of the right-wing paramilitaries, soon captured the drug trade, using rising coca profits to buy arms for a spreading civil war. In the early 1990s, FARC, a Marxist group with its roots in rural struggles dating back to the 1930s, entered the drug trade by cultivating opium in its liberated zone and, encouraged by the extraordinary profits, expanded into protection of cocaine production. By 1992, FARC earned half its income from drugs, reducing kidnapping to a secondary source. As FARC's influence grew, the military countered by backing the violent paramilitaries, particularly the United Self-Defense Forces (USDFC), commanded by Carlos Castaño, a former lieutenant to drug lord Pablo Escobar. In August 1997, the USDFC's reliance on cocaine was confirmed with the seizure of a complex of four sophisticated labs and 700 kilograms of finished cocaine in Cundinamarca (Labrousee 2001: 196–205).

By 2001, the 8,000-strong paramilitary USDFC had assets of some $200 million, largely from coca protection, and was using this illicit income for aggressive counterinsurgency (Forero 2001a, 2001e). Similarly, FARC, with some 17,000 heavily armed guerrillas, used their Switzerland-sized security zone, granted by President Andres Pastrana in early 1999, as a base to expand their coca cultivation, which accounted for 10 percent of national acreage. In a downward spiral, cocaine, insurgency, and counterinsurgency had enmeshed drug dealing in an intractable Colombian civil war whose resolution seems beyond even the enormous increase in U.S. military aid. Whereas the United States had faced only angry peasant unions in its eradication of Bolivia's crop, it would now be forced to confront Colombia's well-armed militias, protected by the country's main political forces (Forero 2000b; Labrousse and Laniel 2001: 186–187). "With the drug trade now an organic part of Colombia civil conflict," read the State Department's 2001 report in opaque diplomatic language, "the question. . . will be how to reduce the supply of illegal drugs without exacerbating local conflicts that threaten regional stability" (Marquis 2001).

Indicative of the failure of this suppression effort, Latin America's coca supply has, over the past 15 years, consistently exceeded U.S. demand, lowering street prices from $400 an ounce in 1982 to only $100 in 1989. Since heroin's wholesale price was 14 times higher than cocaine's, Colombian cartels shifted resources into heroin production for export to the United States. After its introduction in 1991, poppy cultivation spread rapidly but, checked by defoliation, stabilized at 6,500 hectares, yielding some 65 tons of raw opium in the mid-1990s. With skilled chemists from local universities and Southwest Asia, Colombia's cartels began producing high-grade heroin, 80 to 99 percent pure, and soon captured 32 percent of the U.S. market (U.S. Department of State 1994: 103, 1996: 85, 1997: 102, 1999:117; Clawson and Lee 1996: 9, 16–17, 78–79). Moreover, the cartels began promoting opium cultivation in Peru in 1992–1993 and were still, in mid-2001, paying the high price of $800 per kilogram to stimulate production (November 2001: 8). Despite aggressive U.S. defoliation, Colombia's opium production had jumped from zero to 75 tons during the 1990s. By 1999, Colombia was producing 8 metric tons of heroin and had become the leading U.S. supplier, capturing about 65 percent of the American market (United Nations 2000d: 29; U.S. Department of State 2000: 55, 115).

Whereas crop eradication stimulated coca cultivation, covert operations aimed at Colombia's cartels produced few lasting gains. In a striking parallel with Khun Sa's surrender in Burma, the killing of Pablo Escobar in 1993, the collapse of the Medellin cartel, and the breakup of the Cali cartel 2 years later had little discernable impact on the flow of cocaine north to the United States (U.S. Department of State 1995: 81)

By the mid-1990s, Latin America's drug problem had defied conventional methods, and Washington lurched toward a desperate escalation. During its last year in office, the Clinton administration won approval for Plan Colombia—a $1.3 billion military program to train an antidrug battalion, supply helicopters, and defoliate coca fields. From this vast war chest, USAID allocated only $47 million for alternative crops—a clear indication of the program's coercive priorities (Forero 2000a, 2000b).

In December 2000, the United States launched Plan Colombia with a massive defoliation of 75,000 acres of coca in southern Putumayo Province in just 2 months, an eradication that simply pushed cultivation into nearby Nariño Province (Forero 2001b, 2001d). Speaking out against the defoliation in May 2001, the governors of the six southern provinces that produce 75 percent of Colombia's coca called for a gradual crop substitution that would not stimulate such proliferation (Forero 2001d). After formal complaints from indigenous communities, a Bogotá judge ordered a suspension of the U.S.-sponsored aerial spraying in July. "This is one of the most important moments for us," said Armando Valbuena, president of the National Indigenous Organization of Colombia. "The six governors of the south and the Indians and others are saying to the president, 'Please suspend the fumigation because there are other alternatives instead.'" Indeed, the governor of Nariño, Parmenio Cuellar, said defoliation programs "deal with the moment, but not with the root of the problem, the poverty." Responding to these complaints, the UNDCP called for international monitoring to determine the safety of spraying with products like the chemical Roundup, which is used in the United States only under stringent prohibitions against any human contact. But U.S. Ambassador Anne Patterson said manual eradication would be "too dangerous and—frankly—too expensive" (Forero 2001c).

By early 2002, the Bush administration began pressing Congress to lift restrictions on Plan Colombia to allow a shift, as Senator Patrick Leahy put it, from "counter narcotics to counter insurgency." In January, the administration asked Congress for $98 million in aid for the Colombian military to guard a major U.S. oil pipeline and, 2 months later, included an appropriation for Colombian counterterror training in its $27 billion wartime budget, arguing that there is a "significant overlap" between the guerrillas and drug smuggling (Dao and Stevenson 2002; Forero 2002a). As negotiations between President Andres Pastrana and FARC guerrillas collapsed into open warfare, the *New York Times* (January 21, 2002) expressed concern that the paramilitaries' "collaboration with the military is becoming more overt and their involvement in drug traffic is deeper than that of the guerrillas." In early March, as the State Department prepared its annual drug report, bitter infighting over Colombia's coca crop between White House political appointees (who demanded a lower figure) and CIA analysts (who insisted on reporting undoctored data) indicated that the United States was losing this battle in the Andes drug war. Despite massive defoliation and millions in military aid, the release of the final, undoctored figures showed that Colombia's coca area had actually grown markedly, from 122,000 hectares in 1999 to 163,000 in 2000 and then slightly in 2001 to a record-breaking 170,000 hectares (Marquis 2002b; Reuters 2002a).

Even if Plan Colombia were to succeed, both Peru and Bolivia had clearly retained a strong potential to fill any void with increased coca production. Although President Hugo Bánzer, once a protector of the *cocaleros*, halved Bolivia's coca area to 24,000 hectares by late 1999, farmers in the remaining area raised yields per hectare to the point that coca exports to Brazil remained steady. Moreover, Bolivia's capacity for a ruthless eradication is restrained by the political mobilization of the cocaleros, rooted in Indian communities and articulated through mass rallies, that gives them a certain social legitimacy. Although Peru's coca production dropped steadily during the 1990s, yields also rose since farmers abandoned the marginal, defoliated lands and planted coca in better soil. Moreover, opium production persisted, creating the potential for expanded crops in the future (Labrousse and Laniel 2001: 201–206, 209–210). Indeed, after a decade of decline, Peru's coca production, spurred by a doubling of the price for coca leaf to $4 a kilogram, climbed sharply, according to UN figures, from 43,000 hectares in 2000 to 51,000 hectares in 2001 (Forero 2002b).

Not only has the drug war had limited success in the United States, it also has imposed high social costs on source societies. During the 1990s, the CIA's close alliance with Peru's notorious security chief, Vladimiro Montesinos, built an antinarcotics apparatus that was both effective and outrageously corrupt. By allying with Colombian military factions and civilian elites that have long backed the brutal paramilitaries, Plan Colombia has the potential to foster the same corrupting political forces inside Colombia.

This war on supply has had little impact on U.S. demand for illicit drugs. Throughout the 1990s, the U.S. drug market, like its counterparts in Europe and Australia, showed an extraordinary dynamism. Despite intense enforcement efforts, domestic drug use increased significantly. Although cocaine use dropped 70 percent, the number of hard-core users held constant at 3.5 million. Moreover, the number of heroin users surged from 600,000 to 980,000, and their average age dropped from 26 to 17 (Wren 2000; *New York Times* February 2001; Nieves 2001). Despite ample supplies of natural narcotics, the persistent youth drug market experimented with synthetics, notably, MDMA (Ecstasy) and pharmaceutical opiates (OxyContin). By the late 1990s, these synthetics had nurtured new networks of dealers and users outside of established urban markets. Indicative of the scale of the Ecstasy epidemic, U.S. Customs seizures surged from 400,000 pills in 1997 to 9.3 million just 3 years later. Between 1996 and 2000, legal sales of OxyContin rose from $55 million to $1.4 billion, with an estimated 221,000 abusers of this synthetic opium. By mid-2001, pharmacies in the eastern United States were experiencing an epidemic of OxyContin robberies—particularly in Kentucky, with 5.5 percent of its

1,000 drug stores hit (Butterfield 2001; Klam 2001; Rashbaum 2001; Tough 2001). Clearly, the U.S. drug market retained the resilience, first seen in the 1970s, to replace any shortfall in natural narcotics with chemical substitutes.

Although the Clinton and Bush administrations remained committed to the drug war, rising prison populations consumed state revenues and forced local governments to reexamine the nation's prohibition policy. Nearly 70 percent of President Clinton's $19.2 billion drug war budget was committed to enforcement, an emphasis that increased under his successor George W. Bush. After his appointment as Bush's drug policy chief, John Walters announced his commitment to prohibition orthodoxy: "When we push back, the drug problem gets smaller" (Sanger 2001; Wren 2001). Under Bush, the Justice Department remained committed to the drug war and, in March 2002, opposed even a modest reform of the harsh penalties for possession of crack cocaine (N. A. Lewis 2002). Despite Washington's strong antidrug rhetoric, by the late 1990s American voters were weary of the drug war's escalating costs for police and prisons. In 2001, for example, California voters, long known for their social experimentation, passed Proposition 36, mandating outpatient treatment instead of prison for drug possession—a move that Washington State followed a year later. Similarly, New York's conservative Republican Governor George Pataki proposed reform of the repressive Rockefeller drug laws that had filled state prisons with 10,000 nonviolent drug users. In adopting these reforms, states seemed to be taking the first steps, not toward legalization but toward "harm reduction"—a strategy exemplified by the 1990 Frankfurt Resolution of nine European cities, urging criminal sanctions solely against traffickers, decriminalization of drug possession, and medical prescriptions for addicts (United Nations 1997: 188; *New York Times* July 2001; Preusch 2002). Although bipartisan support for the drug war remained strong in Washington, DC, American voters, in state plebiscites and opinion polls across the country, were growing skeptical of a policy whose failure was, after 30 years, more than clear.

Conclusion

Is this history in any sense predictive? Historians usually prefer to wait for the dust of time to settle and then assess the now distant past with a magisterial certainty. Sharing my discipline's biases, let me draw upon the foregoing analysis to offer some tentative predictions, first, about the role of states in narcotics suppression and, more broadly, about the possible impact of such suppression upon global supply.

Even when drugs are produced in remote terrain and consumed in private, the state plays a major role in their political economy. The lessons of the past century indicate that opium cultivation cannot continue to thrive over the long term in a strong state committed to its eradication. Conversely, high-level opium or coca production requires either the attenuation of state power in the producing regions (Afghanistan in the 1980s and Colombia in the 1990s) or extensive official corruption that slows state intervention (Thailand in the 1960s or Burma in the 1990s). Thus, any cluster of policies that increases state control over narcotics-producing regions and simultaneously restrains official corruption may well contribute to a long-term reduction in drug trafficking.

With the end of the Cold War, however, the old Soviet borderlands from the Balkans to Central Asia have experienced an eruption of insurgency in the name of religion, region, and ethnicity that may well lead to the fragmentation of these new nations carved from old empires—a change with implications for future opium production. During insurgency against an established state, rebel groups will become more dependent upon opium finance and resist drug repression. Faced with the threat of regional secessionist movements, nations may become less able to impose unpopular drug control programs upon volatile minority areas. Once the revolt is over and power is consolidated, a weak, war-ravaged state may continue to rely on heroin as its most viable export. In sum, by weakening state structures, the current instability in Central Asia may contribute to increased opium trafficking.

The centrality of the state to drug control raises questions about the efficacy and ethics of the current U.S. and United Nations policy of isolating, even ostracizing, so-called outlaw states. At a pragmatic level, isolating major drug producers from legitimate trade and aid seems self-defeating if the goal is to wean them from economic dependence on illicit drugs. During the 1990s, for example, the international isolation of Burma and Afghanistan, source of over 90 percent of the world's opium supply, hampered the economic engagement necessary to make alternative crops or the shift to labor-intensive industry a success (U.S. Department of State 1994: 20).

More broadly, this punitive approach ignores the very real, though unintended, economic consequences of the prohibition regime. For nearly half a century, global narcotics prohibition has complicated the process of state formation across Asia, slowing the consolidation of central controls over borderlands from Turkey to Thailand. By the late 1950s, the international drug suppression effort had forced opium out of the lowlands into highland margins—home to ethnic or tribal minorities hostile to these new lowland states still struggling to establish their authority. Through a perverse synergy, the temperate opium poppy thrived only at high altitudes in these subtropical latitudes; and highland minorities soon found that opium was, because of its light weight and high value, one of the few crops that could overcome the barrier of distance to compete effectively in lowland markets. As smuggling and drug sales brought arms and cash into these hills, powerful warlords emerged in various guises—as bandits, prophets, militias, mercenaries, rebels, or revolutionaries—limiting the state's authority in these rugged borderlands. Once remote border marches of tribal highlands had now become strategic frontiers, and national security demanded that these new states impose some control. Complicating this process, foreign intelligence agencies, including the CIA, played upon highland-lowland divisions during the Cold War to conduct covert operations along this southern front of communist containment from Turkey to Laos. The mix of illicit opium, ethnic conflict, and covert operations has made these borderlands volatile regions during the Cold War and its aftermath.

Some of these new states—like Ataturk's Turkey, the shah's Iran, or Saddam Hussein's Iraq—had sufficient strength to curb highland resistance with brute force and mass slaughter. But many, like Afghanistan, Pakistan, India, Burma, and Vietnam, lacked such military power and relied instead on a mix of concession and repression—conceding ethnic autonomy and tolerating smuggling at the outset but playing upon internal divisions to slowly break the power of highland warlords. If such intervention is done ineptly, these borderlands could erupt in protracted revolt, draining away revenues and destabilizing the state. But if done deftly, the state could play upon the center-periphery dynamic to strengthen its authority, not just in the borderlands but over the lowlands as well.

Ignoring these realities, the international prohibition regime has placed contradictory pressures upon source nations, whether in Burma or, more recently, in Afghanistan and Colombia. After World War II, global prohibition unleashed market forces that drove drug production into the mountain margins of Asia and the Andes, creating enormous problems for source countries during an early, critical phase of nation building. Let us be clear: None of these countries had development ministers who actually advocated growing opium; none had agricultural extension agents handing out poppy or coca seeds to farmers. The prohibition regime itself unleashed illicit market forces that pushed drug production into these impoverished highlands. Once started, illicit drug production fosters both regional warlords who block suppression and encourage dependence on illicit exports. By generating high foreign-exchange earnings, illicit drug exports strengthen the national currency's value, making legal exports less competitive. Ignoring the ways in which its prohibition policy has stimulated drug production and proliferation, the community of nations, led by the United Nations and United States, has made drug production—like terrorism, genocide, aggression, and chemical-biological warfare—a violation of international norms worthy of serious sanctions (Nadelmann 1990; Crawford 1993; Finnemore 1996: 153–161; Katzenstein 1996: 19–28; United Nations 1997: 143, 2000d: 146).

Burma provides an apt case study of this policy's contradictory impact. For nearly 50 years, the prohibition regime has fostered conditions that made Burma economically dependent upon opium while simultaneously demanding, under international covenants, eradication of a commodity that was now central to the country's economy. As Burma's upland opium production rose from 18 tons in 1958 to 2,430 tons in 1989, its lowland economy collapsed, making this weak state increasingly dependent upon drug trafficking. The ascendance of opium and opium warlords across a vast swath of its northeastern frontier reduced the state's capacities in numerous ways—through a costly military mobilization to battle drug lord armies, the collapse of currency as illicit exports dominated and distorted its economy, strains on national grain supply as land and labor were diverted to opium, and most important, the loss of legitimate trade and foreign aid from the stigma of drug trafficking (Fegan 2002). To contain ethnic revolts that raged for decades across a third of its territory, Burma's military regime, like its early modern antecedents, has been forced to harness its borderland bandits and their illicit trade to the task of nation building—extracting hard currency to finance lowland development and, more important, to buy arms for selective attacks on highland warlords. This tactic of coopting outlaws, with all their violence and criminality, was a common form of state building in the early modern age and is still a necessary one for contemporary drug source nations. But in our own era, when major powers are struggling to build a world order upon shared principles, such an ambiguous state policy has become anathema. By its alliances with drug lords, Burma has become, from Washington's perspective, an outlaw state worthy of diplomatic opprobrium and formal sanctions. And without their close alliance with the United States and its war on terror, Afghanistan and Colombia would soon suffer the same sanctions for their tactical alliances with local drug lords.

Global drug prohibition may well impose similarly contradictory demands on future source nations. The distortions of the drug traffic clearly weaken state capacity to control coca and opium, but the international community, unaware of the economic realities of prohibition, is relentless in its demands for compliance with laws and covenants that require eradication. Those that deviate from the norms of the international community are, like Burma, branded as pariah states and punished with isolation. In the context of the new world order that has followed the Cold War, these international norms have created a new language for political analysis and diplomatic action. During most of the twentieth century, states were generally identified by their internal structures as, for example, communist, authoritarian, or democratic. But at century's close, compliance with international norms has become the determining attribute, creating new categories for analysis and action. Since the Cold War waned in the 1980s, four American presidents have branded midlevel powers that threatened U.S. interests as, variously, "outlaw states" (Reagan, 1985), "renegade regimes " (Bush, 1990), "rogue states" (Clinton, 1995), and "axis of evil" (Bush, 2002) (Klare 1995: 26; Litwak 2000: 2–3; Herring 2000: 189–191; Niblock 2001: 2–13). Washington has usually applied this stigma for involvement in terrorism or weapons of mass destruction, but in expansive moments has extended it to drug trafficking. In 1997, Secretary of State Madeleine Albright branded Burma's leaders as "drug traffickers and thugs," a characterization that relegated the regime to the nadir of her typology of post–Cold War states—advanced industrial, emerging democracies, failed, and rogue. A year later, President Clinton warned of future threats from "a rogue state with weapons of mass destruction, ready to use them or provide them to terrorists, drug traffickers, or organized criminals" (Litwak 2000: xiii, 3).

Although the rogue state concept has no standing in international law or norms, it has, through the weight of American power, gained global currency. In its *World Drug Report 2000*, the United Nations Office for Drug Control and Crime Prevention states that illicit drug production was often found in "failed states"—those "whose institutions are so weak or collapsed that they are unable to provide . . . non-partisan internal regulation (the rule of law)." Such states present "enhanced opportunities for organized crime groupings," which have "a vested interest in making sure that strong, effective and legitimate states are not rebuilt" (United Nations 2000d: 11). Wherever a source nation might fall in this new international rubric, states will remain central, in both their compliance and defiance, to the success of the global prohibition effort, even in an era of rapid globalization.

In a global economy that has shed internal and international restraints to accelerate the circulation of trade, technology, and capital, outlaw states that remain outside the international community, by choice or ostracism, pose a serious threat. Even weak, isolated states can disrupt this new world order through nuclear proliferation, chemical weapons, terrorist attacks, and drug trafficking. In a fragile, interdependent global system, the outcast nations—North Korea, Burma, Iraq, and perhaps Afghanistan—can easily take their revenge by exporting terror, mass destruction, and drugs.

Does this troubled past tell us anything about the future of the prohibition regime? With the collapse of the Iron Curtain, there has been an eruption of ethnic insurgency along southern frontiers of the former Soviet Union. As states fragmented across the vastness of the Eurasian landmass, regional rebels, armed with drug money and fighting for power, smuggled opium and heroin in unprecedented quantities. Just as China's Yunnan and Szechwan Provinces once produced 19,000 tons of opium in 1906, so Afghanistan, Tajikistan, and Uzbekistan are capable, individually or severally, of comparable harvests. If production in both Central and Southeast Asia continues, there are few constraints, except changes in demand, to check the current trend of world opium supply, doubling every decade, from 5,300 tons in 1996 to 10,000 tons in 2007 and 40,000 tons by 2027—in effect, bringing production back to where it had been at the start of drug prohibition in 1906. Despite the end to the Cold War and its superpower rivalries, many of the local and regional conditions that once created Burmese and Afghan drug lords remain— creating a social space for dynamic entrepreneurs who may lead this illicit industry in unimagined directions.

Clearly, there are reasons to question the effectiveness of the current prohibition effort. Perfect coercion has proven effective over the past 2 centuries, but imperfect coercion has unleashed a whirlwind of unforeseen consequences. With their near perfect coercion, European colonial empires were able to promote cultivation where needed (India) and suppress it where not (Southeast Asia), fostering a commodity trade that was by the late nineteenth century integrated into the global economy.

In the twentieth century, global drug prohibition has produced more ambiguous results. In the last half of the last century, the most dramatic development was China's use of coercion, within a closed society, to effect a total eradication of all opium production and use after 1949. Judging by this success, perfect coercion can effect a major reduction in drug trafficking. However, China's experience is historically unique and might not be relevant to the more open political systems that have emerged since 1989. Indeed, China itself has recently experienced a sudden surge in drug trafficking as it lessened social controls during the 1990s to encourage development.

Outside the socialist bloc, the League of Nations and, later, the United Nations have attempted a prohibition on legal opium sales, at first producing a sharp but short-term decline in both drug production and consumption. But from the start of drug prohibition in the 1920s, criminal syndicates have emerged to link highland growers and urban addicts, creating a global illicit market. A half century later, President Nixon's forceful intervention in this illicit market produced another round of unintended consequences. Through bilateral coercion, his drug war crippled the Mediterranean opium traffic, uprooting poppy fields in Turkey and closing heroin laboratories in Marseilles. Over the longer term, however, this exercise in imperfect coercion unleashed global market forces that ultimately stimulated an increase in the supply of drugs on 5 continents.

Market response to imperfect coercion is complex and ultimately counterproductive. Since the 1920s, the syndicate's response to suppression has been supple, sophisticated, and often capable of compromising even the best attempts at coercive intervention. Similarly, even the most effective narcotics suppression efforts can have unforeseen consequences. Over the past quarter century, it has become evident that suppression efforts, particularly bilateral initiatives, can stimulate narcotics production. Even so, the United States and the United Nations have persisted for over 50 years in a quixotic, self-defeating strategy that defies the dynamics of the global drug market. A policy presaged on an assumption of inelastic supply cannot succeed when the market shows repeatedly that the global drug supply is surprisingly elastic. In sum, this attempt to reduce the drug supply through a policy that defies the dynamics of the illicit market has produced unanticipated, unwanted market responses—notably, steady increases in the global drug supply that have sustained rising demand worldwide.

As we saw in Turkey during the 1970s and Thailand in the 1980s, suppression, both bilateral and multilateral, can effect a dramatic short-term reduction in the drug supply that will in succeeding crop years encourage an increase in total global production. The success of the United Nations program in reducing Thai opium cultivation during the 1980s may well have contributed to the simultaneous increase in Burma's poppy harvest. Moreover, by raising the price of smoking opium to addicts in Thailand and thus encouraging the spread of intravenous heroin injection, United Nations suppression contributed to an AIDS epidemic in Thailand. Apparently, heroin supplies, when denied entry into one market, as they were in Southeast Asia during the 1970s, will seek another, resulting in a proliferation of consumption and an overall increase in global demand. Successful United Nations eradication of opium in Asia could thus stimulate a rapid spread of poppies along the Andes, just as U.S. defoliation of poppy fields in the Andes could encourage production in Asia. Should such bilateral and multilateral operations overcome myriad obstacles to effect a long-term reduction in narcotics supply, then domestic dealers, repeating the U.S. experience with amphetamines in the 1970s, could turn to the manufacture of synthetics. In effect, the eradication of both Asian opium and Andes coca could stimulate the production and consumption of chemical substitutes across the globe

Any attempt at solving America's heroin problem by reducing the global opium supply through a war on drugs thus seems unrealistic. Successful bilateral eradication has over the past quarter century stimulated both drug production and consumption. Since America consumes a tiny share of the world's supply and pays the world's highest price, the elimination of the American heroin supply requires that illicit opium cultivation disappear from the face of the globe. In 1985, for example, the United States consumed only 6 tons of opium out of a worldwide harvest of 1,465 tons, just 0.4 percent of the total (U.S. General Accounting Office 1988: 16; U.S. Department of State 1989: 16). In 1997, the White House estimated that the United States still consumed "only 3 percent of the world's [heroin] production" (U.S. Office of National Drug Control Policy 1998: 51). If the illicit drug traffic operates like any other market, then America's drug warriors must eradicate some 97 or 99.6 percent of the world's opium before they finally get to those last few tons destined for the high-priced U.S. market.

As we have seen from past U.S. and United Nations drug control efforts, the illicit market often reacts in unforeseen ways, transforming repression into stimulus. Before launching crop eradication or criminal suppression, antinarcotics agencies need to consider the full range of possible outcomes. Over the past century, each attempt at prohibition has produced an unexpected market reaction that has allowed the illicit traffic to adapt, survive, and in recent years even expand. It may be time to learn from the past and develop strategies for minimizing the negative impact of drug control efforts.

More broadly, it may be time to admit that prohibition's supply-side solution has failed. Since the first U.S. drug war in the 1970s, successful bilateral eradication has stimulated both drug production and consumption. Although U.S. and United Nations drug operations have produced a short-term decline of drug production in target societies, they have simultaneously stimulated an increase in later harvests elsewhere in Asia and the Andes. After 30 years of failed eradication, there is ample evidence to indicate that the illicit drug market is a complex global system, both sensitive and resilient, that quickly transforms suppression into stimulus. If past experience in Turkey is any guide, the possible eradication of opium in Afghanistan, through the United Nations drug program or U.S. intervention, could unleash unpredictable market forces that will ramify invisibly through the global system for years to come, contributing to a spread of narcotics production, drug consumption, HIV infection, and synthetic drugs.

For 30 years or more, US and United Nations drug policy has been wedded to unexamined prohibition. In its 1997 *World Drug Report*, for example, the United Nations warned of dire consequences from any relaxation of prohibition—possibly depriving farmers of their drug crops, creating unemployment among "hundreds of thousands of intermediary" traffickers, conceding political power to drug cartels, and encouraging a massive increase in drug abuse. Although admitting that demand reduction was more effective, the UNDCP insisted on the "many notable achievements" of its supply reduction strategy, arguing that "drugs that would have appeared in the streets are being seized in ever-greater quantities" and financial controls "have the potential to inflict real harm on drug trafficking networks" (United Nations 1997: 189–199, 237). Similarly, the United States has fought 5 major drug wars since 1971, applying localized coercion to the eradication of a global commodity. The White House has used a metaphor of war in each of these campaigns, applying the military logic of rapid-fire campaigns with fixed spatial objectives to the eradication of an elusive global commodity.

Recognizing the power of paradigms to shape concepts and thereby frame policy it might be helpful to abandon the drug war rhetoric and adopt a medical metaphor of treatment and healing. This conceptual change could encourage a replacement of militarized prohibition with long-term global management of a complex drug market. Instead of a metaphor of war, with its rhetoric of maximum force and sudden victory, international drug policy could, in the short term, recognize the complexity of this illicit economy and intervene with the greatest of caution, realizing that every action is likely to produce an unpredictable reaction, greatly compounding the problem. As a first step, we might consider shifting resources from supply eradication to demand reduction through voluntary treatment. Narcotics control could move from the United Nations Drug Control Program to the World Health Organization, from the United States Justice Department to the Department of Health and Human Services. Over the longer term, the international community could dismantle the prohibition apparatus built during the past century and replace it with a more cautious attempt to manage the harm from drugs—not only from the traffic itself but also, above all, from the suppression programs designed to combat it. Such change might not end the illicit traffic in drugs or the spread of consumption. But at least this more modest approach will stop governments from applying coercive measures against both highland producers and urban consumers that often do more social damage than drug use itself.

There are indications that the United States and the United Nations have not seriously explored the possibilities of demand reduction. A 1998 study argued that the 230,000 cocaine users actually admitted to treatment may have reduced U.S. cocaine imports by 35 tons annually, equivalent to one-third of federal seizures. Since these 230,000 patients represented only 7 percent of the country's 3.3 million hard-core cocaine users, this analysis indicates that treatment and other demand reduction programs have an untested potential to reduce global supply (United Nations 2000d: 121–122).

Looking back on this century-long, Anglo-American experiment in drug prohibition, we need to entertain the possibility that this effort has failed—both the international suppression of supply and the domestic control of individual behavior. Over the past 30 years, prohibition has not reduced the production or consumption of illicit drugs. Moreover, the price of this failure has been extraordinarily high: extensive defoliation, forced migration, and military conflict in the source nations; mass incarceration, rising HIV infection, spreading drug use, and social polarization in the consuming countries. Invisible to the panopticon of modern media, the price that highland minorities in Asia and the Andes have paid for their involvement in narcotics production and eradication has been inhumanely high—guerrilla taxes, crop defoliation, military operations, and economic dislocation.

With the end of the Cold War, states have reduced domestic repression and opened their frontiers for free economic exchange, eliminating the coercive mechanisms that once allowed effective narcotics control in colonial, communist, and authoritarian states. Significantly, in the decade since the Cold War's end, the United Nations's only real success has come in Afghanistan, where the Taliban's theocratic rule allowed, momentarily, an exceptional capacity for coercion. As we enter an era of democracy and global exchange, both the U.S. and United Nations drug prohibition efforts may seem more and more like irrational atavisms of an authoritarian age.

Acknowledgments   I am indebted to colleagues for a close reading of this chapter, including John Leake of Adelaide, Dr. Brian Fegan of Sydney, Alain Labrousse of Paris, and Professor Jeremy Suri of the University of Wisconsin–Madison.

References

Abou Zahab, M. 2001. "Pakistan: d'un narco-Etat à une 'success story' dans la guerre contre la drogue?" *Cahiers d'études sur la Méditerranée orientale et le monde turco-iranien* 32 (July-December), pp. 141–158.

Adshead, S.A.M. 1966. "The Opium Trade in Szechwan 1881 to 1911." *Journal of Southeast Asian Studies* 6, no. 2 (September), pp. 93–99.

Ahmed, K. 2001. "Troops Will Target Drugs Stockpile." *The Observer* (London), September 30.

Allan, N. 1974. "Modernization of Rural Afghanistan: A Case Study." In Louis Dupree and Linette Albert, eds., *Afghanistan in the 1970s*. New York: Praeger, pp. 113–125.

———. 1978. "Men and Crops in the Central Hindukush." Ph.D. dissertation, Syracuse University, Syracuse, NY.

———. 1985a. "Human Geo-ecological Interactions in Kuh Daman, a South Asian Mountain Valley." *Applied Geography* 5, no. 1, pp. 13–27.

———. 1985b. "Periodic and Daily Markets in Highland-Lowland Interaction Systems: Hindu-Kush-Western Himalayas." In Tej Vir Singh and Jagdish Kaur, eds., *Integrated Mountain Development*. New Delhi: Himalayan Books, pp. 235–256.

———. 1987. "Impact of Afghan Refugees on the Vegetation Resources of Pakistan's Hindukush-Himalaya." *Mountain Research and Development* 7, no. 3, pp. 200–204.

———. 1991. "From Autarky to Dependency: Society and Habitat Relations in the South Asian Mountain Rimland." *Mountain Research and Development* 11, no. 1, pp. 65–74.

Altman, R. 2001. "H.I.V. 'Explosion' Seen in East Europe and Central Asia." *New York Times*, November 29, p. A16.

Andreas, P. 2000. *Border Games: Policing the U.S.-Mexico Divide*. Ithaca, NY: Cornell University Press.

Antonelli, M. A. 1975. "In Europe: An Incursion of Asian Heroin," *Drug Enforcement*, p. 32.

Apple, R. W. Jr. 2001. "Pondering the Mystery of the Taliban's Collapse," *New York Times*, November 30, p. B2.

Ardila, P. 1990. *Beyond Law Enforcement: Narcotics and Development*. Washington, DC: Panos Institute.

Aspire Films. 1994. *Dealing with the Demon: Part II*. Produced by Chris Hilton, Sydney.

Associated Press. 1989. "Rise in Drug Arrests Is Reported in New York." *New York Times*, 1 November, p. A46.

———. 1999. "Drug Menace Looms Over 14% of Barangays." *Philippine Daily Inquirer*, June 17, p. 2.

———. 2000. "Taliban Poppy-growing Ban Will Measure Afghans' Fear." *New York Times*, November 16, p. A5.

Association d'Études Geopolitiques des Drogues. December 2000. "Peru: The Unsaid in the Montesinos Scandal." *Geopolitical Drug Newsletter*, pp. 1–4.

———. October 2001a. "Afghanistan: Drugs and the Taliban." *Geopolitical Drug Newsletter*, pp. 1–2.

———. October 2001b. "Macedonia Serbia: Dangerous Liaisons." *Geopolitical Drug Newsletter*, pp. 2–4.

———. November 2001a. "Peru: Disastrous Legacy." *Geopolitical Drug Newsletter*, p. 8.

———. November 2001b. "Russia: Central Asia: A Border Under Construction." *Geopolitical Drug Newsletter*, pp. 1–3.

———. May 2002. "Croatia and Bosnia-Herzegovina: Powerful Criminal Political-Military Networks." *Geopolitical Drug Newsletter*, pp. 1–3.

Aureano, G. 2001. "L´Etat et la prohibition de (certaines) drogues." *Cahiers d'études sur la Méditerranée orientale et le monde turco-iranien* 32 (July–December), pp. 15–38.

Balland, D. 1988. "Nomadic Pastoralists and Sedentary Hosts in the Central and Western Hindukush Mountains, Afghanistan." In J. R. Nigel, R. Allan, eds., *Human Impact on Mountains*. Totowa, NJ: Rowman & Littlefield, pp. 265–276.

Bearak, B. 2000. "An Afghan Mosaic of Misery: Hunger, War, and Repression." *New York Times*, February 25, p. A1.

———. 2001a. "At Heroin's Source, Taliban Do What 'Just Say No' Could Not." *New York Times*, May 24, p. A1.

———. 2001b. "Former Inhabitants Trickle Back to Area Ravaged by Taliban." *New York Times*, November 26, p. B2.

———. 2002. "A Warlord Takes His Revenge on a City, Launching an Attack That Kills 25." *New York Times*, April 29, p. A14.

Berridge, V., and G. Edwards. 1987. *Opium and the People: Opiate Use in Nineteenth-Century England*. New Haven, CT: Yale University Press.

Block, A. A. 1989. "European Drug Traffic and Traffickers Between the Wars: The Policy of Suppression and Its Consequences." *Journal of Social History* 23, no. 2, pp. 315–337.

———. 2001. "On the Inestimable Value of the OGD." *Crime, Law & Social Change* 36, nos. 1–2, pp. 1–20.

Bonner, A. 1986. "Afghan Rebels' Victory Garden: Opium." *New York Times*, June 18, p. A1.

Bonner, R. 1997. "Top U.N. Drug Aide Hopes to Rid Globe of Poppy and Coca Crops." *New York Times*, November 14, p. A6.

Brown, R. 1990. "Racism: The Enduring Barrier." In A. S. Trebach and K. B. Zeese, eds., *The Great Issues of Drug Policy*. Washington, DC: Drug Policy Foundation, pp. 83–87.

Burgos, R. 1998. "5,225 Barangays 'Drug Infested'—PNP NarGroup." *Philippine Daily Inquirer*, August 1, p. 5.

Burke, J. 2001. " The new 'Great Game,' " *The Observer*, November 4.

Burns, J. F. 2002a. "Afghan Warlords Squeeze Profits from the War on Drugs, Critics Say." *New York Times*, May 5, p. A14.

———. 2002b. "Warlord Fends Off Warlord, Echoing Afghans' Bitter Past." *New York Times*, February 1, p. A1.

Burns, J. F. and S. LeVine. 1996. "How Afghans' Stern Rulers Took Hold." *New York Times*, December 31, p. A1.

Butterfield, F. 2001. "Theft of Painkiller Reflects Its Popularity on the Street." *New York Times*, July 7, p. A6.

Chao, T. Y. 1987. *The Shan of Burma: Memoirs of a Shan Exile*. Singapore: Institute of Southeast Asian Studies.

Chassagne, P., and K. Gjeloshaj. 2001. "L'émergence de la criminalité albanophone." *Cahiers d'études sur la Méditerranée orientale et le monde turco-iranien* 32 (July–December), pp. 159–190.

Chivers, C. J. 2001a. "400 Demolition Experts Will Try to Harvest Afghanistan's Field of Mines." *New York Times*, December 18, p. B-1.

———. 2001b. "Millions of Afghan Children, and No Ideas About Their Future." *New York Times*, December 4, p. B1.

Chouvy, P.-A. 2001. "L'importance du facteur politique dans le développment du Triangle d'Or et du Croissant d'Or." *Cahiers d'études sur la Méditerranée orientale et le monde turco-iranien* 32, July–December, pp. 69–85.

Chung, T. 1987. "The Britain-China-India Trade Triangle 1771–1840." In Sabyasachi Bhattacharya, ed., *Essays in Modern Indian Economic History*. New Delhi: Munshiram Manoharlal Publishers, pp. 114–130.

Circular no. 875-SAE. 1945. From Resident Superior of Tonkin Desalle to the residents of

Laokay, Sonla, and Yenbay, July 22, 1942. Quoted in *Temoinages et Documents français relatifs à la Colonisation française au Viet-Nam.* Hanoi: Association culturelle pour le Salut du Viet-Nam, p. 115.

Clawson, P. L., and Rensselaer, W. L. 1996. *The Andean Cocaine Industry.* London: Macmillan Press.

Cogan, C. G. 1993. "Partners in Time: The CIA and Afghanistan Since 1979." *World Policy Journal* 10, no. 2 (Summer), pp. 73–82.

Colapinto, J. 1996. "Rock & Roll Heroin." *Rolling Stone,* May 30, pp. 15–20, 58, 60.

Courtwright, D. T. 1982. *Dark Paradise: Opiate Addiction in America before 1940.* Cambridge, MA: Harvard University Press.

Crawford, N. 1993. "Decolonization as an International Norm: The Evolution of Practices, Arguments, and Beliefs." In L. Reed and C. Kaysen, eds., *Emerging Norms of Justified Intervention.* Cambridge: Committee on International Security Studies, American Academy of Arts and Sciences, pp. 37–61.

Crossette, B. 2000a. "Taliban Opens a Campaign to Gain Status at the U.N." *New York Times,* September 21, p. A7.

———. 2000b. "A U.N. Aide Says Taliban Is Reducing Poppy Crop." *New York Times,* December 10, p. A19.

———. 2001a. "Afghan Ban on Poppies Is Convulsing Opium Market." *New York Times,* June 13, p. A15.

———. 2001b. "Cautious U.S. Hope on Report of Lower Afghan Opium Crop." *New York Times,* February 11, p. A14.

———. 2001c. "Taliban's Poppy Ban Seems to Be a Success, U.S. Team Says." *New York Times,* May 20, p. A4.

———. 2002. "Food Aid for Afghans Short of Need, U.N. Agency Says." *New York Times,* March 26, p. A12.

Cusack, J. T. 1974. "Turkey Lifts the Poppy Ban." *Drug Enforcement,* Fall, pp. 3–7.

———. 1976. "A Review of the International Drug Traffic." *Drug Enforcement,* Spring, pp. 34–35.

———. 1979. "Heroin Seized in Europe During 1978." *Drug Enforcement,* February, pp. 20–21.

Dao, J. 2002a. "Afghan Warlord May Team Up with Al Qaeda and Taliban." *New York Times,* May 30, p. A12.

——— 2002b. "Bush Sets Role for U.S. in Afghan Rebuilding." *New York Times,* April 18, p. A1.

Dao, J., and R. W. Stevenson. 2002. "Bush Seeks $27 Billion Emergency Fund." *New York Times,* March 22, p. A20.

DePalma, A. 2001. "Story of C.I.A. and Peru's Former Spy Chief May Soon Be Told." *New York Times,* November 11, p. A7.

Dunn, W. T. 1920. *The Opium Traffic in Its International Aspects.* New York: Columbia University.

Eckholm, E. 2001. "Meet the New Warlord, Same as the Old One." *New York Times,* December 17, p. B5.

Emdad-ul Haq, M. 2000. *Drugs in South Asia: From the Opium Trade to the Present Day.* New York: St. Martin.

Epstein, E. J. 1977. *Agency of Fear: Opiates and Political Power in America.* New York: Putnam.

Erlanger, S. 1990. "Southeast Asia Is Now No. 1 Source of U.S. Heroin." *New York Times,* February 11, p. A26.

———. 1997. "Asians Are Cool to Albright on Cambodians and Burmese." *New York Times,* July 28, p. A3.

Evans, K. 1989. "The Tribal Trail." *Newsline* (Karachi), December.

Falco, M. 1979. "Asian Narcotics: The Impact on Europe." *Drug Enforcement*, February, pp. 2–3.

Fegan, B. Personal communication, Sydney, Australia, October 10, 2000; March 31, 2002; June 5, 2002.

Filkins, D. 2002a. "Afghanistan to Pay Farmers for Uprooted Poppies." *New York Times*, April 5, p. A8.

———. 2002b. "Afghan Officials Arrest Hundreds in Bombing Plot." *New York Times*, April 4, p. A1.

———. 2002c. "Afghan Refugees Allowed to Pass After Poppy Farmers End Protest." *New York Times*, April 11, p. A22.

———. 2002d. "Charm and the West Keep Karzai in Power, for Now." *New York Times*, March 26, p. A1.

———. 2002e. "Disorders Endanger Return of Afghan Refugees from Pakistan and Iran." *New York Times*, April 10, p. A17.

———. 2002f. "U.S. Troops May Keep Order in Afghan Countryside." *New York Times*, March 27, p. A10.

Finnemore, M. 1996. "Constructing Norms of Humanitarian Intervention." In P. J. Katzenstein, ed., *The Culture of National Security: Norms and Identity in World Politics*. New York: Columbia University Press, pp. 153–185.

Fisher, I. 2001. "Europe's East See AIDS on the March." *New York Times*, June 13, p. A3.

Fitzgerald, G. 1990. "Dispatches from the Drug War." *Common Cause Magazine* 16 (January-February), pp. 13–19.

Forbes, A. D.W. 1987. "The 'Cin-Ho' (Yunnanese Chinese) Caravan Trade with North Thailand During the late Nineteenth and Early Twentieth Centuries." *Journal of Asian History* 21, no. 1, pp. 1–47.

———. 1988. "The Yunnanese ('Ho') Muslims of North Thailand." In A. D. W. Forbes, ed., *The Muslims of Thailand: Volume I Historical and Cultural Studies*. Gaya, Bihar, India: Centre for South East Asian Studies, pp. 87–104.

Forero, J. 2000a. "Luring Colombian Farmers from Coca Cash Crop." *New York Times*, November 20, p. A8.

———. 2000b. "Ratcheting Up a Jungle War in Coca Fields." *New York Times*, December 10, p. A22.

———. 2001a. "Colombian Paramilitaries Adjust Attack Strategies." *New York Times*, January 22, p. A3.

———. 2001b. "In the War on Coca, Colombian Growers Simply Move Along." *New York Times*, March 17, p. A1.

———. 2001c. "Judge in Colombia Halts Spraying of Drug Crops." *New York Times*, July 30, p. A4.

———. 2001d."New Challenge to the Bogotá Leadership." *New York Times*, May 6, p. A8.

———. 2001e. "Ranchers in Colombia Bankroll Their Own Militia." *New York Times*, August 8, p. A1.

———. 2002a. "Administration Shifts Focus on Colombia Aid." *New York Times*, February 6, p. A6.

———. 2002b. "Farmers in Peru Are Turning Again to Coca Crop." *New York Times*, February 14, p. A3.

Frantz, D. 2000. "Heroin and Needles: Battling AIDS in Central Asia." *New York Times*, October 16, p. A4.

———. 2001a. "Central Asia Braces to Fight Islamic Rebels." *New York Times*, May 3, p. A1.

———. 2001b. "Pakistan Ended Aid to Taliban Only Hesitantly." *New York Times*, December 8, p. A1.

———. 2002. "Agents Seize Turkey's Largest Haul of Drugs, Said to Be from Afghanistan." *New York Times*, April 2, p. A12.

French, H. W. 2002a. "More Nations Join Afghan Aid Effort." *New York Times*, January 22, p. A1.

———. 2002b. "Pakistani Intelligence Officials See Qaeda Peril in their Cities." *New York Times*, May 29, p. A8.

Gargan, E. A. 1992. "Rival Rebels Fight in Afghan Capital Day After Its Fall." *New York Times*, April 27, p. A1.

Gearing, J. 1999. "Thailand's Battle for Its Soul." *Asia Week*, August 13, pp. 28–29.

Geopolitical Drug Dispatch. November 1991. "Yugoslavia: Balkan Route Fuels War," no. 1, pp. 1, 3.

———. January 1992. "Afghanistan: Aiming to Be the Leading Opium Producer," no. 3, pp. 1, 3.

———. June 1992. "Uzbekistan: Poppy Boom, Enforcement Bust," no. 8, pp. 1, 3–4.

——— (Paris). August 1992. "Afghanistan: Opium and Refugees," no. 10, p. 1.

———. August 1994. "Afghanistan: All Records Shattered," no. 34, p. 5.

———. June 1995. "Azerbaijan: Mafia Groups Settle Scores in Government," no. 44, pp. 1, 3.

———. July 1995. "Italy: Mafia Overhaul in the North," no. 45, pp. 1, 3–4.

———. January 1996a. "Greece: Fall-out from the Balkan Narco-Fraternity," no. 51, pp. 5–6.

———. January 1996b. "Narco-Mafias Move in on Synthetic Drugs," no. 51, pp. 1–3.

———. July 1996. "Albanian Minorities and Heroin Geopolitics," no. 57, p. 6.

———. November 1996. "Turkey: Routes Shift Still Further East," no. 61, pp. 1, 3–4.

———. January 1997. "Afghanistan: The Taliban Face an Opium Dilemma," no. 63, pp. 1, 3–5.

———. March 1997. "Romania: The PKK's Heroin Networks," no. 65, pp. 5–6.

———. May 1997. "Uzbekistan: Stalin's Legacy," no. 67, pp. 1, 3–4.

———. July 1998. "Tajikistan: The Fundamentalists' Opium," no. 81, pp. 1, 3.

———. August 1998. "Indonesia: Ecstasy Market Adapts to Crisis," no. 82, pp. 6–7.

———. February 1999. "Turkmenistan: A New Pipeline for Afghan Drug," no. 88, pp. 5–6.

———. April 1999. "Afghanistan: Deceptive 'Destruction' of Laboratories," no. 90, pp. 5–6.

———. June 1999. "Tajikistan-Kirghizistan: Heroin Contributes to Social Collapse," no. 92, p. 6.

———. September 1999. "Afghanistan: Money Talks to the Taliban," no. 93, pp. 7–8.

———. January 2000. "Trouble in Lin Ming Shin's Organization," no. 97, p. 7.

Golden, T. 2001. "Afghan Ban on Growing of Opium is Unraveling," *New York Times*, October 22, p. B1.

Goodhand, J. 2000. "From Holy War to Opium War? A Case Study of the Opium Economy of North Eastern Afghanistan." *Central Asian Survey* 19, no. 2, pp. 265–280.

Gordon, M. R. 2001. "Gains and Limits in New Low-Risk War." *New York Times*, December 29, p. A1.

———. 2002a. "Fielding an Afghan Army Is Months Off, U.S. Finds." *New York Times*, March 21, p. A18.

———. 2002b. "Saudis Warning Against Attack by U.S. on Iraq." *New York Times*, March 17, p. A1.

Greenberg, M. 1951. *British Trade and the Opening of China, 1800–42*. Cambridge: Cambridge University Press.

———. 2002. "U.S. Fears Afghan Farmers Can't End Cash Crop: Opium." *New York Times*, April 1, p. A1.

Griffin, M. 2001. *Reaping the Whirlwind: The Taliban Movement in Afghanistan.* London: Pluto Press.

Hamill, P. 2001. "Heroin's Ugly Role in Afghanistan." *New York Daily News*, December 10.

Harding, L. 2001. "Taliban to Lift Ban on Farmers Growing Opium if US Attacks." *The Guardian*, September 25.

Harris, P. 2001. "Victorious Warlords Set to Open the Opium Floodgates." *The Observer*, November 25.

Helms, R. [1974] 1992. From U.S. Embassy, Tehran, to Department of State. Subject: "Revised Narcotics Action Plan." Date: March 4, 1974. Airgram, Department of State. In Eric Hooglund, ed., *Iran: The Making of U.S. Policy, 1977–1980.* Washington, DC: National Security Archives and Chadwyck-Healey, 1992, item no. 00849.

Herring, E. 2000. "Rogue Rage: Can We Prevent Mass Destruction?" *Journal of Strategic Studies* 23, no. 1, pp. 188–212.

Hobsbawm, E. J. 1968. *Industry and Empire: The Making of Modern English Society 1750 to the Present Day.* New York: Pantheon.

Hopkins, N., and R. N. Taylor. 20002. "MI5 fears flood of Afghan Heroin." *Guardian* (London), February 21.

Hussain, Z. 1989. "Narcopower: Pakistan's Parallel Government?" *Newsline* (Karachi), December, p. 17.

International Opium Commission. 1909. *Report of the International Opium Commission.* Shanghai: North China Daily News, vol. 2.

Issawi, C. 1971. *Economic History of Iran.* Chicago: University of Chicago Press.

Jehl, D. 2002. "Pakistan to Cut Islamists' Links to Spy Agency." *New York Times*, February 20, p. A1.

Jenkins, P. 1992. "Narcotics Trafficking and the American Mafia: The Myth of Internal Prohibition." *Crime, Law and Social Change* 18, no. 3, pp. 303–318.

Kattoulas, V. 2002. "Crime Central." *Far Eastern Economic Review*, May 30, pp. 48–51.

Katzenstein, P. J., ed. 1996. *The Culture of National Security: Norms and Identity in World Politics.* New York: Columbia University Press.

Klam, M. 2001. "Experiencing Ecstasy." *New York Times Magazine*, January 21, pp. 38–43.

Klare, M. 1995. *Rogue States and Nuclear Outlaws: America's Search for a New Foreign Policy.* New York: Hill & Wang.

Konisberg, E. 1996. "A Model Addiction." *Allure*, July, pp. 90–95.

Krauss, C. 2001a. "From Beachside Mansions to Cold Jail." *New York Times*, July 14, p. A7.

———. 2001b. "Peru's Ex-Spymaster Exercises Power from Jail Cell." *New York Times*, October 27, p. A3.

Kusevic, V. 1977. "Drug Abuse Control and International Treaties." *Journal of Drug Issues* 7, no. 1, pp. 34–53.

Labrousse, A. 2001. "Colombie: conflit de la drogue ou conflit politico-militaire?" *Cahiers d'études sur la Méditerranée orientale et le monde turco-iranien* 32 (July–December), pp. 191–208.

Labrousse, A., and L. Laniel. 2001. "The World Geopolitics of Drugs, 1998/1999." *Crime, Law & Social Change* 36, nos. 1–2, pp. 21–284.

Landler, M. 2002. "Rebuilding the Land Looks More Costly Than Was Thought." *New York Times*, January 21, p. A9.

Laniel, L. 2001. "Communauté des sciences sociales et politique antidrogue aux Etats-Unis." *Cahiers d'études sur la Méditerranée orientale et le monde turco-iranien* 32 (July–December), pp. 209–230.

Leach, E. R. 1964. *Political Systems of Highland Burma: A Study of Kachin Social Structure.* Boston: Beacon Press.

League of Nations. 1923. Advisory Committee on Traffic in Opium. "Raw Opium Statistics." *Application of Part II of the Opium Convention with Special Reference to the European Possessions and Countries in the Far East*, vols. XI–XII. Geneva: League of Nations Publications.

———. 1930. Advisory Committee on Traffic in Opium and Other Dangerous Drugs. *Summary of Annual Reports,* vol. XI. Geneva: League of Nations Publications, XI. 5. Part III: Prepared Opium Statistics, pp. 29–30.

———. 1937. Advisory Committee on Traffic in Opium and Other Dangerous Drugs. *Annual Reports of Governments on the Traffic in Opium and Other Dangerous Drugs for the Year 1935*, vol. XI. Geneva: Series of League of Nations Publications, XI. 5, pp. 72–75.

———. 1940. Advisory Committee on the Traffic in Opium and Other Dangerous Drugs. *Annual Reports on the Traffic in Opium and Other Dangerous Drugs for the Year 1939.* Geneva: League of Nations.

Lewis, A. 1996. "Futility of the Drug War." *New York Times*, February 5, p. A15.

Lewis, N. A. 2002. "Justice Department Opposes Lower Jail Terms for Crack." *New York Times*, March 20, p. A24.

Lifschultz, L. 1988. "Inside the Kingdom of Heroin." *The Nation* (New York), November 14.

———. 1989. "Dangerous Liaison: The CIA-ISI Connection." *Newsline* (Karachi), November.

Lintner, B. 1991. "Triangular Ties." *Far Eastern Economic Review*, March 28, pp. 22–23.

———. 1992. "Smack in the Face." *Far Eastern Economic Review*, November 5, p. 24.

———. 1993a. "Burma: Name Dropping." *Far Eastern Economic Review*, August 19, p. 18.

———. 1993b. "Kicking the Habit." *Far Eastern Economic Review*, July 1, p. 24.

———. 1993c. "Rewriting History: The CIA's First Secret War—Americans Helped Stage Raids Into China from Burma." *Far Eastern Economic Review*, September 16, p. 56.

———. 1994. "Turf War in the Triangle." *Far Eastern Economic Review*, January 20, p. 26.

———. 1997. "Safe at Home." *Far Eastern Economic Review*, August 14, pp. 18–19.

———. 1999. "Drug Tide Strains Ties." *Far Eastern Economic Review*, September 9, pp. 24–27.

Litwak, R. S. 2000. *Rogue States and U.S. Foreign Policy: Containment After the Cold War.* Washington, DC: Woodrow Wilson Center Press.

Lowes, P. D. 1966. *The Genesis of International Narcotics Control.* Geneve: Librarie Droz.

Lubbock, B. 1914. *The China Clippers.* Glasgow: James Brown.

Luhan, J. M. 1991. "Afghan Rebels Revived by a Victory." *New York Times*, April 16, p. A10.

Lupsha, P. A. 1992. "Drug Lords and Narco-Corruption: The Players Change but the Game Continues." In A. W. McCoy and A. A. Block, eds., *War on Drugs: Studies in the Failure of U.S. Narcotics Policy.* Boulder, CO: Westview Press, pp. 177–208.

Maas, P. 2002. "Gul Agda Gets His Province Back." *New York Times Sunday Magazine*, January 6, pp. 34–37.

MacFarquhar, N. 2001. "Iran Shifts War Against Drugs, Admitting It Has Huge Problem." *New York Times*, August 18, p. A1.

Makarenko, T. 2001. "Drugs in Central Asia: Security Implications and Political Manipulations." *Cahiers d'études sur la Méditerranée orientale et le monde turco-iranien* 32 (July–December), pp. 87–115.

Marquis, C. 2001. "Cultivation of Coca Crop Shifts Sharply to Colombia." *New York Times*, March 2, p. A5.

———. 2002a. "Bush's $19 Billion Antidrug Plan Focuses on Law Enforcement and Treatment." *New York Times*, February 13, p. A21.

———. 2002b. "Colombia Says It Cut Coca Crop." *New York Times*, March 1, p. A3.

Martin, J. A. 1990. "Drugs, Crime, and Urban Trial Court Management: The Unintended Consequences of the War on Drugs." *Yale Law & Policy Review* 8, no. 1, pp. 117–145.

Mauer, M. 1991. *Americans Behind Bars: A Comparison of International Rates of Incarceration*. Washington, DC: Sentencing Project.

McCoy, A. W. 1980. *Drug Traffic: Narcotics and Organized Crime in Australia*. Sydney: Harper & Row.

———. 1991. *The Politics of Heroin: CIA Complicity in the Global Drug Trade*. New York: Lawrence Hill Books.

McNeil, D. G., Jr. 2001. "Heroin Users in Europe Don't See Price Drop." *New York Times*, October 24, p. B4.

Merlin, M. D. 1984. *On the Trail of the Ancient Opium Poppy*. Rutherford, NJ: Farleigh Dickinson University Press.

Mintz, S. 1985. *Sweetness and Power: The Place of Sugar in Modern History*. New York: Viking.

Morales, E. 1989. *Cocaine: White Gold Rush in Peru*. Tucson: University of Arizona Press.

Muecke, M. A. 1990. "The AIDS Prevention Dilemma in Thailand." *Asian and Pacific Population Forum* 4, no. 4, pp. 2–27.

Murray, D. H. 1987. *Pirates of the South China Coast, 1790–1810*. Stanford, CA: Stanford University Press.

———. 1995. "Cheng I Sao in Fact and Fiction." In Jo Stanley, ed., *Bold in Her Breeches: Women Pirates Across the Ages*. London: Pandora.

Musto, D. 1973. *The American Disease: Origins of Narcotic Control*. New Haven, CT: Yale University Press.

Mydans, S. 2002. "Burmese Democracy Advocate Is to Be Freed from House Arrest." *New York Times*, May 6, p. A1.

Myers, S. L., and J. Dao. 2001. "U.S. Stokes the Fire, Adding Gunships and More." *New York Times*, November 22, p. B1.

Nadelmann, E. A. 1988. "U.S. Drug Policy: A Bad Export." *Foreign Policy*, no. 70, Spring, pp. 83–108.

———. 1990. "Global Prohibition Regimes: The Evolution of Norms in International Society." *International Organization* 44, no. 4, pp. 479–526.

New York Times. November 25, 1996. Editorial, "American Drug Aid Goes South," p. A14.

———. February 27, 2001. Editorial, "Adjusting Drug Policy," p. A22.

———. May 9, 2001. Editorial, "Worrisome Signals on Drugs," p. A30.

———. July 25, 2001. Editorial, "An Improved Drug Plan in Albany," p. A16.

———. January 21, 2002. Editorial, "The War in Colombia," p. A14.

———. March 27, 2002. Editorial, "Afghanistan at Risk," p. A22.

———. March 24, 2002. Week in Review, "Front Lines," p. 4–2.

Niblock, T. 2001. *"Pariah States" & Sanctions in the Middle East: Iraq, Libya, Sudan*. Boulder, CO: Lynne Rienner.

Nicholson, M. R. 1934. "Survey of Narcotic Situation in China and the Far East." To Commissioner of Customs, Washington, DC, July 12, Annex 2, pp. 2–7. Harry Anslinger Papers, Historical Collections and Labor Archives, Pennsylvania State University.

Nieves, E. 2001. "Heroin, an Old Nemesis, Makes an Encore." *New York Times*, January 9, p. A10.

N.S.W. Parliament. 1978. Joint Committee Upon Drugs. *Progress Report*. Sydney: N.S.W. Government Printer.

Onishi, N. 2001a. "Afghan Warlords and Bandits Are Back in Business." *New York Times*, December 28, p. B1.

———. 2001b. "As 'Southern Alliance' Gels, Many Wonder if It Can Last." *New York Times*, December 1, p. B4.

Owen, D. E. 1934. *British Opium Policy in China and India*. New Haven, CT: Yale University Press.

Pakistan Narcotics Control Board. 1986. *National Survey on Drug Abuse in Pakistan.* Islamabad, Pakistan: Narcotics Control Board.

Parssinen, T. M. 1983. *Secret Passions, Secret Remedies: Narcotic Drugs in British Society, 1820–1930.* Philadelphia: Institute for the Study of Human Issues.

Pear, R. 2002. "House Votes $1.3 Billion in Aid for Afghanistan." *New York Times,* May 22, p. A8

Peat, V. 1998. *The Andean Cocaine Industry: A Maze with No Way Out? Failures of the U.S.' War on Drugs.* Geneve: Institut Universitaire d'Etudes du Developpement.

Prakash, O. 1988. *The Dutch East India Company and the Economy of Bengal, 1630–1720.* Delhi: Oxford University Press.

Preusch, M. 2002. "Washington: Reducing Terms for Drug Offenders." *New York Times,* April 3, p. A14.

Pringle, R. 1970. *Rajahs and Rebels: The Ibans of Sarawak under Brooke Rule, 1841–1941.* Ithaca, NY: Cornell University Press.

Purdy, M. 1995. "New Inmates Reflect Surge in Cheap Heroin." *New York Times,* December 3, p. A49.

Rashbaum, W. K. 2001. "More Than 1 Million Ecstasy Pills Seized." *New York Times,* July 19, p. A24.

Rashid, A. 2000. *Taliban: Militant Islam, Oil and Fundamentalism in Central Asia.* New Haven, CT: Yale University Press.

———. 2002. *Jihad: The Rise of Militant Islam in Central Asia.* New Haven, CT: Yale University Press.

Reid, G., and G. Costigan. 2002. *Revisiting the "Hidden Epidemic": A Situation Assessment of Drug Use in Asia in the Context of HIV/AIDS.* Fairfield, Australia: Centre for Harm Reduction, Burnet Institute.

Renborg, B. A. 1944. *International Drug Control: A Study of International Administration by and Through the League of Nations.* Washington, DC: Carnegie Endowment for International Peace.

Reuters. 1991. "Afghan Rebels Torn by New Quarrel." *New York Times,* April 7, p. A10.

———. 2001. "Taliban Said to Reaffirm Ban." *New York Times,* October 24, p. B4.

———. 2002a. "Colombia's Coca Up, U.S. Says." *New York Times,* March 9, p. A5.

———. 2002b. "U.S. Drug Czar: Years to Go in Afghan Poppy War." April 16. http://lycos.com/news. (site last visited May 5, 2002).

Revkin, A. C. 2001. "Afghan Drought Inflicts Its Own Misery." *New York Times,* December 16, p. B-1.

Rey, L. 1963. "Persia in Perspective." *New Left Review,* March–April, pp. 32–55.

Richards, J. F. 1981. "The Indian Empire and Peasant Production of Opium in the Nineteenth Century." *Modern Asian Studies* 15, no. 1, pp. 59–82.

Rohde, D. 2001. "Afghanistan Redux: Warlords Filling Vacuum Left by Taliban." *New York Times,* November 16, p. B-1.

Rowntree, J. 1905. *The Imperial Drug Trade.* London: Metheun.

Roy, O. 2001. "Afghanistan After the Taliban." *New York Times,* October 7, p. A13.

Rubin, B. R. 1990. "Answers to Questions for Private Witnesses." Testimony Before the Subcommittee on Europe and the Middle East and the Subcommittee on Asia and the Pacific. Foreign Affairs Committee, U.S. House of Representatives, March 7.

———. 2002. "Putting an End to Warlord Government." *New York Times,* January 15, p. A21.

Rupert, J., and S. Coll. 1990. "U.S. Declines to Probe Afghan Drug Trade, Rebels, Pakistani." *Washington Post,* May 13, p. A1.

Rush, J. R. 1990. *Opium to Java.* Ithaca, NY: Cornell University Press.

Sanger, D. E. 2001. "Bush Names a Drug Czar and Addresses Criticism." *New York Times*, May 11, p. A20.

Schemo, D. J., and T. Golden. 1998. "Bogota Aid: To Fight Drugs or Rebels?" *New York Times*, June 2, p. A1.

Schmemann, S. 2001. "Taliban Lose Grip on Wider Regions." *New York Times*, November 15, p. A1.

———. 2002. "Afghanistan Issues Order Taking Hard Line on Opium Production." *New York Times*, January 17, p. A14.

Schmitt, E. 2002. "New Afghan Army Takes Shape, with G.I.'s as Trainers." *New York Times*, May 15, p. A11.

Shahzad, S. S. 2001. "US Turns to Drug Baron to Rally Support." *Online Asia Times*, December 4. http://www.atimes.com/ind-pak/CLO4Df01.html (site last visited on December 11, 2001).

Shihab, S. 2000. "L'Onde de choc de la Guérilla islamiste s'étend en Asie Centrale." *Le Monde*, September 9, p. 2.

Skolnick, J. H. 1990. "A Critical Look at the National Drug Control Strategy." *Yale Law & Policy Review* 8, no. 1, pp. 75–116.

Smith, M. 1991. *Burma: Insurgency and the Politics of Ethnicity.* London: Zed Books.

Smith, W. F. 1982. "Drug Traffic Today—Challenge and Response." *Drug Enforcement*, Summer, pp. 2–3.

Specter, M. 1995. "Highway of Drugs—A Special Report; Opium Finding Its Silk Road in the Chaos of Central Asia." *New York Times*, May 2, p. A5.

Spindler, A. M. 1997. "A Death Tarnishes Fashion's 'Heroin Look.'" *New York Times*, May 20, p. A1.

Stackpole, E. 1954. *Captain Prescott and the Opium Smugglers.* Mystic, CT: Marine Historical Association.

Stelle, C. C. 1940. "American Trade in Opium to China in the Nineteenth Century," *Pacific Historical Review* 9 (December), pp. 427–442.

Stevens, W. K. 1983. "Pakistani-Afghan Area Leads as Supplier of Heroin to U.S." *New York Times*, June 30, p. A1.

Strachey, Sir J. 1903. *India: Its Administration and Progress.* London: Macmillan.

Suvichapouaree. 1993. "Mind Games." *Bangkok Post*, November 7, p. 3.

Tasker, R. 2000. "Flash Point." *Far Eastern Economic Review*, June 1, pp. 24–26.

Tasker, R., and B. Lintner. 2001a. "Nasty Job for Task Force 399." *Far Eastern Economic Review*, April 19, pp. 24–25.

———. 2001b. "No Quick Fix for the Junta." *Far Eastern Economic Review*, November 29, pp. 29–30.

Taylor, A. H. 1969. *American Diplomacy and the Narcotics Traffic, 1900–1939: A Study in International Humanitarian Reform.* Durham, NC: Duke University Press.

Thelwall, A. S. 1839. *The Iniquities of the Opium Trade with China: Being a Development of the Main Causes Which Exclude the Merchants of Great Britain from the Advantages of an Unrestricted Commercial Intercourse with That Vast Empire.* London: Wm. H. Allen.

Thornton, E. M. 1983. *Freud and Cocaine: The Freudian Fallacy.* London: Blond & Briggs.

Torchia, C. 2002. "Poppy-Farmers: Eradication Is Unfair." Associated Press, April 7. http://news.lycos.com/news/. (site last visited May 5, 2002).

Tough, P. 2001. "The OxyContin Underground." *New York Times Magazine*, July 29, pp. 33–37.

Traub, J. 2002. "Questions for Richard C. Holbrooke." *New York Times Magazine*, March 24, p. 18.

Tyler, P. E. 1995a. "China Battles a Spreading Scourge of Illicit Drugs." *New York Times*, November 15, p. A1.

———. 1995b. "Heroin Influx Ignites a Growing AIDS Epidemic in China." *New York Times*, November 28, p. A1.

———. 2000. "Russian Vigilantes Fight Drug Dealers." *New York Times*, March 4, p. A4.

———. 2001. "British Detail bin Laden's Link to U.S. Attacks." *New York Times*, October 5, p. A1.

United Nations. 1953. Department of Social Affairs. *Bulletin on Narcotics* 5, no. 2 (April–June).

———. 1997. United Nations International Drug Control Programme. *World Drug Report*. Oxford: Oxford University Press.

———. 1998a. United Nations Drug Control Programme. "Myanmar Strategic Programme: Executive Summary."

———. 1998b. United Nations International Drug Control Programme. *Afghanistan: Opium Poppy Survey 1997*. Islamabad: United Nations Regional Office for South West Asia.

———. 1998c. United Nations International Drug Control Programme. *Afghanistan: Strategic Study #1. An Analysis of the Process of Expansion of Opium Poppy Cultivation to New Districts in Afghanistan*. Islamabad: United Nations Regional Office for South West Asia.

———. 1998d. United Nations Office for Drug Control and Crime Prevention, Pakistan Regional Office. *Strategic Study #2: The Dynamics of the Farmgate Opium Trade and the Coping Strategies of Opium Traders*. http://www.odccp.org:80/pakistan/report_1998 (site last visited on October 11, 2001).

———. 1999a. United Nations International Drug Control Programme. *Strategic Study #4: Access to Labour: The Role of Opium in the Livelihood Strategies of Itinerant Harvesters Working in Helmand Province, Afghanistan*. Islamabad: UNDCP.

———. 1999b. United Nations Office for Drug Control and Crime Prevention. *Lao PDR; Extent, Patterns and Trends in Illicit Drugs*, May. http://www.odccp.org:80/laopdr/lao_pdr_country_profile.pdf (site last visited on October 31, 2001).

———. 1999c. United Nations Office for Drug Control and Crime Prevention, Pakistan Regional Office. *Strategic Study #3: The Role of Opium as a Source of Informal Credit*. http://www.odccp.org:80/pakistan/report_1999 (site last visited on October 30, 2001.

———. 1999d. United Nations Office for Drug Control and Crime Prevention. *Strategic Study #5: An Analysis of the Process of Expansion of Opium Poppy to New Districts in Afghanistan (Second Report)*, November. http://www.odccp.org:alternative_development_studies (site last visited on October 31, 2001).

———. 2000a. International Narcotics Control Board. *Report of the International Narcotics Control Board for 1999*. New York: United Nations.

———. 2000b. United Nations International Drug Control Programme. *Afghanistan: Annual Survey 2000*. Islamabad: UNDCP.

———. 2000c. United Nations Office for Drug Control and Crime Prevention. *Strategic Study #6: The Role of Women in Opium Poppy Cultivation in Afghanistan*, June. http://www.odccp.org:alternative_development_studies (site last visited on October 31, 2001).

———. 2000d. United Nations Office for Drug Control and Crime Prevention. *World Drug Report 2000*. Oxford: Oxford University Press.

———. 2001a. United Nations International Drug Control Programme. *Afghanistan: Annual Survey 2001*. Islamabad: UNDCP.

———. 2001b. United Nations Office for Drug Control and Crime Prevention. *Country Pro-*

file: Islamic Republic of Iran. 5. Drug Situation. http://www.odccp.org/Iran/country_ profile (site last visited October 31, 2001).

————. 2002. International Narcotics Control Board. *Report of the International Narcotics Control Board for 2001.* New York: United Nations.

U.S. Cabinet Committee on International Narcotics Control. 1972. *World Opium Survey 1972.* Washington, DC: CCINC.

U.S. CIA. 1972. Directorate of Intelligence. "Intelligence Memorandum: Narcotics in Iran." International Narcotics Series no. 13 (June 12) Washington, DC: Central Intelligence Agency.

————. [1983] 1995. Directorate of Intelligence. "Passes and Trails on the Pakistan-Afghanistan Border: A Reference Aid." In Steven R. Galster, ed., *Afghanistan: The Making of U.S. Policy, 1973–1990.* Washington, DC: National Security Archives and Chadwyck-Healey, Item AF01447.

U.S. Congress. 1975a. House of Representatives. 94th Congress, 1st Session, Committee on International Relations. *The Effectiveness of Turkish Opium Control.* Washington, DC: U.S. Government Printing Office.

————. 1975b. House of Representatives. 94th Congress, 1st session, Committee on International Relations. *The Narcotics Situation in Southeast Asia: The Asian Connection.* Washington, DC: U.S. Government Printing Office.

————. 1975c. House of Representatives. 94th Congress, 1st Session, Committee on International Relations. *Proposal to Control Opium from the Golden Triangle and Terminate the Shan Opium Trade.* Washington DC: U.S. Government Printing Office.

————. 1980. House of Representatives. 96th Congress, 2nd Session, Select Committee on Narcotics Abuse and Control. *Illicit Methamphetamine Laboratories in the Pennsylvania/New Jersey/Delaware Area.* Washington, DC: U.S. Government Printing Office.

————. 1986. House of Representatives. 99th Congress, 2d Session, Committee on Foreign Affairs. *Compilation of Narcotics Law, Treaties, and Executive Documents.* Washington, DC: U.S. Government Printing Office.

U.S. Department of Commerce and Labor. 1911. *Statistical Abstract of the United States 1910.* Washington, DC: U.S. Government Printing Office.

U.S. Department of Commerce. 1916. Bureau of Foreign and Domestic Commerce. *Statistical Abstract of the United States 1915.* Washington, DC: U.S. Government Printing Office.

U.S. Department of Justice. 1989. Office of Justice Program, Bureau of Justice Statistics. "Prisoners in 1988." *Bureau of Justice Statistics*, NCJ-116315, April.

————. 1991. Office of Justice Programs, Bureau of Justice Statistics. *Sourcebook of Criminal Justice Statistics 1990.* Washington, DC: U.S. Department of Justice.

————. 2000. Office of Justice Program, Bureau of Justice Statistics. *Correctional Populatons in the United States.* Washington, DC: U.S. Department of Justice.

U.S. Department of State. 1984. Bureau of International Narcotics Matters. *International Narcotics Control Strategy Report.* Washington, DC: U.S. State Department.

————. 1986. Bureau of International Narcotics Matters. *International Narcotics Control Strategy Report 1986.* Washington, DC: U.S. State Department.

————. 1988. Bureau of International Narcotics Matters. *International Narcotics Control Strategy Report.* Washington, DC: U.S. State Department.

————. 1989. Bureau of International Narcotics Matters. *International Narcotics Control Strategy Report, March 1989.* Washington, DC: U.S. State Department.

————. 1990. Bureau of International Narcotics Matters. *International Narcotics Control Strategy Report, March 1990.* Washington, DC: U.S. State Department.

————. 1991. Bureau of International Narcotics Matters. *International Narcotics Strategy Report,* Washington, DC: U.S. State Department.

————. 1993. Bureau of International Narcotics Matters. *International Narcotics Strategy Report, April 1993.* Washington, DC: U.S. State Department.

————. 1994. Bureau of International Narcotics Matters. *International Narcotics Control Strategy Report, April 1994.* Washington, DC: U.S. State Department.

————. 1995. Confidential Cable: "Pakistan's Tribal Areas: How They Are Administered (Or Not)." Origin: U.S. Consulate, Peshawar. Date: October 13, 1986. In Steven R. Galster, ed., *Afghanistan: The Making of U.S. Policy, 1973–1990.* Washington, DC: National Security Archives and Chadwyck-Healey, Item no. 01822.

————. 1996. Bureau for International Narcotics and Law Enforcement Affairs. *International Narcotics Control Strategy Report, March 1996.* Washington, DC: U.S. State Department.

————. 1997. Bureau for International Narcotics and Law Enforcement Affairs. *International Narcotics Control Strategy Report, March 1997.* Washington, DC: U.S. State Department.

————. 1998. Bureau for International Narcotics and Law Enforcement Affairs. *International Narcotics Control Strategy Report, March 1998.* Washington, DC: U.S. State Department.

————. 1999. Bureau for International Narcotics and Law Enforcement Affairs. *International Narcotics Control Strategy Report, March 1999.* Washington, DC: U.S. State Department.

————. 2000. Bureau for International Narcotics and Law Enforcement Affairs. *International Narcotics Control Strategy Report, March 2000.* Washington, DC: U.S. State Department.

————. 2001. Bureau of Public Affairs. Secretary Colin L. Powell. "Statement at Press Briefing on New U.S. Humanitarian Assistance for Afghans," May 17. http://www.state.gov/secretary/rm/2001/2929.htm (site last visited June 3, 2002).

————. 2002. Bureau for International Narcotics and Law Enforcement Affairs. *International Narcotics Control Strategy Report—2001.* Washington, DC: U.S. State Department. http:///www.state.gov/g/inl/rls/nrcrpt/2001/rpt/8483.htm (site last visited March 28, 2002).

U.S. Drug Enforcement Administration. 1972. "Heroin Source Identification for U.S. Heroin Market—1972."

————. 1972–1975. "Heroin Source Identification for U.S. Heroin Market." Washington, DC, manuscript reports.

————. 1975. "Heroin Source Identification for U.S. Heroin Market, January to June 1975."

————. 1996. National Narcotics Intelligence Consumers Committee 1995. "The Supply of Illicit Drugs to the United States, August 1996."

U.S. General Accounting Office. 1988. *Drug Control U.S.-Mexico Opium Poppy and Marijuana Aerial Eradication Program.* Washington, DC: U.S. Government Printing Office.

————. 1996. *Drug Control: U.S. Heroin Program Encounters Many Obstacles in Southeast Asia.* Washington, DC: U.S. General Accounting Office.

U.S. Library of Congress. 1986. "Pushtun Territory: Groups, Tribes, Population Density, and Migration Routes." Washington, DC: Geography and Map Division. (Stamped June 9, 1986; no source is given, but the cartographic style seems similar to those in atlases of the CIA.)

U.S. Office of National Drug Control Policy. 1998. *The National Drug Control Strategy, 1998: A Ten Year Plan 1998–2007.* Washington, DC: Office of National Drug Control Policy.

Van Ours, J. 1995. "The Price Elasticity of Hard Drugs: The Case of Opium in the Dutch East Indies, 1923–1938." *Journal of Political Economy* 103, no. 2, pp. 261–279.

Verhovek, S. H. 2000. "Conference Seeks Ways to Reduce Heroin Deaths." *New York Times*, January 16, p. A16.

Vienne, B. 1998. "De la production d'opium au trafic d'héroine: l'économie du pavot chez les minorités ethniques du Nord de la Thaïlande." In Éric Léonard, ed., *Drogue et reproduction sociale dans le Tiers Monde.* Bondy: Éditions de l'Aube, pp. 66–72.

Virtual Information Center. 2001. *Afghanistan Primer,* September 25. (Sent via email from cschuster@vic-info.org.)

———. 2002a. "Courted by U.S. and Iran, an Afghan Governor Plays One Side Off the Other." *New York Times*, April 3, p. A13.

Waldman, A. 2002b. "A Fertile Valley Left Barren by the Taliban." *New York Times*, January 7, p. A1.

———. 2002c. "A Village at Source of Heroin Trade Fears the Eradication of Its Poppies." *New York Times*, March 12, p. A12.

Weiner, T. 2001a. "Gun Control Policy, Jalalabad Style: He Who Grabs All the Rifles Writes the Rules." *New York Times*, November 23, p. B4.

———. 2001b. "In Latin America, Foes Aren't the Only Danger." *New York Times*, April 29, p. 4–1.

———. 2001c. "Now, the Battle to Feed the Afgan Nation." *New York Times*, November 16, p. A1.

———. 2001d. "Pashtuns in Exile Seem Determined to Fight for Power, if Not for Land." *New York Times*, November 14, p. B1.

———. 2001e. "With Taliban Gone, Opium Farmers Return to Their Only Cash Crop." *New York Times*, November 26, p. B1.

———. 2001f. "Villagers Yearn for the Old, Eternal Afghanistan." *New York Times*, December 3, p. B5.

Wicinski, L. M. 1981. "Europe Awash with Heroin." *Drug Enforcement*, Summer, pp. 14–15.

Wines, M. 2000. "Heroin Carries AIDS to A Region in Siberia." *New York Times*, April 24, p. A1.

Wren, C. S. 1996. "Scouting Trip Brings Drug Czar No Easy Answers." *New York Times*, April 29, p. A18.

———. 1997a. "Drugged Look in Fashion Angers Clinton." *New York Times*, May 22, p. A12.

———. 1997b. "U.N. Report Says Tens of Millions Use Illicit Drugs." *New York Times*, June 26, p. A12.

———. 1998a. "At Dru.

———. 1998b. "International Effort Is Pledged to Curb Demand for Illegal Drugs." *New York Times*, June 11, p. A13.

———. 2000. "Face of Heroin: It's Younger and Suburban." *New York Times*, April 25, p. A22.

———. 2001. "A Drug Warrior Who Would Rather Treat Than Fight." *New York Times*, January 8, p. A8.

Yegar, M. 1966. "The Panthay (Chinese Muslims) of Burma and Yunnan." *Journal of Southeast Asian Studies* 7, no. 1, pp. 73–85.

Zaw, A. 2001. "Drugs, Generals and Neighbors." *The Irrawaddy* 9, no. 5 (June), p. 1.

Zhou Y. 1999. *Anti-Drug Crusades in Twentieth-Century China: Nationalism, History, and State Building.* Lanham, MD: Rowman & Littlefield.

Zucchino, D., and R. Tempest. 2002. "A Cloud of Ruin Hangs Over Poppy Crop." *Los Angeles Times*, April 11. http://www.latimes.com. (site last visited May 5, 2002).

II

Case Studies

3

Opium and the People of Laos

Joseph Westermeyer

This chapter reflects several different studies conducted over 3 decades. The work in Laos was conducted over a single decade, 1965–1975. These studies began with data collection on opium production in Laos, proceeded to opium usage and its functions, then to an epidemiological study of opium addiction, and finally to clinical studies of opium addiction, its treatment, and course (Westermeyer 1982). During the period 1965–1975 (Westermeyer 1971) I spent a total of 3 years in Laos. The first 2 years involved work as a general physician (with the Public Health Division of USAID) and as a graduate student in anthropology. The final 12 months were spent over the period 1971–1975, with several visits of approximately 2 months each. These last visits were funded by grants from the University of Minnesota and consultations to the Ministries of Health and Social Welfare in Laos.

Subsequently, I served as a consultant to the World Health Organization from 1977 to 1997. This role involved about 20 visits to Asia as a research consultant, curriculum developer, and speaker during a time when several countries of Asia were developing their own epidemiological studies and later treatment and prevention programs. During this time, I also had the opportunity to care for and study refugees from Southeast Asia who became addicted (or readdicted) to opium in the United States (Westermeyer, Lyfoung et al. 1989, 1991; Westermeyer and Chitasombat 1995).

Background

In Laos, minorities made up about half the population. To an extent greater than the ethnic Lao themselves, many minority groups were involved in opium production and commerce. Mountaineer minorities grew poppy: Akha, Hmong, Iu Mien, Khamu, Lisu, and the Tai tribes. Expatriate Asians and Europeans, living in towns along the Mekong River, conducted opium commerce; they included ethnic Chinese, Vietnamese, Thai, Cambodians, and French (usually referred to as Corsicans by other French people). Those groups straddling the borders of two or three different countries were in a unique position to smuggle opium, along with legitimate trade in raw products and manufactured goods. For example, the Iu Mien moved opium from Burma and Laos down into Thailand.

In many rural areas occupied by minorities, the topography, geography, and climate augured against central government control. Roads were few, unimproved, and washed away annually by monsoons. Forests, mountains, and rocky crags facilitated armed defense, so that small numbers of armed men—familiar with the terrain and inured to the hardships of life in these remote areas—could hold a superior force at bay. Malaria, liver and lung flukes, dysentery, and sundry other pestilence could disable and kill as many invaders as could missiles. High-technology warfare lost its edge in the vast expanse of the forested mountains.

Some rural minorities did not identify themselves as a Laotian minority but as nation-states in their own right. For example, the Lao classified the Hmong and Iu Mien as Lao Sung, or "High Lao" (high in the sense of high up in the mountains), but the Hmong and Iu Mien saw themselves as autonomous peoples whose destiny was to live in and control their mountains. Likewise, lowland peoples from other cultures maintained their own language, means of writing, and ties with their countries of origin despite residence in Laos for generations, even centuries (e.g., Chinese and Vietnamese expatriates, with their own schools, places of worship, neighborhoods, cemeteries, and business associations).

These minority groups were at a disadvantage in education, job opportunities, advancement, and political power. Certain illegal pursuits, such as opium production or smuggling, might be viewed as legitimate commercial activities (rather than as criminal or immoral acts) within these minority communities. Expatriates tended to view this opium commerce as a necessary exigency; mountaineers were apt to perceive their opium cash crop as their economic birthright. In such a milieu, the central government encountered difficulties in attempting to interdict opium trade conducted by such minorities.

Another politicoeconomic factor in Laos was the remoteness of the countryside, with few means of access to many mountainous areas. Mountaineer farmers cut down and burned the trees and brush as the first step in preparing the soil for planting poppies and other crops (e.g., upland rice and corn). This slash-and-burn agriculture results in soil loss, pollution of surface water, and loss of timber revenues for the country. A central question for the national government and the ethnic minorities was this: How can the forests maintain both people and trees? An answer that would permit the coexistence of both was not obvious.

The political regime during the period of data collection was a constitutional monarchy, the Royal Laotian Government (RLG). The centrist prime minister, Souvanna Phouma, led the government throughout this time. The country was in armed conflict with the government of North Vietnam, which had made armed incursions into the northern and eastern provinces of the country. A small group of Laotian

Communists, under the leadership of the Laotian prince, Souphanna Vong, allied themselves with the Vietnamese. The Chinese government provided material and noncombatant support (other than antiaircraft batteries) to the Communist effort. A consortium of several countries provided material support and expertise to the RLG, including Australia, Canada, England, France, Germany, India, Israel, Japan, the Philippines, Poland, and the United States. International support came from various organizations under the United Nations, including the World Health Organization, and included support of the Laotian currency, food, medical supplies, medical teams, military training (France and the United States), military equipment and supplies (some from France and other countries but most from the United States), and air support (the United States and Thailand). At the beginning of this study, opium poppy was grown in the north, as it had been for decades and perhaps some centuries. By the end, military actions had largely forced poppy farmers out of the northern provinces into central areas of the country. During the last few years of this period, a truce resulted in considerable peace around the country, with a relaxing of wartime stringencies, and with central and leftist leaders cooperating with the governmental ministries. Then suddenly, following the conquest of South Vietnam by the Communist regime, the Vietnamese and Pathet Lao occupied Laos, displaced the RLG, and established the People's Democratic Republic of Laos.

The Agroeconomics of Opium in Laos

Farmers raising poppy in the so-called Golden Triangle employed swidden agriculture, also called slash-and-burn agriculture. Swidden agriculture prevailed where soil fertility was low and population was sparse. Grasses, brush, and trees were cleared from the land (the "slash") and then set aflame (the "burn"). As available land near the village was exhausted, swidden farmers had to travel increasingly greater distances to their fields. As fields were depleted in an ever-increasing circumference around the village, it eventually became too inefficient to walk out to the fields and back to the village in 1 day. Eventually, after several years or so, the swidden agriculturists migrated to lands that had lain fallow for 20 to 50 years.

Prior to planting, the field was carefully prepared. Farmers completed this process by hand-hoeing the field, breaking large clumps into fine granules, and removing weeds. This process required several days of hard, intensive work even for a moderate-sized field. So that weeds did not crowd out the poppies, hoeing would not precede planting by too great a time.

Poppy had a distinct advantage over other crops (such as corn, rice, wheat, and millet) in that it took fewer nutrients from the soil. Some fields had grown poppy continuously over 10 or 20 years. By contrast, an upland swidden rice field might not remain fertile for more than 2 or 3 years and rarely more than 4 or 5 years.

Farmers broadcast the poppy seed, a method favored by the mountain slopes in that locale. Random distribution of the plants over the ground prevented soil and water from erosion caused by rain and high winds. Light hoeing after sowing mixed the seeds into the dirt. Other crops sometimes interspersed included tobacco, cotton, beans, and leafed vegetables.

Timing was all-important. Planting occurred at the end of the monsoon rains, which dominated the climate in this area. Postmonsoon showers—sometimes called the opium rains—and morning dew during the subsequent cool season provided moisture. The sunny cloudless days and cool nights promoted large poppy bulbs and potent sap.

When the flowers were about a foot high, the farmer thinned the plants to avoid crowding, weeding at the same time. Leaves of the discarded young plants were eaten as a salad without ill effects. Rapidly growing crops planted at the same time as the poppy, such as lettuce, were harvested early. A second and sometimes a third weeding, with selective pruning, came next. Each of these weedings continued over a few to several days, with constant bending and stooping. Like the hoeing, it was difficult, tiring toil.

Eventually, the plants reached a height of 2- to 4-and-one-half feet tall, depending on soil, growing conditions, and the subspecies of poppy. When the petals fell from the flowers, they were ripe for harvest. If the flower bulb was incised too early, the resin was thin and ran down the stem. If harvested too late, the sap ran little or not at all.

Southeast Asians harvested the bulb with vertical incisions. Once incised, the bulb exuded a white, runny resin. Several hours then passed before the resin was scraped from the bulb. If harvested too soon, the watery resin would be difficult to collect. If harvested too late, the resin would dry to a powder and be lost to the wind. These constraints required that the incisions be made in the morning, followed by scraping later that day, or that the incisions be made late in the day, followed by scraping the next morning. Regardless of timing, an unseasonable rain could wash away whatever resin clung to the bulb. Between one and three or four incisions were made at a time with cutting instruments containing as many blades. Ordinarily, the bulb was incised on opposite hemispheres at the same time. Depending on size and productivity of the bulbs, a second, third, fourth, or rarely even a fifth set of incisions might be made. Extra effort involved with each subsequent pass through the poppies had to be weighed against the declining harvest of each pass.

Because of the time pressure, every available man, woman, and older child participated in the harvest. Hired help might be brought in from other villages, often people from other tribes who lived at a lower altitude. Frequently in Laos, these helpers were addicts willing to work for small recompense, given as opium. Rather than trust hired help in the poppy field, poppy farmers assigned them to support tasks, such as fetching water, cutting firewood, and cleaning the campsite.

Harvesting was time consuming, often proceeding over 2, 3, or even 4 weeks. Every hour of the day would be utilized. If the poppy field were a few hours' walk from the village, the family moved out to the field for the duration of the harvest, sleeping in a small shelter of sticks and broad leaves. The harvest did not demand as much energy as hoeing and weeding, but it was more pressured, repetitive, prolonged, and grueling. Thousands of bulbs would be rapidly incised and scraped, incised and scraped every day, day after day, from twilight to dusk, sometimes even at night by torch.

Pros and Cons of Opium Agriculture: The Farmer's Perspective

Poppy culture offered some unique advantages in Laos. It was grown at a different time from rice, maize, or other grain crops, so that the farmer had time for its cultivation. There were some overlapping chores to be done between the two crops, so that there were limits to the amount of each that could be grown in the same year. Nonetheless, poppy growing did permit fuller productivity from available land and workers. Substitute cash crops might require work during the rice-growing season or take excessive nutrients from the soil. Opium was a relatively lightweight crop: A family's entire annual harvest could be carried a long distance by a single man or a small pony along a footpath. Other potential cash crops (such as rice) would require two-wheeled carts or trucks, along with roads sufficiently wide and well graded to allow their use. Opium could be kept for many months without deteriorating, unlike most fruits, vegetables, and flowers, which must reach market within hours or days of being picked. Poppy plants did not require years of preparation, pruning, and development, like tea or coffee plants or fruit trees. A poppy farmer could expect to obtain a profit within a half year of planting and could readily set up a poppy field if forced to relocate. These advantages were extremely important in a country where the central government was often unstable or could not guarantee a safe and secure economic future to its citizens.

Against these notable advantages, certain disadvantages also obtained. Too much rain could wash away the young plants, or a drought could desiccate them. Excessive foggy or cloudy weather could stunt their growth. Hail could dash the young pods to the ground. Theft by local addicts or bandits might occur, especially in areas of dense population or those close to roads. A few warthogs or other ungulates with a taste for salad could ingest much of a young poppy field within a few hours. Clear-cut poppy fields provided an excellent sparring field for mating struggles between rival bull elks, elephants, or rhinoceros. Or a tiger or leopard might use the clearing in a dense forest to hunt deer, guar, or elk, with the resultant death struggles mowing down swaths of poppy shoots. During the 1970s, an untimely visit from a defoliating plane or helicopter could waste hundreds of work hours within seconds. As the plants came close to harvest, guards were sometimes posted to dissuade incursions by animal and man.

Poppy growing can be romanticized as a part of the culture among Annamite mountaineers. In an historical sense, it has been part of their economic heritage. Yet in no way is it an obligatory dimension of mountaineer culture. Poppy growing is readily abandoned and just as readily reestablished. A few examples serve to make the case.

Any economic activity that was as remunerative, less difficult, and less risky would induce a poppy farmer to abandon that crop. During the years 1965–1967, when I was working in northern Laos, such circumstances existed in the environs of two burgeoning towns: Sam Thong (a civilian town, with dislocated provincial government offices, schools, and a hospital, where I lived and worked for most of a year) and Long Cheng (a military training and staging center, which I visited on numerous occasions). Farmers in this area had long raised plots of poppy plants. As the towns grew, however, local farmers changed from poppy to vegetable farming and animal husbandry. Selling market produce and meat to the salaried townsfolk was highly preferable to poppy growing. This occurred again during the early 1970s in the area of Ban Son, a burgeoning refugee town. Hmong and Lao associates informed me that this development had formerly occurred around many upland towns, such as the provincial capitals of Sam Neua and Xieng Khouang, where the Hmong and other tribal groups raised farm produce for the townsfolk. During stable times some mountaineers even terraced the mountain, cleared flatland, purchased water buffalo, and established permanent paddy rice farms—in essence, giving up their migratory lifestyle for a settled existence.

Another reason for ceasing poppy culture was any change in occupation. Traders, merchants, soldiers, government wage workers, laborers, and other salaried employees often kept a garden for fruits and vegetables. However, they readily ceased the arduous, risky, and time-consuming poppy farming when other sources of income could replace the poppy crop.

Circumstances, however—such as increased population (as refugees flooded into an area), land scarcity, or access to roads (so that food could be brought in and traded for opium)—could lead to the resumption or increase of opium production. I had had the opportunity to observe this development in Laos during the early 1970s, when military pressure from the North Vietnamese pushed Hmong, Khamu, Tai Dam, and other peoples into a relatively small area—too small to permit subsistence farming by swidden agriculture. During the cool season, the mountainsides in that area became suddenly ablaze with purple, red, white, and variegated poppy. Farmers made $250 to $500 per year (in 1965–1967 dollars) on their poppy crop, whereas in more stable times they earned only $50 to $80 in poppy each year. This greater income from the poppy crop allowed them to purchase rice from lowland areas in a time and place when the scarcity of land would not permit everyone to grow rice by swidden agriculture.

Opium Economics

Farmers might sell the opium fresh from the poppy, or they might mix it in warm water to remove fibers, dirt, and other impurities. People referred to the latter substance as "boiled" or "cooked" opium, or locally as *chandu*. Addicts consumed this refined product, especially when smoking opium. Some households with addicted members consumed all of the opium that they produced. Other families sold their entire crop for profit.

In 1967 the retail price for smoking opium or *chandu* in the valley town of Luang Prabang, Laos, was $39 per kilogram. This price was not the farmer's price at the field but rather the trader's price after bringing it into town (when opium trade was legal in Laos and opium was sold openly in the Luang Prabang market). At the time of high opium prices in 1978 and 1979, a kilogram of smoking opium in Chiengmai town, Thailand (where opium trade was illicit), cost as much as $700 to $800—about 20 times higher than in Luang Prabang, Laos, a dozen years earlier. By late 1983, the time of my last visit to Chiengmai, the price had fallen to less than half of that.

Profits from opium varied greatly from household to household and village to village. Typical annual household profits from opium in Laos (in late 1960s dollars) were $50 to $250 per year. Higher household profits of $250 to $1,000 per year occurred primarily where land pressure forced poppy cultivation as a means to purchase rice.

The daily wage for poppy growing in Laos, based on interviews with poppy farmers in the mid-1960s, was 50 cents to $1 per day, depending on location and other factors. Of course, the profits could fall to nothing if a crop was destroyed or lost. This compared with typical town wages (at that time) of $1 per day in Laos for unskilled or semiskilled work. In many areas of Laos, opium was a prime means, in some cases the only means, for acquiring capital for trade.

Trade items purchased from outside the local community included various metal products. In particular, iron bars—traded for opium—were forged into farm and household implements. In some areas of Laos during my field observations in the mid-1960s, participation in the Iron Age depended on growing opium. Tribes not growing opium had few iron implements, except perhaps for a machete. Some groups still boiled water by dropping heated stones into bamboo that contained water, or they cooked, since they had no metal cooking pots, by inserting food wrapped in banana leaves into hot coals. They hunted with bow and arrow or crossbow since they had no iron to make flintlock rifles.

Silver was another key economic feature in many mountainous areas where poppy was grown. It tided people over when a rice crop failed, when a migration had to be made from an exhausted site to a new one, and when there was sickness or old age. Silver served as a buffer against the often sudden, cruel exigencies of life in an ecological niche that could be as harsh as it was beautiful.

Over time, profits from poppy cultivation made necessities of items that had formerly been luxuries. Factory-made cloth, footwear, dyes, cooking pots, guns, ceremonial paraphernalia, and some foodstuffs—all obtained from the outside—had become part of a long-accepted, minimum standard of living in poppy-producing areas. Even silver and iron no longer were mere economic elements; both functioned as a means for demonstrating social status, for acquiring socioeconomic mobility, for artistic expression, and—when given as a gift—for expressing interpersonal devotion or support.

Commerce

In mountainous Southeast Asia, the opium trade and the itinerant peddler were inseparable. Peddlers ascended the mountains soon after the opium harvest (before the monsoon rains began), accompanied by a small pack train of mules or mountain ponies and a few to several assistants and guards. They carried iron and silver bars, dry goods, and certain foodstuffs (e.g., salt, sugar, tea, and coffee) into the ridges and peaks. On the return trip, opium burdened their ponies and mules.

Poppy farmers often sold their opium to a local trader or merchant whom they knew over a period of time. Often this merchant could be called on to extend credit, make loans, or help in other ways. Some of these rural merchants were indigenous people from a nearby village or small town; they might even be prosperous poppy farmers themselves. More often the merchant came from a nearby town and belonged to other ethnic groups (e.g., Lao or Chinese).

Another system consisted of an entire region or ethnic group selling their opium en masse. For example, in the 1960s the leader of the Iu Mien people in northwestern Laos bargained for and sold virtually the entire crop produced by the Iu Mien. To accomplish this, the leader, Chao Mai, maintained about 40 mules for transportation of the opium crop. A portion of the proceeds went to Chao Mai for the care of orphans, widows, and the crippled and to provide education. This arrangement combined commercial activities with social and political interests.

As rivulets of opium flowed from mountains and plateaus down onto the plains, they converged into lowland mercantile towns. As with any cash crop, local dry goods merchants, crop brokers, moneylenders, and bankers were involved in the sale and resale of opium. Larger volumes of opium accumulated as the rivulets joined each other, requiring either larger mule trains or access to trucks, boats, and planes. During this accumulation phase, other people become involved in the opium trade as truck drivers, boatmen, and coolies. The concentration of such great wealth in one place required the posting of guards.

At this step in the trade, a critical element was the legality or illegality of the opium commerce. When I first went to Laos in the mid-1960s, authorities did not enforce any antiopium laws. Opium trade occurred openly in the markets of many northern towns. The police and political leaders had no more interest in opium than in rice commerce. When a law against the opium trade was passed in the early 1970s, this suddenly changed the conditions of the trade. Police officers and government workers had to be bribed to permit the trade, whereas this had not been true previously. Prices for opium rose dramatically in areas where the police held sway, particularly in the larger towns through which opium flowed.

Epidemiology of Opium Addiction in Laos

Early on I decided to study opium addiction largely for practical reasons. First, it was easy to determine who was addicted to opium in the villages and small towns of Laos. Although addicted people might attempt to hide their addiction for some weeks or months following the escalation to daily use, the addiction soon became apparent to all. Indicators would include the odor of opium about the chronic user and, in time, loss of weight, a pale appearance, slowed movements, an apparent fatigue, devotion of one's resources to opium, and increasing time away from other activities in favor of opium smoking. Rarely could addicts hide their opium habit from family, friends, and neighbors for more than a period of months.

We used several different methods to study the prevalence of opium addiction in Laos. One of these involved making contact with a few addicts in a community, who then provided access to the other addicted people in the village. In several instances, we worked through local district and village chiefs to conduct these interviews. Following the passage of the antiopium law in 1971, addicts in Vientiane were required to register in order to legally purchase opium in the scores of dens.

These data provided epidemiological data for larger towns, where house-to-house surveys were more difficult (Westermeyer 1981a, 1981c).

Opium dens were typically rooms in a private home devoted to the commercial sale of opium. Customers might purchase their opium for consumption elsewhere or consume it there in the den, with paraphernalia supplied by the den operator. In some dens the operator or his spouse might provide light meals for the den habitués to purchase. Dens were located in towns of a few thousand or more people. As described in a study of several dens, the clientele varied from one location to another (Westermeyer 1974a). Dens served many purposes, including social contacts and information about jobs.

The various communities in Laos showed highly variable rates of opium addiction, from zero to 10 percent and above. The denominator in the following rates was the total population of the respective communities, including all adults and children. Rates in these various ecological niches were strongly associated with proximity to opium production and trade (Westermeyer 1981b). For example, mountain villages involved in opium production demonstrated rates of 8 to 12 opium addicts per 100 inhabitants, with a ratio of men to women around 3 to 1 (Westermeyer 1980a, 1988; Westermeyer and Peng 1978). In these settings, the exposure to opium was high since the entire family participated in the harvest, and opium was stored for shorter or longer periods of time in many homes. In these settings, the wives of addicted men were prone to addiction.

Riverside or lowland towns involved in the opium trade had about 4 or 5 opium addicts per 100 inhabitants. These addicts, predominantly men, purchased opium in a market or den. Those involved in the opium trade may have been at higher risk to addiction than those in other occupations, although any or all occupations were affected.

End-use communities were those that were not involved in opium production or commerce. Special commercial efforts were required to transport opium into these communities. The rate of addiction was low in these settings, around zero to 2 opium addicts per 100 inhabitants. These addicts' demographic characteristics were similar to those in the commercial towns, that is, fewer women and more salaried men who smoked outside of the home.

These general findings were similar to those reported elsewhere in Asia, in the Golden Crescent and Gold Triangle countries (Westermeyer 1981b). The one exception in Asia was Turkey, where the rate of opium addiction even among producers was reportedly quite low—less than a fraction of 1 percent of the population. These findings, taken together, strongly suggest that exposure to an addicting substance, with opportunity to use it based on one's own personal decision, functions as a major risk factor in the genesis of opium addiction—at least in those settings in and close to opium poppy production and commerce.

Natural Courses of Opium Addiction

In Laos, when treatment was newly established, most addicts seeking treatment had smoked opium for a few years to a few decades, with 8- to 12-years' duration being the average (Westermeyer 1983). Ethnicity played a role in the duration of use prior to seeking treatment (Westermeyer 1977). Data obtained in Laos at a newly established medical facility showed the following differences among five ethnic groups (Westermeyer 1978a):

		Duration of Opium Addiction (years)	
Ethnic Group in Laos	Number of Patients	Mean	Standard Deviation
A. Lao	280	15.3	10.9
B. Hmong	81	11.6	9.0
C. Expatriate Asians	52	15.5	12.4
D. Other Tribes	25	9.7	8.4

Statistically significant comparisons:
At $P < .05$: C vs. B, C vs. D.
At $P < .01$: A vs. B, A vs. D.
A vs. C and B vs. D were not significantly different.

These data show that poppy agriculturists (i.e., Hmong and other tribes) presented themselves for treatment sooner than the predominantly town dwellers (i.e., Lao and expatriate Asians). Of interest, the Hmong poppy farmers also had a shorter mean duration of preaddictive use (0.4 years) than the Lao addicts (1.4 years) and expatriate Asians (1.1 years). These data suggest that high access to opium, as occurs among poppy farmers, accelerates the course of addiction, leading to both earlier onset of addiction and to earlier problems that prompt seeking treatment. Another explanation could be that the tribal addicts die earlier than the lowland addicts as a result of their addiction, reducing the mean duration in a sample of treatment-seeking addicts.

The type of drug may also influence the rapidity of seeking treatment. A comparison of heroin and opium addicts was conducted at a medical facility in Laos, the National Detoxification Center. Among 51 heroin addicts, the mean duration of use was 3.8 years, whereas 438 opium addicts had a mean duration of 14.3 years before admission to their first treatment (Westermeyer and Peng 1977a, 1977b). These data were probably influenced at least in part by the recent availability of heroin in Laos, so that the independent role of drug type is difficult to assess quantitatively.

Among 56 expatriate Caucasian heroin addicts in Laos, the mean duration prior to first seeking treatment at a medical facility was 2.5 years (Westermeyer and Berger 1977). This was shorter than the mean duration of 3.8 years among 51 Asian heroin addicts (Westermeyer and Bourne 1977) and also shorter than the mean duration of 6.0 years among 100 heroin addicts in the United States (Berger and Westermeyer 1977). These data suggest that status as an expatriate Caucasian hastened seeking treatment, although status as an expatriate Asian did not do so. Probable explanations include a stable residence in Laos, employment, and a larger social network among most expatriate Asians—and the opposite among most expatriate Caucasians. Expatriate Asians had typically been in Laos for generations and had established roles and residences. Expatriate Caucasians, on the other hand, had more recently arrived in Laos and tended to be socially isolated and to have unstable occupations (if any).

Motivations to Cease Addictive Opium Use

When asked, "What brings you here?" addicted people seeking treatment in Laos usually related a personal problem or crisis. For example, addicts in Laos gave me such responses as the following: "My life is caving in on me"; "I feel sick most of the time"; "I have no work or money, and I want to get my wife and child back."

In addition to personal crises, military action motivated addicted people to seek treatment. I had the opportunity of observing this during 1965–1975, when invasion by the North Vietnamese into northeastern Laos forced many Hmong poppy farmers out of their mountain farmlands. Both Hmong addicts and lowland addicts dependent on Hmong opium production had to rely on opium produced elsewhere. This reduced the availability and increased the cost of opium. Insecure transportation compounded the problem of obtaining opium from distant areas still growing the plant. Increased cost and unstable availability greatly increased instances of seeking treatment. For example, by the end of 1971, over 800 opium addicts in Laos had gone voluntarily to a Buddhist monastery in Thailand for a rigorous treatment program, which involved untreated withdrawal.

Treatment Approaches for Opiate Addiction

Before seeking treatment from a healer or institution, most addicts attempted to cease opium use on their own. For example, as opium decreased in availability and increased in price, many addicts tried to reduce their dependence on it. Among 40 opium addicts whom I interviewed in Laos during 1971, all had cut down on their doses (Westermeyer 1974b). Most reported daily dosages that had been reduced from one-half to one-quarter of their previous amounts. This was also reflected in initial treatment doses of methadone, given to withdrawing addicts in 1972: 15 to 20 milligrams ordinarily sufficed, whereas from my experience during 1965–1967 in Laos, 30 to 40 milligrams of methadone (or equivalent amounts of morphine) were required for the withdrawal of addicted opium smokers admitted to the hospital for a medical or surgical emergency. No addicts among the 40 interviewed were using opium more than twice daily, though thrice-daily usage was commonplace in 1965–1967. Three users among the 40 addicts reported occasional once-a-day usage in order to stretch their opium supply, but they complained of malaise and weakness on this lower dosage (Westermeyer and Neider 1982).

A second method of self-help consisted of changing the route of administration. For example, among the 40 addicts referred to above, smoking was the preferred mode of consuming opium. However, by 1971 (when opium availability had dwindled), only 5 well-to-do addicts out of the 40 could afford to take opium entirely by smoking. The remainder used oral opium during the early part of the day and smoked only in the evening—if they had enough opium to smoke at all. This difference is reflected in a comparison of 28 Hmong addicts interviewed in a community survey and a later group of 81 Hmong addicts who were seeking treatment in 1973:

	Number of Addicts		
Mode of Opium Use	Survey	Clinic	Statistical Significance
Smoke only	26	59	$x^2 = 3.76$
Smoking + eating	2	22	$P < .05$

Another method was a change from one drug to another. Opium addicts sometimes used heroin as a means of discontinuing opium, and heroin addicts purchased morphine pills for the same reason. Since herbal medications were sometimes added to alcohol, some addicts become dependent on alcohol.

Caucasian addicts in Laos had undergone self-induced withdrawal more often than had indigenous addicts. Out of 56 Caucasian addicts presenting themselves for treatment at a medical facility in Laos, 44 of them (79 percent) had undergone withdrawal, often many times. With few exceptions, these withdrawal episodes occurred as they traveled from one country to another. To avoid carrying drugs through customs, they gradually discontinued the drug or suddenly stopped them in the country of departure, hoping to obtain opiates in the country of arrival before withdrawal became severe.

Addicts might also employ indigenous treatment methods. Such folk modalities for addiction did not differ essentially from those used for many illnesses, personal problems, or even natural disasters. More than one of these modalities could be employed concurrently, at times even by more than one healer. Spiritual exercises depended on the addict's religious belief to a considerable extent. For example, animist addicts sought the use of charms and exorcisms (Westermeyer 1973). Often these preternatural approaches were used along with herbal medications, counseling, moral education, chanting, or trance. Herbal medications were used widely. Although little is known about many of these compounds, at times raw opium was mixed into these concoctions.

Physical methods applied to the treatment of illnesses included acute drug withdrawal and later symptoms associated with a return to abstinence. These might be applied by family members at home or by healers. Perhaps most common was massage, which varied from superficial rubbing of the skin to deep kneading of the muscles. In some locales, inhabitants used pinching, sometimes to the point of producing sores or even a few hundred bruises. Abrading the skin with a coin resulted in large excoriated patches. Sweat baths were also popular in some areas, consisting of either a sweathouse or tent or a bed arranged over a bed of coals so that heat rose between the slats. Moxybustion, or "cupping," consisted of applying a heated cup —made of glass, gourd, bamboo, or similar materials—to areas of the body. As the warm air cooled, a partial vacuum produced a circular hemorrhage in the skin. Sometimes the hemorrhage was pierced by a needle or knifepoint to release a few drops of the blood, the theory being that this removed "the bad blood" (Westermeyer 1973). Healers have long used acupuncture for addiction.

Buddhist-oriented treatment for opiate addiction was also available. Around 1970 the Buddhist Women's Auxiliary in Laos began opposing opium and heroin addiction. Their movement identified addicts in Laos and supported arrangements for treatment at a Buddhist monastery in Thailand. The abbot there, Pra Chamroon

Parnchan, subsequently received the prestigious all-Asia Magsaysay award, an annual award by the Filipino government to an understanding Asian leader or innovator. He and his staff had treated tens of thousands of addicts, with up to 400 addicts in residence at the monastery. Many of the 100 monks at the monastery were former addict-clients (Westermeyer 1980b). It was expected that each addict seeking admission came voluntarily, with a goal of lifelong abstinence from drugs. No readmissions were accepted. The 5- to 10-day treatment regimen varied little over a score of years. After exchanging his or her clothes for institutional pajamalike garb, each addict received herbal medicine that induced vomiting. The daily regimen consisted of light housekeeping, the morning herbal dose followed by vomiting, sweat baths, free time for relaxation and recreation, religious exhortations and discussion, and a pledge never to resume drug use.

The National Detoxification Center in Laos provided treatment for four years in the early 1970s. Located in Vientiane, the staff there treated several hundred patients per year (Westermeyer, Soudaly et al. 1978). Animist tribal people preferred the secular treatment facility, whereas the Buddhist Lao preferred the religion-oriented program described above. The medical program had a very low mortality, whereas the monastery mortality among elderly addicts was high (Westermeyer 1979). On follow-up, the rate of abstinence from opium was similar in both treatment approaches if one corrected for posttreatment environmental factors (Westermeyer 1979). Among those addicts from rural areas, the recovery rate was highest (80 to 100 percent abstinence at 6- to 12-months' follow-up) in circumstances in which all or most addicts went for treatment within several months of one another. The rate was lowest (under 20 percent abstinence at 6- to 12-months' follow-up) from areas where the percentage of all addicts going for treatment was small. This effect was less remarkable in towns, where about 50 percent of treated addicts were abstinent at 6- to 12-months' follow-up. In urban settings, the presence of a supportive guide or counselor tended to predict abstinence from opium—suggesting that even in urban settings a social network of abstinent persons favored abstinence (Westermeyer and Bourne 1978).

The Politics of Poppy, Opium, and Addiction

The poppy offered many unique advantages as a cash crop in northern Laos despite its many risks, hard labor, and limited profitability for the farmer. Its resilience as a cash crop in the Gold Triangle rests primarily on local farmers' use of it as a cash crop. With poppy, even farmers in remote areas can participate in an international cash economy. With access to silver, they could store wealth, purchase food and medicine, send their children to school, and purchase kerosene lamps and bicycles. Within families, the silver obtained from opium served as financial security against economic hard times. Groups such as the Iu Mien used their corporate poppy crop as a means of social security. In a country with few exportable products, opium was a primary means of participating in the economy of nations.

Poppy growing and opium use were legal in Laos before 1971. During this time, opium-related corruption among public officials was virtually absent (an exception, detailed below, involved army officers in remote areas of northern Laos). Police and government officials benefited little from local production, commerce, or use. Profits from opium commerce devolved to traders, transporters, den owners, and other legal commercial operators. The opium trade functioned much like the rice trade, which was largely dominated by Laotian Chinese traders. Corruption did exist on local, regional, and national levels in Laos during this period but was related to other products and activities. These included government contracts, nonpayment of legitimate debts by governmental officials, tolls paid to soldiers at roadblocks, and fees to government officials to complete various governmental forms.

Opium-related corruption among army officers in northern Laos was directly related to the war. Those people drawn into opium commerce were senior field officers, from majors to colonels. Among those known to me, all were ethnic Lao, not tribal officers. These lowland Lao would ordinarily have no reason to be in the poppy-producing areas since in ordinary times they preferred not to be there and the local tribal people preferred not to have them there. Their common enemy, the North Vietnamese, brought them together, so that their natural preferences were overcome. Military involvement in the opium trade served local needs since farmers had trouble selling their product because of military insecurity. Lowland merchants were unwilling to risk the loss of their goods or being captured and impressed into servile labor by the Vietnamese forces in northern Laos (Westermeyer 1978b).

The army officers in the north not only had direct access to the harvested opium but also the military strength to protect the commodity. In addition, they had the means of transport (via aircraft) to ship it out of the mountains. Shipments of opium could be readily arranged without leaving army circles. Officers could arrange all matters through their own supervisors, thereby assuring confidentiality, safety, payment, and career advancement. As might be anticipated, such an ideal arrangement became difficult to resist, even when the local people did not particularly want or need help with their opium shipments.

Once opium corruption was established, it assumed a life of its own. Low-level corruption, although involving less power and smaller sums of money, was as necessary to the drug trade as high-level corruption. Perhaps it was even more crucial since it created broad-based support for higher echelons of corruption. The local neighborhood policeman who accepted a payoff from drug traders was an integral part of the system and contributed to its strength and resilience (Westermeyer 1983).

It was well known in the 1960s that someone highly positioned in the RLG governed opium matters officially. The opium flowed all too quietly and efficiently out of the mountains into Thailand and South Vietnam. The precise individual was not known. Some thought Prime Minister Souvanna Phouma or the Hmong general for the northern sector, Vang Pao, ran the trade. Certainly they were in a position to do so. However, Souvanna Phouma was a man of considerable principle, who was unlikely to involve himself in this way, and Vang Pao was pursuing the war too avidly to take time for the opium trade. In addition, both were in such close contact with Americans, French, British, and others that it was not likely that they could keep such a major effort secret.

Then in 1971, at a time when the American government was pressuring the RLG to stop the opium trade, the leader of the trade in Laos revealed himself: General

Rachikul, general-in-chief of the RLG army. Paradoxically, his openness in telling what he knew temporarily saved his position. There was no outcry from the Laotian government or the international representatives for him to step down. He retained his position despite his confession.

Once Rachikul was no longer involved in the opium trade, numerous problems resulted as others used their positions to take advantage of large-scale opium commerce. Police officers, who had had no concern with opium addicts, commerce, and dens previously, suddenly became involved with regulating them. The law itself, as written, laid the foundation for corruption. Regulated opium dens were permitted to operate, but all opium commerce was forbidden. Illicit commerce that supplied the legal dens then became a means for obtaining wealth. For example, a new, special narcotics unit arrested the police chief for Vientiane province with over a ton of opium in his bedroom in 1972. Around the same time, the RLG ambassador to France, a former vice president of the Laotian National Assembly, was arrested at Orly Airport in Paris with 60 kilograms of high-grade heroin in his luggage. The French deported him immediately back to Laos, where—as a prince in the royal family—he was not arrested or even prosecuted. These and other events, reported in the international press, lent an atmosphere of dishonesty to the entire venture.

The Proheroin Effects of Antiopium Laws

Before 1971, heroin was virtually unknown in Laos; however, over 4 years in the early 1970s it gradually appeared, to the point that it became as common as opium in Vientiane, the capital city. Pressured by the United States (many of whose soldiers in Vietnam were using Laotian opium), the Royal Laotian government implemented an antiopium law in late 1971. Within several weeks heroin was being sold in the dens and streets of Vientiane (Westermeyer 1974c, 1977).

Officially, the public rationale given for the appearance of heroin in Laos was the chemists, said to be coming from Bangkok to prepare heroin closer to the source. This seems unlikely since the initial supplies of heroin probably originated in Thailand, as there were no known permanent heroin factories in Laos. A few temporary heroin factories had been identified, but these operations were short-lived as they became readily known and were promptly raided by the antiopium authority.

Law enforcement personnel readily interdicted opium because it was tarry, bulky, odoriferous, and not easily disguised. Heroin, on the other hand, was a smuggler's dream: difficult to detect, odorless, powdery, and easily hidden in small volumes. Laws do control opium commerce, especially in populous areas with a police presence and the absence of corruption, but by themselves laws seldom control the heroin trade.

Conclusion

Climatic and topographic features of Laos favored illicit opium production, as well as smuggling opium into and out of the country. Agroeconomics of the region also supported the poppy culture. Ethnic divisions and corrupt government officials contributed to optimal conditions for the drug trade.

Opium poppy culture shared many characteristics with corn or wheat production in the American Midwest, in that all community members supported its production. One major difference was that poppy farmers were at greatly increased risk to addiction from their own cash crop. American farmers can also become addicted to beer or whiskey produced from their products, but in most cases only after commercial fermentation.

Foreign attempts to disrupt these economic endeavors in the early 1970s had effects in all dimensions of Laotian society. Mountaineer farmers perceived that the government was stepping outside of its traditional role, in a country where "the power of government stopped at the village gate." Expatriate Chinese merchants and Corsican smugglers, along with ethnic warlords, perceived governmental interference as a ploy to enrich officials. Indeed, this did occur, with army and metropolitan police officers becoming involved in corrupt practices. At the same time, some moral governmental officials endeavored to obey the law; they arrested or exposed those officials involved in the illicit trade. Absence of roads and a governmental presence in remote areas, lack of resources, a foreign invasion from North Vietnam, and internal politics made antiopium efforts thorny despite a cadre of honest antiopium workers.

Despite the hardy persistence of opium production and commerce, farmers readily surrendered the poppy culture if alternative cash crops or animal husbandry became available. Opium, although valuable, provided limited profits for farm families. Farmers would give up poppy production readily if they had access to markets for other products.

Large profits could accrue to merchant-transporters, who could increase the price for each kilometer away from the poppy field and for each fiefdom or national boundary that was crossed. These merchant-transporters had access to other sources of income, whether legal enterprises (buying and selling, lending, or transshipping) or other illicit enterprises (smuggling items with import duties). If the risks were small (say, in the range of 1 to 3 percent), profits made the effort worthwhile. If the risk of a specific shipment's interdiction increased, alternate investments became desirable.

Opium production and commerce posed its own risks and imposed its own punishments. Communities engaged in the poppy culture gained in wealth but paid a high price in family disruption, neglect of children, and the general human waste associated with opium addiction. Those communities involved in opium commerce paid a somewhat lower socioeconomic tax, but addiction still exacted a high cost as compared to communities not involved in opium commerce.

Opium addicts seldom wanted to abandon opiate use in the early months and first few years of daily opium use. However, with time and consequences, they tried to stop or at least cut down on their own. Probably some were successful and did not go for treatment. Others sought help, using a variety of traditional and modern techniques. Having a social network supportive of continued abstinence from opiates enhanced treatment outcomes.

Numerous factors worked against the ultimate success of antiopium efforts in

Laos. First, the impetus was foreign, not domestic. Second, substitute cash crops and market outlets were not available to the poppy farmer. Third, the presence of soldiers in remote areas and the ready profit from illicit opium transport immediately drew them into an enterprise from which they were not extricated and which undermined the legitimacy of their struggle against a foreign invader that was aided by a local Communist movement. Fourth, the decision to address opium production, commerce, and addiction during a time of foreign invasion and local political change was a poor one. Some notable successes attributed to the antiopium authority indicated that, in better times with more forethought, antiopium efforts might be fruitful.

References

Berger, L. J., and J. Westermeyer. 1977. "'World Traveler' addicts in Asia: II. Comparison with 'Stay at Home' addicts." *Amer. J. Drug Alcohol Abuse* 4(4): 495–503.

Westermeyer, J. 1971. "Use of alcohol and opium by the Meo of Laos." *Amer. J. Psychiatry* 127(8): 1019–1023.

———. 1973. "Folk treatments for opium addiction in Laos." *Br. J. Addict. Alcohol Other Drugs* 68(4): 345–349.

———. 1974a. "Opium dens: A social resource for addicts in Laos." *Archives General Psychiatry* 31(2): 237–240.

———. 1974b. "Opium smoking in Laos: A survey of forty addicts." *Amer. J. Psychiatry* 131: 165–170.

———. 1974c. "The pro-heroin effects of anti-opium laws in Asia." *Archives General Psychiatry* 33: 1135–1139.

———. 1977. "Narcotic addiction in two Asian cultures: A comparison and analysis." *Drug Alcohol Dependence* 2: 273–285.

———. 1978a. "Indigenous and expatriate narcotic addicts in Laos: A comparison." *Culture, Medicine, Psychiatry* 2: 129–150.

———. 1978b. "Social events and narcotic addiction: The Influence of war and law on opium use in Laos." *Addictive Behavior* 3(1): 57–61.

———. 1979. "Medical and nonmedical treatment for narcotic addicts: A comparative study from Asia." *J. Nervous Mental Disorders* 167: 205–211.

———. 1980a. "Sex ratio among opium addicts in Asia: influences of drug availability and sampling method." *Drug Alcohol Dependence* 6(3): 131–136.

———. 1980b. "Two neo-Buddhist cults in Asia: The influence of the founder and the social context on religious movements." *J. Psychological Anthro.* 3: 143–152.

———. 1981a. "A comparison of three case finding methods for opiate addicts. A study among the Hmong in Laos." *Internat. J. Addictions* 16: 173–183.

———. 1981b. "Influence of opium availability on addiction rates in Laos." *Amer. J. Epidemiology* 109: 550–562.

———. 1981c. "Three case finding methods for opiate addicts among the Hmong in Laos." *Internat. J. Addiction* 16: 173–183.

———. 1982. *Poppies, Pipes and People: Opium and Its Use in Laos.* Berkeley: University of California Press.

———. 1988. "Sex differences in drug and alcohol use among ethnic groups in Laos, 1965–1975." *Amer. J. Drug Alcohol Abuse* 14: 443–461.

Westermeyer, J., and L. J. Berger. 1977. "'World traveler' addicts in Laos: I. Demographic and clinical description." *Amer. J. Drug Alcohol Abuse* 4: 479–493.

Westermeyer, J., and P. Bourne. 1977. "A heroin 'epidemic' in Laos." *Amer. J. Drug Alcohol Abuse* 4: 1–11.

———. 1978. "Treatment outcome and the role of the community in narcotic addiction." *J. Nervous Mental Disorders* 166: 51–58.

Westermeyer, J., and P. Chitasombat.1995. "Ethnicity and the course of opiate addiction: American versus Hmong in Minnesota." *Amer. J. Addiction* 5 (3): 231–240.

Westermeyer, J., T. Lyfoung et al. 1989. "An epidemic of opium dependence among Asian refugees in Minnesota: Characteristics and causes." *Br. J. Addiction* 84(7): 785–789.

Westermeyer, J., T. Lyfoung et al. 1991. "Opium addiction among Indochinese refugees in the U.S.: Characteristics of addicts and their opium use." *Amer. J. Drug Alcohol Abuse* 17: 267–277.

Westermeyer, J., and J. Neider. 1982. "Variability in opium dosage—Observations from Laos 1965–75." *Drug Alcohol Dependence* 9: 351–358.

Westermeyer, J., and G. Peng. 1977a. "Opium and heroin addicts in Laos: 1. A comparative study." *J. Nervous Mental Disease* 164: 346–350.

———. 1977b. "Opium and heroin addicts in Laos: 2. A study of matched pairs." *J. Nervous Mental Disease* 164(5): 351–354.

———. 1978. "A comparative study of male and female opium addicts among the Hmong (Meo)." *Br. J. Addictions* 73: 181–188.

Westermeyer, J., C. Soudaly et al. 1978. "An addiction treatment program in Laos: The first year's experience." *Drug Alcohol Dependence* 3: 93–102.

4

Opium Production in Afghanistan and Pakistan

Nigel J. R. Allan

Opium cultivation in Afghanistan and Pakistan is long-standing, probably covering thousands of years. Only in the decades since the 1960s, however, has opium been cultivated and transformed into rough morphine and heroin for export to the world market. Local men have traditionally smoked opium, whereas women eat it. To understand who cultivates opium in Afghanistan and Pakistan and why they cultivate it is the objective of this chapter. The volume of production and spatial distribution of opium cultivation is also discussed. Both Afghanistan and Pakistan have a long tradition of ingesting stimulants, intoxicants, and depressants. These ingestibles are discussed in the context of common consumption and their great cultural, spatial distribution. A brief synopsis of the current scale of opium production in Afghanistan is given.

Post-Taliban Production

With the destruction of irrigation facilities since October 8, 2001, in the major opium-growing regions of southern Afghanistan where the Taliban Pashtuns reside, it is unlikely that cultivators will stop growing opium, the most highly valued crop. On the contrary, 2002 levels have soared to 1990s levels. In 2000, unpublished reports recorded that two Afghan provinces alone, Helmand and Nangarhar—home to the hard-core Pashtun Taliban and former anti-Soviet, U.S.-backed mujaheddin—produced 79 percent of Afghanistan's production, which is 72 percent of the world's opium supply. By 2001, the United Nations Drug Control Programme said that the 1999 production total of 4,581 tons had diminished to a 2002 total of 3,276 tons, and as a consequence of a Taliban enforcement program due to overproduction the amount had dwindled to 185 tons in 2001. These late estimates are not definitive because of the wholesale civic disruption in the poppy-growing regions. International heroin prices have not reflected the dramatic alleged reduction of opium production, with a gram of heroin in London holding steady at around $100. Interdiction programs in Central Asia have confiscated substantial amounts of heroin (Lubin, Klaits, and Barsegian 2002), but the supply continues, leading one to conclude that much of the bumper crop of opium in 1999 and in previous years was held in storage. The Taliban could claim that their eradication program diminished production, but in actual fact there was a glut of opium on the market and the Taliban's program was a smokescreen in an effort to raise the market price. The 2002 harvest indicates that vast areas of southern Afghanistan were already planted to the levels of the 1990s.

Mountain Cropping Systems

Few principles in mountain geography apply to the cultivated agrosystems in the mountains of South Asia. We know that cultivators are willing to grow almost any crop in any place at any altitude in any climatic conditions given the appropriate incentive. Rice grows at over 2,500 meters near Jumla in western Nepal; wheat grows in Tibet at 4,500 meters. Opium cultivation in Pakistan and Afghanistan is possible at 3,000 meters, but the recent surge in cultivation has taken place largely outside of mountains in regions previously cultivated for subsistence food crops, using existing irrigation infrastructure. Consequently, the increase in relatively flatland areas under opium cultivation has been easy to monitor by U.S. and UN agencies. This chapter will analyze the major opium-growing areas in Afghanistan and Pakistan, but more important, it will place the context of opium cultivation within the culture of the people who grow it, especially in the time period of the last 3 decades. Opium and heroin in both of these countries are now major export commodities that generate vast sums of money. The existence of long-standing trading networks and personnel greatly facilitated the expansion of the opium business from the producer to the export market.

In my travels around Afghanistan and Pakistan for over the past 3 decades, I have been struck by the great range of foodstuffs that are consumed. These food crops are arranged in a widely dispersed manner, with some crops, for no apparent reason, absent from some villages and present in others. My early attempt at deciphering these cropping systems revealed a highly idiosyncratic pattern of crop growing in villages belonging to certain ethnic groups. The pattern of ethnic cropping can be regarded as an ethnic iconography on the agricultural landscape (Allan 1978), in which opium cultivation is a feature. There is a great range in the frequency of cropping according to ethnic membership. The major ethnic group that grows the opium poppy is the Pashtuns, originally from the Kandahar area in Afghanistan (figure 4.1) but now also distributed north to the Kabul area and east into the North-West Frontier Province (NWFP) of Pakistan. Another element that enters into the agricultural habits of the population of Afghanistan and Pakistan is

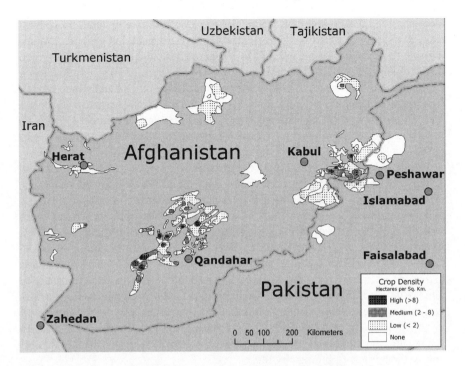

Figure 4.1. Opium poppy–growing areas of northwestern South Asia.

that the people cannot be typed by gross consumption markers such as wheat, rice, millet, or maize eating because they now eat many of these foodstuffs. Some food markers, however, remain. A Pashtun will refer to a Punjabi in a derogatory manner by calling him a *dal* eater, meaning a lowlander from the Indo-Gangetic plains whose protein source is split peas and not meat.

Condiments and spices transform food crops into edible food, but their location varies widely. These are the flavor enhancers. As with all condiments and spices (Schivelbusch 1992), stimulants and intoxicants figure prominently as ingestible consumption items that greatly vary in production and consumption in Afghanistan and Pakistan. It is the latter group, intoxicants—and especially opium—that I wish to examine here. To understand who cultivates opium and where it is cultivated, one has to examine the history of opium production, consumption, and distribution in Afghanistan and Pakistan.

Earlier fieldwork over 3 decades ago in Afghanistan (Allan 1978) and later in Pakistan (Allan 1984, 1987) demonstrated the regional variation in crop production. Opium cultivation is no exception. Figure 4.1 shows the distribution of opium cultivation according to the United States CIA unit that monitors opium cultivation. This cultivation variation was not entirely new because the eminent Russian plant scientist Nicolai Vavilov had noted it in his travels in the 1920s (Vavilov and Bukinich 1923). The material I unearthed for 410 villages in the central Hindukush mountains confirmed Vavilov's observations in a quantitative manner. In Afghanistan, I could predict the mix of crops that an observer could find in a village dominated by a particular ethnic group. My 100 percent sample comprised 25 Pushtun and/or Pakhtun tribes and 10 ethnic groups. With 55 ethnic groups in Afghanistan, as enumerated by Orywal (1986), speaking 45 languages, as listed by the Summer Institute of Linguistics, an observer in Afghanistan could expect great variation in preferences for foods in each village. On the Pakistan side of the border (figure 4.1) it is little different, as the single district of Chitral in NWFP has 14 spoken languages.

Greeting the traveler at any small bazaar or periodic market in Afghanistan and Pakistan (Allan 1985) is a great array of petty merchants of different ethnic groups, offering for sale a variety of spices, stimulants, and intoxicants. Many of these items are gathered from fields and forests, and others are products of local South Asian manufacture. Generally speaking, three items—salt, sugar, and fat—excessively embellish the diet in this part of the world. Unlike the situation in Pakistan or India, not much cooking oil is produced for consumption in Afghanistan. Added to these three items is an array of spices, which allows food crops to be transformed into "real" food. In many instances what we call food is used only to transfer flavorful condiments to the mouth. Stimulants and intoxicants like opium add variety to a mediocre diet of local Afghan and Pakistan food. In contrast to the South Asian situation, opium and heroin in Western countries are consumed as an antidote to the anomie of boring city life.

Stimulants and Depressants

Widespread throughout Afghanistan and Pakistan is the consumption of excessive amounts of tea; 15 to 20 cups a day are common. Shahrani (2002) describes how a Kirghiz group once resident in the Pamirs of the Soviet Union fled to China and then to the Wakhan corridor of Afghanistan, where they traded in opium, but they also introduced tea into many northwestern Afghanistan Badakhshan communities. Vast amounts of scarce money in these impoverished valleys were spent on this nonfood item. Its stimulant qualities are well known, as the International Olympic Committee considers caffeine to be a drug if the concentration in an athlete's urine exceeds 12 micrograms per milliliter, which is about three or four cups of tea or coffee. A cultural boundary does exist between Afghanistan and Pakistan, although it does not lie along the Durand Line, the present-day eastern boundary of Afghanistan, adjacent to Pakistan. In the roadside teahouses of Jalalabad and Kandahar, tea is drunk Indo-Pakistani style, where it is made with hot milk and not water. In Kabul, south of the Hindukush, however, tea is drunk sometimes with milk but often without. North of the Hindukush, tea is drunk Russian style, without milk. These widespread food habits are indicative of the regional variation in stimulant use, which for tea means excessive consumption.

Other Intoxicants

Cannabis

Charas, or the exudent of cannabis plants, is consumed throughout the region. Its existence is so prevalent that no official statistics are kept of its production and use either by Pakistani offices or United Nations agencies. It is the most widespread narcotic substance found in common use. Cannabis plants line the roads of many districts. Even the Christian church on the Mall in Rawalpindi has profuse cannabis growth in its cemetery. Another product from cannabis is bhang, a liquid drunk in the evening and at festive occasions.

Alcohol

General statements about the use of alcohol in Muslim countries rarely provide any insight into the actual use of locally distilled alcohol, called country liquor in Afghanistan and Pakistan. Muslims consume several types of alcohol. The further a person is from the centers of religious orthodoxy, such as Peshawar and Kandahar, the tendency to indulge in prohibited behavior is greater. Outside major cities in Afghanistan and Pakistan, country liquor consumption is common. In northern Pakistan and adjacent Badakhshan Province in Afghanistan, there are large numbers of heterodox Isma'ili ("Sevener") Muslims. Their fidelity to orthodox Islam is much reduced when compared to Sunni Muslims or even the Wahabi, or rather Deobandi "Taliban" Pushtuns, centered in Kandahar who emanate from the same Pakistani *madrasahs*—religious schools.

In mountain areas, tree fruit is seen as a drought crop because trees continue to yield fruit in dry years that affect field crops. Fruits include oleaster, jujube, and mulberry. This last fruit, of *Morus nigra* (Pers. = *tut*), is often gathered and processed just like the wine grape. More frequently, the fruit is dried on the flat rooftops and ground into scarce supplies of wheat and millet to make flour for bread. Wine, however, is made and consumed in the homes of Kuhestanis, the dwellers in the Hindukush mountains. Traditionally wine was kept in large clay pots and drunk during the winter, which was an ideal way to store food calories. No mention of wine making appears in the literature on Pushtun ethnography, perhaps because Pushtuns are less able agriculturalists.

Early historic *vitus vinifera* vines appear in Chitral District in Pakistan. A recent expedition sponsored by the U.S. Department of Agriculture found grape germ plasm in the eastern Hindukush in Pakistan, from where it was taken to Napa Valley, California, where 40 vines survive today in one of the best vineyards in the world. The theory behind the search for these vines was based on the idea that wine making originated in the Caucasus 7 millennia ago and that these vines and wine making were diffused to the west, into Europe. Almost no knowledge, however, of vine varieties exists to the east of the Caucasus because Islam proscribed drinking wine in recent times. Textual evidence in the annals of the first Mughal emperor, Baber (Beveridge 1970), reveals that wine and spirits were consumed in plentiful amounts 5 centuries ago in this area. This is still the case, for example, in Kabul Kuhestan (Krochmal and Nawabi 1961), the area to the north of Kabul, where there are extensive vineyards (Dawlaty et al. 1968). These are mostly used for raisin production and for a few years, until the 1973 coup d'état in Kabul, supplied grapes to an Italian winery in Kabul. Almost all of these vineyards were eradicated by the Pashtun Taliban in 1999. Across the border in Pakistan, intoxicants include locally made wine and *araq*, a spirit made from grapes. In the Hunza Valley in northern Gilgit district, however, consumption of homemade wine and liquor made from grapes and tree fruit (similar to the Austrian mountain farmer's *obstler*) was a simple way of storing food calories for winter consumption (Allan 1990).

Western-style liquor consumption is tolerated in Afghanistan, whereas in Pakistan spirits ("whisky" and "gin") are manufactured by a firm owned by a prominent Parsi (Zoroastrian). Public consumption is severely constricted by the Pakistani government although large shipments of European distilled alcohol are smuggled into Pakistan, mostly through Afghanistan or the free port of Dubai in the Persian Gulf. In 1993, for example, an entire 20-foot shipping container containing nothing else but Queen Anne Scotch whisky appeared in Peshawar, having been brought through Central Asia conduits.

Historical Context

Most attention in this section will be devoted to Afghanistan, which, as I will make clear, can best be regarded as a "space" and not a "place." There is a fundamental difference in the cognitive occupancy of territory in Afghanistan between the dominant Pushtun ethnic group and almost all the others (Nuristanis are one exception). This distinction is of prime importance to the current pattern of opium cultivation, especially the conduits that take opium and heroin out of the country.

From Morocco to the Hindukush mountains there exists the notion of *manteqa* in the settlement pattern (Allan 2001). *Manteqa* is found almost throughout this area and can best be termed "neighborhood," although not in the English sense, where it simply means "nigh" or "next to." It is used in the Italian sense or in the German *gemeinschaft* usage of the word, meaning a place where people share a common culture and values. In India one can think of *mohalla*, which would be an equivalent. One can dissect the problem of Israel and Palestine according to the fact that Israelis (i.e., Ashkanazim) have fidelity to the nation-state, whereas Palestinians are loyal to an indigenous folk territory, *manteqa*. This spatial phenomenon exists in Afghanistan also. Pashtuns have no notion of *manteqa*; their fidelity—and a fierce one at that—is to the code of their ethnic group. "Place," then, means little to Pushtuns; they are an ethnic group that traverses and establishes long-distance links of their kinship through space. That space means more than just Afghanistan: In the past 5 centuries, for example, Pushtuns have developed trading networks far into Russia. In the nineteenth century, Russia established the railhead at Orenberg to tap into the two-way trade between Central Asia, across the Hindukush mountains, and South Asia. Earlier, these long-distance networks had been established for trading hundreds of thousands of horses brought across the

Hindukush to India. There they were sold to princely states of India for their cavalry forces (Gommans 1997). Pushtuns also migrated through the Peshawar valley across the Punjab into the fertile land that became known as Rohilkhand (*Rohilla* means people from *roh*—the hills). In the 1931 census of India, for example, in one district in present-day Uttar Pradesh State, the dominant "caste" was listed as Pathan, meaning that Pashtuns dominated this district at that time. Parenthetically, it is worth mentioning that the dominant Islamic ideology of the Taliban is called Deobandi, Deoband being a town in Saharanpur district in Uttar Pradesh where many Pushtuns settled centuries ago. Now the Islamic *madrasahs*, religious schools, are merely exporting back to Afghanistan and Pakistan Pashtun Islamic ideology, albeit of some antiquity and much modified in recent times. These historical features, placelessness, ethnic fidelity, and long-distance trading networks, underpin the cultivation and distribution of opium outside of Afghanistan into adjacent regions.

To this traditional trading network one must add another lesser avenue—through the small harbors along the Makran coast of Pakistan into the Gulf of Oman. Several of these small harbors came under British jurisdiction in the nineteenth century when they were administratively linked with Muscat and Oman on the southern Arabian coast. Also brought into the orbit as a harbor of small craft— dhows sailing across the Arabian Sea to the Indian subcontinent—was Dubai, today a Persian Gulf state free port of considerable size and regional prominence. Dubai's current link in the drug-trading network is confirmed by its status as the third-largest Afghan (Pushtun) city, after Peshawar and Karachi. The reader should not infer from these remarks that Pushtuns are large consumers of drugs; on the contrary, according to the United Nations Drug Control Programme their personal consumption is minor. What has to be emphasized, however, is that Pakhtuns, Pushtuns, or Pathans—or Afghans, as they are often called in the literature—have had extensive trading networks for all goods, licit and illicit, for centuries.

Regional trade from Central Asia to the Indian subcontinent through what is now north Pakistan was relatively minor with most trade coming from Badakhshan over the Dorah pass into what is now Chitral district, then over the Lowarai (Lahore) pass down through the Pushtun area of Bajaur and lower Dir and Swat to the Grand Truck Road, and finally to the great city of Mughal India, Lahore. Trans-Himalayan trade went from the Vale of Kashmir to Leh in Ladakh and then via the infamous Five Passes route—five passes, all over 18,000 feet—to Chinese Turkestan. Early twentieth-century geographers like Huntington (1907) and Lattimore (1994: 323–360) put the opium trade from India to China on this route. Contrary to some contemporary academic positions (Stellrecht 1997: 3–22), there is little evidence of any historic trade through north Pakistan because the route was impassable for pack animals.

The emphasis on external trade, largely smuggling for many people in Afghanistan today, stems from the fact that the country simply cannot support itself. It does not have enough water to support a surplus-producing agrosystem and the biophysical environment is inelastic. Kabul for centuries acted as a break-of-bulk point for goods being conveyed across the Hindukush from fertile India to Central Asia. It had served in this role for millennia, as excavations in the Kabul area record.

Alexander the Great stopped here to replenish his army's supplies before crossing the Hindukush in 329 B.C., and Timur the Great built at the end of the fourteenth century the large Mahagir irrigation canal in the Kabul Kuhestan to grow food and fodder for his army (Hookham 1962: 120). All crossings of the Hindukush between Central Asia and South Asia used Kabul as their caravanserai. Kabul was not the Afghanistan we know today; it was a cosmopolitan city peopled by Jews, Hindus, Sikhs, Zoroastrians, Turks, Armenians, and Russians. It was not an "Afghan" city; it was the frontier of Hind and Sind, meaning India, as the tenth-century map in the *Musalik wa Mamalik* chronicles showed.

It was often trade in local products to far-off places that sustained Kabul. In the 1830s British India sought to buttress its position on this Indian frontier against incursion by expanding Tsarist Russia. With a bloated, ill-led East India Company "army" in Kabul in 1839, it sent young English officers into and beyond the Hindukush to scout out routes that Russia might use to invade India, as well as routes that were capable of being used to further British trade into Central Asia (Garbett 1878: 1–11). By 1878 the British had fully reconnoitered the Indian subcontinent frontier of the Hindukush (the "mountains of India") and published the magisterial six-volume set *Routes in Asia,* volumes 2 (Mackenzie 1878) and 5 (Seward 1878) cover Afghanistan, Pakistan, and northwest India in today's territorial context. These volumes laid out all the routes passable by a mounted army or by pack animals.

This topographical and political exercise had far-reaching effects. Prime Minister Disraeli, who had advocated the "Forward Policy" of a British presence in the "Scientific Frontier" of India in Kabul, was defeated by Gladstone in the 1880 British general election, thereby forcing the British Resident in Kabul, Sir Lepel Griffin, to hand over control of the Kabul area to a local chieftain. After completing this transaction, the British withdrew to Kandahar, where they took control of that city and handed it over to the same chieftain, who thereupon proclaimed himself amir of Afghanistan—a country that was still in the making. The Afghans never adjudicated a single inch of the borders of what became known to us as the nation-state of Afghanistan. It was a largely British imperialist concoction. It became a space, offering a buffer zone between Central Asia and British India. Kabul, and to a lesser extent Kandahar and Herat, still continued to act as they had always done, as trading stations along the routes of Asia. Notwithstanding the construction of illogical Afghanistan borders, cross-border trading networks flourished, sustained by external trading, now smuggling, to this day.

Opium Cultivation

Opium poppy growing in Afghanistan and Pakistan undergoes great cycles according to the external demand. There has always been local use, often for medicinal purposes, and that is steadily increasing; but it is the external demand, especially in the last 30 years, that has provoked concern in European—and lately American—governments. The archetypal European heroin scene would depict the drug addicts in Switzerland, in Zurich's public park of Platzspitz, injecting heroin in full view of the passing public. Scenes like this today appall many of the citizenry.

It is the scale of drug consumption that concerns the public now. Decades ago it was acknowledged in Europe and America but did not seem to be a major problem. Forty years ago in the United States I had a job in college, driving student nurses to the heroin junkie's detoxification hospital, a U.S. Public Health Service facility, in Lexington, Kentucky. I met its inmates: TV performers, jazz musicians, and public officials. My own hometown of Edinburgh, Scotland, is the largest pharmaceutical morphine-processing center in the world. As a boy I knew what a junkie was because there was always apparent leakage from these facilities. Today Edinburgh is awash in heroin addicts. As a recent survey of illegal drugs in the *Economist* (2001) highlighted, attitudes toward drugs vary according to contemporary norms. That is, attitudes toward drugs labeled illegal vary according to the public's perception of their harm to society and individuals.

The great impetus for so much drug addiction in Europe with Asian-derived drugs was the large-scale travel of youths from Europe to South Asia that began around the end of the 1960s. This is contrary to the popular myth promulgated by relatively young Westerners reporting on the past 20 years (Rashid, 2000) that opium cultivation in Afghanistan surged when the Soviets reinforced their already sizable Afghanistan forces in December 1979. The impetus in fact came a decade earlier. Zurick's (1995) excellent book *Errant Journeys* chronicles the pilgrimage of disaffected European youths along the route from Europe through Turkey, across Iran, to Afghanistan and then Pakistan, to India, and finally to Kathmandu, where the trail ended. Drugs, not scenery, provided escapism. Afghanistan, and Kabul in particular, provided a welcome respite for these youths. Three decades ago it was possible to walk into the Kabul Hotel restaurant in downtown Kabul at any time and purchase any drug known in the world, including imported exotica from America like LSD. Local pharmacies could oblige a morphine user by giving him an injection in the shop. The amoral behavior and dress of the Europeans was repulsive to many Afghans.

Many urban Afghans with knowledge of trading took advantage of the demand by increasing production through contacts in the countryside. In addition to the traditional traders, members of the extended royal family in the diplomatic service freely admitted smuggling heroin into Washington, D.C., and New York City in their diplomatic pouches. The diffusion of opium and heroin found ready outlets through all the existing external trading routes. Enforcement of antiopium edicts by the Kabul regime was totally ineffective in rural areas. The photograph of a household opium patch in figure 4.2 was taken during the spring opium harvest in April 1970 in the Konar valley north of Jalalabad, the main town in eastern Afghanistan. At that time I accompanied a vice president of the World Bank on a field trip and in answer to a question about opium cultivation being illegal, the provincial governor, a Pushtun, said that without gratuities in opium from local cultivators he would not be able to hold his job as governor. From the highest to the lowest station in life, Afghans grew opium. Women ate it, and men invariably smoked a tiny sphere, the size of a ball bearing, mixed in with tobacco in a cigarette.

Generally speaking, opium cultivation for export is found on irrigated fields formerly devoted to grain production. For household consumption, the small opium patch is grown close to the farmhouse, interspersed by other crops. In the high

Figure 4.2. Household opium field, Konan Province, April 1970.

mountains in Badakhshan Province and in north Pakistan, an outside supplier usually imports opium for domestic household consumption. Exceptions may occur. A
highly regarded development project in north Pakistan, Aga Khan Rural Support
Project (AKRSP), had its genesis in an antiopium project. Former U.S. Congress-
man Stephen Solarz obtained a large amount of federal funding for antidrug efforts
in the 1970s, much of which were aimed at crop substitution for drug plants around
the world. With U.S. Department of Defense remote-sensing imagery, the village of
Imit in Gilgit district was identified as a opium-growing village and targeted for a
U.S.-funded effort through the United Nations Development Programme, with the
United Nations Food and Agricultural Organization as the operating agency. A
Drills and Dynamite program, aimed at bringing peripheral villages in north Pakistan into the central government orbit by constructing jeep tracks, cable bridges,
and later small irrigation and agricultural projects, proved to be a great success. The
AKRSP assumed some of the basic features of the Food and Agricultural Organization program in the mid-1980s and complemented the basic project by introduc-
ing other community self-help credit schemes, such as women's programs and agricultural extension. Isma'ili Muslims populated most of the settlements involved in
the initial project. With the expansion into other parts of Gilgit and into the Chitral
and Baltistan regions of northern Pakistan, the AKRSP project now embraces
Sunni Muslims, although it has to be admitted that the receptivity of some villages
to the project has been lukewarm. Opium use, most likely from outside sources, is
still found in some remote villages in North Pakistan, as Mock (Mock and O'Neil
1996: 176)—the most traveled person in northern Pakistan—reports.

Afghanistan

Considerable variation in land tenure systems between Afghanistan and Pakistan accounts for diverse production systems. Surveys have been made into the reasons for production in excess of household consumption.

Much of the increase in production of opium and its conversion into morphine and heroin have been attributed to the civil wars that have engulfed Afghanistan since the coup d'état of 1973. This date is a more precise estimate of the increase in general civil carnage in Afghanistan because it was the year in which King Zahir Shah was ousted in a long awaited coup d'état while he was vacationing in Italy. Several leaders of various political factions went into exile at that time, including Gulbuddin Hekmatyar, a Kharoti Ghilzai Pashtun, the leader of the Hezb-i-Islami party—later a favorite of American arms supplied by CIA director William Casey —and Ahmad Shah Masood, the assassinated leader in September 2001 of the Jamaat-i-Islami (Northern Alliance), the principal group that routed the erstwhile Taliban regime. Masood was a Kuhestani from the Panjshir Valley in Kabul Kuhestan. Often termed Tajiks by Pashtuns and foreigners, these people relate to their *manteqa*, which can be a common grazing ground, an irrigation source, a valley, or a kin group. There is not much tradition for opium export from their territory where men occasionally consume *charas*. A surge in planting and now consumption occurred in 2002.

Increasing political strife in 1978 brought a Pashtun leftist regime into power in Kabul, but factions within that group caused anarchy throughout much of Afghanistan as various land reforms were proposed. Afghanistan, like Mongolia, had been a preferred buffer state for the Soviet Union, which had maintained a substantial military and civil presence in the country since the 1950s. Consequently, in summer into early winter 1979, the Soviets reinforced their presence in Afghanistan, for the first time moving large numbers of forces through the Salang Tunnel under the Hindukush crest from Central Asia to South Asia into the Kabul and Kandahar "scientific frontier" of the onetime British-Indian subcontinent. The United States, a long-time operator of electronic listening posts in Pakistan beamed at China and the Soviet Union, initiated multibillion-dollar support for Pakistan to further the anti-Soviet regime activities. The continuing civil war brought to the surface long-standing grievances between ethnic, regional, and religious groups aided and abetted by their two international patrons, the Soviet Union and the United States, and complemented by regional political players like China, Iran, Pakistan, and its antagonist, India.

During the civil war, opposing factions would mine the underground irrigation aqueducts known as *karez* and surface irrigation ditches. This tactic would essentially starve out the opposing factions because they would be unable to clean out the sediment that accumulates annually in the irrigation ditches and canals. With little land to cultivate and diminishing water, cultivators had to either migrate to the refugee camps in Iran, Tajikistan (an SSR—Soviet Socialist Republic) and Pakistan or grow a high-value crop, opium, with a limited amount of water.

As the civil war intensified, local periodic markets ceased to function normally as brokerage points for grain and other basic food staples, thereby forcing itinerant traders to opt for high-value opium transactions. These traders, mostly members of the Ghalji Pushtun tribes, always had access to credit for purchases and hence had no problems in shifting to a more lucrative crop. Tenant farmers, particularly in the Helmand-Arghandab River Authority (HAVA) region—a place that had received much agricultural infrastructure development from America starting in the 1950s through the 1970s (Cullather 2002), found it more profitable to receive rent in kind, invariably wheat, and cultivate opium for absentee landlords. It should be noted at this juncture that Helmand Province produced 40 percent of the world's opium in the year 2000. By storing the opium, a crop that does not deteriorate with time, growers are able to weather the fluctuations in prices or periodic bans on its growth. Estimates of opium cultivation in 2001 indicated a substantial decrease in cultivation, but that had little to do with Taliban edicts on banning opium cultivation and more to do with a saturation of the market. The interim government premier of Afghanistan, Hamid Karzai, a Popalzai Pushtun feudal landlord in Helmand province, issued another ban on opium cultivation in January 2002. Notwithstanding this injunction, opium cultivation was expected to rise in 2002 because of the almost total breakdown in the irrigation and agricultural systems in the old opium regions of Nangrahar in eastern Afghanistan and in the Arghandab-Helmand valleys. Moreover, American observers who have blown up the storage sites have detected stored opium during the glut years of 2000 and 2001. International emergency food supplies brought to eastern and southern Afghanistan will allow cultivators to obtain subsistence food but at the same time will free up the land for opium cultivation.

Opinions expressed by opium-growing cultivators that attribute the dramatic increase in opium cultivation to the almost 3-decade-long Afghan civil war should be placed in the context of the time in which they are made. Opium has always been cultivated, but external international demand for processing it into heroin and the subsequent sales abroad have never been so high. Figure 4.3 exhibits the increase in opium production during the 1990s. Overproduction in the previous years has resulted in a reduction and then increase in the price of dry opium, oscillating to a low of PRs15,000/kg (December 2000) from a high of PRs2200/kg (August 2000) in less than a year (the 2001 exchange rate was PRs62=$1). Consequently, many of the claims by the Taliban regime in 2000–2001 that they had instituted a ban on poppy cultivation because of international pressure should have been greeted with a great deal of skepticism.

Prices of wet, newly harvested opium have customarily varied according to the seasonality of the crop. The calendar for opium cultivation varies according to altitude and latitude. Regional areas planted to opium during the 5 years prior to 2000 are given in figure 4.4. Most of the low-altitude-growing regions are in the south. Seeds are planted in October and November, laying dormant throughout the winter and growing and flowering in February, March, and early April. Because opium poppies mature at different times, it takes almost a month to harvest a field, from late April into May and perhaps even into June. During this slightly later period, the crop is harvested in the Kabul River Valley regions in Laghman and southern Konur and in Nangrahar Province south of the main Kabul-to-Peshawar road, running through the Khyber Pass. This latter opium-growing region (figure 4.1)—once the stronghold of Osama bin Laden and his bodyguards—is the second-largest

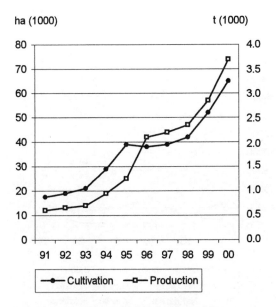

Figure 4.3. Opium production in Afghanistan.

growing region in Afghanistan. For the small amount of opium that was once grown in the low- and high-altitude areas of Badakhshan Province in the northeast, the outlet is into Tajikistan through a Russian military-defended border or through Termez, Uzbekistan, a major freight conduit with Afghanistan.

The dramatic 2002 increase in poppy planting and consumption in Badakhshan province in Afghanistan can be attributed to a unique set of factors. American officials agreed to pay $350 per jerib (one fifth of a hectare) to poppy growers in eastern Afthanistan if they destroyed their poppy fields. This action was generally successful. But poppy growing in eastern Afghanistan is a winter crop. When farmers in Badakhshan province heard how substantial sums of money could be made by destroying an opium crop, many of them planted opium—for the first time—hoping that they too would be paid a generous fee to destroy the crop. Badakhshan is colder than eastern Nangrahar province, hence the lag time allowed Badakhshi farmers to plant their opium as a spring crop. But the Americans never extended their generous eradication program to north of the Hindukush into Badakhshan; consequently a huge crop of opium was available on the market. Development agencies, like the Aga Khan Development Fund, have been active in eliminating the large opium crop's deleterious effects in production and consumption in Isma'ili communities in Badakhshan.

Other small outlier areas of opium cultivation are given in figure 4.1. All of this opium poppy is a summer crop, planted in February and March and harvested in August and September. Yields vary considerably according to the degree of irrigation, with high yields up to 60 kilograms per hectare for wet opium on well-irrigated land to 20 kilograms per hectare for fields with marginal irrigation, if any,

ha

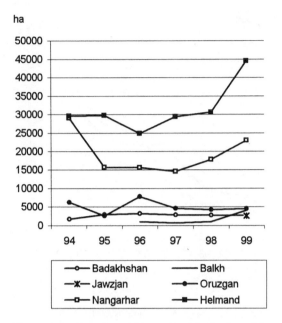

Figure 4.4. Area devoted to provincial planting of the
opium poppy, Afghanistan.

but supplementary rains assist the moisture level. At the end of the 1990s, Helmand
and Kandahar provinces and adjacent provinces were the largest producers, and the
Jalalabad plain area, adjacent to the west of the Khyber Pass, was the second most-
prominent production area. Upstream of Helmand is Uruzgan Province, where
dams constructed by USAID in the 1950s provide water storage for Tennessee Valley Authority–type water management facilities that now supply irrigation water
for new opium fields.

Poppy varieties and harvesting methods demonstrate a high level of agronomic
knowledge. In low-altitude areas in the east and south it is possible with a crop like
the poppy, which has a short growing season, to plant another food crop like maize
or, better yet, rice, thereby performing double cropping for the calendar year. Poppy
varieties correlate with yield, water availability, soil conditions, fertilizer and dung
application, climate and weather, and labor availability. It may take 1 month of harvesting to completely obtain all the available opium from plants in an opium field.
The seed is sown and then, upon sprouting, is thinned (occasionally by women, if
they are not Pushtun), with a plant density of about 20–30 per square meter, according to variety. After about 4 months' growth, a bud containing a red, white, or
even purple (according to the variety) flower appears and, after a few days, blooms;
then the petals fall, and the remaining capsule swells to a size larger than a golf ball
for a few days, at which point it becomes firm and ready to lance for the opium exudate. Within a week of the petals' fall, cultivators, sometimes assisted by itinerant workers, start scarifying the outside of the poppy head, which bleeds a fluid that

coagulates overnight. In the morning the coagulated substance, or gum, is scraped off with a homemade knife. This procedure is repeated several times every few days until no more exudate is produced by the poppy. The moisture content of wet opium is about one-third of its weight; the opium dries out during storage and transportation to more central facilities, awaiting further transportation to laboratories for processing into heroin. For refining into heroin, about 1 kilogram of brown heroin requires 10 kilograms of quite dry opium.

Financial returns on opium are relatively lucrative for the cultivator. Compared to wheat cultivation, which yields about PRs15/kg (the 2001 exchange rate is PRs62=$1), opium can fetch PRs1000 to PRs4000/kg at 2001 prices, according to informants. This variation in price may be due to local standards and opinions about quality and moisture content. The income to the cultivator from 1 hectare (2.4 acres) of opium is $1,500 to $3,500, which is three to four times as much as wheat can accrue from a similar-sized plot of land. If the cultivator is a *dehgan*, a sharecropper, he may keep 20 percent of the income; the absentee landowner receives the rest. Various middlemen deal with the opium from the producer to the processor. Extensive networks of Pashtun traders who smuggle consumer goods just arrived in Afghanistan across to Pakistan handle much of the opium traffic once it leaves the village retailers.

Pakistan, with many processing laboratories in the Federally Administered Tribal Area of NWFP—an area where, dating back to British India days, no central authority exists—has conduits out of the country through the southern port of Karachi. It is important to remember that there is an Afghanistan boundary with Pakistan but no Pakistan boundary with Afghanistan. Technically speaking, there is nothing to prevent Pakistanis, the successors to the British, who constructed the Durand Line in the 1890s and created the treaties between the nascent nation-state of Afghanistan and British India (and now its successor state, Pakistan), to have free travel into Afghanistan without facing Afghan border controls. Although there are border checkpoints at Torkham, at the western end of the Khyber Pass, and at Chaman, the border control between Quetta in Pakistan and Kandahar in Afghanistan, it is appropriate to think of this border as being open between Afghanistan and Pakistan. Proximity to the border assists the passage of Afghan opium and heroin. The southern outlet for heroin is through Baluchistan Province, bordering the Arabian Sea, where it is conveyed to the gulf states or into Iran for transport to Turkey and ultimately to Europe. Many different traffickers are involved in this route, including various Israeli crime syndicates. Other routes are increasingly to the north, into the emerging Central Asian states of Tajikistan, Uzbekistan, and Turkmenistan. Russian crime syndicates, as well as Central Asia's emerging crime groups, garner much of this trade, which flows into former eastern Europe states, especially Poland, where it is conveyed to the large consumption nations of Germany, the Netherlands, France, and the United Kingdom. Within the past decades, with civil disruption in the Balkans, there are reports that Albanians are acting as conduits into Europe.

Table 4.1 Production trends of opium and heroin in Afghanistan and Pakistan, 1996–2000

	1996	1997	1998	1999	2000
Cultivation (hectares)	41,350	43,250	44,750	53,070	65,025
Afghanistan	37,950	39,150	41,720	51,500	64,510
Pakistan	3,400	4,100	3,030	1,570	515
Potential production (metric tons)	2,175	2,269	2,406	2,898	3,667
Afghanistan	2,099	2,184	2,340	2,861	3,656
Pakistan	75	85	66	37	11
Potential heroin (metric tons)	217	226	240	290	366
Afghanistan	210	218	234	286	365
Pakistan	7	8	6	4	1

Pakistan

In Pakistan, opium production has decreased dramatically during the past decade. Table 4.1 demonstrates the effectiveness of the eradication efforts of Pakistan compared to Afghanistan. Some traditional growing areas like Momand Agency, Bajaur Agency (the principal area), and Buner and southern Dir in NWFP (figure 4.1) are declared poppy-free by the government. There is no doubt that the local eradication efforts spurred by American authorities have proved successful.

Pakistan, unlike Afghanistan, has had for many years legal production of opium for ultimate pharmaceutical use. Initially grown outside of NWFP, production shifted there in 1957 when the Federal Government Opium Department and its staff were moved to that area. With this shift in authority, the illicit amount of poppy grown in NWFP surpassed, by 1975, the licit production. Under General Zia's regime in Pakistan during the 1980s, the Islamic Hadd Ordinance was proclaimed, specifying that drug laws in Pakistan had to conform to the prescriptions of acceptable Islamic moral behavior. In the history of poppy cultivation in NWFP, the renewal of an 1857 British order did little to reduce illicit production because the injunction against consuming opium extended to the settled area of Pakistan and not to the autonomous—one might say autarchic—Tribal Areas of NWFP. Little production has been found in the southern districts of NWFP; most of it is concentrated in those tribal areas immediately south and north of the Khyber Pass, with the gateway of trading in Peshawar immediately available.

Summary

Several features stand out in the production of opium in Afghanistan and Pakistan. For Afghanistan, the principal aspect is the inability to be self-sufficient in food production. Agriculture is almost all subsistence with little expectation of dramatic increases upon reconstruction. Furthermore, although there is the Karakul sheepskin trade in the Central Asian northwestern provinces, fruit and nut production (as comically portrayed by travel writer Paul Theroux in *The Great Railway Bazaar* many decades ago) is not an option except in some southern provinces, in Kabul Kuhestan, and in the Jalalabad plain in the east. Agricultural export crops to Pakistan and India, once the recipients of the fresh grape trade, are no longer possible. These two countries have developed their own domestic markets. In some northern Afghanistan provinces like Baghlan and Kunduz, some cash crops, especially cotton and sugar beet, were processed. These uneconomic crops are now defunct because of the destruction of facilities. Dupree (1973: 634–642) provides a good account of all the failed agroindustries in the country.

Barring a huge discovery of oil and gas—a small amount is presently exploited in the Central Asia provinces—Afghanistan will remain dependent on transfer payments from bilateral and multilateral foreign aid agencies for decades. It simply cannot support itself. The carnage of internally inspired anarchy and corruption, largely attributed to the Pashtun ethnic group, now approaching 3 decades' duration, has meant that any brainpower it once had is now safely ensconced in Western countries. Furthermore, any developing country needs to marshal 100 percent of its potential labor pool in expanding agricultural production. Traditional Pashtun culture, such as that exhibited by the Taliban, prevents the majority Pushtun from using its female population in agricultural tasks because the Pushtun insist on the seclusion of women. Subsistence agriculture for them cannot exist without some form of subsidy from elsewhere, be it transfer payment, rent, or remittances from relatives abroad. Migration to Pakistan is customary in this situation, which is not unusual, as has been pointed out in this chapter. Afghans, especially Pushtuns, have always migrated from the margins of the northwestern Indian subcontinent to the more fertile regions of the Indo-Gangetic Valley, now Pakistan and India. In this context refugees from Afghanistan must be allowed to settle permanently in a place like Pakistan. Pretending that refugees will return permanently to the ravaged home territory in Afghanistan, (Allan 2003) as the world community thinks now, is flying in the face of all evidence (Turton and Marsden 2002).

Proposals and financial commitments for reconstruction in Afghanistan by the Asia Development Bank and the United Nations World Bank fail to acknowledge the disastrous development record prior to the 1973 coup d'état. At one time (omitting Israel), Afghanistan reputedly received the highest per capita foreign aid of any country in the world. With impoverishment and destitution facing the remnants of the rural population, it is perfectly understandable that cultivators turn to high-value opium production. These features, combined with the increasing demand for drugs in the Western world, are the primary reason for increased opium production. Although the civil war is to be blamed for the shortfall in food supply in Afghanistan, it has to be remembered that opium and heroin sales financed the strife between warring ethnic factions opposing Soviet suzereignty of this buffer state in the 1980s. At that time Western powers looked in the other direction.

Another feature involved in the continuing cultivation of opium is that there is a fundamental difference in the manner in which U.S. and United Nations authorities attack the growing cultivation of the poppy. The United States, after trying a number of crop substitution programs in the early 1980s, which were quite successful, withdrew its support as employees and funds were redirected toward fighting the proxy war with the Soviet Union. (Local Afghans and Pakistanis refer to their civil war as the American War.) Antinarcotics authorities looked the other way when it became evident that proceeds from the civil war by the mujaheddin, the largely Pushtun forces, were being derived from illicit opium cultivation. Nowadays, the U.S. authorities, through their Pakistan counterparts, use satellite imagery of a very high-quality resolution—the poppy flowers are easily identified—to direct U.S.-paid Pakistani eradicators, driving small farm tractors with dozer blades, to plow up the Pakistani opium poppies before maturity. It is essentially a search and destroy mission.

By contrast, the United Nations Drug Control Program (UNDCP) uses ground survey teams guided by local informants to persuade cultivators to switch to alternate crops. Americans in Pakistan are more effective than the people who direct this strategy of reducing crop production. The UNDCP also attempts to persuade cultivators to refrain from cultivating opium, but, as described above, this is not a satisfactory solution because a cultivator can be given Pakistani grown wheat imported into Afghanistan as part payment for growing opium. Nevertheless, a great reduction in large-scale opium cultivation in Pakistan has been achieved (table 4.1).

What cultivation remains is usually in very small plots often obscured from sight by satellites by being grown in forested mountain areas away from prying eyes. New cultivation was reported in 2000 in the forested areas of several Pakistan mountain districts, Swat, Dir, Chitral, and Kohestan, places where no previous incidence of poppy growing was ever found. It appears that the successful eradication program in the low hill areas has pushed cultivation higher up into the Hindukush. *Charas* may have been processed for moderate local consumption, but opium, especially heroin, was virtually unknown in these areas until 20 years ago. In southern Swat, for example, heroin injection by youths with needles, as reported by a Pakistani narcotics officer 2 decades ago, was completely unknown before that date. These same officers recorded opium addicts at that time. Concurrent with that registration system, the American Embassy also regularly sent a narcotics officer to Landi Kotal in the Khyber Pass tribal area of NWFP to monitor supply and prices. Little enforcement by federal or even provincial authorities was present. Newspaper accounts of local drug barons, working in collusion with government officials, attest to the links between authorities and opium and heroin trafficking.

As explained in this chapter, different ethnic groups in Afghanistan grow different crops. When looking at the map of opium cultivation, one is struck not by the incidence of poppy growing but by the existence of many places on the map where it is not grown. Eastern Afghanistan in Nangrahar and the Kandahar and Helmand areas are well populated by Pushtuns, who dominate the opium-growing areas. Despite millions of dollars of infrastructure investment in these two areas, the Nangrahar area by Russians and the HAVA area by Americans (Cullather 2002), little success was obtained in raising agricultural production. The basic livelihood in Afghanistan is trading in licit and illicit goods, and it will remain so as long as external demand exists.

Acknowledgments Many informants during 2000–2002 were kind enough to answer my probing questions. Thanks are also due to the staff of the two United States Embassies and various United Nations agencies for supplying unpublished data on opium yields and prices around Afghanistan and Pakistan. Funds for fieldwork and travel were provided by the United States Department of State Council of Applied Overseas Research Centers, the University of California, Davis, Academic Senate, and by Andrew Wilder and the Afghanistan Research and Evaluation Unit in Kabul.

References

Allan, N. J. R. 1978. Men and Crops in the Central Hindukush. Ph.D. dissertation, Syracuse University, Syracuse, NY.

———. 1984. Changing Crop Complexes in North Pakistan. *Geography* 69: 261–263.

———. 1985. Periodic and Daily Markets in Highland-Lowland Interaction System, Hindukush-Western Himalaya. In *Integrated Mountain Research and Development*, edited by T. V. Singh and J. Kaur, pp. 239–256. New Delhi: Himalayan Books.

———. 1987. Ecotechnology and Modernization in Pakistan Mountain Agriculture. In *Western Himalaya, Environment, Problems and Development*, vol. II, ed. Y. P. S. Pangtey and S. C. Joshi, pp.771–787. Nainital: Gyanodaya.

———. 1990. Household Food Supply in Hunza Valley, Pakistan. *Geographical Review* 80: 399–415.

———. 2001. Defining Place and People in Afghanistan. *Post-Soviet Geography and Economics* 42: 545–560.

———. 2003. Rethinking Governance in Afghanistan. *Journal of International Affairs* 56: 193–204.

Cullather, N. 2002. "Damming Afghanistan: Modernization in a Buffer State." *Journal of American History* 89: 512–537.

Dupree, L. 1973. *Afghanistan*. Princeton, NJ: Princeton University Press.

Economist. 2001. A Survey of Illicit Drugs. July 28, pp. 3–16.

Garbett, H. 1878. Report on the Passes into Turkestan. *Routes in Afghanistan*, Vol. 2 by F. J. N. MacKenzie. In *Routes in Asia,* ed. Fred. S. Roberts, pp. 1–11. Calcutta: Superintendent of Government Printing.

Gommans, J. 1997. *The Rise of the Indo-Afghan Empire, 1710–1780*. New York: E. J. Brill.

Hookham, H. 1962. *Tamburlaine the Conqueror*. London: Hodder & Stoughton.

Huntington, E. 1907. *The Pulse of Asi: A Journey in Central Asia Illustrating the Geographic Basis of History*. New York: Houghton Mifflin.

Krochmal, A., and A. A. Nawabi. 1961. A Descriptive Study of the Grapes of Afghanistan. *Vitus* 2: 241–256.

Lattimore, O. 1994. *High Tartary*. New York: Kodansha.

Lubin, N., A. Klaits, and I. Barsegian. 2002. *Narcotics Interdiction in Afghanitan and Central Asia: Challenges for International Assistance*. New York: Open Society Institute.

MacKenzie, F. J. N. 1878. *Routes in Afghanistan, vol. 2, Routes in Asia,* ed. F. S. Roberts. Calcutta: Office of the Superintendent of Government Printing.

Mock, J., and K. O'Neil. 1996. *Trekking in the Karakoram and Hindukush*. Hawthorn, Australia: Lonely Planet Publications.

Orywal, E., ed. 1986. *Die Ethnischen Gruppen Afghanistans*. Wiesbaden: Ludwig Reichert Verlag.

Pickett, L., M. Q. Ma-Yar, and Z. Saleh. 1968. Bibliography of Materials Dealing with Agriculture in Afghanistan. Technical Bulletin no. 8, Faculty of Agriculture, Kabul University, Kabul.

Rashid, A. 2000. *Taliban: Islam, Oil, and the New Great Game in Central Asia.* London: I. B. Tauris.

Roy, O. 1995. *Afghanistan: From Holy War to Civil War.* Princeton, NJ: Darwin Press.

Sahibzada, R. A. 1991. *Poppy Cultivation in Northwest Frontier Province: Its Past, Present and Future.* Islamabad: USAID.

Saward, M. H. 1878. *Routes in the Territories of the Maharaja of Jummoo and Kashmir, and Adjacent Countries. vol. 2.* In *Routes in Asia,* ed. Fred Roberts. Calcutta: Superintendent of Government Printing.

Schivelbusch, W. 1992. *Tastes of Paradise: A Social History of Spices, Stimulants, and Intoxicants.* New York: Random House.

Shahrani, M. N. 2002. 2nd ed., *The Kirghiz and Wakhi of Afghanistan: Adaptation to Closed Frontiers.* Seattle: Univeristy of Washington Press.

Stellrecht, I. 1997. Dynamics of Highland-Lowland Interaction in Northern Pakistan since the 19th Century. In *Perspectives on History and Change in the Karakorum, Hindukush and Himalaya,* pp. 3–22. Cologne: Ruediger Koeppe.

Theroux, P. 1975. *The Great Railway Bazaar.* Boston: Houghton Mifflin.

Turton, D., and Marsden, P. 2002. *Taking Refugees for a Ride? The Politics of Refugee Return to Afghanistan.* Kabul: Afghanistan Research and Evaluation.

Vavilov, N. I., and D. D. Bukinich. 1923. *Agricultural Afghanistan.* Supplement no. 33 to the *Bulletin of Botany and Plant Breeding,* Leningrad.

Zurick, D. 1995. *Errant Journeys: Adventure Travel in a Modern Age.* Austin: University of Texas.

5

The State and the Ongoing Struggle Over Coca in Bolivia

Legitimacy, Hegemony, and the Exercise of Power

Harry Sanabria

The planets and stars are in alignment to take Bolivia out of the drug circuit.
Head of the Drug Enforcement Administration, Bolivia (cited in Krauss 1999)

*D*angerous Harvest, the title of this volume, is an especially appropriate metaphor with which to begin to discuss and understand the ongoing, protracted, and increasingly violent struggle over coca in Bolivia—the third most-important coca leaf–producing country in the world (BINM 1998: 65). Such a metaphor—which suggests the reaping of a product that is potentially precarious, menacing, ominous, and even deadly—points to the fact not only that coca is an inherently conflict-ridden arena or social space but also that the most enduring and significant upshot of the current drive against coca, what is being "harvested" by recent counternarcotics efforts, is the potential for long-term structural instability and conflict in Bolivian society.

In this chapter I pay special attention to this struggle over coca in Bolivia, particularly from the late 1980s to the early part of 2000. I will argue that the contest over coca in Bolivia reflects and embodies numerous and inherently conflictive claims and counterclaims (social, political, economic, and ideological) by different segments of Bolivian society, many of which entail fundamental questions about legitimacy, hegemony, and challenges to the exercise of power by elites and state elites. That is, to view the coca conflict as essentially one between "evil" or "criminal" coca growers and traffickers, on the one hand, and enlightened, law-abiding authorities and citizens, on the other—precisely the criminal justice perspective that ideologically informs, guides, and justifies current anticoca policy by U.S. and U.S.-funded counternarcotics agencies and programs—is not only not enlightening but also fundamentally counterproductive in that it fails to provide the necessary insights with which to grapple with and arrive at a just solution to some of the most important roots of the current coca strife in Bolivia.

I will also try to understand and explain the seemingly successful coca eradication efforts in the late 1990s and first half of the year 2000, as well as how and why resistance to these efforts by coca cultivators in the Chapare appear to have been particularly ineffective in recent years. Specifically, I will suggest that the apparent success of the drive against coca in recent years is not the result of a propitious alignment of "planets and stars"—as the head of the DEA in Bolivia has suggested—but of increasing repression, greater capacity of the state to maneuver around resistance strategies by coca cultivators, and growing inability of coca cultivators to bridge deepening divisions with other societal sectors that also challenge state elites and shield themselves from divisive tactics by the Bolivian state.

The Struggle Over Coca and the Arming of the State in the 1980s

It is important to situate the contemporary struggle over coca in Bolivia in a broader political-economic and historical context in order to understand and underscore the fact that the coca leaf (*Erythroxylum* spp) has been an enduring feature of the physical, sociocultural, and economic landscape of Bolivia (and Peru) since its domestication in the eastern Peruvian Andes thousands of years ago (Plowman 1984a, 1984b). Large areas of the eastern flanks of the Bolivian and Peruvian Andes have always been dedicated to the growing of the coca leaf; the various ways in which coca has been consumed have always been deeply rooted in and constituted an important dimension of (mainly Bolivian and Peruvian) Andean culture and social relations; and the planting, harvest, and commercialization of the coca leaf has historically constituted a crucial pillar of local, regional, and state economies since the colonial period and, as a result, has been supported (although sometimes not unanimously) by ruling political-economic elites (Soux 1993; Sanabria 1993: 37–48; Spedding 1994, 1997; Lema 1997; Léons and Sanabria 1997).

Historically, coca cultivation in Bolivia has been centered in two main subtropical regions in the eastern flanks of the Andean foothills: the Yungas, east of the city of La Paz, and the Chapare region, east of the city of Cochabamba (figure 5.1). From the early colonial period—mid- to late sixteenth century—through the mid-1960s, the Yungas remained Bolivia's primary coca-producing area, whereas coca cultivation in the Chapare began to rapidly increase and would eventually outpace Yungas coca only after (and as a direct result of) colonization (land settlement) policies and programs in the 1960s and 1970s. Land settlement programs during the 1960s and 1970s had two closely related political-economic objectives. The first was to further the emergence and consolidation of agroindustrial enterprises by sponsoring the flow of labor to the sparsely populated eastern lowlands (which constitute 70 percent of Bolivia's territory). The second objective of these programs was to grapple with the shortcomings of the 1953 agrarian reform and, more specifically, the declining terms of trade of highland peasant crops and the potential for social unrest, given the rising population and land fragmentation in the densely populated intermountain highland valleys and inter-Andean plains (altiplano) (For a detailed discussion of these policies, see Gill 1987; Sanabria 1993: 48–53).

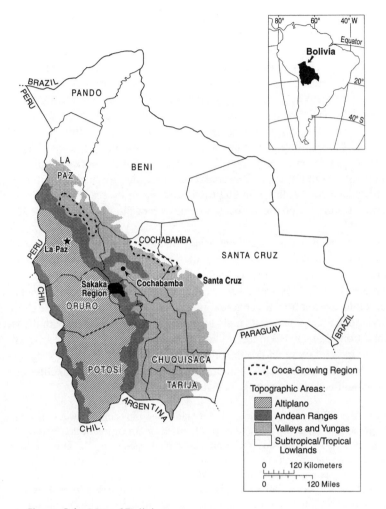

Figure 5.1. Map of Bolivia.

A massive migration of peasants to the Chapare—primarily from the nearby and heavily populated Cochabamba valleys and highlands—led to an accelerated increase in coca cultivation, partly because it was and still is so highly adaptive (socially and environmentally) to the Chapare landscape, but also because the cultivation of coca was encouraged by state policies and was uniquely positioned to provide peasant cultivators with a secure income. Furthermore, migration to and coca cultivation in the Chapare would intersect with and be fueled by political-economic policies in Bolivia that undermined peasant household economies but favored capital accumulation by agroindustrial elites in other parts of the Bolivian eastern lowlands; progressive involvement by elite segments in Bolivian society in drug trafficking; and the increasing demand for cocaine and, later, crack, by North

American consumers, especially during the 1980s and 1990s (Sanabria 1993: 48–55; Bourgois 1996; Léons and Sanabria 1997).

Throughout the late 1970s and most of the 1980s, coca cultivation increased dramatically, especially in the Chapare. For example, between the late 1970s and 1983, coca cultivation in the Chapare increased from about 15,000 hectares to over 58,000 (Sanabria 1993: 59). During this period Bolivia's economy steadily deteriorated, and the nadir of coca cultivation in the mid-to-late 1980s coincided with and was inscribed within a context marked by the collapse of the Bolivian economy in mid-1982 (hyperinflation and erosion of wages and income, as well as widespread shortages and escalating social unrest were lasting memories of this period); protracted inter- and intraelite class conflicts; increasing pressure from the United States to reduce coca cultivation and the beginning of the "war on drugs" in the Chapare and Bolivia; and the almost total paralysis of the Bolivian state (Sanabria 1997).

Indeed, the intensity of the current onslaught against coca in Bolivia is a direct result of this political-economic context, marked by profound cleavages and conflicts in Bolivian society, as well as challenges to the authority of the Bolivian state during the early 1980s, all which threatened to engulf Bolivia in chaos and anarchy. Indeed, while the neoliberal economic program instituted in mid-1982 (NEP, or New Economic Policy) had as its main objective to effectively cope with the structural conditions that had led to the collapse of the economy, it also had an overt political goal: to restructure and reconsolidate the state apparatus at the verge of collapse—which in turn implied a regrouping of economic and political elites around a core political-economic project. As I've suggested earlier:

> Viewing the NEP as simply a program for stabilizing the economy would not only prevent us from capturing the fundamentally *political* dimension of this historic undertaking. . . . The NEP was above all a last-ditch attempt by the elites to avert political-economic anarchy and state collapse . . . facing a serious social threat from "below," a key political objective of the NEP has been to "arm" an "obsolete state" and reestablish its control over a (supposedly) weak, lethargic, fragmented, and disintegrating society that nevertheless wanted to be "modern, vigorous and strong." (Sanabria 2000: 62–63)

Within a relatively brief period of time, the newly reconstituted state—which would, not incidentally, also play a renewed role in the consolidation of capitalism in Bolivia—would center its attention on the two most menacing sectors that openly challenged its rule: miners and coca cultivators. Miners posed an especially dangerous threat to the social order—partly because of their crucial role in one of the most important sectors of the Bolivian economy, how they went about challenging newly emerging patterns of capital accumulation in the mining sector, and also because historically they had so openly challenged powerful elites aligned with the state—and they would be the first to receive the brunt of furious state repression. Unable to forge meaningful alliances with other sectors of Bolivian society, highly dependent on state mining for their income and supplies, and laboring in easily accessible (and therefore weakly defensible) work sites for their livelihood, miners were unable to resist the onslaught against them. In just a few months the state-owned mining company had been virtually shut down, and one of the most politically engaged, militant, and combative working-class movements in Latin America was destroyed (Sanabria 1999; Gill 2000: 67–85). It is ironic and tragic that after losing their jobs, thousands of former miners would migrate to and settle in the Chapare to grow coca—only to once again face a fierce onslaught of state repression and once again lose their livelihood.

Before and after the NEP, coca cultivators, unlike miners, had not so much openly challenged the social order or fundamentally questioned the structure of privilege in Bolivian society and had therefore rarely posed a direct political threat. Nevertheless, they continued to grow coca at a rapid pace and allowed most coca crops to be funneled (at least in the Chapare) into the production of illegal coca paste and cocaine. Coca cultivators also openly confronted antidrug effects (particularly in the Chapare), which were centered not only on drug interdiction but also, increasingly, on eradicating coca plants when coca planting was still legal. They also continued to resist alternative development programs courted and sponsored by the United States and designed to entice coca cultivators to grow alternate crops in lieu of coca. It is in these ways that coca cultivators in the Yungas and the Chapare began to openly clash with the agendas and policies of state agencies and institutions (Léons 1997; Léons and Sanabria 1997; Sanabria 1997; Spedding 1997). A few years after the NEP, in 1988, a new law was passed, outlawing new coca cultivation (and eventually eradicating all coca) in the Chapare and restricting legal cultivation to 12,000 hectares in the Yungas. It was this law—and the judicial infrastructure that would soon follow—that signaled a new phase and commitment by the Bolivian state against coca cultivators. Ongoing attempts have been made to reform Bolivia's judicial infrastructure to allow the state to more effectively cope with drug trafficking and coca cultivation (BINM 1997: 67, 1999: 80).

Throughout the late 1980s and the 1990s, coca cultivators, especially in the Chapare, waged an ongoing and increasingly protracted struggle against the state and its attempt not only to curb illegal drug trafficking but also to eradicate coca. It is important to stress that this heightening struggle was not waged in a political-economic vacuum but was firmly inscribed within wider conflicts that pitted different (elite and nonelite) segments of Bolivian society against the state and sometimes against each other—such as former miners; urban wage workers; the regional and national labor and peasant organizations; politically powerful "civic committees," representing elite interests at the departmental level; informal organizations in peripheral urban spaces; other (noncoca cultivating) peasant organizations; the Catholic Church; nongovernmental organizations (NGOs); and indigenous (non-Andean) ethnic groups in the eastern lowlands (see, e.g., Sanabria 1993, 1995, 1997, 1999, 2000; Léons and Sanabria 1997; Gill 2000). If, as many scholars have suggested, the formation of a legitimizing ideology partly underpins successful state rule and hegemony (see, e.g., Lears 1985; Eagleton 1991; Kurtz 1996), then clearly the gamut of social conflict during the late 1980s and the 1990s within which the drive against coca was situated pointed to a moral and legitimizing chasm between the state and state elites, on the one hand—including their exercise of power—and broad sectors of Bolivian society, on the other hand. The ways in which Chapare coca cultivators in late 1994 understood a much publicized yet eventually fleeting *opción cero* (zero option) plan to forcibly relocate them to other regions of Bolivia, do away with coca, and transform the Chapare into an investment zone, provides a particularly poignant example of how state legitimacy was actively contested: Coca growers associated the plan with a direct threat to their livelihood and their claims to land they had labored on, a deepening of the highly unequal class relations characteristic of Bolivian society, the massive dislocation suffered by miners, and Bolivia's political and economic dependency on the United States (Sanabria 1995).

Despite the intensity of conflict in the Chapare—and the zeal with which the state would eventually and progressively move against them—in many respects and until quite recently coca cultivators retained the upper hand. They did so not by openly confronting the state but by engaging in a wide gamut of resistance tactics not easily suppressed by state security forces and by therefore maneuvering around the state's repressive tactics and programs. Indeed, such apparently successful "everyday forms of resistance" (Scott 1985, 1990) would account for the fact that the number of hectares under coca production continued to increase through 1996, despite record amounts of illegal drugs seized and record numbers of hectares under coca destroyed (see Sanabria 1997; BINM 1998: 70, 1999: 84). The expansion of coca cultivation in the Chapare continued unfettered during the 1990s, peaking between 1996 and 1997 at around 40,000 hectares (BINM 1998: 70). Such seemingly successful strategies, however, seem to have reached their limits by late 1997 and early 1998. It is to this more recent, concerted, and apparently successful drive against coca—as well as how and why coca resistance in the Chapare seems to have run its course—that I now turn.

State Repression and the Onslaught Against Coca Growers, 1997–2000

I predicted only recently that coca growers in the Chapare, unlike miners, were structurally in a far more advantageous position to engage in successful resistance efforts against state policies and programs designed to undermine their livelihood, and I emphasized five closely intertwined configurations that could explain their successful resistance: (1) the ability of coca cultivators to elude state surveillance, given the nature of the terrain on which coca cultivation takes place; (2) the inability of the Bolivian state apparatus to solidly unite against coca growers; (3) the important role of coca in the Bolivian economy and in popular consciousness; (4) the ability of coca cultivators to forge intraclass alliances with other politically important sectors of Bolivian society; and (5) the fact that (as I have suggested above) historically coca growers—unlike miners—have not posed a direct and overt political threat to the state and state elites (Sanabria 1999).

It would appear, however, that it is the Bolivian state that now has the upper hand. Indeed, U.S. State Department publications point to a substantial drop in coca cultivation and a corresponding increase in coca eradication, especially in the Chapare, since 1997. The State Department's Bureau of International Narcotics Matters, for example, estimates that coca cultivation in Bolivia decreased from a high of

55,612 hectares in 1996 to about 52,800 in 1997. Official U.S. estimates place the upper limit of Bolivian coca cultivation in 1998 at slightly over 49,000 hectares (BINM 1998: 70, 1999: 84). More recent estimates not only agree with what appears to be an accelerated trend in forced coca eradication but also point to an even more pronounced decline in coca cultivation over the last 2 to 3 years. Some sources suggest that about 12,000 hectares were eradicated between 1996 and 1998 (Farah 1999), and others suggest that an additional 14,000 hectares were destroyed between 1998 and 1999 (Wren 1999). According to Barry McCaffrey, U.S. drug czar, "These are absolutely astounding changes in both Peru and Bolivia. . . . The main reason is the political will of the democractic governments there. . . . The United States has played a modest supporting role, but these countries now see eradication as in their own national interests" (Farah 1999). Of course, many would argue that Alberto Fujimori's authoritarian government in Peru was anything but "democractic."

By mid-1999, 38,000 hectares were "being devoted to coca throughout Bolivia" (*Latin American Weekly Report* 1999a). In the first 6 months of 1999, state security forces—antinarcotics police and army troops, among others—eradicated 9,000 hectares in Chapare (*Latin American Weekly Report* 1999b), and by the end of the year a record 17,000 coca hectares were razed (Thorpec 2000). And whereas one recent report claims that at the beginning of 2000 there were only 8,000 hectares of coca left in the Chapare (*Latin American Weekly Report* 2000a), another source claims that there were only 3,000 left (Thorpec 2000). Regardless of the absolute accuracy of these slightly divergent estimates, the fact remains that, unimaginable only a few years ago, the total eradication of coca in the Chapare looms just over the horizon. Paradoxically, but not unexpectedly, the imminent destruction of all coca in the Chapare has led to the manufacture of smaller amounts of coca paste (an intermediary product between coca leaves and cocaine hydrochloride). Also not unexpectedly, prices have tripled over the past 3 years, and there is little evidence that the success against coca in the Chapare has led to a reduction of cocaine smuggled into the United States (Thorpec 2000).

The successful drive against coca cultivation in recent years can be traced to—and is partly a direct outcome of—the election of former dictator General Hugo Bánzer to Bolivia's presidency in June 1997. Although implicated in drug trafficking during his dictatorial rule in the 1970s (Sanabria 1993: 58–59), Bánzer, apparently viewing coca cultivators as a significant political threat, vowed upon appointment as president to wipe out coca cultivation in the Chapare by 2002. Bolstered by tens of millions of dollars in U.S. "aid," Bánzer's government quickly intensified the low-intensity conflict that had been raging in the Chapare for the last 15 years by saturating the area with unprecedented numbers of police, army, and other security personnel dedicated to drug interdiction and coca eradication. Plans by late 1998 to shift Bolivia's military high command from La Paz to Cochabamba —and thereby much closer to the conflicted Chapare region (*Economist* 1999)— and proposals to establish military bases directly in the Chapare (Andean Information Network 2000) are just two indicators of the determination by the Bánzer and U.S. governments to intensify repression. These renewed efforts at a military and coercive "solution" to Bolivia's "coca problem" have been, not unexpectedly, often under the careful watch of U.S. military "advisors." Indeed, according to Otis (1998), "U.S. involvement is so obvious that a Bolivian army officer asked permission from an American advisor before taking reporters along on a helicopter tour of eradication sites."

At the political-economic and ideological plane, these renewed efforts at eradication have been paralleled by and have been part of a (supposedly national) "Dignity Plan" (*plan de dignidad*) that calls for not only the total destruction of all coca in the Chapare but also the resettlement of Chapare peasant families elsewhere, as well as capital investment in the region—and carries a $1 billion price tag in U.S. "aid" (*Latin American Weekly Report* 1999a). In an eerie reminiscence of the zero option plan of 1994 (see above), this new plan entails relocating "hundreds of families to farming areas outside the Chapare and will target more money for crop substitution, packing plants, roads and other infrastructure." At the same time, greater investments would be made for alternative crops, such as palm hearts, pineapples, and citrus (Otis 1998).

The scheme of relocating coca-cultivating peasants in the Chapare was formally institutionalized in May 1998 with the enactment of the Transmigration and Human Settlements (Transmigración y Asentamientos Humanos) plan, which according to official discourse was necessary because of the "high levels of ecological fragility represented among certain sectors of the Chapare" (*alto índice de la fragilidad ecológica que representan algunos sectores del Chapare*) (CEDIB 1999: 224). Interesting enough (and not unexpected), at about the same time the Bolivian defense minister also claimed that, although "totally voluntary," by means of this plan the government would seek to "relocate all coca out of the Cochabamba tropics" (*relocalizar a toda la hoja de coca del Trópico de Cochabamba*) (CEDIB 1999: 224). The government predicted that some 15,000 families would leave the Chapare to seek out "new sources of subsistence" (CEDIB 1999: 209).

The supposed concerns over the environmental effects of peasant settlement and coca cultivation in the Chapare were not only paralleled by national security issues but also intersected with elite interests in investments and capital accumulation in the area—hardly novel issues. Indeed, it should also come as no surprise that ostensible environmental and national security concerns (as shown above by Defense Ministry statements) also took place in a political-economic and ideological context that ushered in new laws and projects encouraged and promulgated by elites and their business allies—such as Bánzer's personal representative (Delegado Presidencial) to the Chapare region, also a leading businessman—seeking to encourage investments in the Chapare and transform it into a huge industrial park (CEDIB 1999: 50–51). Two examples of these new laws and projects are Beneficios para Inversiones en el Chapare Tropical and the Proyecto de Ley de Incentivo Económico al Trópico de Cochabamba. These laws and elite-centered projects—which, it is worth again emphasizing, presumes the (involuntary) departure of tens of thousands of coca cultivators from the Chapare and the eventual eradication of coca there—are apparently deemed necessary to "stimulate investment in the region by national and international business interests" (*imprescindible para incentivar al empresariado nacional e internacional a invertir en la región*) (CEDIB 1999: 245). In fact, despite the intensity of conflict in the Chapare (see below) and its transformation into an essentially military zone, elite investments are already well underway. By the second half of 1999, almost $20 million had been invested in the Chapare by foreign and local companies (Otis 1998). And what better way to be fully cognizant of the class dimensions of the conflict in the Chapare—and of the "modernizing" projects of the political-economic elite class that is spearheading anticoca efforts—than to learn that "one investor is building a $5 million country club with an 18-hole golf course" in the area (Otis 1998)?

When the zero option plan first surfaced in 1994, coca cultivators, by stating that "the lands [in the Chapare] will be sold to big capitalists . . . that will come from the United States" and that "all the coca in the Chapare will disappear and . . . the United States will take advantage . . . of all the Chapare" (Sanabria 1995: 91), were able to see through and uncover the transparent elite and class interests in the region—and there is no reason to assume that the present relocation plan is any different. Indeed, peasant organizations in the Chapare vigorously opposed such a plan, and they were joined by their counterparts (as well as elite sectors) in the departments of Santa Cruz and Beni—the likely targets or relocation points—who claimed the absence of "surplus" land and who were also worried about the possibility of the conflicts in the Chapare spilling over into their areas (CEDIB 1999: 225)

The increasingly repressive coca eradication campaign, especially that of the Bánzer government, has been met with fierce resistance on the part of coca cultivators. Throughout 1997 and 1998, coca cultivators repeatedly clashed with security forces in and out of the Chapare, and between 1997 and the early part of 1999 dozens of coca cultivators, police officers, and soldiers have been killed, hundreds more have been wounded, and over 1,000 coca cultivators have been arrested and/or forced to flee the Chapare (Otis 1998; CEDIB 1999: 160–161, 217–218; Krauss 1999; *Latin American Weekly Report* 1999a, 1999b). Unlike what appears to have been the case just a few years ago (see Sanabria 1997), current resistance to eradication efforts during the past 3 years seem to have taken a radically different turn—from primarily small-scale, sporadic resistance tactics to increasingly large-scale, open confrontations with state security forces—thereby heightening the possibility of many more fatalities. As historically has been the case, the resistance tactic favored by coca cultivators when openly confronting security forces has been to block key roads in and out of the Chapare and other important urban centers. I am not necessarily suggesting that coca cultivators have given up on the array of resistance tactics that had, until recently, allowed them to bring the conflict to a standstill. And, as has historically also been the case, they have fared poorly when openly confronted with thousands of heavily armed troops. Some examples of these open, massive confrontation tactics include the 1998 and 1999 blockade of the major roads linking the major cities of Cochabamba and Santa Cruz by thousands of peasants (CEDIB 1999: 217–218; Krauss 1999).

Escalating conflict in the Chapare was paralleled by and inscribed within the context of much broader levels of social conflict that reached dangerous proportions in the early part of 2000—partly because of the dramatic economic implosion reverberating throughout the Bolivian economy as a result of the anticoca drive, along with a variety of unpopular measures enacted by the state that directly affected broad sectors of the Bolivian society—prompting Bánzer's government to once again impose a state of siege. For example, at the beginning of the year, the government announced the sale of Cochabamba's public water system to a U.S. corporation, who in turn steeply hiked water rates. In addition, the government was proposing to directly intervene in and control rural irrigation systems—long under the control of small rural communities and a symbolic marker of communal autonomy. An "enormous, often violent, civil uprising" (Shultz 2000:1) by local citizens soon followed, prompting the government to fly in troops from other parts of the country (McFarren 2000). Yet after a week, the government rescinded the sale of Cochabamba's public water system.

In fact, a wave of protests rocked Bolivia in the first months of 2000. Thousands of Aymara-speaking peasants clashed with police officers in the towns of Achacachi and Batallas near the capital city of La Paz, storming government offices and reportedly setting some building on fire (*Dominion* 2000). Other Aymara-speaking coca cultivators in the Yungas east of La Paz were also "manning barricades on the highway to the Yungas, demanding that the government cease in its attempts to eradicate 3,000 hectares of allegedly 'surplus' coca plantations . . . and rescind regulations imposing quotas on the amount of coca leaf which can be brought to market" (*Latin American Weekly Report* 2000b). According to Bolivian Law 1008, enacted in 1988, 12,000 hectares of coca are legally allowed in the Yungas region for "traditional" consumption. In the midst of escalating conflicts, the police in La Paz and Santa Cruz went on strike and took over local jails, joining other protestors and strikers in different parts of the country. At about the same time, members of Bolivia's nationwide peasant federations were also in the process of blocking roads and confronting the army, and coca cultivators almost literally "paralyzed Cochabamba" (McFarren 2000) by blocking all roads in and out of the city (see also Krauss 1999). More recently (October 2000), Bánzer's government faced once again waves of protests led by Aymara-speaking peasants, demanding that he "reverse a land titling process that would have raised taxes, and return water rights from the government to Indian peasants" (Krauss 2000). These protests—which were so effective that food shortages and looting quickly spread to major cities—were paralleled by other, widespread protests and demonstrations by teachers and other wage workers (McFarren 2000). It is interesting that the government agreed to meet the demands by the Aymara-speaking peasants but has so far refused to back down in its incessant drive against coca cultivators in the Chapare.

The (admittedly reluctant) willingness of the Bánzer government to occasionally back down and compromise with some societal sectors laying claims to and openly challenging the state contrasts starkly with its aversion to doing the same with coca cultivators in the Chapare. This inconsistency suggests that the struggle over coca in Bolivia is, politically and economically, of a rather different order than other societal struggles currently permeating Bolivian society. The unwillingness to negotiate—and the unrelenting, fierce repression that such refusal has entailed—would seem to suggest that ideologically and politically coca cultivators now seem to pose a threat to the state as serious as that posed by miners over 15 years ago. The determination of the Bánzer regime to eradicate coca—the "incredible amount of commitment by this government," according to a U.S. State Department official (Otis 1998)—also suggests that now coca cultivators, as did miners years ago, are confronting a much more unified state apparatus than they did some years ago (see Sanabria 2000).

Conclusion

In this chapter I have argued that the last few years have witnessed a dramatic reversal of the fortunes of coca cultivators in Bolivia, especially in the Chapare—the volatile region that for so long supplied most of the coca leaves for the production of illegal drugs in Bolivia. The stark reality is that only a few thousand hectares of coca remain in the Chapare, and assuming that the pace and intensity of current coca eradication efforts do not lose steam, these remaining hectares of coca are likely to be gone in a year or two.

The inability of coca cultivators to stem the onslaught against them—a sharp (and in so many ways a surprising) reversal of their fortunes of just a few years ago—is the result of a concatenation of forces working against them. One of the most important, of course, is the sheer determination and seemingly unified stance of the state apparatus, as well as its seeming ability to saturate the Chapare with troops and other instruments of repression and surveillance. Indeed, the success of a variety of everyday tactics of resistance that worked so well for coca cultivators in the past (see Sanabria 1997) were partly contingent on maneuvering between the interstices of a fractured state apparatus, as well as their ability to slip beyond the grasp of the state, to take advantage of the Chapare's extremely difficult subtropical terrain in order to elude detection and arrest, and to conceal new coca plantings (Sanabria 1999). Although much more research is needed to fully substantiate this claim, it would appear that such an advantage has been lost.

It is also quite possible that domestic public opinion is turning against coca cultivators. For example, according to the *Economist* (1999), "The growers have few influential supporters, and public opinion is largely hostile—especially among those who travel abroad." It is certainly quite difficult to ascertain the validity and reliability of this claim, the extent to which such an opinion may be in the process of entrenching itself across different class and societal sectors, and/or whether it is part of an elite-centered ideological campaign. Nevertheless, such a possibility cannot be discounted without further research. In addition, such a possibility may in fact account for what appears to be some evidence of a lack of ability of coca cultivators (as was the case of the miners) to sustain alliances and solidarity with other societal groups—precisely one of the reasons for the inability of the miners to resist the state onslaught against them in 1985–1986. For example, once the government met the demands of Aymara protestors in early October (see above; cf. Krauss 2000), the latter apparently refused to continue their roadblocks in solidarity with Chapare coca cultivators who were also engaged in similar types of protest. Krauss (2000) therefore suggests that Chapare coca cultivators may be in the process of becoming increasingly isolated from other "Indians" and peasants.

Coca cultivators have historically been grouped into several powerful "federations" (*federaciones*) linked to Bolivia's main peasant organization (the CSTCB, the Confederación Sindical de Trabajadores Campesinos de Bolivia), which in turn has formed part of Bolivia's central labor union (Central Obrera Boliviana). Although this organizational structure suggests the potential for a great deal of cohesion and solidarity (and thereby the capability of successfully confronting the state along multiple fronts), in fact the coca federations are inchoate social movements lacking an overriding, all-inclusive sense of identity and a solid ideological stance, and as such they are easily prone to discord and divisions, ideologically and in terms of organizational practices and resistance strategies. I should point out that whereas coca cultivators do in fact have a strong sense of identity that emerges from their social position as *coca* cultivators (*cocaleros*), this is only one of the multiple identities that they ascribe to themselves, and thus there is a greater likelihood of social practice and resistance being diffused along multiple—and even conflicting—paths. To my knowledge, possible ethnic divisions within the *cocalero* movement have yet to be sufficiently explored, although I suspect that ethnicity does not play a crucial role in intra-*cocalero* divisions. There is, in fact, some evidence that suggests that the Bolivian state, through a variety of tactics, has been able to sow divisions and conflicts within and between different coca federations over the course of several years (e.g., Léons 1997; Sanabria 1997) and thereby impede the formation of a politically and ideologically coherent front by coca cultivators. The recent deployment in the Chapare of members of a CIA-funded counterintelligence agency (Krauss 1999)—and more specifically, the use of informants and undercover agents to sow rumors, gather sensitive information, and engage in divisive tactics—not only speaks to the ever-increasing surveillance and repressive tactics of the Bolivian state but also to the inability of coca growers, as members of social movements, to shield themselves, politically and ideologically, from the penetrating strategies of the state.

All said, the destruction of coca that looms over the horizon, will probably be short-lived. Hegemonic projects—political, economic, and ideological undertakings by cohesive elite factions with the objective of instilling generalized (though not, of course, unanimous) compliance to rule through consent and coercion—are often short-lived (Rosberry 1994; Sayer 1994). In the case of Bolivia, the hegemonic project established after the 1952–1953 revolution and agrarian reform pretty much came to an end in 1985; and although the post-1985 neoliberal political-economic program has yet to be challenged from within elite sectors of Bolivian society, it is constantly being seriously contested by nonelite sectors (Sanabria 1999; Gill 2000). Long-term or permanent eradication of coca in the Chapare would necessarily entail ongoing, sustained ideological, political, and economic cohesiveness—and history (particularly Bolivian history) suggests that such prospects are quite unlikely. As a result, if given the chance—and assuming little change in the international (but primarily U.S. and European) demand for cocaine and in national policies aimed at redressing the profound economic, political, ideological, and cultural cleavages in Bolivian society—we can expect that peasants in the Chapare and elsewhere will once again take up the cultivation of coca. The future of coca in Bolivia and of coca cultivators in the Chapare is still an open question.

References

Andean Information Network. 2000. "US policy and the Current Situation in Bolivia," January.

BINM. 1997. *International Narcotics Control Strategy Report*. Washington, DC: United States Department of State, Bureau of International Narcotics Matters.

———. 1998. *International Narcotics Control Strategy Report*. Washington, DC: United States Department of State, Bureau of International Narcotics Matters.

———. 1999. *International Narcotics Control Strategy Report*. Washington, DC: United States Department of State, Bureau of International Narcotics Matters.

Bourgois, P. I. 1996. *In Search of Respect: Selling Crack in El Barrio*. Cambridge: Cambridge University Press.

CEDIB. 1999. *Anuario Coca-Press 1996–97–98*. Cochabamba: Centro de Documentación e Información—Bolivia.

Dominion. 2000. (Wellington). "Cocaine War Sparks Violent Rampage in Bolivia," April 11, p. 5.

Eagleton, T. 1991. *Ideology: An Introduction*. London: Verso.

Economist. 1999. "Clashes to Come" 350 (February 20, 1999), p. 34.

Farah, D. 1999. "Coca Crop Shrinking in Key Andean Nations." *Washington Post*, January 7.

Gill, L. 1987. *Peasants, Entrepreneurs, and Social Change: Frontier Development in Lowland Bolivia*. Boulder and London: Westview Press.

———. 2000. *Teetering on the Rim: Global Restructuring, Daily Life, and the Armed Retreat of the Bolivian State*. New York: Columbia University Press.

Krauss, C. 1999. "Bolivia, at Risk of Some Unrest, Is Making Big Gains in Eradicating Coca." *New York Times*, May 9.

———. 2000. "Bolivia Makes Key Concessions to Indians." *New York Times*, October 7, p. A5.

Kurtz, D. V. 1996. "Hegemony and Anthropology: Gramsci, Exegeses, Reinterpretations." *Critique of Anthropology*, 16, no. 2: 103–135.

Latin American Weekly Report. 1999a. "Bánzer Sets Record Eradication Target," June 1, pp. 248–249.

———. 1999b. "Coca Eradication Ahead of Target," July 27, p. 345.

———. 2000a. "Bolivia Within a Whisper of Proving That Coca-Farming Can Be Eradicated," February 8, p. 61.

———. 2000b. "Promises of Talks Defuse Protests," April 18, p. 182.

Lears, T. J. J. 1985. "The Concept of Cultural Hegemony: Problems and Possibilities." *American Historical Review* 90, no. 3: 567–593.

Lema, A. M. 1997. "The Coca Debate and Yungas Landowners During the First Half of the 20th Century." In M. B. Léons and H. Sanabria, eds., *Coca, Cocaine, and the Bolivian Reality*, pp. 99–116. Albany: State University of New York Press.

Léons, M. B. 1997. "After the Boom: Income Decline, Eradication, and Alternative Development in the Yungas." In M. B. Léons and H. Sanabria, eds., *Coca, Cocaine, and the Bolivian Reality*, pp. 139–168. Albany: State University of New York Press.

Léons, M. B., and H. Sanabria. 1997. "Coca and Cocaine in Bolivia: Reality and Policy Illusion." In M. B. Léons and H. Sanabria, eds. *Coca, Cocaine, and the Bolivian Reality*, pp. 1–46. Albany: State University of New York Press.

McFarren, P. 2000. "Indian Farmers Continue Protests in Bolivia." *Chicago Sun-Times*, April 10, p. 25.

Otis, J. 1998. "Coca Confusion: Eradication Effort Strikes at a Way of Life in Bolivia." *Houston Chronicle*, September.

Plowman, T. 1984a. "The Ethnobotany of Coca (Erthroxylum spp., Erythroxylacae)." *Advances in Economic Botany* 1: 62–111.

———. 1984b. "The Origin, Evolution, and Diffusion of Coca, Erythoxylum spp., in South and Central America." In D. Stone, ed., *Pre-Columbian Plant Migration*, pp. 126–163. Cambridge, MA: Papers of the Peabody Museum of Archaeology and Ethnology, vol. 76.

Roseberry, W. 1994. "Hegemony and the Language of Contention." In G. M. Joseph and D. Nugent, eds., *Everyday Forms of State Formation: Revolution and the Negotiation of Rule in Modern Mexico,* pp. 355–366. Durham, NC, and London: Duke University Press.

Sanabria, H. 1993. *The Coca Boom and Rural Social Change in Bolivia.* Ann Arbor: University of Michigan Press.

———. 1995. "Elusive Goals: 'Opción Cero' and the Limits of State Rule and Hegemony in Eastern Bolivia." In M. M. Snipes and L. Giordani, eds., *Indigenous Perceptions of the Nation-State in Latin America,* pp. 83–112. Williamsburg, VA: College of William and Mary.

———. 1997. "The Discourse and Practice of Repression and Resistance in the Chapare." In M. B. Léons and H. Sanabria, eds., *Coca, Cocaine, and the Bolivian Reality,* pp. 169–194. Albany: State University of New York Press.

———. 1999. "Consolidating States, Restructuring Economies, and Confronting Workers and Peasants: The Antinomies of Bolivian Neo-Liberalism." *Comparative Studies in Society and History* 41, no. 3: 535–562.

———. 2000. "Resistance and the Arts of Domination: Miners and the Bolivian State." *Latin American Perspectives* 27, no. 1: 56–81.

Sayer, D. 1994. "Everyday Forms of State Formation: Some Dissident Remarks on 'Hegemony.'" In G. M. Joseph and D. Nugent, eds., *Everyday Forms of State Formation: Revolution and the Negotiation of Rule in Modern Mexico*, pp. 367–377. Durham, NC, and London: Duke University Press.

Schultz, J. 2000. "Uprising in Bolivia." Andean Information Network, May.

Scott, J. C. 1985. *Weapons of the Weak: Everyday Forms of Peasant Resistance.* New Haven, CT, and London: Yale University Press.

———. 1990. *Domination and the Arts of Resistance.* New Haven, CT: Yale University Press.

Soux, M. L. 1993. *La coca liberal: Producción y circulación a principios del siglo XX,* La Paz: CID/COCAYAPU.

Spedding, A. L. 1994. *Wachu wachu: Cultivo de coca e identidad en los Yunkas de La Paz,* La Paz: CIPCA\2COCAYAPU\2HISBOL.

———. 1997. "Cocataki, Taki-Coca: Trade, Traffic, and Organized Peasant Resistance in the Yungas of La Paz." In M. B. Léons and H. Sanabria, eds., *Coca, Cocaine, and the Bolivian Reality,* pp. 117–138. Albany: State University of New York Press.

Thorpec, N. 2000. "Leabes on the Line." *Guardian* (London), August 25.

Wren, C. 1999. "U.N. Says It Is Getting Farmers to Replace Their Coca Crops." *New York Times,* July 11.

6

The Marijuana Milpa
Agricultural Adaptations in a Postsubsistence Maya Landscape in Southern Belize

Michael K. Steinberg

oreign fieldwork always presents interesting and unique challenges; however, fieldwork that involves illegal activities on the part of the study group is "ethnography" like no other. The typical fieldwork tools such as tape recorders, cameras, statistical models, and formal questionnaires are often not an option. Instead, great caution and sensitivity must be maintained to protect the identity of informants, as well the researcher's personal safety. Informants may be willing to talk about illegal activities, but in this study no one was willing to go on record or have their photographs taken with their illegal marijuana (*Cannabis sativa*) crop. As a result of these cautious methods, much of the information contained in this chapter is based on interviews with unnamed informants in unstructured interviews whom I came to know and trust mainly during the late 1990s while conducting fieldwork with the Mopan and Kekchí Maya in southern Belize on various cultural ecological topics. There was no intention to assist informants in illegal activities by hiding their identities, but similar to investigative journalism (which in many ways these chapters resemble), informants must have sufficient trust in the investigator in order to provide reliable information.

This chapter discusses a situation that the Drug Enforcement Agency (DEA), the U.S. media, and most citizens would consider a success story in the so-called war on drugs — small-scale marijuana producers who, through the actions of interdiction authorities, were largely driven out of business. However, this chapter presents a slightly different angle on the war on drugs in that it examines the recent history of marijuana production among Maya farmers in southern Belize: why seemingly traditional and conservative peasant farmers turn to drug production in the first place, how these activities affect village life and culture, and some implications and lessons this case study provides on the larger battle over what crops, legal or illegal, smallholder farmers produce. This chapter provides some useful lessons for the larger war on drugs because the Mopan and Kekchí Maya are quite similar to other smallholder farmers who grow most of the commodities that are then consumed in raw form or manufactured into narcotics. These are economically poor farmers who perceive psychoactive plants as cash crops, much like coffee or cacao, that are consumed in distant lands by unknown peoples. Certainly some farmers worry about the ultimate consequences of their dangerous harvest, but most have immediate economic needs to fulfill, which drug plants often help to meet. This chapter does not portray farmers as victims; however, it does illustrate the ground-level complexities of the drug trade and the war on drugs in indigenous agricultural communities. As will be discussed, interdiction authorities have won the war on drugs in southern Belize, and lessons may be gained from this small victory. However, this victory is not likely to be duplicated on a larger scale.

Cultural Economic Background of the Maya Landscape in Southern Belize

When one first enters Mopan and Kekchí Maya villages in southern Belize, they appear as unlikely settings for groups who would have participated deeply in the risky venture of marijuana production for export. Most villages appear to be geographically, economically, and thus culturally isolated. Simple thatched roof and dirt-floor dwellings dominate in all villages except San Antonio and San Pedro Colombia, and commercial activities remain limited to small shops at which mainly basic household items can be purchased (figure 6.1) (Steinberg 1996). This apparent isolation would seem to be an ideal setting for peasant agriculturalists, who according to the classic peasant model "produce just enough to satisfy their subsistence needs, are generally averse to producing significant surpluses for the market, and consequently avoid cash or exchange relations" (Sanabria 1993: 5). However, although appearing to be isolated, the Mopan and Kekchí Maya have a long history of sporadically interacting with economies beyond the village level. Similar to many indigenous groups in Latin America, the Mopan and Kekchí Maya have experienced a series of boom-and-bust economies over the past century and earlier (Nietschmann 1973; Gregory 1984; Wilk 1991). In Belize and other indigenous landscapes these economic cycles have included natural, resource-related extractive activities such as timber cutting, plantation agriculture, nontimber forest products, and minerals (Nietschmann 1993).

Thus the participation in marijuana production in the Maya landscape, the most recent example of a boom-and-bust economy, is not surprising upon closer cultural-historical examination. In fact, I argue that ideal economic and social conditions existed in the early 1980s to drive the new marijuana boom economy. These conditions included rapid integration into a national, more commercial economy, thereby fostering a need for cash incomes, and internal social changes such as a rejection of traditional social structures in favor of more Western models, especially by the younger generation. Besides occasionally working for commercial-oriented interests such as timber harvesting, the Maya of southern Belize have a long history of

Figure 6.1. Mopan Mayan village (photo by Michael K. Steinberg).

being smallholder agriculturalists. Like most farmers, the Mopan and Kekchí are economically rational about the activities in which they invest precious labor and financial resources. Thus, when presented with a guaranteed market and cash income for a new commodity (marijuana), not surprisingly many seized the opportunity. These same or similar cultural and economic conditions exist today in many indigenous, peasant landscapes in transition, thereby making the war on drugs a difficult proposition in many regions.

Recent History of the Marijuana Economy in Southern Belize

The rapid expansion or boom economy of marijuana production began in southern Belize around 1980 (Wilk 1991; Wilk and Chapin 1991). Before 1980, marijuana was grown in southern Belize but on a small scale, to be sold locally in villages and to non-Maya mainly in Punta Gorda. How and when marijuana first arrived in southern Belize is unclear. It was probably brought to Belize by East Indian immigrants who arrived between 1861 and 1891 via Jamaica (Hartshorn et al. 1984) or perhaps by one of the many other cultural groups who have entered Belize over the past 150 years. Given the many cultures that have come to Belize in the past 2 centuries, coupled with relative inattention paid to rural areas and especially southern Belize by colonial officials, marijuana's exact origins in Belize will probably remain a mystery.

The Mopan and Kekchí Maya residents do not use marijuana in any religious rituals. Its use is limited to the younger generation, who smoke it for recreational purposes. As more Maya have interacted with outside cultural forces in locations such as the regional high school in Punta Gorda or travel beyond villages to work in the tourism industry, marijuana and alcohol consumption has increased. The boom in marijuana production has also resulted in more young people smoking it (it was simply available in greater quantities than at any time in the past), but, again, this use is recreational, not spiritually oriented. However, the recent boom in marijuana production has not been fueled by internal consumption but instead by demand for the drug in the United States.

After 1980, marijuana production became organized, which set in motion one of the most recent and profitable boom economies in the southern Belize Maya land-scape. It is interesting that this economic boom was largely initiated and organized by a single non-Maya individual living in the Kekchí village of San Pedro Colum-bia. This individual, although a cultural outsider, had lived in the village for many years and so was well known to local farmers. This "drug lord" in southern Belize, albeit on a much smaller scale than the Colombian cocaine drug lords so often dis-cussed by the media, largely acted in a very similar manner as his large-scale coun-terparts. He provided farmers with necessary inputs, such as seed and fertilizer, and a guaranteed market for the harvested crop. This single individual coordinated the entire marijuana economy in the Maya villages around San Pedro Columbia, which included the Kekchí villages San Miguel and Silver Creek and nearby Mopan vil-lages San Antonio, Santa Cruz, San Jose, and Crique Jute (figure 6.2). The villages that produced the greatest quantity of marijuana were San Pedro Columbia, San Miguel and Silver Creek—again, all Kekchí Maya villages. This is not surprising, given that the coordinator of this economy lived in San Pedro Columbia. On the na-tional level, an affluent Belizean family that had economic interests in transporta-tion supported this individual, which made the movement of marijuana to export points, particularly in the Dangriga area, quite easy. During the 1980s and most of the 1990s, the Southern Highway, which runs between the Maya villages and Dan-griga to the north, remained unpaved and very rough, with little police presence. Thus contraband could be moved easily between the far southern villages and the export points to the north, with little fear of prosecution. This is particularly true when passenger bus lines were used as modes of transportation for the marijuana crop. Rural highways were also used as collection points via airplanes. I was told that it was not uncommon for airplanes to actually land on certain less-traveled highways at designated collection points and times.

By the middle of the 1980s, Belize annually produced around 1,300 tons of mar-ijuana, making it the fourth-largest producer in the world at the time (Taswell 1985; United States International Narcotics Control Strategy Report, 1997). This is an as-tounding figure, given that the total population of the country at that time was no more than 150,000 people overall. Thus by per capita measures, Belize was the largest producer of marijuana in the world. The amount is significant because the marijuana crop was not grown on large, plantation-scale levels, controlled by a few families or commercial interests. Instead, smallholder farmers were growing al-most all of this tonnage in rural Belize (other regions of the country other than the Maya south contributed significant amounts, with the northern region along the

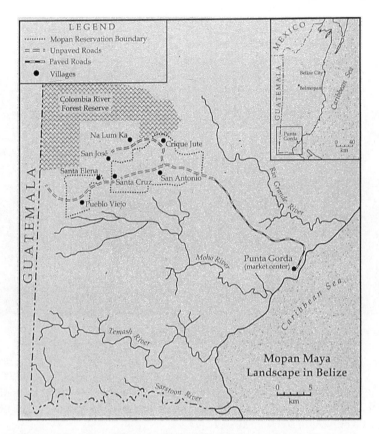

Figure 6.2. Maya villages in southern Belize that participated in a marijuana economy (map by Michael K. Steinberg).

Mexican border leading the way). The small overall population of Belize, coupled with the large amount of marijuana being produced, indicates the importance and popularity of marijuana among Belizean farmers in the 1980s.

For many farmers, marijuana became an important part of their *milpa*—a slash-and-burn agricultural (figure 6.3) crop complex—along with maize and beans, the traditional food crops among the Maya. Often, marijuana was intercropped with maize. The inclusion of marijuana into the Maya crop complex is interesting because maize is the most important crop in the Maya agricultural world. Many Mopan cannot separate their personal identities from that of maize farmers. As one informant told me, "the Maya [Mopan] are farmers, without our *milpa* and corn, we are nothing." Almost all adult men and many widowed or single women create *milpas* and plant maize. Even villagers who are considered well off and involved in other economic activities such as shopkeeping maintain a *milpa* with maize. Traditionally, many religious rituals and beliefs have incorporated maize or have been performed in order to appease the spirits associated with this crop plant (Steinberg

Figure 6.3. Slash-and-burn plot (photo by Michael K. Steinberg).

1998, 1999). Therefore, for the Maya to experiment with a new plant by dedicating time and space usually reserved for maize indicates the economic value of the marijuana harvest in southern Belize.

Marijuana was perceived by local people to be a get-rich-quick type of product, unlike any other crop grown by the Maya. The Maya landscape is home to many examples of failed cooperatives and other development efforts centered on agricultural products (Wilk 1981, 1991; Gregory 1984). Previous efforts that were focused on honey, maize, rice, and beans failed to find the rare combination (rare in many rural, tropical landscapes) of consistently high demand, high product price, and easy access to market. The marijuana crop contained all of these characteristics, thus making it very attractive to farmers who had seen previous development efforts fail many times in the past because of poor planning, lack of research, or many other factors that help determine success or failure in agricultural development economics.

Because of the large number of people involved in the production and sale of the marijuana crop, this new industry was discussed openly, and the identities of the individuals who were organizing its export from the region were common knowledge in southern Belize. Virtually overnight, marijuana became such a conspicuous crop in many Maya villages that villagers were even seen smoking marijuana in public. One story claims that two Maya women were seen smoking marijuana on a public bus traveling to Punta Gorda. These acts, along with the open discussion of the plant, are unthinkable today, or would have been before the economic boom, when a more traditional Maya cultural setting dominated. According to informants, an air of excitement surrounded this new economy because of the income it generated.

Southern Belize is a difficult landscape on which to earn a living. Swidden agriculture continues to be the economic mainstay for Maya villagers (and has been for a millennium), with maize beans and rice the focal crops of this ancient agricultural system. Because most villagers grow these crops, the markets are saturated and prices are consistently low. Local people believed (before law enforcement took notice of the new economy) that their financial troubles were over or were at least significantly relieved by the marijuana economy.

Southern Belize was ideally suited for the production of an illicit crop in the early and mid-1980s (some of these same reasons continue to exist today), and the Maya were ideally suited to grow it. First, in the early 1980s, drug producers in Colombia, the world leader in marijuana production at the time, began to shift into the more lucrative cocaine industry. The marijuana production void left by Colombia was filled by drug organizers and producers to the north in Belize and Mexico (Taswell 1985). As Alfred McCoy discusses in chapter 2 of this volume, drug economies are elastic; thus when one production area is either targeted or shifts to another crop, in this case marijuana production in Colombia, production is stimulated and shifts to a region where the political, legal, and economic conditions are right for an expansion of an illegal crop, in this case southern Belize.

Second, before this expansion of marijuana production in the early 1980s, little effort was put forth by local or national authorities to eradicate or criminalize the crop. Marijuana was not widely grown, so little negative social stigma was associated with it, creating an environment ripe for the expansion of its production. Enforcement was lax, fines for growing marijuana were small, and convictions were rare. Initially at least, few institutional factors to discourage marijuana's rapid expansion existed. Southern Belize and the Toledo district are seen as backwater zones by most Belizeans, especially civil servants working in Belize City and Belmopan. Because of this perception, the central government's presence in the district is small because most personnel are reluctant to be stationed there. There are only two police stations or outposts in the Maya region, one in San Antonio and another in San Pedro Columbia, the two largest Maya villages. Because these two stations were not expanded until the boom in marijuana production began, it was relatively easy for individuals in Maya villages to participate in illegal activities, especially at the onset of the new economy.

Third, the physical landscape where the main production villages are located is conducive to illegal activities. Much as other geographic locations where illegal drug or alcohol production takes or has taken place—such as the remote tropical, forested landscape of the Golden Triangle or the rugged hollows of Appalachia—the physical environment is an important factor in an individual's or group's ability to participate in illegal activities. The main production area is found at the southern end of the Maya Mountains, which are made up of low but rugged limestone hills (Hartshorn et al. 1984). Ground reconnaissance for illegal activities of any kind are difficult in this physical setting (figures 6.4 and 6.5). Outside interdiction authorities would need the help of local Maya villagers to negotiate the terrain, and with so many individuals participating in marijuana production in the 1980s, there was little incentive for a villager to disrupt the boom times. Fellow villagers would not have looked favorably on assisting enforcement authorities.

Figure 6.4. Physical landscape in southern Belize (photo by Michael K. Steinberg).

Last and probably most important, the lack of alternative employment in villages and the low prices paid for more traditional crops such as maize and beans lured large numbers of Maya farmers into the marijuana economy. The Toledo district in southern Belize is the most economically depressed region in the country. This was true in the early 1980s, and it remains true today (Gregory 1984; Steinberg 1999). There were (and are) few economic activities in villages beyond slash-and-burn agriculture, and none were as lucrative as marijuana production. Not surprisingly, many farmers eagerly embraced the new crop, given that the buyer supplied seed, technical support, cash upon delivery, and such perquisites as the use of vehicles. Farmers also found they could intercrop marijuana with maize, therefore producing their stable food along with a new and lucrative cash crop without expending much more labor in the form of clearing land for *milpas*. This agricultural adaptation indicates how flexible these seemingly conservative "peasant" farmers actually are. In contrast to the traditional definition of smallholder peasant farmers, the Maya in southern Belize and many groups involved in drug plant production are extremely adaptable to the changing economic conditions presented by illegal economies (Sanabria 1993).

The Boom Turns Bust

Like past boom economies, the profits gained from the boom in marijuana production did not last. The frenzy over this new and increasingly important economic ac-

Figure 6.5. Forest landscape in southern Belize (photo by Michael K. Steinberg).

tivity began to draw interest from beyond the confines of southern Belize. By the mid-1980s, Belize had caught the attention of the United States Drug Enforcement Administration (DEA) because it was producing substantial amounts of marijuana bound for the United States (United States International Narcotics Control Strategy Report, 1997). Again, by the middle of the 1980s, Belize was annually producing around 1,300 tons of marijuana, making it the fourth-largest producer in the world at the time (Taswell 1985; United States International Narcotics Control Strategy Report, 1997). Because of the substantial size of this crop, Belize began to receive greater attention from the DEA, resulting in greater pressure on the Belizean government to crack down on marijuana producers. This attention by the DEA set in motion the end of the high times in southern Belize.

The increasing pressure on the Belizean government led to the criminalization of the plant, with stricter enforcement and harsher penalties if one was caught producing or selling it. In the early 1980s, an individual found guilty of marijuana possession or production received a relatively minor fine; however, by the late 1980s and early 1990s, the penalty had increased to a 3-year jail term and/or a fine of around $2,000. In villages where the per capita income ranges roughly between $500 and $1,000, large fines and jail time proved to be a serious economic hardship. Most Mopan and Kekchí Maya were and continue to be slash-and-burn farmers; therefore when the head of the household was removed for an extended period of time, other family members, including children, had to devote greater amounts of time and labor to creating and maintaining a family's *milpa*. Unlike smallholder producers in states such as Colombia, Afghanistan, and Burma, Maya farmers in southern Belize were not protected from interdiction authorities by a larger political or military shield (McCoy 1999). In Colombia, for example, many smallholder coca growers are largely untouchable because of the protection they receive from various rebel, military, or paramilitary interests (Steinberg 2000). Certainly Maya farmers benefited from economically established and politically connected individuals who organized the marijuana economy, but these individuals could do little to protect the farmers and became targets themselves when criminalization of the new economy began.

The DEA also began a direct eradication campaign that included aerial spraying with defoliants. The rugged terrain that makes ground detection extremely difficult is overcome easily from the air. Because marijuana often was intercropped with maize, a farmer lost not only his marijuana cash crop but also his family's maize crop. Again, among the Mopan and Kekchí, maize remains the staff of life (Steinberg 1999). This is true even among those who leave villages for extended periods while working for wages or among the wealthier villagers, who can afford to buy store-bought foods. For economically marginal villagers, losing a single season's food is devastating. When aerial spraying occurred, it sent an unmistakable message to Maya farmers that the DEA and Belizean government had declared an unconditional war on drug production in southern Belize.

With funding and logistical help from the DEA and British military (whose air and ground forces were stationed in various camps around Belize, including an outpost in the south), the Belizean military and police began aggressively enforcing the newly criminalized marijuana policies. Roadblocks were established, and public buses traveling into Punta Gorda were searched regularly. A marijuana siege took place in southern Belize in that individual's activities and movements were monitored as never before. Buses taking Maya high school students into Punta Gorda were searched. When students were found with marijuana, they were arrested promptly and expelled from school. This was another deterrent because attending the Toledo district's only high school is an honor in rural villages. Being expelled for a criminal activity, even one that was profitable, brought disgrace to offenders' families because receiving a diploma is the most likely manner by which an individual may find employment opportunities beyond slash-and-burn agriculture.

Not only was greater pressure exerted on villagers, but also the DEA sought out the individuals who controlled marijuana trade within Belize. Because those who purchased the crop became entangled in legal problems, the organizer responsible for purchase at the village level was forced to leave San Pedro Columbia and seek more legitimate employment. One member of the family who controlled marijuana's movement and export from southern Belize was arrested by the DEA while in the United States, and another was made a prisoner in Belize by the threat of arrest upon leaving the country.

By the early 1990s, with the help of outside technical and financial support and stricter enforcement of domestic laws pertaining to drug production and use, the criminalization of marijuana was complete. Thus in a very short time marijuana went from an openly grown, sold, profitable, and socially acceptable commodity to one that presented troubling social, economic, and ecological (because of aerial spraying) dilemmas for individuals taking part in this economy. Today, marijuana remains in a bust state. Although it continues to be grown by some villagers, it is cultivated in small quantities, with an unorganized distribution process. A small market remains in villages among the young (particularly males) and in Punta Gorda, where it is often sold to tourists passing through southern Belize. But today's marijuana economy is a mere shadow of that which existed during the 1980s. In contrast to the 1980s, marijuana is no longer openly discussed and certainly not used in southern Belize.

Cultural Consequences of the Marijuana Boom

The boom economy in the early 1980s resulted in widespread cultural changes in the production villages, especially the Kekchí village San Pedro Columbia (the production and collection center among Maya villages). Generally speaking, traditional Maya culture was further marginalized under the influence of a sudden influx of large amounts of cash. Certainly by 1980, the concept of a "traditional" Maya culture must be used cautiously, for the Mopan and Kekchi cultures hardly resembled the classic "closed corporate communities" in Guatemala described by anthropologist Eric Wolf (1957). However, many economic- and social-leveling mechanisms were still in place on the eve of the marijuana boom. For example, traditional cultural traits, such as pole-and-thatch huts, still dominated in villages. No individual or family stood out from his or her neighbors because of living quarters; thus these structures represented public symbols of cultural solidarity. Villagers, in fact, did not want to stand out because they were then accused of various deviant activities such as witchcraft or abstaining from participation in the expensive cargo system.

The traditional civil-religious cargo system consisted of a hierarchy of offices that most or all adult men were expected to participate in. The cargo system involved such activities as organizing and financially supporting the village fiestas and patron saint feast days, maintaining the village church, and organizing various other community events like cleaning and clearing the village green. As individuals move up the chain of cargos, the cost associated with each office increases; thus individuals spend large sums of money as each cargo office is completed. Those who can afford to move up in the cargo system are rewarded with personal respect and political power within a community. But as the economic boom took hold, traditional thatch and dirt-floor structures were increasingly replaced by modern concrete, two-story structures (Steinberg 1996), often with electricity. In fact, various individuals told me that *every* concrete house in San Pedro Columbia built before 1990 was built with drug money. The construction of these types of house represented a radical break with the past, given that public expressions of wealth were discouraged in more traditional times (Wilk 1983).

Vehicles also became common in villages (especially San Pedro Colombia) because the organizer provided trucks to productive farmers. Thus a dependent, coercive relationship developed between the buyer and the farmers, resulting in a situation in which the former could exert pressure upon the latter. For example, one farmer told me that he believed that he could not stop planting marijuana after receiving a vehicle because the buyer would demand payment for its use. However, most individuals were quite happy to receive vehicles, particularly before law enforcement became an issue. Their desire is understandable because in any agricultural setting a vehicle is vital in order to carry crops, supplies, livestock, and so on to markets or fields.

New houses and vehicles were the most visible physical signs of the economic boom in many Maya villages in the 1980s. A less visible result of marijuana production was the erosion of the *alcalde* legal-political system. In the past, *alcaldes* had the authority and responsibility to enforce laws and report illegal activities to national authorities. However, given the amount of wealth generated by the new crop, they had little power to enforce laws because of pressure placed on them by friends, family, and neighbors who were earning income through marijuana production. Also, I was told that some *alcaldes* were even involved in the marijuana economy, producing a serious conflict of interest. Also, as villagers involved in marijuana production became wealthy by local standards, some felt that traditional political and legal structures no longer applied to them. This challenge to the *alcalde's* authority further undermined a traditional institution that had already begun to lose power in villages for a variety of reasons, such as growing numbers of Protestant converts and the intravillage squabbles that resulted between them and the Catholics (Steinberg 1996).

Lessons and Larger Implications of the Marijuana Economy in Southern Belize

The marijuana boom-and-bust economy in southern Belize provides important lessons for the current war on drugs. First, similar to Maya farmers of southern Belize, many indigenous and other peasant groups exist on the margins of national economies with few opportunities beyond semisubsistence agriculture, low-wage labor on commercial agricultural plantations (many of which have laid claim to the most productive agricultural lands), or participation in sporadic boom-and-bust economic opportunities. However, while continuing to exist on the economic margins of national economies, most indigenous groups are increasingly incorporated into and dependent on cash incomes and market economies. For example, today more Maya villagers are attending the regional high school in Punta Gorda than at any time in the past. Most villagers correctly perceive that a secondary education will create opportunities for their children that surpass career options open to previous generations. However, school uniforms, school supplies, and transportation to and from school—or room and board in Punta Gorda—all demand greater amounts of income. Also, as groups such as the Mopan and Kekchí interact with the larger national culture and economy, a self-perception of material poverty has developed. Although the Mopan and Kekchí produce abundant food supplies and malnutrition is rare in southern Belize, they are certainly poor in terms of material objects associated with the modern world.

Many Maya, especially the younger generation, have grown frustrated with the prospects of living the materially poor lives of many of their parents and grandparents. As a result of this real and perceived need for greater cash incomes, there is growing pressure to earn wages to pay for the perceived necessities of modern life. It is not surprising that where these conditions exist many indigenous people, such as the Mopan and Kekchí, often turn their agricultural efforts to the production of marijuana, coca, and opium poppies (Sanabria 1992; Thongtham 1992; Hobbs 1998; Wilson 2001; Reuters 2002). Yes, the marijuana economy went bust in southern Belize, but if the opportunity presents itself for a resurrection, many villagers will probably again eagerly participate. And although this illicit economy was largely destroyed in southern Belize, it simply moved to another location, where similar socioeconomic conditions exist. In the case of marijuana, the Peten in neighboring Guatemala and Mexico both expanded their production as Belize reduced its own.

Smallholder farmers are rational actors in that they invest labor and other inputs such as fertilizer. Given that earnings from few commodities in southern Belize and elsewhere could or can compete with the wages earned from marijuana or other psychoactive drug plants in many Third World landscapes, it is not surprising that so many smallholder farmers embrace illegal commodities. This conflict strikes at the heart of present-day development policies. On the one hand, national governments, international development agencies, and international trade agreements emphasize global markets and free trade zones; yet in many Third World indigenous landscapes, these agreements and policies are postmodern in that present-day farmers have little ability to compete and earn a livable wage in the new global economy. Therefore, many turn to illegal commodities, which provide earnings that far exceed those from legitimate agricultural activities.

The lesson here is simple. Until smallholder farmers in Belize, Colombia, Afghanistan, Burma, and other states are given economic opportunities that rival the returns provided by marijuana, coca, and poppies, the war on drugs will never be won. There are precedents for apparent success. Crop substitution efforts have been successful in Thailand, where a large-scale alternative development plan has sought to replace poppy cultivation with various crops such as coffee, strawberries, and kiwi fruits (Hobbs 1998). Known as the Royal Northern Project, this multidimensional development strategy has sought to modernize the poppy-growing region with new crops, infrastructure such as roads to effectively move crops to markets, and refrigerated trucks to transport perishable items (Hobbs 1998). Critics claim that efforts like the Royal Northern Project are expensive, and initially they are. However, the traditional approach to drug interdiction cannot be called cheap by any economic or social indicator. For example, the U.S. Congress just raised the stakes by approving a $1.3 *billion* military and interdiction aid package for the Colombian government. It is unlikely that a *global* crop replacement and education strategy would add up to such a huge amount of money.

Certainly small "victories" (by DEA standards) in the larger war on drugs, such as the destruction of the marijuana export economy in southern Belize, will occur with the help of intensive spraying, surveillance, and enactment of stiff legal penalties and fines. But the same conditions that led to the marijuana boom remain in place in southern Belize and in many other indigenous and peasant landscapes. As Alfred McCoy demonstrates in chapter 2, when criminal activity (drug production) "is squeezed and crushed in a vice-grip of coercion," that stimulates the economic conditions elsewhere for the start of a new drug production zone. Drug crops such as marijuana, coca, and opium poppies are fairly adaptable and tolerant plants. Thus the landscapes in which they can be grown are limitless compared with the ability of interdiction authorities to eliminate them. A recent *New York Times* article states that coca farmers in Bolivia are saving coca seeds for future plantings when the political and legal atmosphere is more conducive to growing this now banned crop (Kraus 2000). So although the DEA and Bolivian government have been successful in largely eliminating commercial coca production, this "vice-grip" has stimulated production in Colombia, where the current war on drugs rages on. Similar to a wildfire that flairs up in various locations, seemingly without warning, when environmental conditions are right, drug production zones are equally difficult to extinguish as long as smallholder farmers continue to struggle in landscapes where the right (or wrong) socioeconomic conditions exist. Based on this case study, these conditions include lack of markets for legal commodities that rival the economic returns of drug plants and increasing penetration of national and international market economies, which often force indigenous groups into poverty-stricken existences because they are not presented with appropriate tools nor have the political power to make decisions regarding desired paths of local or regional development.

The DEA seems intent on attempting to replicate the success in southern Belize on a global scale. Eradication campaigns that involve aerial spraying, criminalization of drug plants, military involvement, and targeting of drug organizations' infrastructure may be effective in the immediate sense. Certainly these policies were effective in southern Belize. However, where poverty exists on one end of the drug production line and there is high demand on the other, individuals will continue to grow crops like marijuana, coca, and poppies. If host governments and the United States are serious about reducing the competitive advantages drug plants have over legal means of income generation in the long term, they must address the social and economic conditions that have drawn indigenous farmers into this often destructive economic activity, such as financial incentives and initial subsidies for nontraditional crop plants, development of nature tourism, greater access to regional and national markets for agricultural products in general, and greater political autonomy and control of local resources (Smith 1992; Thongtham 1992; Hobbs 1998). Until then, eradication victories similar to that in southern Belize will probably remain ephemeral and generally limited in the global production of illicit drug plants.

References

Allen, C. J. 1988. *The Hold Life Has: Coca and Cultural Identity in an Andean Community.* Washington DC: Smithsonian Series in Ethnographic Inquiry, no 12.
Bagley, B. M., and W. O. Walker III. 1996. *Drug Trafficking in the Americas.* Miami, FL: North-South Center Press.
Booth, M. 1998. *Opium: A History.* New York: St. Martin's.
Celia Toro, M. 1995. *Mexico's "War" on Drugs : Causes and Consequences. Vol. 3. Studies on the Impact of the Illegal Drug Trade.* Boulder, CO: Lynne Rienner.
Gregory, J. R. 1984. Cooperatives: Failure Versus Success. *Belizean Studies* 12: 1–15.

Hartshorn, G., et al. 1984. *Belize: Country Environmental Profile*. Belize City: USAID Contract, Robert Nicolait and Associates, Ltd.

Hobbs, J. J. 1998. Troubling Fields: The Opium Poppy in Egypt. *Geographical Review* 88 (1): 64–88.

Kraus, C. 2000. Bolivia Wiping Out Coca at a Price. *New York Times*, October 23, p. A10.

McCoy, A. W. 1999. Lord of Drug Lords: One Life as Lesson for U.S. Policy. *Crime, Law, and Social Change* 30(4): 301–331.

Nietschmann, B. Q. 1973. *Between Land and Water*. New York: Seminar Press.

———. 1993. The Conservation of Biological and Cultural Diversity. Paper presented at the Eighty-ninth Annual Association of American Geographers, Atlanta, Georgia.

Reuters. 2002. Afghan War Hikes Thai, Myanmar Opium Production.

Rohter, L. 1999. With U.S. Training, Colombia Melds War on Rebels and Drugs. *New York Times*, July 17, p. A1 and 6.

Rohter, L., and C. S. Wren. 1999. U.S. Officials Propose $1 Billion for Colombian Drug War. *New York Times*, July 17, pp. A7.

Sanabria, H. 1992. Holding Their Ground: Crop Eradications, Repression, and Peasant Resistance in the Chapare of Bolivia. Paper presented at the Seventeenth International Congress of the Latin American Studies Association,

———. 1993. *The Coca Boom and Rural Social Change in Bolivia*. Ann Arbor: University of Michigan Press.

Smith, M. L., ed. 1992. *Why People Grow Drugs*. London: Panos Publications.

Steinberg, M. K. 1996. Folk House-types as Indicators of Tradition: The Case of the Mopan Maya in Southern Belize. In D. Hopkins and S. Driever, eds. *Yearbook, Conference of Latin Americanist Geographers* 22: 87–92.

———. 1998. Political Ecology, Cultural Change, and Their Impact on Swidden-Fallow Agroforestry Practices Among the Mopan Maya in Southern Belize. *The Professional Geographer* 50(4): 407–417.

———. 1999. Maize Diversity and Cultural Change in a Maya Agroecological Landscape. *Journal of Ethnobiology* 19(1): 127–139.

———. 2000. Generals, Guerillas, Drugs, and Third World War-making. *Geographical Review* 90(2): 260–267.

Taswell, R. 1985. Marijuana, an Overview. *Cultural Survival Quarterly* 9 (4): 5.

Thongtham, C. N. 1992. Fruitful Harvest from Alternative Crops. In C. L. Smith, ed., *Why People Grow Drugs*. London: Panos Publications.

United States International Narcotics Control Strategy Report. 1997. http://www/state/gov/www/global/narcotics_law/1997_narc_report/camex97.html.

Wilk, R. R. 1981. Pigs Are Part of the System: A Lesson in Agricultural Development. *Belizean Studies* 9: 122–129.

———. 1983. Little House in the Jungle, the Causes of Variation in House Size Among Modern Kekchi Maya. *Journal of Anthropological Archaeology* 2: 99–116.

———. 1991. *Household Ecology: Economic Change and Domestic Life Among the Kekchi Maya in Belize*. Tucson: University of Arizona Press.

Wilk, R. R., and M. Chapin. 1991. *Ethnic Minorities in Belize: Mopan, Kekchi, and Garifuna*. Belize City: Society for the Promotion of Education and Research.

Wilson, S. 2001. Peru's Shining Path Rebels Resurface. *Miami Herald*, December 16.

Wolf, E. R. 1957. Closed Corporate Peasant Communities in Mesoamerica and Central Java. *Southwestern Journal of Anthropology* 13: 1–18.

Zhou, Y. 1999. *Anti-Drug Crusades in Twentieth-Century China*. Lanham, MD: Rowman & Littlefield.

7

Sacred and Profane Uses of the Cactus *Lophophora Williamsii* from the South Texas Peyote Gardens

Clarissa T. Kimber
Darrel McDonald

The white man goes into his church and talks about Jesus. The Indian goes into his tipi and talks to Jesus.
Quanah Parker

Peyote is one of the best-known plant sources for a psychedelic experience. This small cactus is also associated in the popular mind with North American Indians and Hippies. Although its ritual use is thought to be over 7,000 years old (Furst 1989, cited in Schaefer 1996: 141), its use by Indians of the Native American Church (NAC) is less than 100 years old. The peyote button is the essential ingredient in the ritual ceremony associated with NAC meetings and is referred to as "the medicine" by those who regard the button as a god-being and ingest it as a sacrament (Slotkin 1956: 29; Smith and Snake 1996: 80, 91, 105–6). Even more recently, non-Indians have formed churches (the Neo American Church) to follow the Peyote Way or Road (Trout 1999: 47). Secular uses of peyote are as medicine, especially for topical application to the skin on open wounds (Schultes 1940), for divination to discover something lost or when possible attacks of the enemy will occur; or for mind-altering experiences of a nonreligious nature, that is, for recreation. These nonritual (profane) uses have a long history, but peyote's more significant sacred use in the United States, as measured by numbers of participants, has been in force for little more than 100 years.

Various plants are called peyote in Mexico (Schultes 1938: 157), and their usage in the public and official literature of Texas and the United States has not been precise over the years (Morgan 1976: 12, La Barre 1975: 14–17). The major confusion over the common name among field anthropologists and government officials has been with the mescal bean, or Texas mountain laurel [*Sophora secundiflora* (Ort.) DC]. This hardy, small tree produces a hard, highly toxic, red seed, which has had a long history of ritual use by Amerinds (La Barre 1975: 15). The distribution of the mescal bean is on the southern edge of the Edwards Plateau, on the caliche cuestas in the Rio Grande Plains, and in the mountains of the Trans-Pecos. The native Americans of this region strung the beans into necklaces or bracelets, and a shaman might have passed down to another shaman some of these items as important paraphernalia. Another plant that adds to the confusion is mescal (*Agave americana* L.), which is used to prepare the intoxicating drinks of pulque and tequila but is not a source of mescaline. In the popular literature, one hears of the peyote mushroom. This is not peyote but a series of Mexican fungi within the *Basidiomycete* group with hallucinogenic properties, especially the *Psilocybe mexicana*, often called by its vernacular name, *teonanacatl* (Schultes 1963: 188–232), which was made famous by Wasson (1968: 7–17). Other species of *Psilocybe* are occasionally called *teonanacatl*; other members of the Agaricaceae family are *Panaeolus campanulatus* (var. *sphinctrinus*), *Stropharia cubensis*, and *Conocybe* spp. (Anderson 1996: 164–165). Our concern is with the cactus beautifullly illustrated for the first time in *Curtis's Botanical Magazine* (1847, plate 4296), reprinted in *Peyote, the Divine Cactus* by Edward F. Anderson (1996: 156).

The peyote cactus, *Lophophora williamsii* (Lemaire) J. Coulter, is endemic to an area that extends northward from central northern Mexico to the plains immediately north of the Rio del Norte (Rio Grande) in South Texas (Anderson, 1969: 300; Rouhier 1927: 11); (figure 7.1). Spontaneous in the understory of the shrub-dominated lands on dry, gravely, limestone soils, it is easily overlooked until one penetrates the spiny thickets. The above-ground portion, the so-called button, is very small in comparison with its parsnip-shaped root (figure 7.2). Inconspicuous in the best of weather, during long drought periods the button may retreat underground and be almost invisible, only to surface after a rain. Varying in color from dark green to a gray-green, the button has a variable number of segments on which are tufts of hairs instead of the spines found on other cacti. Bearing a single or occasionally a double white to deep pink flower, the fruit is red and contains numerous small black seeds, which are dispersed by birds who roost in the brush that characteristically arches over and covers the individual plants.

Virtually all of the cactus buttons eaten in the United States come from the "peyote gardens" on the Mustang Plains of South Texas. The Smithsonian ethnographer James Moony (1892) reported that peyote grows in the breaks along either side of the Rio Grande from El Paso to Eagle Pass and Laredo south to Starr County. This corresponds to Lumholz's (1902) reports. Three physiographic divisions extend across Starr, Jim Hogg, Webb, and Zapata Counties (figure 7.3), and the modern commercial collectors of peyote exploit the western face of the Bordas Escarpment, the Aguilares Plain to its west, and the Breaks of the Rio Grande farther west (Morgan 1983: 320–321).

Pilgrimages by Amerindians to the region to harvest peyote for use in rituals were reported as early as the eighteenth century (Beals 1932: 216; Stewart 1944: 64; Slotkin 1955: 205). Later, especially when the Indians were relocated from Texas to the Oklahoma Territory, local hispanos called *peyoteros* began to harvest the peyote populations and provide the medicine to the pilgrims coming down from the north (Morgan 1976: 4–5). As a result of these relationships, the peyote trade of Texas with the rest of the United States and Canada was established. Close bonds

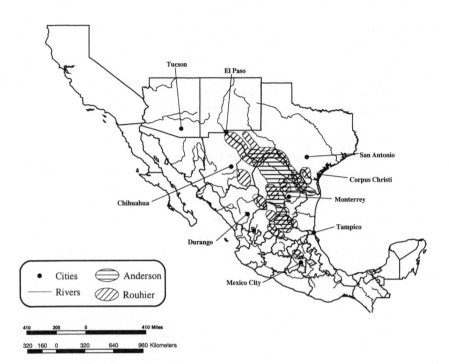

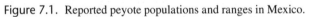

Figure 7.1. Reported peyote populations and ranges in Mexico.

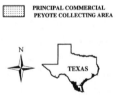

Figure 7.2. Commercial peyote-collecting areas in south Texas.

Figure 7.3. A peyote plant from south Texas (photo by Darrel McDonald).

emerged between Native American tribal elders, the *peyotists*, who ventured to South Texas, and the local *peyoteros*, who supplied the sacrament. The *peyoteros* often guided the Indians for free to the fields to harvest some buttons and to conduct a private ceremony with the peyote (Morgan 1976: 136; A. Cárdenas 1992, personal communication). Tales of the pilgrimages to South Texas grew as the membership in the Native American Church grew. Over time the stories created the vision in the minds of many church members of vast fields of peyote tucked into the stark landscape of South Texas. So, to many adherents, the Mustang Plains became the home of "peyote gardens," although no one knows who put this name on this landscape (Morgan 1976: 24). The name first appears on a J. H. Young Texas map dated 1835 (Meinig 1993: 136). By the first third of the twentieth century, the Mustang Plains had become widely recognized as a sacred landscape to those who practiced the peyote religion and followed the Peyote Road.

The new seekers of the second half century focused on this same region as a place where they might find a mind-expanding experience. During the last half of the twentieth century, peyote became a pseudosacrament for the hippie generation and often a recreational drug for individuals looking for alternative world perspectives (Grinspoon and Bakalar 1979: 59; Schaefer and Furst 1996: 507). Although this nonritual, profane use of peyote has been documented over the last century, it is in the decades of the 1960s and 1970s that nonreligious use had the most impact on the peyote landscapes and culture of South Texas. In that period the larger social community became aware of and began to associate hallucinogenic properties with the cactus and the counterculture.

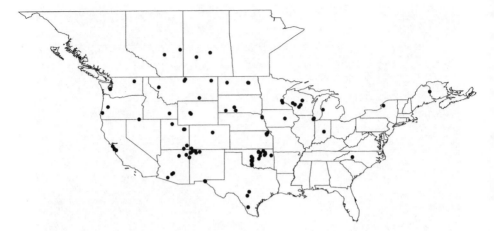

Figure 7.4. Locations of Native American Churches registered with the Texas Department of Public Safety.

In the 1910s, when the first church charter for the Native American Church was recognized, there were several thousand members, and by 1922 there were an estimated 13,2000 members (Schultes and Hofmann 1973: 121). Since the 1950s and particularly in the last 25 years, the Native American Church has experienced a rapid increase in membership. It is estimated that about 250,000 –300,000 Amerindians are registered members of the NAC (Echo Hawk 1999, personal communication; Smith and Snake 1996: 172; figure 7.4). This equates to a need for several million peyote buttons to be harvested annually to meet the demand for medicine in religious ceremonies. This demand has resulted in two important developments. First, the peyote population is reputedly under stress in the United States (Morgan 1983a,b; Anderson 1995). Second, the attachment to the sacred gardens of South Texas has changed in nature as many young, second- and third-generation Amerindian pilgrims to South Texas have a different perspective from that of the earlier, traditional pilgrims. The history of ritual usage and the rise and subsequent fall in profane, recreational uses of peyote indicates to us that it is the ritual practices that currently account for most of the use of peyote from South Texas.

Among Amerindians, all psychotropic drugs were traditionally used in controlled, guided religious contexts. Accounts of Huichol and Tarahumara use of peyote in tribal ceremonies described the shaman-led trips, suggesting that the practice dates from early times (Schaefer and Furst 1996: 26–30; La Barre 1975:29–39, 131–132; Lumholz 1902, vol. 1: 358–372; vol. 2: 128–144). Among those using peyote for recreation, little thought in the beginning was given to guiding the participants in its use. This difference in how participants were initiated is partly a function of the different meanings associated with the use of the peyote buttons.

The recreational or profane use of peyote in Texas and the United States has occurred in several documented eras, or cycles, associated with the general use of the drug (Jonnes 1996: 443–444). There was the great era of cocaine and morphine addiction at the end of the nineteenth century that extended into the early part of the twentieth century. There was the notorious expansion of drug use by antiwar activists of the 1910s; marijuana and then the psychedelics joined heroin and cocaine as the drugs of choice. However, it was the hippie movement in the late 1960s and 1970s that brought the use of the peyote for its hallucinogenic effects to the attention of the general public (Grinspoon and Bakalar 1979: 54–55). The practice was associated with persons interested in personal, mind-expanding, and recreational uses (Schaefer and Furst 1996: 507). Underground newspapers carried notices and articles, but the regular press gave accounts as well. As a result, peyote became recognized as a hallucinogen by most Americans during those years.

Although there had been numerous legal constraints on the use of peyote by Amerindians since the 1880s, the most stringent prohibitions and sanctions date from the second half of the twentieth century that culminated in putting peyote on the notorious Schedule 1 in 1997 (*US Code of the Federal Regulations 1997* §1308.11. (22): #7415). Such opposition had only marginal effectiveness among tribal members of the church. At other times, more compassionate individuals cared less about prohibiting Amerindians from practicing the peyote religion. Thus, it was not until the beat and especially the hippie periods that serious efforts were made to reestablish controls on the use of peyote in the United States, especially in Texas, where it grows naturally. For example, see La Barre (1975: 236) for a 1964 ruling by the California Fourth District Court of Appeals and Smith and Snake (1996: 128–153) for a historical treatment to 1994 that ends with the American Indian Freedom Act.

Nature of Intoxication by Peyote

The physiology of the peyote intoxication is complex. Many different chemical compounds are found in the plant as it is chewed and ingested. There are over 60 alkaloids, divided into the phenethylamine and the isoquinoline compounds (Anderson, 1996: 220–225). Mescaline is the only one known to have psychedelic characteristics. The very number of these secondary metabolates or complex plant compounds may moderate the effects of ingesting mescaline directly from the plant. According to Grinspoon and Bakalar (1979: 20), mescaline is a 3,4,5 trimethoxyphenethylamine and belongs to the largest group of psychedelic compounds, the phenylalkylamines. Mescaline is the simplest of the plant's compounds and the only psychedelic one so far discovered (Grinspoon and Bakalar 1979: 21). The effective dose is about 200 milligrams, or three to five peyote buttons. Habitual participants in the peyote ceremony report eating as many as 20 buttons in an evening. Tolerance develops, as with psilocybin and LSD: "There is cross-tolerance between any two of the three drugs in all sequences of administration" (Rech et al. 1975: 265–266).

Physiological effects described in the scientific literature are likened to those of LSD. The chewed button and pure mescaline derived from it can cause nausea and vomiting (Grinspoon and Bakalar 1979: 21). Vomiting is a common result of eating as few as three or four buttons. It takes 30 to 40 times as much mescaline as psilobybin to produce effects, depending upon the individual's physiology. The psychological effect, according to Grinspoon and Bakalar (1979: 21), is more sensual and perceptual, "with less change in thought, mood, and the sense of self." There are many anecdotal reports of people who, while under the influence, refuse to engage in routine psychological tasks because they seem to be absurd. Some subjects go into long fits of laughter. Hollister and Martman (1962: 240–241) reported that in clinical trials subjects apparently could not distinguish mescaline from LSD at "appropriate doses."

The experience lasts from 6 to 12 hours (Gottlieb 1997 on Erowid): "After being absorbed by the blood stream, the mescaline has a half-life of around 6 hours. Peak concentrations of mescaline occur about 2 hours after oral administration; this corresponds to the time period of highest psychedelic effect. Drug levels in the blood drop gradually over 10 hours, with 87% of the dose eliminated after 24 hours." According to the *Visionary Cactus Guide* (Erowid 2000), the average experiences of different participants for different doses are as follows:

1. Low dose, 100–200 milligrams: a mild buzz to good trip with some visuals
2. Moderate dose, 200–300 milligrams: average dosage, strong visuals
3. High dose, 300–500 milligrams: intense visuals, ego dissociation possible
4. Extreme dose, 500–800 milligrams: for *"experienced, competent explorers only"*

The first stage of intoxication as described ethnographically by La Barre (1975: 17) is that of "physical and mental exhilaration." Euphoria is followed by depression and usually vomiting. There is a stimulant quality in the plant and no desire for sleep during the ceremonies, which are conducted at night. A person may feel the need to vomit, thus purging or cleansing the body. After the less comfortable experiences, "pleasure effects"—including colored hallucinations and a desire to sing—are often experienced. Red and yellow colors are frequently reported. People then become quieter, and by morning, with water and food, the effects wear off. The use of peyote is neither harmful nor habit-forming (Siskin 1983: 84)), and no case of addiction has been associated with peyote chewing and ingesting (La Barre 1975: 222–223). There is considerable discussion in the literature of peyote as a narcotic substance, but the prevailing scientific opinion is that it is not a narcotic, not habit-forming, and not harmful (Grinspoon and Bakalar 1979: 5–9, 176). However, the habit of preconceived assumptions among federal and state officials is strong, and much of the legislation is based upon the belief that button chewing is harmful and not in the best interests of the persons ingesting it (see numerous citations to the literature in Schultes 1938; La Barre 1975; Stewart 1956).

The sacramental button is eaten whole, either green or dried. A young person may chew a dried button until is soft for the use of an elderly or toothless participant. Also a kind of tea is made from the dried peyote: The fresh or dried button is cut into pieces and then ground on a metate or, more recent, in a food processor. The ground peyote is then mixed with water and is drunk during the ceremony. This form of the medicine is absorbed into the system more rapidly than by chewing since free mescaline in an aqueous solution is absorbed faster than mescaline that is entrapped in an organic matrix of cactus tissue, which must be broken down to free the mescaline.

Peyote in Ritual and the Growth of the Native American Church

The Native American Church ceremony has religious practices that incorporate traditional elements interwoven with Christian rituals and American patriotic themes. Church members are encouraged to maintain high moral principles. Among the mores stressed are responsibility to family and abstinence from alcohol abuse. Meetings are usually held on a weekend. The ceremonies take one night followed by a feast the next day. Occasionally meetings may be held on consecutive days for special reasons. Because of the large number of adherents who travel to South Texas for the annual Presidents' Birthday Meetings, ceremonies may be held on two or even three nights. These church meetings bring together a diverse group of adherents, who sing and pray together. At times this brings about a sharing of religious practices during a meeting, and an innovation may be carried on or dropped at the next meeting.

The arrangement of the furnishings within a tepee is carefully circumscribed and stylized (La Barre 1975: 44–75; Smith and Snake 1996: 75–101). There are specific paraphernalia: a fire and fire caretaker, drum, gourd rattle, staff, and feather fan. The roadman, who directs the ceremony and generally keeps order, looks out through the opening of the tepee to watch the stars and note the passing of time. He is assisted by a drummer, a cedar man, and a fireman, as well as informally by other persons. The roadman may be the organizer of the ceremony or someone he wishes to honor. The timing and the order of the ceremony vary but seem to be constant with each roadman or with the particular "way" adopted by the group leader. The smoking of cornhusk tobacco cigarettes usually proceeds the eating of several peyote buttons. Fire is necessary to cleanse the mind and the body and to burn the incense. Cedar, sage, and other aromatic plants are used in the ceremony, but cedar is the Plains Indian holy native incense (Marriott and Rachlin 1971: 25). Feathers in bundles or fans were made to brush the incense over the worshipers. Participants may bring specific paraphernalia, considered personal items, to be used during prayers. The bundle generally includes at least a rattle, a staff, and a feather fan. These may be gifts from fellow peyotists and are held in high regard. It is also common for individuals to bring pads, blankets, cushions, and a few other items for personal comfort.

The Ritual Described

The following observations are based on personal accounts of two meetings by Darrel McDonald. The first was a funeral meeting for Dr. George R. Morgan held in Slim Buttes, South Dakota, on the Weasel Bear home place in November 1984. The second meeting was held on the property of Amada Cárdenas in Mirando City,

Figure 7.5. Raising of the teepee on the Cárdenas grounds, Mirando City, 1995 (photo by Darrel McDonald).

Texas, in honor of her ninetieth birthday in October 1995. The meetings are described in the singular. Occasional references are made to differences between the two meetings and to reports in Stewart (1944: 65) and other investigators in the Plains Indian context.

Sometime in the late morning or early afternoon before the meeting, the raising of the tepee took place. This was a group effort, with the provider of the tepee organizing the project (figure 7.5). Later, the half-moon altar was prepared inside the tepee, and firewood was stacked outside the tepee for the meeting. As dusk settled in, people began taking personal bundles into the tepee; they visited and shared information about the theme for the meeting (see the description of the tepee's layout in Stewart 1944: 65). Shortly thereafter, members lined up to formally file into the tepee. Inside the teepee, low conversation among the participants drifted off into quietness.

Once all was in order, the roadman reverently placed the chief peyote on the altar. He began the meeting by offering instructions on how it was to be run. He gave the appearance of teaching rather than making authoritarian pronouncements. While this part of the meeting was taking place, the fire was stoked and cedared (cedar shavings were placed on the flames). Next, the roadman reminded everyone about the purpose of the meeting. In both cases, he also asked a sponsor of the meeting to comment on its purpose. Following a few moments of reflective thought, a smoke was sent around the tepee in a prescribed direction; during these meetings it was clockwise. This was followed by comments and questions from the roadman, making sure his helpers were ready for the meeting.

After the initial settling in activities, the sacrament (peyote) was passed around to the participants. No comment was made on the amount taken or if one chose not to ingest the medicine. At Slim Buttes, ground buttons were passed in a glass jar and tea was available. In South Texas, fresh peyotes were passed, as well as the tea. The roadman continued with a reminder to members about the protocol for moving around the fireplace if one had to move to another position or desired to leave the tepee. Again, the environment gravitated toward an unrequired but understood quiet. At this juncture in the meetings, the roadman rose to a kneeling position and began to pray, using his rattle and staff and accompanied by a drummer. Four songs were offered; then the staff was passed clockwise to the next individual. If that person chose to sing, the drummer or a requested drummer relocated to support the new singer. This sequence made a complete cycle, but not all chose to sing. There were approximately 25–30 adherents, including women, at each meeting.

Following the prayers, the peyote sacrament was offered a second time. Quiet conversations ensued as the medicine made its way to all at the meeting. Shortly thereafter, the roadman again began to pray, and a second round of singing continued the meeting. Besides making up individual prayers, members also sang traditional songs and others joined in. These activities were somewhat equal in pace at both meetings. Around midnight, the roadman interrupted the meeting to go outside to perform the task of acknowledging the four directions. To do this, he left the tepee in the prescribed manner and, while facing each of the cardinal directions, blew an eagle-bone whistle. During this intermission of activity within the tepee, individuals stepped out of the tepee; some left and did not return, but the majority returned or remained seated. The roadman returned to his seat directly across from the chief peyote and conferred for a few moments with the cedarman and other participants seated nearby. The roadman initiated the third round of prayers. After the third round, the medicine was offered to each person. The fourth round of prayers ensued. After this, the roadman offered each person the opportunity to reflect on the purpose of the meeting or to comment on a personal situation.

After all had spoken, the roadman expressed his thanks for all the cooperation from the members. He then asked the fireman to call for the morning water. The water was brought in and placed on the other side of the tepee from the roadman at the base of the fireplace near the tepee opening. After each woman waterbearer had offered the Morning Prayer, the water was passed; later gruel was passed for all to sample. The last activity before the meeting ended was a final series of prayer songs. The participants then made their way outside the tepee. Immediately, conversations arose that related to the meeting, as well as general social interactions, often with humorous interjections. In the late morning or around noon a picnic feast was held in South Texas (figure 7.4). Because of the wintry temperatures during the funeral meeting in South Dakota, the postmeeting activities took place inside the Weasel Bear home.

Diffusion of Peyote Use and Creation of Cult and Religion

In the process of diffusion from Mexico, many older Mexican ceremonies were modified, so the ceremonial use of peyote in the United States was changed substantially from the rites practiced by the Huichole, Cora, and Tarahumar (Lumholz 1902; LaBarre 1975; Schaefer and Furst 1996). Anthropologist Omer C. Stewart (1977: 19; 1987: 40–41) made numerous cross-cultural studies of the peyote rituals among North American Indians, and he asserted that, in fact, nearly all cults north of Mexico are probably identical in most respects. We suggest that the conditions that led to the original peyote ritual as practiced in the church arose early and that the rites were codified quickly. Throughout the twentieth century, as more churches were established, each roadman would introduce minor variations as he understood the rites, contributing to the variations that exist in the practices of the different churches today.

The earliest accounts of the northern activities date from Velasco, who wrote in 1716 that the Indians of Texas drank "pelotte" when dancing (cited in La Barre 1975: 110). According to Opler (1938: 271–285), the Lippan got the peyote from the Carrizo before white contact, about 1870. He maintained that the Carrizo from the Laredo area was an early group, perhaps the group that developed important peyote rituals outside of Mexico in the nineteenth century (M. E. Opler, 1938: 280). The naturalist Berlandier (1980: 590) reported in his journal, written in the early 1830s, of finding peyote on the rocky hills along the Rio Grande upstream from Reynosa: "The peyotl today corrupted to peyote is still highly esteemed by the indigenes along the banks of the Rio Bravo. They never celebrate any fiesta without drinking the intoxicating decoction of that singular plant. . . . We heard [near Matamoros] the songs of the indigenes, who were dancing to the sound of their monotonous but expressive music." These people may have been the Lippan Apache. Mooney (1896b: 7–9) saw peyote in use by the Kiowa around 1886, but he thinks that they knew about it from the Mescalero by 1850. According to La Barre (1975), the Tonkawa peyote ceremony may be as old. Stewart (1987: 46–53) made a case that the Carrizo of northeastern Mexico were using peyote in rituals that lasted all night as early as 1649. He dates the appearance of the Lippan into that area about 1770, having obtained the peyote complex from the Carrizo (Stewart 1987: 49). Some new usages were being developed in southern Texas and the borderlands of northern Mexico.

After the Civil War, expansion by Euro-Americans into the western grasslands of the United States put them into direct conflict with the Plains Indians. The Americans considered the Indians heathens and uncivilized. Both by arms and culture, the native people were subjected to violence and bloodshed and forced onto segregated lands. These lands were generally smaller in territory and often a different environment than that of their original homelands. Then followed a period of official "assimilation," which meant the forced loss of Indian culture, a disruption of their cultural ecologies, and an imposition of a foreign, Euro-American culture. Thus, in the late 1800s and early 1900s, reservation life and conditions provided a fertile ground for new converts to the Peyote Way. A number of responses within the Indian groups were efforts to come to terms with the new contexts of their lives. One famous cult was the Ghost Dance. But since the Ghost Dance was not repelling the expansion of settlement into tribal lands, and the repressive actions of settlers and soldiers were demoralizing the Amerinds, many individuals were seeking some other spiritual solace. The Peyote Road offered that solace. This was especially apparent in the Oklahoma area and the regions directly to the north. La Barre (1975: 217) quoted an early summary of the movement: "By 1906, a loose intertribal association of local Peyote groups, known as the 'Mescal Bean Eaters,' had spread from Oklahoma in the south to Nebraska in the north. In 1909, in an attempt to accommodate White patterns of religious organization, the 'Mescal Bean Eaters' name was changed into the 'Union Church.'" (Slotkin 1956: 57–58). During the period 1890–1910, the peyote religion diffused into the heartland of the United States, and peyotists brought a complex of plant, ritual, and spiritual renewal to the dispossessed.

The attraction of peyotism, according to Vincenzo Petrulo (1934: 1), was that it held no impossible dream of the imminent extermination of the dominant culture and the return to a pre-Columbian world, such as in the Ghost Dance. Rather it taught the acceptance of a new worldview and an attitude of resignation. It directed Indian thought away from the loss of mundane aspirations to a "loftier spiritual realm which is beyond the reach of the Whites to destroy." It provided a rational psychological and religious adjustment to the changes imposed by the larger culture.

During this period of peyote religious expansion, concerted efforts by the federal and state authorities were organized to stamp out the religion. The 1899 statute (Oklahoma Session Laws, Section 2652) further fueled their zeal. In spite of these attacks, the peyote religion persisted and gained more members. Several attempts at church formation with various names resulted. The year 1918 brought a determined effort by the Bureau of Indian Affairs to have an antipeyote law passed by Congress. To counter this effort, intertribal conferences were held in Oklahoma during the summer to discuss incorporating a Pan-Indian Peyotist Association as a defense measure and to form a church that could be accepted because its organizational structure bore some relationship to American churches of the frontier. With the advice and assistance of James Mooney, studying Kiowa Peyotism at the time, the Native American Church was incorporated in Oklahoma on October 10, 1918 (La Barre 1989: 168–169). Stewart (1987: 224) quoted the Articles of Incorporation as follows:

> The purpose for which this corporation is formed is to foster and promote the religious belief of the several tribes of Indians in the state of Oklahoma, in the Christian religion with the practice of the Peyote Sacrament as commonly understood and used among the adherents of this religion in the several tribes of Indian in the State of Oklahoma, and to teach the Christian religion with morality, sobriety, industry, kindly charity and right living and to cultivate a spirit of self-respect and brotherly union among the members of the Native Race of Indian, including therein the various Indian tribes in the State of Oklahoma.

In the immediate years after 1918, when the first charter was written and recognized by the United States government, a flurry of other charters were established among tribes that had embraced the peyote road. In 1944 the articles of incorporation were amended so that the association became a national organization with the name The Native American Church of the United States. With the spread of Peyotism into Canada in 1955, the name was again changed to The Native American Church of

North America (Stewart 1987: 239–243). In June 23–26, 1960, nearly 200 members of the Native American Church met at Greenwood, South Dakota, to reorganize and to include the Yankton, Rosebud, and Pine Ridge groups under the state charter of the Native American Church of South Dakota.

The proliferation of church charters continued in the succeeding years as less pressure was exerted toward prohibition of peyote use. Following World War II, even though antipeyote laws were on the books, federal agencies like the Bureau of Indian Affairs did not feel inclined to prosecute peyotists. Among the reasons cited was that the peyotists seldom caused problems. In more recent decades, an even more favorable position for the Nature American Church arose when the Drug Abuse Controls Act Amendments implicitly allowed members to carry out their ceremonies. This was further enhanced with an explicit exemption for NAC in the Controlled Substances Act of 1970 under the efforts of Frank Takes Gun, president of NAC in the mid-1950s.

It was during the 1950s that legal issues on state and national levels about possession and distribution of the "narcotic" cactus resurfaced after being carefully worked out in the 1920s and 1930s (Patchen 1991, personal communication). In South Texas, the law was tested and enforced occasionally. This was the case in 1953 when Claudio Cárdenas was taken into custody. The Cárdenas family had long been important *peyoteros*. The Cárdenas and the Sanchez families lived in Los Ojuelos, where along with the Canales family, the first peyote trade had been set up for Amerind pilgrims to South Texas. As soon as Cárdenas was arrested, NAC officials came to his aid with legal council. Allen P. Dale, an Omaha, secured legal help for him. After some legal maneuvering, Cárdenas went before the grand jury in Laredo, where the charges were dismissed (Texas Department of Public Safety 1969–1999), and he gained much personal status among peyotists. In 1967, Texas outlawed peyote possession, most likely in response to the hippie movement (Svehlak 1999, personal communication), and NAC began to negotiate an amendment. Frank Takes Gun, a Crow, took matters on a more direct path. He convinced David Clark, a Navajo, to get arrested for possession so that the law could be tested. Clark won and the law was amended (A. Cárdenas 1994, personal communication). Shortly after this event, Claudio Cárdenas became ill and died not long after. This left Amada Cárdenas, who had publicly sold the peyote medicine to Clark, to act on her own as one of the primary *peyoteros* in the area. Both hispanos and the Indians in Texas were thus involved in the legal fight to protect their rights to use peyote legally.

In the 1970s American Indian prison inmates in Nebraska sought the right to practice their religions in prison; the initial result was the Consent Decree (Grobsmith 1994: 38). The Native American Rights Fund, based in Boulder, Colorado, played an important role in gaining this decision. The wording included the right to have spiritual leaders come to the prison to perform ceremonies and later allowed sweat lodges to be built. However, inmates who were NAC members sought the right to have access to peyote for ceremonies, and their cases were less successful (Grobsmith 1994: 43). In essence, the courts sided with the prison administration that no prisoners would have access to "dangerous drugs" while "behind the wall" (Grobsmith 1994: 48).

In 1990, the pendulum abruptly swung away from religious tolerance once again. In a chilling decision not only to the NAC but also to the religious communities across the country, an Oregon court prohibited peyote use and also implied in the decision that other religious activities might be suitable for prohibition. The Clinton administration sponsored the 1993 Religious Freedom Restoration Act, which restored the integrity of religious activities. A framed copy of this act hangs on an inner wall in the recently built hogan on the Cárdenas' property. However, the Supreme Court nullified this act in their decision on *Boerne, Texas vs. Flores* (case no. 95-2074, June 25, 1997). In 1994, Congress passed a much narrower and less controversial amendment to the Native American Religious Freedom Act of 1978, now designated Public Law 103-344 (Smith and Snake 1996: 149–155). These decisions illuminate the fact that the NAC must constantly be alert to legal decisions that could jeopardize their use of peyote in ceremonies. A number of very competent lawyers, not just members of the tribe, have come to their aide. The NAC believes it is important to defend by law the cultural and religious accommodations made within their culture as a response to the turmoil created in the late nineteenth and the early twentieth centuries.

Secular, or "Profane," Uses of Peyote

Nonritual uses of peyote are documented back to the early contact period, with references in Fray Bernardino de Sahagun (1950–1969) concerning Aztec uses and in Hernandez (1651, vol. 3: 70) among the Chichimeca (cited in La Barre 1975: 23 and Schaefer and Furst 1996: 141). "The peyotl, Sacatensis, causes those Chichimeca devouring it to be able to foresee and to direct things, such as for instance, as whether on the following day the enemy will make an attack upon them, or whether the weather will continue favorable, or to discern who has stolen from them some utensil or anything else; and other things of like nature which the Chichimeca really believe they have found out" (Padre Arlegui, cited in Urbina 1900: 26; Hernandez, 1900b, vol. 3: 22). The Spanish Inquisition was so concerned about peyote use among the Indians that the priests were required to ask those in confession, "Hast thou drunk peyotl, or given it to others in order to discover secrets, to discover where stolen or lost articles were?" (Hernández 1900b, vol. 3: 70). Other references to peyote in works by Hernando Ruiz de Alarcón ([1629] 1984), Jacinto de la Serna (1656), and Francisco Hernández (1651) are cited by Schaefer (1996: 141). The early chroniclers reported some medicinal uses, as well as its use for divination and prophesy (La Barre 1975: 23).

Lumholz (1902, vol. 1: 33; vol. 2: 72–74) said that the Tarahumara peyote was good "to drive off wizards, robbers, and Apaches and to ward off disease." In the plains, the "father peyote" may be carried as a fetish (Kroeber on the Arapaho, cited in La Barre 1975: 25), and the Commanche report in their origin tale of peyote that the Apache told them that the peyote foretold his arrival. In another Commanche tale, peyote permitted one to hear an enemy coming (La Barre 1975: 251). There are reports of peyote and other herbs being used as amulets. Witchcraft is fought with peyote among the Mescalero Apache and Tonkawa (La Barre 1975: 27). Numerous instances of medicinal uses of peyote are noted among the Wichita, Winnebago, Kiowa, and Shawnee (Schultes 1940). Trout (1999: 105) lists 42 different medicinal uses, including antiseptic decoctions, childbirth, cuts and bruises, infections, paralysis, and tuberculosis. Outside of ritual, peyote was consumed by the Huichole of Mexico "to restore energy, stay awake, ward off hunger and pain, and alleviate intestinal disorders" (Schaefer 1996: 167). The button can be cut and applied directly to the skin (McLeary et al. 1960: 247; Schaefer and Furst 1996: 20–21). Some authors published articles that reached a large number of readers. Notable among them was Wier Mitchel (1896), who wrote a paper on the effects of the mescal button [peyote] for physicians in *Lancet* that intrigued the medical profession of England. Havlock Ellis (1897) fired the imaginations of many with his article, provocatively entitled "Mescal, a New Artificial Paradise," which was widely distributed and quoted in America.

Lumholz (1900, 1902) reported that Texas Rangers during the Civil War, when deprived of liquor, would resort to white whiskey, a drink of water and ground-up peyote buttons. Between 1915 and 1918 James Mooney frequently made formal statements to congressional committees to support the noncriminalization of peyote when used in Indian ceremonies, as did others (Slotkin 1956: 55, 132–160; La Barre et al. 1951). Leon Diguet wrote three articles between 1899 and 1911, the most accessible of which is his 1907 article in the *Journal of the Americanists*. Near the turn of the century there was widespread interest in sampling the hallucinogens being discovered among Indians by the anthropologists, by the literati, and by Bohemian types.

Peyote was introduced into the group of drugs taken in nonritual situations in Bohemian circles in Europe toward the end of the nineteenth century. Louis Lewin, who had received the first specimens from America, began publishing on peyote in 1888 with "Uber *Anhalonium lewinii*," published in *Archives der Experimentalen Pathologischen Pharmakologie* (1888, vol. 24: 401–411; cited in Furst and Schaefer 1996: 507). His classic work *Phantastika* was published first in German in 1927 and then in English in 1964. Heinrich Kluever published *Mescal: The Divine Plant and Its Psychological Effects* in 1928. In the first third of the twentieth century, the fascination with the supernatural and the occult led to experimental and then habitual use of hallucinogens to arrive at states of enlightenment. Ravenscroft (1973: 77) reports that Adolf Hitler was introduced to peyote by Ernst Pretzsche, owner of a bookshop in the old quarter of Vienna, the same man who introduced him to ancient astrological and alchemical symbolism of the search for the Holy Grail. References to peyote use in Vienna and Munich drop out after the 1940s.

The bored society types, those interested in the occult and others just interested in trying Indian medicines, seized upon this information. One socialite wrote about her experiences with the peyote as an interesting excursion. Mabel Dodge Luhan (1936: 265), in her book *Movers and Shakers*, describes a peyote meeting conducted in her apartment in 1914 for her friends, guided by a Raymond Harrington, who had been living with the Indians in Oklahoma while doing ethnological research:

> Now Raymond told us about a peculiar ceremony among the Indians he lived with
> that enabled them to pass beyond ordinary consciousness and see things as they are in
> Reality. He said they used an Indian medicine called *peyote* in the ceremony, and sang

all night long. He told us that the Indians that belonged to the Peyote Cult were the most sober and industrious of all, that they made better beadwork and seemed to be able to recover old designs through their use of the stuff and to become imbued with a nobility and a religious fervor greater than those who didn't use it.

Despite careful preparation and construction of the proper setting, the meeting was not successful, and one participant became very ill and almost suicidal (Luhan 1936: 270-278). She reported her anxious moments when she thought they might be investigated by the police for drugs or for holding a "dope party" (Luhan 1936: 276–277). The Lawrencites, part of her crowd in Santa Fe, were reported to sample and regularly use peyote for recreational purposes, as well as other Indian-derived drugs.

By the late 1950s and early 1960s there developed a burgeoning interest, mainly among young people, and not only in the United States, in exploring "inner worlds" and "alternate realities" through the use of psychedelic substances (Schaefer and Furst 1996: 508). Scientists were discovering and studying these substances in the laboratory, as well as in the natural world. Still others found evidence for the long-time use of psychedelics in the historic literature, not the least in the accounts of sixteenth-century Spanish chroniclers in Mexico. The first edition of Weston La Barre's *The Peyote Cult* appeared in 1938. Aldous Huxlely's the *Doors of Perception* appeared in 1954. The Swiss chemist Albert Hofmann unknowingly created a revolution with his discovery of LSD in 1938, and there were numerous articles about its effects during the 1950s. R. Gordon Wasson (1968: 10) "rediscovered the magic mushrooms of Mexico" and reported on them in a 1957 issue of *Life*; and he and his wife, Valentina, published their first book, on the Siberian fly agaric cult, in 1957. *The Peyote Religion* by J. S. Slotkin, a prominent anthropologist who joined the Native American Church and became its secretary, came out in a commercial edition in 1956. Richard Evans Schultes, former director of the Harvard Botanical Museum and the ranking botanical authority on New World hallucinogens, published numerous articles on peyote in the 1930s and 1940s. His study of *ololiuhqui*, the Nahuatl name for the inebriating seeds of the common morning glory, *Rivea coryumbosa* (now *Turbina corymbosa*) (Schultes 1941), which dates to 1941, had 1960s graduate students at the University of Wisconsin talking to Clarissa Kimber about chewing morning glory seeds to get into a state of altered consciousness (Gade 1963, personal communication).

The hippie use of peyote has been reported in many newspaper accounts and was the target of investigation by Texas, Arizona, and New Mexico drug enforcement officers. It was in the 1960s that America lost its innocence, and alternative routes, like the Peyote Way, were attractive to many young people. The public interest in peyote was so high that the National Association of Retail Druggists (1970) published a guide for pharmacists with up-to-date information on hallucinogens. Some reprints of technical articles were made for responsible professionals who encountered demands for information about recreational uses (Marriott and Rachlin 1971: 101). The methods for preparing peyote were described: fresh, dry, powdered, or as a tea or an extract. At this time, peyote was readily available in the Indian schools run by the Bureau of Indian Affairs. It was available to the Indian students, and non-Indian teachers would be offered peyote for their own use (Shafer 1999, personal communication).

Figure 7.6. Number of registered peyote distributors (*peyoteros*) authorized in Texas, 1966–1999.

Numerous investigators appeared before federal and state courts in attempts to keep the United States from criminalizing the use of peyote, to remove sanctions put into law, and to stifle enforcement (La Barre 1975: 225). Unwittingly, Indians and those who investigated them became targets for requests for information and participant observation by people who had lost their "spiritual center." These people became footloose, without direction, and went to areas where peyote was known to exist. Some went to the Huichole in Mexico; others went to South Texas to see for themselves the Indian people's special access to some eternal wisdom. This is still going on (Price 2000, column 4) but in lesser numbers. It has become such a state in Mexico that the previously benignly neglected Huichole are now the brunt of some very negative actions by the *federales*.

There are stories told by ranchers of non-Indians (not the *peyoteros* they had lived with for many years) who would wander on ranchers' property without permission and have a peyote party, often staying several days, "making a mess," and generally making a nuisance of themselves. Some ranchers who had been tolerant of the harvesting of peyote on their lands and an occasional open-air ceremony by Indians on their property became hostile and threw everyone off the land, including the *peyoteros* who had been collecting on the land for years (A. Cárdenas 1999, personal communication).

The interesting jump in the numbers of distributors in the 1970s suggests that many local *peyoteros* and traders were perhaps selling to casual eaters of peyote (Texas Department of Public Safety 1969–1999; figure 7.6). There are persistent rumors that even members of this Texas department ingested peyote and entered the tepee to participate in the NAC ceremonies. Interest in peyote peaked and then declined very swiftly as LSD and later drugs like Ecstasy (MDMA, 3,4 methylenedioxymethamphetamine) delivered a hallucinogenic and related (entactogenic) experiences without the discomfort of the vomiting associated with eating peyote (Grinspoon and Bakalar, 1979: 61). Interest in the nonritual use of peyote declined.

A survey of three underground newspapers, *Ann Arbor Sun*, *Berkeley Barb*, and *Eugene Augur*, for the years 1964 to 1978 did not yield much information in the form of articles on peyote. The plant emphasis was almost entirely on marijuana— how to procure it, use it, and stay free of the law. However, in nursery advertisements there were clues to its availability. Occasionally pictured, along with marijuana, was a stylized, low, rounded cactus that could be taken for a peyote button and a columnar cactus that resembled San Pedro (*Trichocereus pachanol*), an Andean cactus that is also a source of mescaline and is often suggested as a substitute for peyote. It is as if the two images were symbols of the availability of both peyote and San Pedro and thus eliminated the need to spell it out in the text of the advertisement. Curiously, there were more of these advertisements in the *Ann Arbor Sun* (1974), than in the other two West Coast newspapers.

Peyote is available at the beginning of the twenty-first century in head shops— especially in the Netherlands—through the mail from nurseries, and over the Web. Although the control over the peyote trade by the state of Texas is very strong, sources are available. However, we estimate the importance of these sources for nonritual uses to be vastly reduced from the time of the turbulent 1960s and early 1970s (see articles in *High Times* and *Shaman's Drum*). This is an impression since we have as yet not located a good source of data in support of this assessment.

Growth of the Religious Movement Among Non-Indians

In the early 1930s some of the Hispanos began to take part in celebrations with their Indian clients and became adherents of the Peyote religion. Both Claudio and Amada Cárdenas became members of the NAC, as did a number of the other *peyoteros*. The Cárdenas became members of the Board of Trustees of NAC, and since 1957 their home became the "official headquarters in Texas of the Native American Church of North America" (Morgan 1976: 127). It is so today, and most Indians consider Amada Cárdenas the matriarch of the church. There seems to have been little objection from Indians about *peyoteros* presence at peyote ceremonies.

A number of scientific ethnographers and anthropologists became involved through participant observation and were converted to *peyotism*, notably Mooney and Slotkin. A strong stand is now being taken by *peyotists* in Texas and Arizona to encourage non-Indian churches in the two states, at least to give legal status to non-Indian *peyotists*. For example, the Peyote Foundation, begun in 1996 by a small number of *peyotists* in Arizona under the leadership of Leo Mercado, has a Web site and publishes a hard-copy edition of the newsletter under different names: *Peyote Awareness Journal, Peyote, Medicine Journal*, and *Peyote Foundation Journal*. Mercado's story is an interesting example of the difficulties experienced by non-Indian followers of the Peyote Road: He has had all his peyote plants confiscated, has been put in jail, and has had a running battle with the local law enforcement officials that has brought him in and out of court. The ambiguities and contradictions of the body of laws (federal and state) make for a lawyer's paradise, and there has been much litigation in Texas and in Arizona. The bulletin of the Multidisciplinary Association for Psychedelic Studies, *MAPS*, is devoted to raising the money to fund research in the medical uses of psychedelic substances. A recently published article urges that NAC *peyotism* has been useful in the treatment of alcoholism (*MAPS* 1997: 7).

K. Trout (1999), a strong advocate for the Peyote Way for all peoples, recently completed and published an encyclopedic reference book of the cactus, *Trout's Notes on Sacred Cacti*. He graciously gave a copy of the book, which has been an introduction to the non-Indian *peyotists*, to Clarissa Kimber. A quote from one of the contributors reveals one man's response to the cactus:

> The Peyote has never misrepresented itself to me as a god. It is a face of "God." I love it, fear it and respect with religious awe and sincerely venerate it, but I do not worship it anymore than a mainstream Christian worships their communion sacraments, the Bible or their priests. It is living, dynamic vehicle who desires to teach me so that I can learn and grow and it can live in a larger way. (Chien 1999: 69)

Indians speak of the medicine. Although non-Indians call peyote medicine, they also call it teacher or refer to it as the teacher. This may be a subtle difference in the way in which the two groups use peyote in ritual. A few non-Indians have also mentioned that they no longer use the peyote button; they find the memory or the resources within themselves to conjure up the experiences they cherish. It will be interesting to follow this development in peyote use and to see whether it grows substantially or remains in use by a small group of intense advocates.

At times these non-Indian *peyotists* are invited to share in the services of some churches of the Native American Church of North America. Other churches in the NAC are adamantly against their participation at all—opposed to non-Indians having anything to do with their ceremonies. It is possible that this is a response to the idea than peyotism is a pan-Indian cultural tradition, sustaining Indians, and that non-Indians might pollute or in some way vitiate the congregational experience that helps maintain their cultural identity. In the 1990s the use of peyote by non-Indians in a religious context may have increased. No numbers have come to us, but our sense is that some very active people in Texas and Arizona are spearheading the legal and public relations fight for the right to be legal *peyotists*.

Implications

The use of peyote in the Native American Church of North America is not traditional. It is a consequence of the actual disruption of their traditional *genre de vie* by the dominant society that occurred over a period of not more than 200 years, and the church itself is less than 100 years old. Although Amerinds in the United States will say that the peyote road is traditional, for most Indian groups the usage has been around for considerably less than 100 years. The peyote cult reached a poor, socially marginalized people that had little stake in the larger society and who had been consistently denigrated and deprived of their own language, their symbols of integrity, and their own lands. Its importance lies in its role as a symbol of pan-Indianism and its use in a religious context that is communal and group reinforcing. The very fact that some Indians refuse non-Indians even the right to use peyote is evidence of how important the peyote has become as a symbol.

Peyote is a drug of ancient use in Middle America. Within the last few centuries, Amerindians carried it into North America. This diffusion has been reasonably well documented as it pertains to Texas, and the principal actors can be identified in the diffusion of this drug and changes in its meaning as it crossed between cultures. The migration has coincided with a debasement of the drug's use by nontraditional peoples. The Americans who came into contact with the Indians of the Mexican border regions began using it as a substitute for whisky during the Civil War and the decades following. In the twentieth century, some non-Indians began experimenting with the same ingestion practices of Indians and other native peoples to experience hallucinogenic effects, but for a nonreligious experience. Others tried it to gain the superior knowledge that native peoples have about the inner life. As Kent Mathewson (1999b) has said, this is not uncommon worldwide, and "disenchantment and—usually debasement—of sacred substances, especially drugs, is one of the markers of the transition from traditional worlds to global modernity."

Very early, Amerinds recognized that religion and religious practices were being redefined by the conquerors. Deloria and Lytle (1983:162) point out that in the United States freedom of religion is protected by the Constitution but not religious practices. Beginning in the nineteenth century, members of the peyote religion had freedom of religion at the federal level, but they were subject to control of their religious practices, particularly the ingestion of the peyote as a sacrament. A partial explanation may come from the fact that early in the history of the Bureau of Indian Affairs, the agents appointed were often missionaries, not only imbued with zeal for Christianizing the heathen but also advocates of the temperance movement (Marriott and Rachlin 1971: 33). The ecstatic visions of the Indians were interpreted as inebriation. These early bureau men were determined to stamp out these practices, not to mention the efforts of several determined women with a cause.

North of the Rio Grande, the ritual use of peyote varies in fine detail from group to group, a reflection of the changes in ceremonies that come with the migration of peoples and the diffusion of ceremonial practices between them over the twentieth century. There has grown up a usage among anthropologists of identifying several gross variant types: The most basic one is considered to be the Plains type, identified by Mooney (1898, 1905) in his work among the Kiowa, and Lipan Apache, to which the ritual described above belongs. The Southwestern Pueblo and the Navajo peoples have a variant type. The Washo of Nevada took on the Plains type, but made modifications of their own. Since each roadman has much authority to make changes in the ceremony, the possibilities for innovation and change are great and to be expected. However, the eating of peyote is the central fact of the peyote cult, and the sacred plant is referred to as "the medicine" (Gilmore 1919: 165). The memory of the early charismatic leaders has been a strong force for conservatism in ritual.

As tribal and traditional societies come into direct and abrasive contact with more modern and, usually, colonial societies, the use of the drugs, especially the psychoactive ones, can lose their religious connotations. Peyotism was already established in Texas and Oklahoma by the time of the 1890s Ghost Dance (Stewart 1972). It is not surprising that as the Sun Dance cult declined in effectiveness as a Plains Indian rite, peyote use began an explosive diffusion associated with several charismatic individuals (La Barre 1975: 261). The trade in the drug becomes necessary as traditional people migrate beyond the native region of the drug plant or as some peoples acquire the ritual use through its migration. When the trade becomes obvious to those in authority who do not sanction the drug use, efforts to control the trade begin. Laws are passed to control the use, to criminalize the use and trade, and to make difficult the possession of the drugs. Such laws may make the illegal use more enticing to rebellious youths.

Native Americans have had a strong interest in freedom of religion. In large part this position was based on the fact that Euro-American colonization introduced religions that were unyielding in their desire to convert all the people encountered in the places they invaded. Indigenous belief systems were quite different from organized churches of the Europeans. In North America, native religions often made plant and animals central to the religious experience and pantheon. Among these were psychotropic plants that gave participants vehicles with which to see visions or complete rites of passage or provided the medicine needed to regain physical and mental health, whether for an individual or a group. In the North American area, religious freedom was sharply curtailed for indigenous belief systems after the Spaniards and northern Europeans arrived. As a result, native practitioners retreated to isolated areas or took on a cloak of secrecy to maintain their traditional, individual, and collective spiritual practices. Other groups integrated native practices with the dominant church as a way to avoid being discriminated against and to gain credibility. These syncretic religions took many forms. In some cases, Catholicism took on elements of the native beliefs among the Indians of the Andes. In others, new religions were based on old customs but modified by the acquisition of Catholic or Protestant behaviors or elements, as in the NAC.

The Indians know that collecting of peyote is a problem, but there is no agreement about how to solve the biotic degradation. The Indians no longer use moral arguments against the cultivation of peyote, as they did 30 years ago (Morgan 1976: 118), nor do they say out loud that a divine plant should be harvested from God's garden. Efforts to grow peyote commercially have been successful, and it is legal to do so in Arizona but not in Texas. The time may come when peyote is a plantation crop; however, we suggest that it will never be an important one.

Most mind-altering drugs used around the world are and were derived from plants. Cultural anthropologists, ethnobiologists, and economic botanists have long been involved in documenting the uses and meanings associated by traditional societies with these drugs. More recently, geographers have become interested in looking at the distribution of different psychoactive drugs and the migration of these plants and their uses over time and space. The use of the peyote button as a sacrament by members in the NAC has led us to think of it not only as a reverent act but also as partaking of the sacred because its use is for reaching the deity through a hallucinogenic experience. It is considered medicine; it is teacher. It is sacred because it is part of the theology of the church members, however imperfectly expressed by them. Not only is the content sacred, so is the experience. In the profane use of the plant, the physiological experience is not directed toward reaching the deity but to the hallucinogenic experience in itself. This is a more mundane, even irreverent act. Therefore, the sacred peyote is a "denotation of an objective attribute, not merely a denotation of subjective appraisal" (J. Smith 1999: 1). This is why we consider that "sacred" and "profane" are indeed useful terms in discussing peyote as it is used today in North America.

Acknowledgments   Claudio Cárdenas, longtime *peyotero,* living most of his life in Mirando City, Texas. Provided space in the grounds about the home for tepee and hogan in which Native Americans regularly conduct NAC ceremonies.

Walter B. Echo-Hawk, Pawnee lawyer, staff attorney for the Native American Rights Fund, specializing in First Amendment Rights for Native Peoples.

Daniel W. Gade, Latin Americanist, cultural geographer, Professor Emeritus in geography, University of Vermont.

Jerry D. Patchen, Attorney at Law, has represented Native American Church for over 20 years. He is a member of the Arapaho Chapter of the Native American Church of Oklahoma and an officer in the Native American Church of the United States.

Losee Peloquin, Narcotics Section, Texas Department of Public Safety, has consistently provided archival information to the authors since she assumed responsibility in 2000.

Amada Sanchez Cárdenas, wife of Claudio Cárdenas, born in 1904 in Los Ouelos, Texas. Revered as the matriarch of the NAC. She has been a long-time friend of Darrel McDonald.

Richard Shafer, Ph.D., Associate Professor of Journalism, North Dakota State University North Forks. A keen observer of social life in western America, he taught school in Utah and has reported on Native American life in the 1950s and 1960s. He has been a Fulbright Scholar in the Philippines and in Uzbekistan.

Tracie Svehlak, Director of Controlled Substances Registration, Texas Department of Public Safety, Austin.

Frank Takes-Gun, Crow, saved several lives as leader of the Native American Church. Under his leadership, the office has become more active politically, interacting at both the state and federal levels.

References

Archives

Microfilm records of applications by peyote distributors, employees of distributors, and copies of their sales slips as provided for by the Narcotics Service, Controlled Substance Registration, Texas Department of Public Safety (DPS) Austin, Texas.

Publications

Anderson, E. F. 1969. "The Biogeography, Ecology, and Taxonomy of *Lophophora* (Cactaceae)," *Brittonia* 21(4): 299–310.

———. 1995. "The 'Peyote Gardens' of South Texas: A Conservation Crisis." *Cactus and Succulent Society Journal* 67:67–73.

———. 1996. *Peyote, the Divine Cactus,* 2nd edition. University of Arizona Press.

Ann Arbor (Michigan) Sun, 1974, April 19–May 33. Also Microfilm Reels 9, 32, 41, 70. Underground Newspaper Collection. Produced by Micro-Photo Division Bell and Howell and the Underground Press Syndicate.

Beals, Ralph L. 1932. *The Comparative Ethnology of Northern Mexico Before 1750. Ibero-Americana*, no.2. Berkeley: University of California Press.

Berkeley (California) Barb, 1964–1978. Microfilm Reels 1, 2, 5, 15, 42, 71, 92 Underground Newspaper Collection. Produced by Micro-Photo Division Bell and Howell and the Underground Press Syndicate.

Berlandier, J. L. 1980. *Journey to Mexico During the Years 1826 to 1834.* 2 vols. Translated by S. M. Ohlendorf, J. M. Bigelow, and M. M. Standifer. Introduction by C. H. Muller. Botanical Notes by C. H. Muller and K. K. Muller. Austin: The Texas State Historical Association in Cooperation with the Center for Studies in Texas History, University of Texas at Austin.

Cárdenas, A. 1994. Personal communication to Darrel McDonald, Mirando City, TX.

Chien, C. 1999. "The Peyote 'Crisis' and Some Suggestions." In Trout and Friends, 1999. (eds.), *Trout's Notes on Sacred Cacti, Botany, Chemistry, Cultivation & Utilization (Including Notes on Some Other Succulents)*, 2nd ed. rev., pp. 67–70. Austin, TX: Better Days Publication.

Curtis's Botanical Magazine. 1847. Figure 8.1, plate 4296. Beautiful illustration, reprinted in Anderson 1996.

de la Serna, J. 1656. Cited in Schaefer and Furst; see D. G. Brinton, "Nagualism," *American Philosophical Society Proceedings,* 1894, vol. 33, p. 28.

Deloria, V., Jr., and C. M. Lytle. 1983. *American Indians, American Justice.* Austin: University of Texas Press, Austin, TX.

Diguet, L. 1907. "Le 'Peyote" et son usage rituel chez les Indiens de Nayarit." *Journal de la Société des Américanists de Paris* 4: 21-29.

Echo Hawk, W. B. 1990. Personal communication to Darrel McDonald, Mirando City, TX.

Ellis, H. 1897. "A Note on the Phenomenon of Mescal Intoxication." *The Lancet* 75(1): 1540–1542.

———. 1989. "Mescal, A New Artificial Paradise," pp. 537–548. Washington, DC: *Annual Report of the Smithsonian Institution.*

Eugene Augar. 1970, Jan–Dec. Microfilm Reels N/427, reel 54, title 2. Underground Newspaper Collection. Produced by Micro-Photo Division Bell and Howell and the Underground Press Syndicate.

Fikes, J. C. (ed.). 1996. *Reuben Snake, Your Humble Servant: Indian Visionary and Activist.* As told to J. C. Fikes. Foreword by J. Botsford. Afterword by W. Echo-Hawk. Santa Fe, NM: Clear Light Publishers.

Furst, P. T. 1989. "Review of *Peyote Religion: A History*, by Omer C. Stewart." *American Anthropologist* 16(2): 386–387.

Gade, D. 1963. Personal communication to Clarissa Kimber, Madison, WI.

Gilmore, M. R. 1919. "The Mescal Society Among the Omaha Indians." *Nebraska State Historical Society* 19: 163–167.

Gottlieb, A. 1997. *Peyote and Other Psychoactive Cacti.* Berkeley, CA: Ronin Publishing.

Grinspoon, L., and J. B. Bakalar. 1979. *Psychedelic Drugs Reconsidered.* New York: Basic Books.

Grobsmith, E. S. 1994. *Indians in Prison: Incarcerated Native Americans in Nebraska.* Lincoln: University of Nebraska Press.

Hernández, F. 1651. *Nova Plantarum, Animalium et Mineralium Mexicanorum Historia . . .* Rome: B. Deuersini et Z. Masotti.

———. 1790. *De Historia Plantarum Novae Hispania Opera cum Editalum Inedita ad Autographi Fidem et Integratem Expressa.* Madrid: Imp. Ibarra Herendum. Cited in Stewart.

———. 1900a. "De Historia Plantarum Novae Hispaniae." *Anales del Instituto Médico Nacional* 4(11): 204. Reprint of 1790.

———. 1900b. *Historia 1577. Rerum Medicarum Novae, Mineralium Mexicana Norum Historia.* Rome: Mascardi. Reprint of 1651. Cited in Stewart.

High Times. Individual issues as cited. Furnished by Martin Terry and purchased by Clarissa Kimber.

Hollister, L. E., and A. M. Martman. 1962. "Mescaline, LSD, and Psilocybin Comparison of Clinical Syndrome Effects on Color Perception and Biochemical Measures." *Comprehensive Psychiatry* 3(4): 235–241.

Hollister, L. E., and B. M. Sjoberg. 1964. "Clinical Syndromes and Biochemical Alterations Following Mescaline, Lysergic Acid Diethylamide, Psilocybin, and a Combination of the Three Psychotomimetric Drugs." *Comprehensive Psychiatry* 5: 170–178.

Huxley, A. 1954. *The Doors of Perception.* New York: Harper.

Jonnes, J. 1996. *Hep-cats, Narcs, and Pipe Dreams: a History of America's Romance with Illegal Drugs.* Baltimore: Johns Hopkins University Press.

Kluever, H. 1928. *Mescal: the Divine Plant and Its Psychological Effects.* London: Kegan, Paul, Trench, Trubner.

La Barre, W. 1938. *The Peyote Cult.* Yale University Publications in Anthropology, no. 19. London: Oxford University Press.

———. 1975. *The Peyote Cult,* 44th ed. Hamden, CT: Anchor books, Shoe String Press.

———. 1989. *The Peyote Cult,* 5th ed. Norman: University of Oklahoma Press.

La Barre, W., D. P. McAllester, J. S. Slotkin, O. C. Stewart, and S. Tax. 1951. "Statement on Peyote." *Science* 114(2970): 529–583.

Lewin, L. 1927. *Phantastika—Die Betaubenden and erregenden Genussmittel.* Berlin: G. Stilke.

———. [1927] 1964. *Phantastica—Na.* English translation. London: Routledge & Kegan Paul.

———. 1988. "Über *Anhalonium lewinii.*" *Archiv der Experimentalen Pathologischen Pharmakologie* 24: 401–411.

Light, A. and J. M. Smith. 1998. *Philosophies of Place: Philosophy and Geography III.* Lanham, MD; Boulder, CO; New York; Oxford: Rowman & Littlefield.

Luhan, M. D. 1936. *Movers and Shakers,* Vol. 3. *Intimate Memories*, pp. 265–279. New York: Harcourt, Brace.

Lumholz, C. G. 1900. *Symbolism of the Huichol Indians.* New York: American Museum of Natural History.

———. 1902. *Unknown Mexico,* 2 vols. New York: Scribner's.

MAPS. Bulletin of the Multidisciplinary Association for Psychedelic Studies. 2121 Commonwealth Ave., Charlotte, NC 28205.

Marriott, A., and C. K. Rachlin. 1971. *Peyote.* New York: Crowell.

Mathewson, K. 1999a. "Cultural Landscape and Ecology II: Regions, Retrospects, Revivals." *Progress in Human Geography* 23(2): 267–281.

———.1999b. "Double Agents: Illicit Drugs, Cultural Identities, Indigenous Moral Geographies." Unpublished manuscript.

———.1999c. "Sacred to Profane: Illicit Drugs in Traditional Cultures and Landscapes." Unpublished manuscript.

McLeary, J. A., P. B. Sypherd, and D. L. Walkington. 1960. "Antibiotic Activity of an Extract of Peyote *Lophophora Williamsii* (Lemaire) Coulter." *Economic Botany* 14: 247–249.

Meinig, D. M. 1993. *The Shaping of America,* vol. 2. New Haven, CT: Yale University Press.

Mitchell, S. W. 1896. "The Effects of *Anhalonium lewinii* (The Mescal Button)." *Lancet* 2: 1625–1628.

Mooney, J. 1892. "A Kiowa Mescal Rattle." *American Anthropologist* 5: 64–65.

———. 1896. "The Mescal Plant and Ceremony." *Therapeutic Gazette*, 3rd series, 12: 7–11.

———. 1898. "Calendar History of the Kiowa Indian." *Annual Report, Bureau of American Ethnology* 17(1): 129–444.

———. 1907. "Peyote." In F. W. Hodge, ed., *Handbook of American Indians North of Mexico, 1905–1910,* p. 237. Washington, DC: Bureau of American Ethnology, Bulletin 30, 2: 237. Reprinted New York: Rowman & Littlefield, 1971.

Morgan, G. R. 1976. "Man. Plants, and Religion: Peyote Trade on the Mustang Plains of Texas." Ph.D. thesis, Department of Geography, University of Colorado, Boulder.

———. 1983. "Hispano-Indian Trade of an Indian Ceremonial Plant Peyote (*Lophophora williamsii*), on the Mustang Plains of Texas." *Journal of Ethnopharmacology* 9: 319–321.

National Association of Retail Druggists. 1970. *A Community Challenge and Opportunity for You—The Pharmacist.* Bethesda, MD: National Institutes for Mental Health.

Opler, M. E. 1936. "The Influence of Aboriginal Patterns and White Contact on a Recently Introduced Ceremony, the Mescalero Peyote Rite." *Journal of Amercan Folk-lore* 49: 143–166.

———. 1938. "The Use of Peyote by the Carrizo and Lipan Apache Tribes." *American Anthropologist* 40(2): 271–285.

Patchen, J. 1991. Personal communication to Darrel McDonald.

Peloquin, L. 2000. Telephone conversation with Clarissa Kimber, October 21, followed by a FAX.

Petrullo, V. 1934. *The Diabolic Root: A Study of Peyotism, the New Indian Religion Among the Delaware.* Philadelphia: University of Pennsylvania Press.

Peyote Awareness Journal. Official Publication of the Peyote Foundation, P.O. Box 778, Kearny, AZ 85237.

Price, N. 2000. "Tinseltown and Tiny Village Both Bank on *The Mexican.*" *The Bryan-College Station Eagle,* June 11, pp. B1, B5.

Public Law No. 33. 1897. United States Act, prohibit the sale of intoxicating drinks to Indians and providing penalties therefor and for other purposes. Cited in Marriott and Rachlin 1971.

Public Law No. 103-344. 1994. United States Amendment to the Native American Religious Freedom Act of 1978, making it legal at the federal level for Native Americans to possess, transport, and use peyote in the cause of traditional religious ceremonies.

Ravenscroft, T. 1973. *The Spear of Destiny.* York Beach, ME: Samuel Weiser.

Rech, R. H., H. A. Tilson, and W. J. Marquis. 1975. "Adaptive Changes in Behavior After Repeated Administration of Various Psychoactive Drugs." In A. Mandell, ed., *Neurological Mechanisms of Adaptation and Behavior.* Vol. 13. *Advance in Biochemical Psychopharmacology,* pp. 263–286.

Rouhier, A. 1927. *La Plante qui fait les yeux émerveilles, le peyotl (Echinocactus williamsii Lem).* Paris: Gaston Dloin.

Ruiz de Alarcón, H. [1629] 1984. "The Treatise on the Heathen Superstitions That Today Live Among the Indians Native to this Narcotic Mescal Button of the Indians" New Spain, 1629. Translated and edited by J. R. Andrews and R. Hassig. Tulsa: University of Oklahoma Press.

Sahagún, B. de. 1950–1969. *Florentine Codex: General History of the Things of New Spain.* In A. J.O Anderson and C. E. Dibble, trans. (from Aztec to English). Monographs of the School of American Research, no. 14, part 7VII, 1969. Santa Fe, NM: School of American Research and the University of Utah.

Schaefer, S. B. 1996. "The Crossing of the Souls: Peyote, Perception, and Meaning Among the Huichol Indians." In S. B. Schaefer and P. T. Furst, eds., *People of the Peyote*, pp. 138–168. Albuquerque: University of New Mexico Press.

Schaefer, S. B., and P. T. Furst, eds. 1996. *People of the Peyote*. Albuquerque: University of New Mexico Press.

Schultes, R. E. 1938. "The Appeal of Peyote (*Lophophora willliamsii*) as a Medicine." *American Anthropologist* 40: 698–715.

———. 1940. "The Aboriginal Therapeutic Uses of *Lophophora williamsii*." *Cactus and Succulent Journal* 12: 177–181.

———. 1941. *A Contribution to Our Knowledge of* Rivea eoymbosa, *the Narcotic* Ololuique *of the Aztecs*. Cambridge, MA: Harvard Botanical Museum.

———. 1963. "The Botanical Sources of the New World Narcotics." *Psychedelic Review* 1: 145–166.

———. 1969. "Hallucinogens of Plant Origin." *Science* 163: 245–254.

———. 1972. "An Overview of Hallucinogens in the Western Hemisphere," pp. 3–54. In P. T. Furst, eds., *Flesh of the Gods: The Ritual Use of Hallucinogens*. New York: Praeger.

Schultes, R. E., and A. Hofmann. 1973. *The Botany and Chemistry of Hallucinogens*. Springfield, IL: Charles C. Thomas.

———. 1979. *Plants of the Gods*. New York: McGraw-Hill.

———. 1992. *Plants of the Gods,* 2nd ed. New York: McGraw-Hill.

Shafer, R. 1999. Personal communication to Clarissa Kimber in North Fork, ND.

Shaman's Drum. Various issues. Cross-cultural Shamanism Network, Berkeley, CA.

Siskin, E. E. 1983. *Washo Shamans and Peyotists: Religious Conflict in an American Indian Tribe*. Salt Lake City: University of Utah Press.

Skye, D. 1997. "Peyote Visions." *High Times*, July, pp.10–11.

Slotkin, J. S. 1955. "Peyotism, 1521–1891." *American Anthropologists* 57: 202–230.

———. 1956. *The Peyote Religion: A Study in Indian-White Relations*. Glenco, IL: Free Press.

Smith, H., and R. Snake, eds. 1996. *The Triumph of the Native American Church*. Santa Fe, NM: Clearlight Publishers.

Smith, J. 1999. Letter to Clarissa Kimber, August 2.

Spindler, G. D. 1952. "Personality and Peyotism in Menomini Indian Acculturation." *Psychiatry* 15: 151–159.

Stafford, P. 1992. "Peyote, Mescaline, and San Pedro." In *Psychedelics Encyclopedia,* 3rd ed., pp. 103–155. Berkeley, CA: Ronin Publishing.

Stewart, O. C. 1934. "The Northern Paiute Bands." *University of California Anthropological Records* 21: 127–149.

———. 1956. "Peyote and Colorado's Inquisition Law." Colorado Quarterly 5: 79–90.

———. 1972. "The Peyote Religion and the Ghost Dance." *Indian Heritage* 5(4): 27–30.

———. 1973. "Anthropologists as Expert Witnesses for Indians: Claims and Peyote Cases." In J. Officer, ed., *Anthropology and the American Indian*, pp. 35–42. San Francisco: Indian Historical Press.

———. 1974. "Origin of the Peyote Religion in the United States." *Plains Anthropologist* 19(65): 211–223.

———. 1977. "Ute Peyotism." *University of Colorado Studies Series in Anthropology,* no. 1, pp. 1–42.

———. 1987. *Peyote Religion: A History*. Norman: University of Oklahoma Press.

Svehlak, T. 1999. Director of Controlled Substances Registration, Texas Department of Public Safety, Austin. Personal communication to Clarissa Kimber, March 10.

Texas Department of Public Safety. 1969–1999. File on peyote, with manuscript and fugitive materials. Narcotics Service, Controlled Substances Registration, Austin.

Trout, K. (pseudonym). 1999. *Trout's Notes on Sacred Cacti: Botany, Chemistry, Cultivation & Utilization (Including Notes on Some Other Succulents*, 2nd ed. Austin, TX: Better Day's Publishing.

Urbina, M. 1900. *El Peyote y el Ololiuhqui.* Mexico. Cited in Rouhier 1927:10.

Wasson, R. G. 1957. "Seeking the Magic Mushroom." *Life* 42(19): 100.

———. 1968. *Soma: The Divine Mushroom of Immortality.* New York: Harcourt, Brace & World.

Wasson, V. P., and R. G. Wasson. 1957. *Mushrooms, Russia, and History,* 2 vols. New York: Pantheon.

Web sites

www.erowid.org

8

Desert Traffic
The Dynamics of the Drug Trade in Northwestern Mexico

Eric P. Perramond

The semiarid expanses of northern Mexico have long been a haven for drug trafficking and shipment into the southwestern United States. During the past 3 decades, a more specialized and dedicated drug industry has used the long U.S.-Mexican border to move illicit narcotics. Northern Mexico is not a heavily indigenous zone, and yet some native populations have been adversely affected by this recent industry, and not just a few have taken a role in it.

Two states in northern Mexico that still have indigenous peoples are Sonora and Chihuahua. Both of these semiarid states are more sparsely populated than the rest of Mexico, yet both share a long, expansive border with the United States. Thus, neither state has escaped the activities of the drug industry, and some of the major drug cartels are located in this region (figure 8.1), the largest in urban areas such as Ciudad Juarez in the state of Chihuahua and Culiacán in the state of Sinaloa. Although these urban areas are the economic and logistical centers of two large cartels, an aspect frequently ignored in the literature, and certainly in policy circles, is the variety of scales of production in this industry.

Aside from these giant cartels, drug cultivation, production, and transportation are also common at lesser scales, and the difficulties and dangers associated with drug production and trafficking extend to these small farmers. Small plots of marijuana (*Cannabis sativa*) and poppies (*Papaver somniferum*) dot the northern Mexican landscape, especially in the foothills and high peaks of the Sierra Madre. Most of the poppy production lies further south, in the states of Michoacan, Guerrero, and Oaxaca. Marijuana (*Cannabis*) is by far the more common of the two illicit crops grown in Mexico, partly because of its longer history of cultivation in the country's mountainous regions and partly because of its greater ease of integration into agriculture. Poppy fields are a lot harder to hide, both from neighbors and from

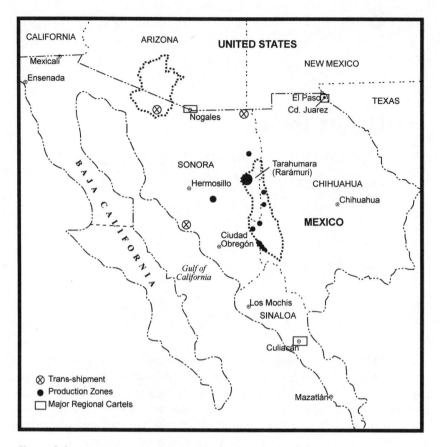

Figure 8.1. Physical geography of northwestern Mexico.

more interested authorities. Marijuana is also more easily intercropped with more common agricultural crops. Intercropping is the practice of growing two or more crops in the same field or parcel of land, and it is common when farmers need to maximize total output per unit of area (Wilken 1987: 248). I have seen marijuana integrated with corn, bean, squash, sunflower, and tomato plants. Poppies, on the other hand, do not fare well in competition with these other food crops. Every single poppy field I saw in 1996 and 1997 was growing on its own and not intercropped with more common food crops. As of 1995, Mexico produced only about 2.4 percent of the world's refined opium, most of it as heroin (Booth 1996: 324). More recent figures also suggest that the total cultivated area given over to opiates has shrunk dramatically, from 5,500 hectares in 1990 to 3,600 in 1999 (ODCCP 2000: 26). If these data are to be believed, Mexico stands in sharp contrast to Guatemala and Colombia, where the cultivation area of opiates increased. It should be noted, however, that claims of seizures and eradication from Mexico's General Attorney's Office may be inflated. According to the latest figures, some 14,050 hectares of opiates were eradicated between January and November 1999 (ODCCP 2000).

Affected Peoples

Unlike most of the regions discussed in this volume, the states of Sonora and Chihuahua in Mexico are not a hub of indigenous populations, the great majority of whom have largely been integrated into the wider *mestizo* culture of the region. Two persistent native groups, however, are subject to effects of narcotrafficking. The Tarahumara, or the Rarámuri, as they call themselves, inhabit the high Sierra Madre Occidental range that runs between the states of Sonora and Chihuahua (figure 8.1). The other group discussed here, the Tohono O'odham (commonly referred to as the Papago), also live in a border region between Arizona in the United States, where the majority of them live, and the state of Sonora. These two indigenous groups are subject to quite different sectors of the drug economy in their respective regions. The term *sector* is used rather than *industry*, as it is more precise and specific. There are indeed complex sectors within the industry of narco-trafficking: regions and specialists who focus on production, shipment, government monitoring, or enforcing cartel boundaries. The Tohono are much more affected (and occasionally involved) with the trafficking and transshipment of narcotics, rather than being directly involved in the production (cultivation) of illicit goods. The Rarámuri, on the other hand, play a direct role in small-scale production of illicit goods without much of a hand in the transportation aspects of narco-trafficking. Because of their geographic situations, however, they are both implicated in this complex and sometimes dangerous industry. The costs of marijuana production and transshipment, the degree to which these peoples are involved, and the intertwining of economic interests in each region are quite distinct. The forms of resistance to the drug industry by each group are also distinctive.

The Rarámuri: Cultivation in the Sierra Madres

The Tarahumara, or the Rarámuri, as they call themselves (and used hereafter), occupy the foothills and high mountains of the Sierra Madre Occidental range bordering Chihuahua and Sonora. The vast majority of this group resides on the Chihuahuan side, and yet the effects of the drug trade are both familiar and deeply felt on both sides of these Mexican state borders. Drug trafficking has been common in the region for decades, as landing strips located throughout the mountainous ranges have been used by large-scale operations since the 1960s. It is the lesser drug traffickers, ironically, who have created the greater problems for the Rarámuri.

The reasons for growing illicit crops in the Sierra Madres are economic. One kilo of marijuana, for example, is worth about $280 (in 2002). This is about 100 to 200 times more than similar corn or wheat harvests are worth in the region. The temptation is clear for native growers, but with increased surveillance and enforcement by Mexican authorities, so are the consequences. For those not directly cultivating these crops, there is still the attraction of working in the fields, and a poppy cultivator can make the equivalent of $40–$50 in 1 day, although usually not in cash. More frequently, payment is in kind with alcohol, foodstuffs, or nonperishable items (axes, tools, and other hardware). The level of direct participation by

Table 8.1. Rarámuri *Cannabis* Field Sizes and Yields

Cultivator	Size of Cannabis Plot (ha)	Yield (kg)
1	.8	6
2	1.4	9.5
3	.4	2.5
4	.5	3.0
5	.5	3.5
6	.25	2.0

Source: Author's fieldnotes, v. 7.

the Rarámuri, however, is minor. Most of these people are involved or forced into production ventures by traffickers in the region, and they typically do not plant more than a hectare of *Cannabis* or *Papaver*. Conditions for growing *Cannabis* are also climatically poor in the Sierra Madre, and a young crop must be constantly supervised, and watered. Table 8.1 provides a general idea of the less successful crops of *Cannabis* at high elevations, in plots I observed, than of other marijuana yields in Mexico (Drake [1979] 1986). The size of the plots was determined by direct measurement, whereas the yields were provided by the field owners and should be interpreted as estimates only.

As seen in the data, the yields of marijuana plots in the sample provided are notably poor (figure 8.2). There are two reasons for this. First, the production of marijuana is difficult at high elevations, when farmers fight off late spring frosts or when locust plagues are common in the early fall. Second, and more important, when production is forced onto the Rarámuri, they are more preoccupied with their food crops than with their illicit ones. This is also a way to quietly resist the local or regional traffickers: by refusing to care for the crop properly. Although this is a dangerous strategy for native farmers, as they may then be subjected to punishment, it is one that is commonly used because traffickers may have a difficult time checking on remote drug fields throughout the year. Some Rarámuri, although perhaps reluctant to grow poppies or marijuana, may gladly join the practice over the long run for the extra income or goods that traffickers may provide. As one local told me:

> At first, they didn't give me a choice, you know . . . they told me to grow it, or they would harm my family or take away my land. They know the local police, so it was no good to report it. After I grew one crop of marijuana [yerba buena was the preferred term used during interviews with the Raramuri], I had over 30 kg of food on my doorstep the next morning and some Buchanan's whiskey, which is really expensive. . . . I'd never had it before. So I keep growing it, it helps my family, and the police haven't bothered me yet. Source: Author's fieldnotes, v. 8

The environmental conditions in the Sierra Madre also preclude extensive areas of poppy cultivation. Only a small window of opportunity exists, between late April and September, for possible production. Late winter frosts and early fall cold wind patterns prevent more widespread cultivation, and certainly at no higher than 1,500

Figure 8.2. Chihuahua landscape.

meters in elevation. Marijuana, however, will thrive in most locations if properly cared for. The main limiting factor for the cultivation of *Cannabis*, aside from non-cultivation by the Rarámuri, is water. Indeed, a dozen of the fields (out of the 53 visited) I saw in November 1996 were being watered by hand from water sources at least 5 kilometers away from the fields.

The effects of drug production and trafficking on the Tarahumara stem more from local, microscale efforts of production than from the larger operations that use these mountains for shipment or storage. Small-time *mafiosos* (gangsters) from the region, especially in Chihuahua, are directly influential (figure 8.3). These same infamous characters may also be involved with illegal logging operations in the Sierra Madre, a common companion in illicit affairs in this mountainous region. *Corridos*, popular folk songs, in Sonora and Chihuahua mention by name some of the more influential and ruthless mafiosos of the Sierra Madre.

The Tohono: Desert Crossroads

The Tohono O'odham, whose tribal name literally translates as the "Desert People," have experienced a rather unique sector of the international drug-trafficking economy. The Tohono's main reservation stretches over 200 miles along the Arizona-Sonora border. There are four separate reservation areas for the group, totaling 2,854,881 acres. The main section, which appears in figure 8.1, contains the bulk of this land and stretches across the international boundary into Mexico (Nabhan

Figure 8.3. Drug trafficking in Chihuahua.

1982). The challenge for the Tohono (Papago) is the transportation of illicit narcotics across and around their ancestral lands of the Sonoran Desert. The scale of
trafficking witnessed by the Papago is much smaller than the more urban and organized cartel passages in Ciudad Juarez (Chihuahua) or in Tijuana (Baja California Norte). Much of what passes overland or in dry river channels on the Papago
reservation lands is packed on domesticated livestock or carried by migrant couriers. The areas of activity involved in trafficking may appear innocuous indeed,
sometimes passing for simple livestock corrals, and the frequent stacking of marijuana packages in corrals is not an uncommon sight. Among those Tohono con-
tacted in July 1997, eight informants were especially helpful and knowledgeable
about the problems and opportunities of trafficking within their tribal lands. Six of
the eight informants had been directly involved in drug smuggling in the past, although all but one were inactive at the time I interviewed them. Even those not involved, however, had family members still participating. Those eight informants
put me in touch with eight smugglers on Tohono lands, or near them, and these data
appear in table 8.2. Names were neither asked for nor given by these informants.
Discussions were frank, once the informants were assured (and felt assured) that
their responses were confidential and that I had no links to either the U.S. or Mexican government.

Table 8.2 suggests the relative sizes and importance of transshipment sites in
Tohono country, although this was not a random sample of trafficking depots in the
region. The informants provided the figures.

Table 8.2. Transshipment Points in Tohono O'odham Lands

Site	Amount Transferred (kg)	Permanent? (Yes/No)[b]	Rotation of site (Days)
1	100	N	2
2	50	Y	10
3	30/2–5[a]	Y	5
4	60/1–3	N	3
5	40	Y	6–7
6	110	N	daily
7	10	Y	14
8	15	Y	5

[a]Denotes small shipments of heroin.

[b]Permanent sites or structures used by the smuggler.

Clearly, the amounts of narcotics transferred at each site vary, although certain trends are evident if these figures are at all indicative of more widespread practices. The largest transfer points (in terms of weight) seem to be the most ephemeral; rarely are they permanent sites used by traffickers and are most commonly areas rented on a short-term basis by users. The rotation basis for these larger shipment and storage points is also more frequent.

However, the smallest sites are usually safer to keep as permanent locations for transshipment, and they are also used for longer periods of time before being rotated out of a transshipment location schedule. The key to survival for these smaller smugglers is the flexibility in locations for transfer and the timely rotation of sites, so that there is no predictable pattern of use. All the informants I consulted revealed that their particular site, listed in table 8.2, was only one of a dozen points they commonly use for transferring illicit goods to other purchasers or smugglers. They are, however, the last points in Mexico before crossing the border into Arizona.

With sparse fencing in Tohono lands stretching across the international border, these areas are favorable to the smaller operations. The units of transportation for smuggling of these goods into the United States are likely to be small. Pack animals are especially common for the crossings in this region, and a train of mules (10–12) can move 500–600 kilograms of goods in about 2 days' time. Most of this travel is done at night, following small canyon washes or deeper gullies to elude detection. The animals are then unburdened of their loads near ranches or along rural highways in southern or southeastern Arizona for further transportation. The latter is trickier to coordinate because constant communication is necessary between the packers (*burreros*) and the truckers arranging for pickup, so this option is only open to those with a larger scale of operations.

The distinguishing characteristic of drug trafficking on Tohono lands is its discretion. Large amounts of narcotics, up to 5 metric tons (5,000 kilograms), may be on Tohono lands at any given time. The movement of this mass of goods, on the other hand, is swift. Shipments spend no more than a day on the native lands before crossing into Arizona. The biggest problem for the Tohono, in their opinion, is the indiscriminate police tactics used by both federal and state authorities in Sonora, Mexico. Almost all of the transfer points on Tohono lands occur within the Mexican state's boundaries. Similar to the parallel activity of trafficking and logging in the Sierra Madres, as well as what the Rarámuri experience, the Tohono witness a great amount of collusion between drug traffickers and human trafficking by *coyotes*, a term given to those who smuggle illegal immigrants across the Mexican-U.S. border. Many of the larger migrant smuggling operations are also involved in small-scale drug trafficking, although not competing at levels similar to the full-blown drug cartels of Ciudad Juarez, Culiacán, or Tijuana.

Our academic understanding of trafficking belies the specialization and separation of drug sectors as an overall industry. The largest drug operators vertically integrate their sources, transportation (and transshipment), and storage sectors. Small producers and smugglers, such as those discussed here, are organized horizontally. In other words, there are specialists in transportation, transshipment, receiving, and storage, and this specialization is much more common among smaller producers and traffickers. These individual, specialized sectors seldom venture into other competing sectors, but when they do, violence erupts. Three Tohono transshipment traffickers were purportedly killed in 1997 because they attempted to establish direct links to Oaxacan suppliers of poppies, and middlemen from the latter state were dispatched to quell this effort. The most lucrative product for smugglers in and around Tohono lands is cocaine. Marijuana, indeed, is so common that large amounts of it are sacrificed to the state and federal police on a weekly basis, to throw them off larger shipments, or more common, to provide the Mexican authorities with a symbolic victory in the "drug war" of the region.

Conclusion

Both the border region of the Tohono and the high Sierra home of the Rarámuri are now increasingly affected by drug production and trafficking. A rising wave of low-level drug warfare has been apparent during the last decade, affecting those operating at the bottom of the larger drug industry, frequently hitting these native people the hardest. The Mexican federal government has recently militarized both of these zones in northern Mexico, and along the border the involvement of U.S. officials is even more pressing on the Tohono. Enforcement in the hyperarid expanse of the Tohono lands on the Sonoran side is almost nonexistent. Yet, unlike drug production in other areas, other economic activities occur in these regions (c.f. Hobbs 1998).

Colleagues in Mexico suggest that the drug situation has become more violent because of more stringent enforcement measures by both Mexico and the United States. Several of them refer to this as the Colombianization of Mexico. What they mean is that, like Colombia, Mexico has become increasingly violent as the levels of corruption have decreased in the Mexican government. With less cooperation of Mexican officials, traffickers are resorting to intimidation or outright violence, in an effort to keep their production and transportation lines intact. Traffickers have also begun to flexibly produce and move their products, in some ways imitating the corporate strategy of just-in-time production, perhaps becoming the most timely of capitalist enterprises. The greatest irony of drug trafficking is the source of its profit. Every attempt to escalate enforcement by the U.S. and Mexican authorities leads to higher drug prices, both in Mexico and in the United States. The drug war is adding most of the value to these highly value-added products.

More disconcerting, in light of recent events, is the so-called war on terrorism declared by the U.S. government. There are clear indications that narcotrafficking and production rights have been used or controlled by insurgent groups, from Colombia to Afghanistan. These illicit sources of funding have underwritten arms purchases and questionable regional political alliances. There is simply not enough evidence yet to suggest that northern Mexico's drug routes will be affected by the war on terrorism. To be sure, border crossings will be increasingly monitored, but the long-term consequences are unclear. If the U.S. administration's war on drugs is tied to the war on terrorism, illicit smuggling will face difficulties in crossing the Mexico-U.S. border. Given that northern Mexico has traditionally not been linked to funding terrorist activities, however, other nations and regions will most likely be targeted for the link between narcotics and violent political dissention.

References

Booth, M. 1996. *Opium: A History*. London: Simon & Schuster.
Drake, B. [1979] 1986. *Marijuana: The Cultivator's Handbook*. Berkeley, CA: Ronin Publishing.
Hobbs, J. J. 1998. Troubling Fields: The Opium Poppy in Egypt. *Geographical Review* 88(1): 64–85.
Nabhan, G. P. 1982. *The Desert Smells Like Rain*. Berkeley: University of California Press.
ODCCP (United Nations Office for Drug Control and Crime Prevention). 2000. *World Drug Report 2000*. New York: Oxford University Press.
Wilken, G. C. 1987. *Good Farmers*. Berkeley: University of California Press.

III

History and Drug Plants

9

Cannabis in Colonial India
Production, State Intervention, and Resistance in the Late Nineteenth-Century Bengali Landscape

James H. Mills

When approaching the subject of rural producers and their environments in nineteenth-century India, it is necessary to be mindful of the range of studies during the last 30 years or so that have emphasised the importance of resistance to colonial projects. These studies, most notably those published in the Subaltern Studies project (Guha 1982), have focused on the strategies and agendas of peasants in South Asia and have emphasized their importance in shaping rural developments and relationships during the period of British rule. This work has shown how these agendas and strategies often led to conflicts of interest with the colonial state. Importantly, however, these studies have insisted that resistance to colonial designs was not always expressed in confrontation and rebellion. Resistance could often be subtle, difficult to detect, localized, and small scale, coming in forms such as "foot dragging, dissimulation, false compliance, pilfering, feigned ignorance, slander, arson, sabotage and so forth," which have been called "the weapons of the weak" (Scott 1985: 29).

Such perspectives are important in this study as it focuses on the ways in which Indian rural producers of hemp (*Cannabis sativa*) narcotics transformed their environments in the process of producing the drugs for the domestic market in the nineteenth century. Definitions of the various preparations of hemp varied from place to place, and indeed different officials and administrators would give differing accounts. The preparations that are mentioned might broadly be understood as follows: *Ganja* is the dried flower head of the *Cannabis sativa* variation of the hemp plant, which is mixed with tobacco and smoked, often in a *chillum* (clay pipe). *Bhang* is the ground leaves and stalks of the *Cannabis sativa*, mixed into a paste and drunk with milk and sugar or taken neat with black pepper. *Charas* is the dried, sticky exudation of the sativa, smoked with tobacco in a *chillum*. *Majum* is a green sweetmeat made with the ground leaves of the plant and mixed with butter, milk, and sugar and baked. *Muddat* is a preparation of hemp and opium. After a brief introduction to the hemp narcotics market in India during this period, the chapter will consider the modes of production in the rural areas of the main hemp products. The main objective of the piece, however, is to look at the ways in which drug production affected the environment of rural Bengal. It will be argued that it was not simply the ecological requirements of cultivated hemp that shaped landscapes in India. It was also resistance to the ambitions of the colonial state to control and regulate the *ganja* trade that determined these landscapes, and indeed it was the low-level, localized strategies of resistance that were most important here.

Consumers and Markets

Consumption of cannabis seems to have been common to Indians, regardless of income or status. Consumers of the many preparations of the drug could be found across the subcontinent, in urban and rural contexts and throughout the many castes and classes of South Asia. In the cities, the example of Delhi seems fairly typical:

> Both the rich and the poor among Hindus indulge in this narcotic, whereas only the lower class of Muhammedans partake of it. The habitual indulgers are to be found in saises [grooms and riders], dhobis [washermen], faquirs [itinerant mystics], labourers, kahars and halalkhors [the lowest castes]. They may be found in groups of 20 or 30 from three to five in the afternoon in the Kerdun Shuraf, Panch Kua, Eed Ghar or on the banks of the Jumna, clubbing together for a smoke at from a dumrie to a pic [copper currency of the lowest value] or two a head. The pipe is passed round until they become merry or angry and too often quite intoxicated. Brahmins [the elite caste], mahajuns [merchants] and bunyas [moneylenders] generally smoke charas at their own houses every day in the afternoon. (Government of India 1872: 14)

Elsewhere in the country similar groups seem to have taken hemp narcotics. As in Delhi, where workers like the *saises* and the laborers resorted to the drug, it was felt in Hyderabad that "these drugs are taken by the labouring poor as a means to lighten their daily work" (Government of India 1872: 23), and in the Central Provinces it was reported that "persons whose employment subjects them to great exertions and fatigues, such as palki bearers [carriers of palanquin carriages] etc are solely enabled to perform the wonderful feats that they not unfrequently do by being supported and rendered insensible to fatigue by *ganja*" (Government of India 1872: 11). The working population of India resorted to narcotic preparations as a sort of combination of intoxicant and medicine to combat the effects of a hard life and to aid rest and recovery, or as one British official wrote, "to dull the pain of exposure and starvation and . . . to induce a pleasant languor and stupor" (Government of India 1872: 59).

As mentioned in the Delhi account above, hemp narcotics also had a place in the religious life of Indian society. The faquirs (itinerant mystics) are mentioned as smoking it there, and in the Bombay Presidency it was noticed that "*ganja* appears to be chiefly used by 'gossavees', 'faquirs' and other mendicants [members of India's range of quasi-religious healers and mystics], generally of a low class" (Government of India 1872: 55); in Bengal it was considered an act of charity to supply religious wanderers with *ganja* (Government of India 1872: 141). Preparations of the drug were also used by the wider society in their religious and cultural rituals. In Hyderabad it was the case that "some people, except Marwaris [inhabitants of Jodhpur in Rajasthan], offer it first to their gods" (Government of India 1872: 26), and in Uttar Pradesh it was noticed that "there is also a concoction of bhang and sweetmeats called majum, which is an accompaniment at festivals" (Government of India 1872: 45). One such festival was that of the goddess Durgá, which was celebrated with most energy in Bengal. There, drinks prepared with hemp narcotics were integral to the celebrations: "On the last day of the Durgá Pujá it is religiously offered to every guest and member of the family, and those who do not like to take it put a drop of it on their tongue by way of acceptance" (Government of India: 105).

Indeed, it is also evident that it was not just the wealthier and elite groups of Delhi who used the narcotics. Members of high-income or high-status groups elsewhere in India were also consumers. In Bombay it was asserted that "all classes of the community make use of hemp, and all castes of Hindus from the Brahmin downwards," the Brahmin being the highest caste in the Hindu order. In Bengal the elites seemed to prefer to drink their hemp preparations, as "bhang is used in the shape of a drink prepared in various ways and chiefly consumed by the better classes" (Government of India: 81). In short, intoxicating preparations of the hemp plant were taken for pleasure, as medicine, and in rituals all over British India by all groups in society.

Cultivation and the Physical Transformation of the Landscape

Although found wild across India, the hemp plant that was cultivated for the production of narcotics for Indian markets had certain specific environmental requirements. The British were convinced that in India they were dealing with a distinct strain of the hemp plant, which they christened *Cannabis indica*. This appears to have been since abandoned, and Indian strains are recognized as simply being variants of the *Cannabis sativa* plant (Chopra et al. 1958: 84–85). The soil was preferably a light sandy loam (called *poli* in Bengali), able to maintain moisture and situated in a region where water was accessible and controllable throughout the winter, as irrigation of the crop took place at least twice between November and January. In other words, the regional ecosystem needed to be capable of retaining water from the monsoon until the beginning of the following calendar year but not regularly susceptible to rains in the period from October to March. Rain in late September or October killed the newly transplanted seedlings, and prolonged rain in December and January disrupted the flowering of the female plants. Rain in this period encouraged new shoots that weakened the budding flowers and also created conditions for the growth of insects that attacked the plants. Strong winds at any time of the plants' life cycle threatened to uproot them.

These requirements meant that the plants were cultivated only in certain regions of India. By the 1870s the crop was known to be produced at Solapur, Ahmadnagar, and Khandeish in what is now Maharashtra; at Salem, Tanjore, Nellore, Arcot, Coimbatore, Kurnool, and Bellary; straddling the modern-day states of Tamil Nadu, Andhra Pradesh, and Karnataka; and across Uttar Pradesh in districts around towns such as Bareilly, Gorakhpur, and Moradabad. In Bengal the crop was grown in the Ganja Mahal, a tract of land made up of parts of the old districts of Bogra, Dinagepore, and Rajshahi (now across West Bengal, Bangladesh, and Assam) that totaled about 60,000 acres and that had as its headquarters the town of Nowgong.

This chapter will focus on the last area, the Ganja Mahal, the Indian hemp trade of which was the subject of an extensive survey in the 1870s. Hem Chunder Kerr (1877), a deputy tax Collector, toured the area from November 1876 to March 1877 on behalf of the Board of Revenue of the Lower Provinces of Bengal and his account of his observations is the most complete available on the system of *ganja* production in India in the nineteenth century. Most of the details in this chapter are taken from his report.

From this report it seems that Indian hemp was chief among the range that made up the local agricultural producer's portfolio of crops. In any one field, *ganja* was sown once every 4 years. It was reaped in March, and the field was turned over to the cultivation of jute, which was planted in May and harvested in October and which was closely followed by mustard, which was harvested in February. Other crops raised from the field in the interval between hemp yields included potato, turmeric, tobacco, early rice, and ginger. In other words cultivated hemp was deeply embedded in the ecology of the Ganja Mahal, as it was included in both the annual crop production cycle and in the longer term planning of land use rotation systems.

The whole process of cultivating hemp for narcotics and manufacturing the *ganja* products shaped the ecology of the areas in which it was an important part of the economy. Land was carefully managed through the processes of plowing, applying manure, and irrigation, and the soil was doctored to prepare it for the hemp crop. Hydromanagement systems were devised to preserve and make accessible the water in the ecosystem. Where wells were available, a complex of narrow irrigation channels was dug in the fields, and water was raised by using a bamboo lever at one end of which was a basket for the water and at the other end a counterweight to lift the basket from the well when full. Where the water table could not be relied upon, tanks were constructed near the fields to capture and keep rainwater, and this was then distributed through baling by hand. Trees were removed to ensure that no shade fell on the crop because the plants needed constant exposure to sunlight to develop the resin in the leaves. Fields were dug into narrow ridges into which the seedlings were placed. Farmland was set aside for the nursery and for the *chátor*, the area of manufacture.

In short, cultivating hemp that was destined to be turned into *ganja* for the narcotics markets of India entailed a range of physical transformations to the landscape. The land was carefully prepared, and a series of elaborate environmental interventions were planned and carried out to ensure that the crop was successful and that facilities existed for manufacturing *ganja* from it.

Resistance and the Imaginative Transformation
of the Landscape

The British had throughout the nineteenth century raised duties on the consumption of *ganja* and in the later decades began to actively consider its prohibition (Mills 2000: 43–65). The wholesaler was taxed on his holdings of *ganja*. Earlier in the nineteenth century he was expected to pay tax at the point where he collected the *ganja* from the cultivators. He had to present himself and his stock of *ganja* at the headquarters of the British officer (known as the Collector) of the district and to pay the duty on the amount that he had purchased. The problems with this system however, became obvious: "There was some difficulty in collecting the tax in the manner just mentioned, for the byaparis [traders] might come, make their whole transaction in a single night, and clandestinely export large quantities of *ganja* without paying tax" (Kerr 1877: 107). The system in operation by the time of Kerr's report was to tax the wholesaler in his place of business rather than at the point of purchase or production. In other words, once the stock of *ganja* was in the wholesaler's warehouse, the District Collector there would be able to assess his approximate holdings and maintain surveillance of how much the retail buyers were taking from the wholesaler. The amount sold by the wholesaler to the retailer was therefore taxed.

The key to the success of levying this duty was an accurate knowledge of the amount of *ganja* in the system. To this end, the British had introduced a series of licences under Act II of 1876. The peasant producer of the hemp plant had to approach the authorities to obtain a licence to cultivate the crop. This was intended to inform the District Collector which peasants in his area of supervision were producing hemp so that he might keep these people under watch. He employed an establishment specifically for this purpose in Nowgong, which was the headquarters of the Ganja Mahal. Among the duties of this staff were regular tours of the area in order to form estimates of the area under cultivation and to watch the progress and health of the crop, thereby supplying approximations of how much *ganja* might reasonably be expected to come onto the market in February and March. When the crop was ready and the *ganja* had been processed, the cultivator (or the wholesaler who had purchased the standing crop and prepared it with his own staff) applied for a licence to store the drug. To be granted this licence, he stated how much of the drug he intended to store, and the permit was made out to cover this amount.

The wholesaler, meanwhile, had gained a permit to export the crop from the Ganja Mahal back to his home district, where he intended to sell the *ganja* to retailers. This permit, completed by the Collector of his home district, stipulated how much of the drug he could legally take back with him. He also had a licence to purchase the drug once in the Ganja Mahal, and to comply with the requirements of this licence he needed to present his purchases to the supervisor of the staff employed to look after the district's *ganja* trade. Here his stock of the drug was weighed and checked against the amount that he was allowed to import back into his home district. Once all was in order, the wholesaler's carts or boats were searched to make sure that he was not smuggling. Once this was completed, the authorized bales, each marked with an excise stamp, were loaded and the wholesaler headed for home with his stocks.

Although this was the system as the British intended it to operate, it does not necessarily follow that this was how it did operate. The Subaltern Studies school of historians and anthropologists like James Scott have been keen to point out that where peasants interacted with the state or with other elite groups, the outcome of these interactions was not simply either the compliance or the confrontation that were commonly focused on by historians (Dhanagare 1983; Hardiman 1992). In other words, these historians and anthropologists counsel against the language of official documents and of elite social groups that holds the peasantry to be a lumpen mass, the "ignorant cultivators" of Kerr's report, capable only of mulelike forebearance or sudden, violent protest. Instead they assert that members of "subaltern" groups, those that experience subordination in their societies (Guha 1982: vii), have complex and autonomous agendas and strategies of their own (Guha 1982: 4). These often lead to resistance to state or elite designs but not necessarily the spectacular resistance of a peasant revolt or riot (Scott 1985: 31–32). Rather it is resistance through the unspectacular methods of avoidance, sabotage, or land encroachment. These historians and anthropologists point out then that to find evidence of resistance agendas among subaltern groups, it is necessary not simply to look for violent reactions but also to seek out the sly and often undisruptive actions of those in subordinate positions.

Such perspectives, although problematic (Spivak 1988: 308; Gandhi 1998: 1–3), are useful in understanding the actions of one subaltern group, the peasant producers of the Ganja Mahal. It seems that they resisted the British desire to regulate and monitor the trade in preparations of the hemp plant, and they did this through the unspectacular method of manipulating the advantages given to them by their local environment. The peasant producers pursued their politics of resistance to the colonial state through interactions with their ecologies and local geographies. They did not transform their local landscapes physically in order to resist British designs. Rather, in seeking to use these landscapes in surreptitious ways, they transformed them imaginatively, as they began to look at their local environments in novel ways for the new purpose of avoiding the state's planned interventions.

It is possible to trace in the historical records three ways in which the subaltern did this. The first was by exploiting the sheer extent of the suitable land available to them to grow hemp in the knowledge that the apparatus of the state for enforcing its policies was limited. The establishments set up by the British to supervise the *ganja* trade were expected to have a working knowledge of how much hemp was being grown in any one year. They were supposed to gain this knowledge by pursuing what one Collector called their "out-door inquiries," which involved walking in the villages and arriving at estimates of the scale of hemp cultivation by observation and by taking information from the cultivators themselves.

Hem Chunder Kerr quickly discovered, on ordering a measurement of the fields, that there was a considerable difference between the area that the cultivators were declaring as set aside for hemp and the area that was actually made up of plots of the crop:

No one on behalf of Government surveyed the fields and there was nothing to prove that the area alleged was really what was under cultivation. The difference between the reported area (2113 bigás and 2 cottás) last year and the actual (3111 bigás 9 cottás) found by measurement showed a difference of 998 bigás and 7 cottás . . . this would amount to an annual loss of revenue to the extent of Rs 478 852. There is nothing to show that there has not been a similar disparity between the total of the reported area and the actual under cultivation in former years; on the contrary, the presumption is strong that there was marked disparity. (Kerr 1877: 143)

Quite simply, the cultivators knew that the representatives of the colonial state were too few in number to accurately and regularly assess the large areas devoted to hemp cultivation and, indeed, that those representatives were dependent upon them for information. As Kerr (1877: 121) recorded, an independent assessment was impossible because "the supervisor has not the means of making such an inquiry, as he has not men enough to go to the *chators*, or to the houses of about 200 men." Indeed it was a prominent feature of the recommendations of Kerr's report that considerable alterations should be made to the staff of the *ganja* supervisor's office, including mounted police to increase patrols of the Ganja Mahal and the stationing of officers of the supervisor's establishment every 16 square miles:

They will find no difficulty from June to September to measure every inch of the fields proposed to be devoted to hemp and submit a report to the Collectorate. After transplantation it will be their duty to visit the fields from time to time and see how the cultivation is progressing and submit progress reports. In December and January they should prepare an estimate of the probable yield of each field. The work during the manufacturing season will be heavy; it will then be their duty to visit the chátors frequently, to take note of the quantity daily manufactured, and to see that the produce is regularly and promptly forwarded to store houses. (Kerr 1877: 146)

These elaborate expansions of the *ganja* supervisor's responsibilities were designed, then, to overcome one of the main peasant strategies of resisting the colonial state's determination to tax the *ganja* trade. This was to declare that a certain amount of land was being cultivated, in order to appease the state's representatives and not arouse the suspicion of the authorities by asserting that no hemp was being produced. However, the peasant producers then brought supplementary, undeclared areas under cultivation for hemp, at once taking advantage of the fertility of the local land and also of the geographical extent of that ground, which they knew was beyond the surveillance of the colonial state's limited machinery. It is little wonder, then, that Kerr (1877: 122) noticed activity on the peripheries of the area that he was surveying: "In the northern and western parts of the Ganja Mahal there are jungles which the people are gradually clearing and bringing under cultivation." The regional environment and local geography were central here to the politics of resistance and to the strategies of defiance, and encroachment and undeclared land use were as common in the Ganja Mahal as in other areas where the environment was incorporated into resistance strategies. Atluri Murali (1995), for example, noted similar actions in the hills of Andhra by local communities when threatened by the colonial state's assertion of power over the forests. Here, "the first and spontaneous individual peasant protest against forest regulations took the form of a violation of government restrictions . . . there was an increase in cases of unauthorized grazing and the removal of grass and other produce" (Murali 1995: 119).

Second, subaltern groups were also quick to incorporate the river systems of their areas into these strategies of resistance (Gadgil and Guha 1992: 168–169; Chattopadhyay 2000: 125–126). This was certainly the case in the Ganja Mahal, where "the river Jabuna runs through the *ganja* tracts; it is navigable all the year and smugglers have every opportunity for taking away *ganja* of any description with very little risk of detection" (Kerr 1877: 144). Kerr (1877: 146) mentioned a system designed to combat this, "to prevent smuggling from the houses of the cultivators." This involved a guard boat on the river Jabuna and "a preventive station at Sahebgunge on the Atraie river," as these waterways provided the ideal means of removing illicitly produced hemp narcotics from the area without having to pass along the roads, which were patroled by the colonial police and which passed through the towns of the district administrators. Smuggling, in this case along the rivers, was a key means of evading the demands of the colonial state in the Ganja Mahal, as it had been with other narcotic substances earlier in the colonial period (Farooqui 1998).

Evidence of this smuggling trade was of course difficult to come by because of the secretive nature of the processes involved. Some instances, however, point to the involvement of the cultivators in the trade. It is difficult to imagine who else but local peasants would be able to pick their way across the land in the dark, as the men described here did:

> In December following, a couple of police constables and a village watchman belonging to thana [district subdivision] Manda in Rajshahye were, about 9pm on their way to Bálihar, when they saw two persons crossing the field with something on their heads. On their shouting out, the men dropped their loads and ran off. It was then found that they had dropped 36½ *kutcha* seers of flat hemp. The drug was taken possession of by the constables but the culprits were never traced. (Kerr 1877: 142)

These units varied considerably from region to region, so it is impossible to accurately render them in modern measurements (Yule and Burnell 1996 discuss the problems with these terms). Similarly, a tantalizing glimpse of the cultivator in the smuggling trade is caught in another example cited by Kerr (1877: 142): "In the first week of January last two men were seized with seven tolás of round *ganja* at the Táherpore Haut. Their defence was that they had received them from a *ganja* grower, who however denied having ever given it to the men, who were found guilty of the offence and punished." In this example, there is every reason for the cultivator to deny knowledge of the smugglers' claim. He could be prosecuted for participating in the illegal trade. He had no doubt already received payment and thus he had no reason to care about the fate of the arrested men and good reason to deny any connection to them.

The colonial state could not prove that the crop was the grower's because the cultivators deliberately exploited the geography of their farms to make sure that the state's representatives had no way of knowing how much *ganja* the cultivator had actually manufactured. The crop that had been processed on the farm was not gathered together in one warehouse or barn but was deliberately spread around the various buildings and lean-tos erected across the farm. Consider the observations on storage in the report:

> During my stay at Nowgong I took the supervisor with me and visited several places used for the storage of ganja. I found it stored at every convenient nook or corner, without any care or guard. I saw a quantity of flat ganja kept in a cowshed situated in an open place and without any doors in the house of one Fakir Bakhsh. In one Piru Mandal's place I found some hemp lying in an open verandah of a room in the house. In the homestead of one Chhedor Mandal there was a large quantity of round ganja lying in an open hall of the house on planks placed on the floor. I also saw some flat hemp in an open room and inside a cowshed in the house of a respectable ryot [small-holder] named Kukur Sardár. (Kerr 1877: 121)

The objective of this dispersal was to make the job of the state's representatives almost impossible. Even if a visit was made by the supervisor or one of the staff of the *ganja* establishment, he would not be able to accurately assess the amount of the drug that had been produced. Kerr was well aware of this: "There is nothing to prevent the concealment of a portion of what has been prepared or to prevent some of it being taken away secretly at night, before the supervisor or his chuprasees visit the khullian [property]. If the ryot has stored the prepared produce, the supervisor can examine 'the store', he cannot search the several houses of the cultivator" (Kerr 1877: 144).

The third defence, fire, used more commonly in acts of sabotage or in the assertion of customary rights in other instances of peasant resistance (Guha 1991: 107; Gadgil and Guha 1992: 169), was combined with these decentralized warehousing arrangements in the strategies of the Ganja Mahal producers. The heat and dryness of that part of Bihar and West Bengal from March to July and the ad hoc storage facilities meant that "accidental" fire provided an ideal story to cover for anomalies in *ganja* stocks:

> Even of the quantity reported a good portion might disappear without any let or hindrance. Fires are frequent, and reports frequently sent in of quantities of the drug having been destroyed thereby. An open shed or cowhouse where ganja is stored is of little value. Ten rupees suffice to replace one, and yet a couple of bales burnt in it is equal to a duty of over Rs. 212. There is nothing to prevent the removal and sale of the drug and the subsequent firing of the hut to cover the nefarious transaction. Every such transaction would amount to a clear gain of nearly Rs. 200. (Kerr 1877: 145)

Quite simply, then, Indian cultivators fully incorporated the geography and ecology of their farms and of the Ganja Mahal region into their strategies of resisting the colonial state and its officers. They made use of the opportunities for concealment presented by the extensive spaces available to them on their land. Therefore, they deliberately spread their holdings of the narcotic across the full extent of their farms to prevent accurate assessment of their stocks. They exploited the fact that fire was a common hazard in the local ecology. This meant that no one could legitimately blame them for the misfortune of a sudden blaze in the tinderbox conditions created by the summer sun; therefore, quantities of the drug that had already disappeared into smuggling networks could be passed off as lost in fires that were in fact far from accidental. They made use of the rivers of their region as a transportation system to send drugs out from the Ganja Mahal and into smuggling networks designed to get the narcotics to the markets without the state being able to exact its toll.

Conclusion

Cultivation of hemp for narcotic preparations physically transformed the landscapes of the producers, as the crop demanded specific farming methods, the spatial reorganization of farms, and the expansion of cultivated areas into previously unused territories. But the production of hemp and *ganja* for nineteenth-century Indian consumption also demanded an imaginative transformation of indigenous landscapes as subaltern producers began to look at ways of using their environments to evade the interventions of the colonial state. Peasants began to see river systems as smuggling routes, outhouses as contraband storerooms, and peripheral land as full of potential for concealed cultivation. The landscape was transformed through the preparation of hemp for the narcotics markets both in the real world of field systems and irrigation networks and in the imaginative world of those who lived in the rural areas and who began to see their local environments in new and powerful ways.

Acknowledgments　Thanks are due to Crispin Bates of Edinburgh University and Peter King of University College Northampton for their roles in the development of this research as well as to David Washbrook of St Anthony's College, Oxford and David Arnold at SOAS for helpful comments at various stages of my work. Research on this topic was completed with the support of the British Academy, the Carnegie Trust for the Universities of Scotland and the Wellcome Trust for the History of Medicine and with the kind assistance of the staff at the India Office Library, the National Archives of India and the Maharashtra State Archives.

References

Chattopadhyay, B. 2000. *Crime and Control in Early Colonial Bengal, 1770–1860*. Calcutta: Bagchi.

Chopra, R. N., I. C. Chopra, K. L. Handa, and L. D. Kapus. 1958. *Chopra's Indigenous Drugs of India*. Calcutta: U. N. Dhur.

Dhanagare, D. 1983. *Peasant Movements in India 1920–1950*. Delhi: Oxford University Press.

Farooqui, A. 1998. *Smuggling as Subversion: Colonialism, Indian Merchants and the Politics of Opium*. Delhi: South Asia Books.

Gadgil, M., and R. Guha. 1992. *This Fissured Land: An Ecological History of India*. Delhi: Oxford University Press.

Gandhi, L. 1998. *Postcolonial Theory*. Edinburgh: Edinburgh University Press.

Government of India. 1872. Papers relating to the consumption of *Ganja*. In United Kingdom. House of Commons. *Parliamentary Papers 1891–2,* vol. 66.

Guha, R. 1982. On Some Aspects of the Historiography of Colonial India. In *Subaltern Studies,* vol. 1, ed. R. Guha, pp. 1–8. Delhi: Oxford University Press.

———. 1991. *The Unquiet Woods: Ecological Change and Peasant Resistance in the Himalaya.* Delhi: Oxford University Press.

Hardiman, D. 1992. *Peasant Resistance in India, 1858–1914.* Delhi: Oxford University Press.

Kerr, H. M. 1877. Report on Cultivation of and Trade in *Ganja* in Bengal. In United Kingdom. House of Commons. *Parliamentary Papers 1891–2,* vol. 66.

Mills, J. 2000. *Madness, Cannabis and Colonialism: The "Native Only" Lunatic Asylums of Colonial India.* Basingstoke: Macmillan.

Murali, A. 1995. Whose Trees? Forest Practices and Local Communities in Andhra, 1600–1922. In *Nature, Culture, Imperialism: Essays on the Environmental History of South Asia,* ed. D. Arnold and R. Guha, pp. 100–121. Delhi: Oxford University Press.

Scott, J. 1985. *Weapons of the Weak: Everyday Forms of Peasant Resistance.* New Haven, CT: Yale University Press.

Spivak, G. 1988. Can the Subaltern Speak? In *Marxist Interpretations of Culture,* ed. C. Nelson and L. Grossberg, pp. 200–215. Basingstoke: Macmillan.

United Kingdom. 1891. House of Commons. Papers relating to the consumption of *Ganja.* *Parliamentary Papers 1891–2 ,* vol. 66.

Yule, H., and A. Burnell. 1996. *Hobson-Jobson: the Anglo-Indian Dictionary.* Ware: Wordsworth.

10

Suppressing Opium and "Reforming" Minorities

Antidrug Campaigns in Ethnic Communities in the Early People's Republic of China

Zhou Yongming

In China, the term *minority nationalities* is used to refer to all ethnic groups that are not Han Chinese. According to the 2000 census, a total of 55 minority nationalities numbered in total 106 million people, or 8.4 percent of the total population in the mainland (Zhu 2001). However, the size and composition of minority nationality populations in China is extremely heterogeneous. In terms of population, based on the 1990 census, the smallest, the Lhoba, numbered only 2,312, whereas the most populous, the Zhuang, were 15.5 million strong (National Statistics Bureau 2000: 38). Socially and culturally speaking, the differences among the minority nationalities are large: Some are hunter-gatherers or slash-and-burn cultivators, whereas others are highly sinicized Chinese-speaking groups like the Hui and the contemporary Manchu. Minority nationalities are spread all over China, and 90 percent of them live in mountainous areas (Li 1994: 72). Because of this geographic distribution, isolated minority areas became safe havens for poppy planting and opium production, especially after the opium suppression campaign of 1906–1911 by the Qing dynasty (1644–1911).

In most cases, opium was introduced into minority communities in the late nineteenth century and early twentieth century. Opium's effects on minority communities have varied considerably. Generally speaking, there have been three possible types of effects. First, members of some minorities have become addicted to opium but relied on others to obtain the opium supply. Second, members of other minority groups have acted mainly as poppy cultivators and raw opium suppliers but have been less involved in consumption and trafficking. Last, members of yet other minority groups have become involved not only in poppy planting but also in opium trafficking and consumption. Opium has thus come to play an important role in a minority's social and economic lives in those areas affected by the drug. By exploring how antidrug campaigns were carried out in the Jiayin Erlunchun community in northeast China and the Liangshan Yi and Aba Tibetan areas in southwest China, I will explore all three types of the effects of drugs on minority communities up to the late 1950s.

The People's Republic of China was established in 1949. To Mao Zedong and the Chinese Communists, drugs were remnants of capitalist and feudal culture and had no place in the new China to which they looked forward. After the establishment of the new government, drugs were among the first targets of the mass campaigns that were part of Communist state building. However, the antidrug campaign of 1952, carried out mainly in cities, towns, and drug-distribution centers, did not touch most minority areas (Zhou 1999: 93–111). Although antidrug ideology applied to all Chinese, the authorities decided to conduct drug suppression in minority areas in a different way from those used in Han areas in the 1950s. This decision arose from several contributing factors.

One important factor was that the Communists had adopted a clear and conscious nationality policy well before they took power in 1949. Unlike previous regimes in Chinese history, they took a nonassimilationist view, at least theoretically and ideologically, to the minority issue. Although their policies were deeply influenced by official Soviet views based on Stalin's nationality theory, as some scholars have observed, "the policy of the Chinese Communist Party towards minority nationalities in the early 1950s was cautious and gradualist, providing an interesting contrast with the Soviet Union" (Brugger and Reglar 1994: 313). In addition, the Communists had come to realize the importance of gaining the support of the minorities in the process of struggling for power. The nationality issue had been a key part of the party's United Front work. In the early 1950s, many minority areas were yet to be "liberated," or were not under firm government control. The authorities thus had to carry out the antidrug campaign within the framework of nationality policy and remain alert to practical concerns.

Another important factor was the Communists' strong belief that minority nationalities were "backward" people who needed to be reformed to become members of society in a socialist new China. This belief was based on the Marxist doctrine that sees the progress of human society as unilinear, starting from primitive communism; progressing through slavery, feudalism, capitalism, and socialism; and eventually reaching the ultimate destination of communism. According to the official classification, most of China's minority societies were in the first three stages of social development, and thus it was urgent to reform them to fit them into the socialist system the People's Republic was constructing. From this perspective, suppressing drugs was always a small part of a much bigger social reform project. As we will see in the following discussion, the movement against drugs was in all cases achieved in connection with other "reform" initiatives advocated by the government.

Opium and the Jiayin Erlunchun Community

The Erlunchun were historically a group of hunters living in the vast mountainous areas of northern Manchuria, located in today's Inner Mongolia Autonomous Region and Heilongjiang Province. Though the traditional tribal organization had been destroyed by efforts to put the group under government administration in the late Qing dynasty, the group had kept much of its previous egalitarian lifestyle. According to the aforementioned Marxist gauge of social development, the group was thus classified as being at the end phase of primitive communism and therefore still a classless society. The group had a total population of 4,100 in the 1910s, but this decreased to 3,700 in 1934 and again to about 3,000 in 1938. The first census data of 1953 showed that the number had further fallen to 2,256 (Inner Mongolia Compilers 1984: 2–3). Among the various causes of the population decrease—including warfare, epidemics, and intragroup marriage—opium and liquor were identified as major factors in the decline (*Erlunchunzhu jianshi* 1983: 5; Inner Mongolia Compilers 1984: 3).

It is difficult to pinpoint the exact time that opium was first introduced into the Erlunchun communities. Though most have blamed the Japanese for their role in spreading opium among the Erlunchun during their occupation of Manchuria from 1931 to 1945, it is more likely that the problem started in the early years of the republican era (the Qing dynasty fell in 1911 and the Republic of China was established in 1912). One scholar has pointed out that opium smoking and alcohol abuse were very common among adult Erlunchun males in the republican era (Du 1993: 129). Fur traders and other merchants might well have played a big role, using opium and liquor to facilitate their exploitative unequal trade with the Erlunchun, who had little knowledge of commercial exchange (*Erlunchunzhu jianshi* 1983: 93–94). In addition, a large number of Han migrants were also responsible for the spread of opium into the Erlunchun area in the late Qing and early republican era.

It is certain, however, that the opium problem worsened during the years of Japanese occupation. In 1933, the Japanese and their puppet government imposed an opium monopoly in Manchuria. Every Erlunchun over 20, male and female alike, was allotted a fixed opium ration daily (*Erlunchunzhu jianshi* 1983, 130; Qiu 1987: 197; Gu 1997: 275). Furthermore, the Japanese adopted a policy of mollification toward the Erlunchun in wartime, recruiting them to join the Mountain Teams that were fighting against the anti-Japanese forces in the area. Japanese intelligence agencies were put in charge of dealing with the Erlunchun, dispatching so-called instructors to the Mountain Teams as supervisors (*Erlunchunzhu jianshi* 1983: 121–124). Those who provided the Japanese with information about resistance activities, true or false, were rewarded with opium (Gu 1997: 275). In combination with the dramatic social changes inflicted on the Erlunchun, opium and alcohol addiction put the population on the brink of total social and physical collapse in the early 1950s.

However, compared with the cases of the Tibetans and the Yi (to be discussed later in this chapter), the Communist authorities faced a less complex situation because the Erlunchun were only opium users and were not involved in poppy planting and opium trafficking. As migrating hunters, they did not plant poppies themselves. In Jiayin County, where there were 67 Erlunchun in 1953 (Inner Mongolia Compilers 1984: 3), the addicts relied on Han poppy planters to obtain their supply. Those Han planters had migrated into the area at the end of the nineteenth century, along with bandits and gold miners, and these three groups remained outside of governmental control in the area before 1949 (Gu 1997: 274). After the Communists took power, the new authorities realized that to solve the Erlunchun opium problem they needed first to cut off the supply. Thus the Han poppy planters became the first target of the government drug suppression campaign.

The authorities needed 3 full years to solve the problem at the supply end. The county government waited until August 1950, after other major campaigns (including the land reform and bandits suppression) were completed, to launch the operations against poppy planters. The operation was designed to eradicate poppies and arrest planters at the same time, but the news leaked out and most planters escaped into the mountains in advance. Though the authorities eradicated more than 10 hectares of poppy fields and seized 3.5 kilograms of opium, after the operation was over these planters returned and resumed business as usual. Clearly, the first operation did not achieve its goal (Gu 1997: 275–276).

One year later, the county police and militia conducted a second operation against poppy planters. This time, they did a better job in collecting leads and information about their targets and in keeping their operation secret. A force of more than 100 men silently entered the mountains and launched the operation simultaneously in different locations during September 1951. The planters offered strong resistance and suffered casualties. The operation team eradicated 7 hectares of poppy fields and caught 16 planters. They were held together in a village inn under the surveillance of the police and militia. What the police did not know was that among those planters captured, many had planted opium for the Erlunchun hunters, and some of them had even forged partnerships with the latter. The Erlunchun provided to the planters food and other necessities of life in exchange for a portion of harvested opium. The eradication of the poppies and the arrest of the planters thus meant the loss of their opium supply. One night, several Erlunchun hunters armed with guns stormed the village inn and drove off the militia. In the chaos, all the captured poppy planters escaped, with the exception of one who was injured. The second operation had failed miserably.

Having learned its lesson, the county government now turned its attention to the Erlunchun. First, the authorities investigated the relationship between each individual poppy planter and his Erlunchun food suppliers and opium buyers. Next, the county government invited several influential Erlunchun figures to meet with the county party secretary and mayor. The Erlunchun were urged to persuade their opium suppliers to abandon the business and come down from the mountains. Only after they had gotten the guarantee from the county authorities that those planters who abandoned their occupation were not to be put in jail did the Erlunchun agree to do so. With the cooperation from the Erlunchun secured, the county conducted a third drug suppression operation, from July 15 to August 14 in 1952, which was successful. In the operation, 54 poppy planters were forced to give up their business and 11.2 hectares of poppies were eradicated. This operation basically wiped out poppy planting in the whole county (Gu 1997: 276–278).

The next task was to suppress opium consumption and to rehabilitate opium addicts. In Jiayin, the county authorities rounded up over 20 Erlunchun addicts and put them through a rehabilitation session at the county seat. Local cadres and doctors used persuasion and compulsion alternately as methods of rehabilitating the addicts. Most addicts were thus rid of their habits after three 10-day rehabilitation sessions, and the authorities sent several unrehabilitated addicts to the prefecture rehabilitation center the following spring to get further treatment. Meanwhile, rehabilitation sessions were also conducted among the Han gold miners, and over 100 were cured. It is said that by the spring of 1954, opium addiction had essentially ceased to exist in the whole area (Gu 1997: 279–280).

The operation in Jiayin involved only a small portion of the Erlunchun. For the whole group, spread across vast areas of northern Inner Mongolia Autonomous Region and Helongjiang Province, the opium addiction problem was solved after the implementation of a planned program aimed at transforming the Erlunchun from migrant hunters to dwellers in fixed settlements. The program was the key part of the authorities' efforts to "reform" or "improve" Erlunchun life. Though both the late Qing and the republican administration had failed to get the Erlunchun to settle down and to induce them to begin agricultural cultivation, the Communist rulers insisted that sedentization of Erlunchun was necessary for them to learn a "civilized and progressive" way of life and become a "modern nationality." The settlement process was carried out from 1953 to 1958. At the same time, the authorities acknowledged that the settlement of the Erlunchun would facilitate government administration, in general, and would make compulsory rehabilitation of opium addicts and control of alcoholics easier, in particular (Du Yonghao 1993: 147–151). Retrospectively, we can see that the authorities were successful in suppressing opium consumption, but they still have to fight a high rate of alcoholism today in Erlunchun settlements (Du Yonghao 1993: 202–203).

Opium and Liangshan Yi Society

From all accounts, the introduction of opium into the Liangshan Yi area had such a profound effect that it changed many aspects of Yi society in just a few decades. Opium not only became a part of the Yi people's everyday life but also was a catalyst for the dramatic social changes that the Yi experienced in the early to the middle years of the last century. To discuss the antiopium campaign in the Yi area, it is necessary to first trace the origin, spread, and effects of opium in Liangshan.

The Liangshan Yi Autonomous Prefecture is located in the southwestern part of Sichuan Province. Before 1978, this prefecture encompassed 19,000 square kilometers in the mountainous area between the Dadu and Jinsha Rivers. In 1978, the former Xichang Prefecture was incorporated into the Liangshan Prefecture, making today's Liangshan much larger (63,000 square kilometers) and more populous (Editors of Liangshan 1985: 1–2). In the mid-1950s, the total population of Liangshan was 973,000, of which 706,000, or about 72 percent, were Yi (Cheng 1987: 152).

Chinese scholars agree that the existence of slaves was one of the main characteristics of the Yi social system before it was fundamentally changed by the "democratic reform" carried out in the 1950s (Wang 1987: 49–52). Yi society had a rigid hierarchy and was divided into two major groups: black Yi and white Yi. The black Yi (about 7 percent of the population) made up the aristocratic ruling class. Within the white Yi, however, there were three subgroups: Qunuo, Anjia, and Jiaxi. The Qunuo were defined as semiindependent peasants, whereas the Anjia and Jiaxi were slaves. Clan organizations had a dominant role in Yi society, and clans were often involved in various feuds, which were extraordinary in frequency and scale. Frequent clan feuds also made Yi society very militarized, and the Yi used this strong fighting power to descend from the mountains and capture Han villagers, taking them away as slaves. The dominance by the Yi was a rare exception in the relationship between the Han and other nationalities in southwest China, in which the Han usually played the dominant role.

All these social features were affected by the introduction of opium into the Liangshan area in the early twentieth century. According to several sources, opium poppy planting began around 1910 and was started by Han people as a way of evading the antiopium campaign conducted by the Qing dynasty (Du Yuting 1987: 220; Shao 1987: 51; Zhang 1987: 144). By 1950, in the area of the current Liangshan, 50–80 percent of the households, both Yi and Han, engaged in poppy planting, and 50–60 percent of the local population smoked opium (Sun, Shi, and Zhu 1993: 198). Simultaneously, the price of opium increased dramatically. Though the black Yi received a large share of the opium wealth, the massive inflow of silver enriched the entire Yi society, which in turn played a big role in creating further stratification in the Yi social hierarchy. For example, it became common for rich Qunuo to use newly accumulated money to buy land and slaves. Conversely, both Anjia and Jiaxi were able to use silver to redeem themselves from their black Yi masters, moving themselves one rung up the ladder of the social hierarchy.

With opium came an inflow of rifles and handguns into the Liangshan Yi area. By 1950, about 100,000 guns of various kinds were held by a Yi population of 600,000, representing approximately 1 gun in every household (Editors of Liangshan 1985, 91). The prevalence of guns dramatically increased the fighting power of the black Yi, enabling them to consolidate their ruling position. In addition, the possession of modern weaponry changed the nature of clan feuds, making them more frequent and more deadly. The large quantity of guns possessed by the Yi made them militarily superior to other ethnic groups, and the nearby Han Chinese and Tibetans became easy targets. It is estimated that before 1950, among a total Yi population of over 600,000, about 10 percent were Han who had become slaves (Hu 1987: 20). This fact could explain why the slave population increased so quickly in the years after opium was introduced into Liangshan and why hatred and distrust between the Yi and Han communities had become deeply rooted by the time the Communists arrived in 1950.

The Antiopium Campaign in Liangshan: 1950–1959

From the very beginning, opium suppression was carried out separately in the Han and Yi areas of Liangshan, and with very different approaches. The Han area made up the majority of the former Xichang Prefecture. Drug suppression started from spring 1950 and was conducted within the Han area only. Though contained by the middle of 1952, the opium problem was still a headache to the authorities. In 1952,

Xichang authorities conducted their antidrug campaign in the same manner that the campaign was carried out in the rest of the country. After three waves of massive arrests, more than 70 public trials were held, in which 26 drug offenders were sentenced to death and more than 300 were sent to prison (Sun, Shi, and Zhu 1993: 200–203). The campaign was very effective at the time in the Han area.

The effectiveness of the 1952 campaign was compromised in the following years because opium produced in the Yi area found its way back to the Han area through both Han and Yi traffickers. Therefore, in 1954, the local authorities decided to deal with the resurgence of opium on two fronts. In addition to cracking down on opium trafficking by Han Chinese in the Han area, the authorities also tried to cut off the outflow of opium from the Yi area. Yi traffickers, however, were only subject to "education," compared to the severe punishment the Han traffickers faced at the time. By the end of 1954, after 466 arrests of non-Yi offenders, the authorities claimed that the resurgence of opium in the Han area had been suppressed (Sun, Shi, and Zhu 1993: 204–205).

Thus, the Liangshan Yi area was not touched by the antiopium campaign of 1952. In the following years, the authorities tried to accomplish their goals step by step. Major attempts to curtail opium planting and trafficking were thus first carried out in Yi areas in the Xichang Prefecture, where the Han constituted the majority. Before April 1954, when Yi or other ethnic minorities were caught bringing opium into the Han area, the authorities would merely point out the harmful effects of opium to the traffickers, asking them to take it back. In areas with large opium outflows, the authorities also tried to persuade Yi clan heads to tell their subordinates not to sell opium in Han areas. After April 1954, however, the authorities started to temporarily seize opium brought in by minority people. The seized opium was eventually turned over to the owner's local authorities, letting the latter work with the local clan head on the issue. By the second half of 1954, the authorities finally started to confiscate opium brought into Han areas by the Yi (Sun, Shi, and Zhu 1993: 204–207).

Suppressing poppy planting in the Yi area turned out to be a much tougher issue than merely curtailing the outflow of opium. Many Yi depended on the opium income to acquire food and other necessities of life. Without a change of agricultural practice from opium planting to crop cultivation, it would thus be very difficult for the Yi to stop planting poppies. This issue touched upon the interests of Yi of varying social statuses, especially those black Yi with large investments in poppy fields and slaves. Understandably, the authorities approached the issue carefully. They worked to educate and persuade Yi to voluntarily increase crop cultivation and to decrease poppy planting. Without resort to any form of coercion, the propaganda and persuasion seemed to work quite well in several Yi areas (Sun, Shi, and Zhu 1993: 207–208).

In contrast, the authorities met strong resistance when they used force to uproot poppies in the Yi area. After achieving the encouraging eradication of the opium poppy from two Xichang counties in 1954, the prefecture authorities asked that the task be carried out in five other counties, and they set the spring of 1955 as the deadline for eradicating poppy planting in both Han and Yi areas. To meet this deadline, poppy eradication was carried out hurriedly by force, an action that became the catalyst for a large-scale disturbance in Miyi County in January 1955, which lasted for 5 months and cost more than a dozen government cadres' lives. Immediately following the outbreak of this disturbance, the prefecture authorities ordered the poppy-eradication teams to be dismantled, and the forced eradication of opium in the Yi area was halted (Sun, Shi, and Zhu 1993: 208).

From 1950 to 1954, the authorities left the essential elements of Yi society intact. Government teams were ordered not to liberate slaves or to propagandize land reform (Lin 1995: 205–206). However, allowing a slave-based society to remain intact within a socialist China was not congruent with Communist ideology. After consolidating their presence in the Yi area for several years, the authorities finally launched a so-called democratic reform in 1956. This was actually a revolution forced upon Yi society, demanding the confiscation of slave owners' land and its redistribution to the public. It also forbade ownership of slaves and granted all present slaves freedom. Slave owners, most of them black Yi, resisted the democratic reform by rising against the government. The revolts started in December 1955 and were finally put down in October 1957.

In many aspects, the democratic reform utilized the same techniques that the Communists had used in other areas to establish their rule, involving massive propaganda campaigns and mass mobilization. As a result, hundreds of thousands of former slaves participated in the democratic reform and fought alongside 10,000 People's Liberation Army (PLA) troops and 5,000 militia members against those who revolted. In this process, the authorities cultivated 35,000 activists, including 2,300 Yi cadres. The Communist Party recruited 2,380 new members and established 251 party committees. In that way, the Liangshan Yi area was finally brought under the firm control of the Communists (Lin 1995: 223–229).

Fundamental changes in the Yi society from 1956 to 1958 provided a new opportunity for the authorities to carry out opium suppression. Since slave owners were the main cultivators of the opium poppy, when their land was confiscated, the poppy ceased to be planted. Authorities had considerable leverage over the newly liberated slaves to prevent them from planting poppies: After all, they had just received land from the government and did not want to jeopardize their acquisitions. The policy of suppressing opium planting in parallel with the process of democratic reform was clearly elaborated by a government document of 1957. By the second half of 1957, the authorities had eradicated 469 hectares of poppy fields in Liangshan and 315 hectares in Xichang—70 percent and 55 percent of the total acreage, respectively (Sun, Shi, and Zhu 1993: 209). In July 1957, for the first time, the authorities proclaimed that no nationality would be allowed to plant poppy, to sell opium, or to operate opium dens (Sun, Shi, and Zhu 1993: 210). The differentiation between policies on opium suppression between Han and Yi was thus finally abolished.

The final phase of opium suppression in Liangshan Yi area was carried out, from 1958 to 1959, concurrently with the campaign to suppress counterrevolutionaries. A total of more than 3,000 arrests was made in the latter campaign, and some of those arrested were also found guilty of drug offenses. In addition, the authorities tackled 17 opium cases and made 27 arrests. As far as poppy planting was concerned, the fact that 85 percent of Yi households had joined cooperatives by the spring of 1958 enabled the eradication of all poppies in Liangshan during the campaign. Meanwhile, with the seizure of 56,000 *liang* of stock opium in the Liangshan Yi area and another 55,000 *liang* in Xichang, opium was finally declared to have been wiped out in the Liangshan area (Sun, Shi, and Zhu 1993: 210–212; Lin 1995: 229).

Opium Suppression in the Aba Tibetan Area in the 1950s

The Aba Tibetan Autonomous Prefecture is located in the northwestern part of Sichuan Province, where Tibetans, Qiang, and Han are the main ethnic groups. According to a survey conducted in 1952, there were about 190,000 Tibetans in this area, accounting for about 48 percent of the area's total population of 400,000 (Research Office 1985a: 2, 1985b: 178). Within Aba, an area of 82,000 square kilometers that covered 13 counties, Tibetans were concentrated mainly in the western and northwestern parts, whereas the Han and the Qiang inhabited the eastern and southeastern parts, adjacent to the Han-dominated area of Sichuan Province (Editors of Aba 1985: 1, 11).

It is believed that opium planting started in the area in the 1860s. After the Qing dynasty established an "official" opium outlet in Maoxian in 1909, opium consumption appears to have been common in the area. After the fall of the Qing dynasty, poppy planting started to spread through the whole area, though poppy planting in the eastern and southeastern parts was more apparent than in the western and northeastern parts of Aba. According to a survey of one district of Maerkang over several years before 1950, out of a total of 2,156 hectares of arable land, 228 hectares, or 10.6 percent, were devoted to opium planting. Planting in Maerkang started in 1935 and reached its peak during 1947–1949 (Sichuan Nationality Survey Team 1985b: 258, 260; Maerkang Working Committee Survey Team 1985: 281). Coincidentally, 1935 was the start of the Six-Year Opium Suppression Plan under the Nationalists. It is possible that the opium cultivators in the Han area were under pressure and turned to the Tibetan area as a safe haven for opium cultivation.

The introduction of opium into the Tibetan area in Sichuan (mainly an agricultural area) brought a series of changes to local society. First, opium became a catalyst of commercial exchange, something that had previously scarcely existed in the mostly self-sufficient Tibetan economy. Maerkang, the current capital of the Aba Prefecture, was transformed from a small village into a bustling commercial market because of the opium trade. Although Han and Hui businessmen from both Sichuan and Gansu Provinces dominated opium transactions, Tibetan businessmen and stewards of Lamaist temples were also involved in exchanging opium for salt, tea, and other everyday necessities (Sichuan Nationality Survey Team 1985b: 261–262). As in Liangshan Yi society, opium also brought more guns into the Aba area.

But the opium did not enrich and empower ordinary Tibetans to the same extent that it had empowered members of the Yi community in Liangshan. The huge profits from opium were realized mostly in the process of commercial exchange. When Aba opium reached Gansu, the price would be quadrupled, and it would be even higher if the drug was sold as far away as Xinjiang Province. Though the profit margin was extremely high, few members of the Tibetan community benefited. Except chieftains (*tusi*), headmen, stewards of Lamaist temples, and a small number of wealthy people, the majority of Tibetans were not involved in the opium business because of its capital-intensive nature (Sichuan Nationality Survey Team 1985a: 334). Generally speaking, Han and Hui opium merchants controlled transactions in opium; the ordinary Tibetan role was limited to that of opium producer.

The Communists entered the Aba area in 1950. Facing complex social and ethnic problems, they used caution in dealing with the local opium issue, tackling it step by step and differentiating the Tibetans from the Han and other ethnic groups. It took much longer to eradicate the opium problem in Aba than in the rest of country. In 1951–1953, opium suppression was carried out in areas cleared of remnants of the Nationalist forces. In 1954, the campaign was conducted in the Chuosijia and Heishui Counties, signaling the extension of the campaign to the whole Aba area. In the same year, land reform was carried out in the Han and Qiang areas, reducing poppy planting further. From 1956 to 1959, the democratic reform deprived landlords of their land holdings in Tibetan communities. In 1959, the whole area was collectivized, and poppy planting was virtually eradicated in Aba. For the authorities, the remaining task was to seize opium still in peoples' possession. A detailed plan for this was devised in 1959, and the task was finally accomplished in 1963 (Editors of Aba 1985: 139–140; Yang 1993: 321–322).

The step-by-step strategy was used concurrently with one of differentiating and stratifying different ethnic groups in opium suppression. Theoretically, with the exception of the Han Chinese, all ethnic groups belonged to minority nationalities and were entitled to certain rights under the so-called nationality policy of the Communist Party. It is interesting that in the antidrug campaigns of the 1950s, differentiation was made not only between the Han and non-Han but also among the three other main ethnic groups—Tibetan, Qiang, and Hui—in the Aba area.

Before 1950, the majority of Aba-produced opium was sold to Gansu and Sichuan, the trade to the two provinces being controlled by Hui and Han trafficking groups, respectively. From the very beginning of the campaigns, therefore, the Han and Hui were the main targets of opium-suppression policies. At the end of 1951, the public security bureau of what was then Maoxian Prefecture ordered a crackdown on Han and Hui traffickers. However, in dealing with Tibetan and Qiang opium merchants who sold their products in the Han area, the local authorities were instructed to use persuasion only and to let the chieftains and headmen handle the issue. Paradoxically, as far as opium trafficking was concerned, the Hui were obviously deprived of their rights as a minority nationality, whereas the Qiang enjoyed the same lenient treatment as the Tibetans. However, since the majority of the Qiang lived in Maoxian (currently the Maowen Qiang Autonomous County) and had close contact with the Han, the authorities did not differentiate the Qiang from the Han when they conducted land reform in the fall of 1954 and thus at that time subjected them to the same standard of opium suppression as in the Han area.

Tibetans occupied the extreme low end in the ethnic stratification during the campaign, and they therefore enjoyed more tolerance in the opium suppression attempts. The national antidrug campaign of 1952 was directed at only the Han Chi-

nese in Aba. The local authorities presented suggestions on forbidding poppy planting to the provincial authorities on September 28, 1952, but the latter were cautious
and waited more than a year before instructing the local authorities to carry out
antidrug campaigns through a combination of propaganda and education. Furthermore, the instructions emphasized that opium suppression should be strictly limited
in its target to the Han and Hui opium trafficking groups, especially those Han traffickers from outside Aba areas (Yang 1993: 321). Since in many areas opium was
still the main source of income for ordinary households, the authorities clearly realized that without full control of those areas and without replacement of poppies
with other crops, conducting opium suppression would have provoked strong resistance and even riots, as had happened in the Liangshan Yi area. It is therefore
understandable that only after the democratic reform and collectivization in Tibetan areas was opium planting finally stopped in 1959.

Conclusion

The antidrug campaigns conducted among Erlunchun, Yi, and Tibetans reflect a
consistent policy on opium suppression in the minority areas by the People's Republic of China. The policy was based on two assumptions within the framework of
the state's nationality policies. One was that minority nationalities were different
from the Han Chinese and thus needed to be treated with sensitivity by the authorities. The other was that most minority peoples were at a "backward" stage of social development and thus needed to be "reformed" to enter the new socialist China.
Opium was one of the social evils to be eradicated in minority communities. The
first assumption, however, made the authorities adopt a gradualist approach, and in
most cases antidrug campaigns were conducted in minority areas only after they
had succeeded in Han areas. The second assumption prompted the government to
implement radical political and social policies to change the lives of minority peoples. As we have seen, opium suppression was never conducted as an isolated issue
but treated as an integral part of overall "reforms" and was accomplished in the
processes of those "reforms."

As far as the first assumption was concerned, the Chinese government from the
beginning tackled the opium problem in minority communities step by step, applying different tactics to different ethnic groups. Although applying a harsh policy to
the Han Chinese, the authorities used lenient policies, with some degree of variety,
toward other ethnic groups. The ethnic stratification of these policies is intriguing.
Ostensibly, it seems as if the more sinicized an ethnic group was, the more likely
it would be to get the same treatment as the Han in drug suppression, as in the case
of the highly sinicized Hui opium traffickers. In the case of Aba, the Tibetan,
Qiang, Hui, and Han communities were all treated differently according to a hierarchy of ethnic stratification in opium suppression in the 1950s.

This pattern, however, needs further scrutiny. In fact, the application of different
policies had more to do with the level of the government's actual control over particular ethnic groups in particular areas at particular times than with a theory of societal differentiation. Both the Yi in Liangshan and the Tibetans in Aba were not

under the firm control of the newly established People's Republic, and so the authorities had to conduct the opium-eradication campaigns step by step in connection with the completion of political and social transformation in these areas. The standard of ethnic differentiation was thus established mainly out of practical concerns, according to the degree of potential threat posed by such communities to the authorities.

Unfortunately, the cautious and gradualist approach of the nationality policy in the early 1950s did not last long. The desire to transform old, backward societies into new, civilized ones that fit a vision of the new socialist China prompted the Communists to launch "democratic reforms" in the mid- and late 1950s in most minority communities. Among the three cases discussed, the Erlunchun did not experience the democratic reforms. Because Erlunchun society was classified as classless, the official policy was that the authorities did not have to conduct "democratic reforms" as it did in Yi and Tibetan societies (Zhao 1987: 180). But the government viewed the settlement of this group of migrant hunters as the most effective way to advance them into socialism, and this move to permanent settlement totally changed their previous lifestyle. At roughly the same period of time, the new settlers were pushed to collectivize their labor, and they eventually became members of people's communes in 1959 (Du Yonghao 1993: 169–172). In the process of settlement and collectivization, even though the authorities' policy might have been well intentioned, and although antidrug efforts were helped by the settlement program, the rapid destruction of the old social and cultural composition of the Erlunchun caused unforeseeable social and psychological damage that has still to be redressed today. Alcohol abuse, for example, has never been solved in the Erlunchun society after their settlement. In the 1980s, it was still a major cause of nonnormal deaths that accounted for 50 percent of total deaths in some communities, an extraordinarily high rate (Du Yonghao 1993: 202–203).

In the Yi and Tibetan communities, it was in the years of "democratic reforms" that the government's antidrug campaigns finally achieved their goals. In the wave of collectivization, the authorities abandoned their previous cautious and gradualist approach. Even the Tibetans, who had been previously exempted from reform for 15 years, were collectivized at the end of the 1950s. Reform met strong resistance from the Yi and Tibetan communities, and its success was ensured by the military and political power of the authorities. Drug suppression gained effectiveness from the reform campaigns, and at the same time it contributed to their successful completion. By the end of the 1950s, opium had therefore become more of a social issue, as it had been among the Han Chinese for some time, than a minority issue that was to be tackled with sensitivity. Thus, a high-pressure reform approach finally prevailed, an approach that would exert its influence on the history of the People's Republic of China for the remainder of the century and into the new millennium.

References

Brugger, B., and S. Reglar. 1994. *Politics, Economy and Society in Contemporary China.* Stanford, CA: Stanford University Press.

Cheng Xianmin. 1987. Liangshan Yizu renkou wenti qianxi (A Preliminary Analysis of Liangshan Yi Population). In *Xinan minzu yanjiu* (*Study of Southwest Nationalities: Special Issue on Yi*), ed. China Association for the Study of Southwest Nationalities, pp. 151–179. Chengdu: Sichuan minzu chubanshe.

Erlunchunzhu jianshi (*A Concise History of Erlunchun*). 1983. Harbin: Helongjiang renmin chubanshe.

Du Yonghao. 1993. *Erlunchunzhu youlie, dingju, fazhan* (*Erlunchun: Hunting, Settlement, and Development*). Beijing: Central Nationality University Press.

Du Yuting. 1987. Banfengjian banzhimindi de jiuzhongguo yu Liangshan de nulizhi (On the Relations Between the Liangshan Yi Slavery and the Semi-feudal, Semi-Colonial Society of the Old China). In *Xinan minzu yanjiu* (*Study of Southwest Nationalities Special Issue on Yi*), ed. China Association for the Study of Southwest Nationalities, pp. 219–236. Chengdu: Sichuan minzu chubanshe.

Editors of Aba. 1985. *Aba Zangzu zizhizhou gaikuang* (*A General Description of the Aba Tibetan Autonomous Prefecture*). Chengdu: Sichuan minzu chubanshe.

Editors of Liangshan. 1985. *Liangshan Yizu zizhizhou gaikuang* (*A General Description of the Liangshan Yi Autonomous Prefecture*). Chengdu: Sichuan minzu chubanshe.

Gu Zeng. 1997. Jiayin Erlunchunren de jinyan (Opium Suppression among Erlunchun in Jiayin). In *Jindai zhongguo yandu xiezhen* (*Opium and Drugs in Modern China*), 2 vols., ed. Editorial Office of Wenshijinghua, pp. 274–280. Shijiazhuang: Hebei renmin chubanshe.

Hu Qingjun. 1987. Lun Liangshan Yizu de nuli zhidu (On the Yi Slave-Owning System in Liangshan). In *Xinan minzu yanjiu* (*Study of Southwest Nationalities: Special Issue on Yi*), ed. The China Association for the Study of Southwest Nationalities, pp. 10–46. Chengdu: Sichuan minzu chubanshe.

Inner Mongolia Compilers. 1984. *Erlunchunzhu shehui lishi diaocha* (*A Survey of Society and History of Erlunchun*), vol. 1. Hohalt: Neimenggu renmin chubanshe.

Li Jiaxiu. 1994. Shaosu minzu shanqu jingji fazhan tanwei (Reflections on Economic Development in Minority Inhabiting Mountainous Areas. In *Shanqu minzu jingji kaifa yu shehui jingbu* (*Ethnic Economy Development and Social Progress in Mountainous Areas*), ed. He Yaohua, pp. 72–84. Shanghai: Xuelin chubanshe.

Lin Yaohua (Lin yueh-hua). 1995. *Liangshan yijia de jubian* (*Tremendous Changes of Liangshan Yi People*). Beijing: Commercial Press.

Maerkang Working Committee Survey Team. 1985. Zhuokeji dubu xiasizhai shehui diaocha (A Social Survey of Four Villages of the Dubu District in Zhuokeji). In *Sichuansheng abazhou zangzu shehui lishi diaocha* (*A Survey of Tibetan Society and History in the Aba Prefecture of Sichuan Province*), ed. Sichuan Editors, pp. 271–300. Chengdu: Sichuan Academy of Social Sciences Press.

National Statistics Bereau. 2000. *Zhongguo tongji nianjian 2000* (*Statistical Yearbook of China, 2000*). Beijing: Zhongguo tongji chubanshe.

Qiu Pu. 1987. *Erlunchun shehui de fazhan* (*Development of Erlunchun Society*). Shanghai: Shanghai renmin chubanshe.

Research Office, Southwest Nationality College. 1985a. Caodi shehui qingkuang diaocha (A Social Survey of the Grassland Society). In *Sichuansheng abazhou zangzu shehui lishi diaocha* (*A Survey of Tibetan Society and History in the Aba Prefecture of Sichuan Province*), ed. Sichuan Editors, pp. 1–74. Chengdu: Sichuan Academy of Social Sciences Press.

———.1985b. Jiarong Zangzu shehui qingkuang diaocha (A Social Survey of Jiarong Tibetan). In *Sichuansheng abazhou zangzu shehui lishi diaocha* (*A Survey of Tibetan So-*

ciety and History in Aba Prefecture of Sichuan Province), ed. Sichuan Editors, pp. 178–257. Chengdu: Sichuan Academy of Social Sciences Press.

Shao Xianshu. 1987. Jiefangqian yapian zai jinyang diqu de zhongzhi, xiaoshou jiqi dui Yizu shehui jingji de yingxiang (The Effects of Opium Planting and Sales on the Yi Society and Economy in the Jinyang Area Before the Liberation) In *Sichuan Guizhou Yizu shehui lishi diaocha* (*A Survey of Yi Society and History in Sichuan and Guizhou Provinces*), ed. Yunnan Editors, pp. 51–54. Kunming: Yunnan renmin chubanshe.

Sichuan Nationality Survey Team. 1985a. Chuosijia shehui diaocha (A Social Survey of Chuosijia). In *Sichuansheng abazhou zangzu shehui lishi diaocha* (*A Survey of Tibetan Society and History in the Aba Prefecture of Sichuan Province*), ed. Sichuan Editors, pp. 332–353. Chengdu: Sichuan Academy of Social Sciences Press.

———. 1985b. Zhuokeji tusi tongzhi diqu diaocha (A Survey of the Area under the Zhuoheji Chieftains). In *Sichuansheng abazhou zangzu shehui lishi diaocha* (*A Survey of Tibetan Society and History in Aba Prefecture of Sichuan Province*), ed. Sichuan Editors, pp. 258–270. Chengdu: Sichuan Academy of Social Sciences Press.

Sun Xingsheng, Shi Tangxi, and Zhu Changhe. 1993. Jinyan jindu zai Liangshan (Anti-Opium Campaign in Liangshan). In *Jinchang jindu* (*Abolish Prostitution and Eradicate Narcotics*), ed. Ma Weigang, pp. 197–217. Beijing: Jingguan jiaoyu chubanshe.

Wang Yingliang. 1987. Liangshan Yizu shehui de lishi fazhan (The Historical Development of Liangshan Yi Society). In *Xinan minzu yanjiu* (*Study of Southwest Nationalities: Special Issue on Yi*), ed. China Association for the Study of Southwest Nationalities, pp. 47–74. Chengdu: Sichuan minzu chubanshe.

Yang Guangcheng. 1993. Aba de jinyan sudu (Anti-Opium Campaign in Aba). In *Jinchang jindu* (*Abolish Prostitution and Eradicate Narcotics*), ed. Ma Weigang, pp. 316–322. Beijing: Jingguan jiaoyu chubanshe.

Zhang Chengxu. 1987. Liangshan Yizu yige nuli shichang de diaocha baogao (A Survey of a Slave Market in the Liangshan Yi Area). In *Xinan minzu yanjiu* (*Study of Southwest Nationalities: Special Issue on Yi*), ed. China Association for the Study of Southwest Nationalities, pp. 143–150. Chengdu: Sichuan minzu chubanshe.

Zhao Fuxing. 1987. *Erlunchunzhu yanjiu* (*Study of Erlunchun*). Huhehot: Neimengu renmin chubanshe.

Zhou Yongming. 1999. *Anti-Drug Crusades in Twentieth-Century China: Nationalism, History, and State Building.* Lanham, MD: Rowman & Littlefield.

Zhu Jianhong. 2001. Woguo zong renkou wei 12,9533 yi (China's Population Is 1.29533 Billion). *People's Daily*, March 29.

IV

Environmental Issues

11

Environmental and Social Consequences of Coca/Cocaine in Peru

Policy Alternatives and a Research Agenda

Kenneth R. Young

T he demand for illicit drugs can leverage dramatic changes in land cover and associated native biological diversity. These changes, in turn, can lead to loss of critical habitats and rare species of plants and animals, in addition to the degradation of remaining habitats and the contamination of water bodies. Concomitantly, demand can transform social and economic processes, acting against the interests of long-time residents, such as indigenous groups, by attracting new colonists and fomenting crime and violence.

Given these potential interconnections between illicit drugs and grave social and environmental consequences, it is more than peculiar that so much scholarly work on environmental transformations does not consider drug-related causes in those countries that supply or transship the drugs. Examples of this myopia include most of the literature on tropical deforestation, where illicit drugs are ignored (e.g., Anderson 1990; Wood 1990; Dove 1993; Myers 1993; Place 1993; Rudel 1993; Brown and Pearce 1994; Jepman 1995; Goldsmith 1998; Barraclough and Ghimere 2000; Horta 2000). The chapters in this book partly correct this deficit and I provide here information for the case of Peru and for "coca/cocaine."

In this chapter, I provide an overview of the way these processes have acted in Peru in relation to the demand for coca leaves, which are transformed into cocaine paste and cocaine. I find great spatial heterogeneity in the negative impacts, at least some of which can be explained by the values and practices of particular social groups. A political ecology approach is helpful in this assessment because by definition illicit drugs intermix the power of governments and economic forces with outcomes toward and resistance by local peoples. I begin by characterizing "coca/ cocaine," first disaggregating the two words and then showing how the associated processes have affected geopolitics acting upon and within Peru. Then, I examine the evidence available for the effects of coca/cocaine on local landscapes inhabited by indigenous and other social groups. Finally, I outline the known environmental consequences. In the conclusion, I provide the elements necessary for a more complete research agenda that, in turn, could provide the information needed to explore policy alternatives for the social actors involved.

Coca/Cocaine

Coca

Coca is the common name in Spanish of two shrub species of the genus *Erythroxylum*, *E. coca* and *E. novogranatense*, which were domesticated in the tropical Andes (Rury and Plowman 1983; Plowman 1984a, 1984b, 1986). There are approximately 325 named species in this genus (http://mobot.org), which is particularly diverse in the lowlands and foothills of humid environments in South America. The two domesticated species were probably found to be useful several millennia ago, as their leaves appear in archaeological contexts from as much as 5,000 to 7,000 years ago (Piperno and Pearsall 1998). The leaves traditionally are picked and dried, then chewed, usually with the addition of lime to the wad. The result is a gradual dosing with dozens of alkaloids and a physiological response of reduced sensations of hunger and fatigue. This was obviously a useful plant product for subsistence agriculturalists who needed to walk great distances and work long hours. In addition, the leaves are used medicinally in places where coca is grown, for example, in the form of an infusion.

The traditional use of coca for chewing appears to have no negative social consequences (Duke et al. 1975; Martin 1975; Morales 1989). There are probably several million daily users of coca who show no ill effects at all. In fact, the sharing of coca leaves and group sessions of coca chewing reinforce ties of friendship and kinship in the Andean highlands (figure 11.1; Martin 1970; Isbell 1985; C. J. Allen 1986, 1988; Morales 1989). Coca is symbolic of the ancient ties of Andean peoples to the powerful natural forces that surround them; offerings of coca leaves are traditionally made to request safe passage through high mountain passes. Coca has been important economically for at least a thousand years; because it is grown in the Andean foothills but consumed principally in the highlands, the interchange of products in order to obtain coca leaves has long tied highland and lowland communities together (Osborne 1973; Rostworowski 1988). It was also an important commodity during colonial times (Stern 1993).

Cocaine

It was in the late 1800s that a process was developed to chemically separate cocaine from the coca leaf (MacGregor 1990; Gagliano 1994). This purification creates a narcotic that is both addictive and in demand by people other than traditional coca users. In fact, the demand for cocaine is principally from outside of Peru and the

Figure 11.1. These Andean farmers are taking a break to chew coca leaves during a long day of harvesting and threshing wheat in northern Peru (photo by Kenneth R. Young).

other tropical countries where coca is grown: Bolivia and Colombia. This changes the market forces and connects this once traditional crop to social entities that collect the leaves, process them into cocaine, and move that cocaine to drug users primarily living in the United States and Europe. This was first important from the 1880s to the 1920s. When the addictive nature of cocaine became obvious, controls were put on its commerce (Gagliano 1994; Spillane 2000). The only legal international trade in most of the twentieth century was for cocaine as a pharmaceutical product and the coca leaf as a flavoring for drinks such as Coca-Cola (F. Allen 1994).

The demand for illicit cocaine increased markedly in the 1970s and resulted in more plantings of the shrub. Coca can be grown below about 2,400 meters in the Andes, mostly on the eastern, Amazon side, but also with irrigation in coastal or inter-Andean valleys. Most of the new areas for cultivation were in isolated places, where there was little access or oversight by the government (Poole and Rénique 1992). The eastern slopes of the Peruvian Andes were ideal in this regard (figure 11.2). Coca fields were increased in the areas where coca had been grown for traditional usage since colonial days: in the central Huallaga River Valley and near Quillabamba. New areas of cultivation were established in areas opened for colonization by government-sponsored programs in the 1960s, 1970s, and 1980s. Without exception, every area with new roads and colonists became centers of coca leaf production for the illicit market: the entire upper Huallaga River Valley, the upper Pachitea River Valley, and the Ene River Valley.

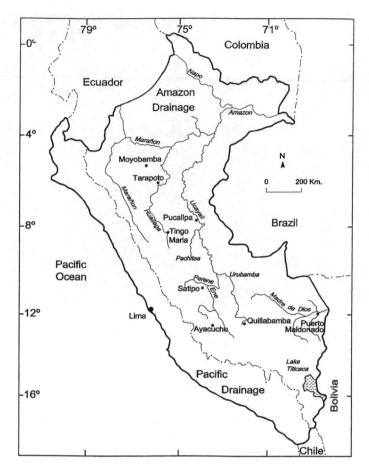

Figure 11.2.   Cities and rivers in eastern Peru.

When Coca Becomes Cocaine

Coca grows especially well on humid and steep slopes at 500- to 1,500-meter elevation (figure 11.3; Young 1996). Places with these characteristics, which were accessible to colonists but without much governmental control, were deforested and occupied over a 20-year time period. Most settlers were from the Andean highlands or the Amazon lowlands. They grew coca because they could and because there was a market for the leaves. Typically, the coca plants form only part of the agricultural landscape, with other fields supporting maize and beans, some coffee and oil palm plantations, and rough pasture for raising cattle (Aramburú 1989). The amount of coca grown is a function of the area of suitable land, the price paid for the picked leaves, the degree to which the cultivation and gathering of leaves is controlled or punished by law enforcement agencies, and the attitudes and aspirations of local people.

Figure 11.3. Tropical forest fragmented for the establishment of coca fields and pastures in central Peru's eastern Andean foothills (photo by Kenneth R. Young).

Leaves are picked three to six times a year from the perennial coca shrub (Morales 1989; MacGregor 1990). After drying, they are sold by the weight to either the legal, controlled market (for flavoring or pharmaceutical use) or to wholesalers connected to the illicit narcotics trade. For the latter, the leaves are soaked and trampled in pits, using solvents, acids, and a neutralizer such as lime, in order to extract cocaine paste. The paste is then typically moved to another site, where the cocaine is extracted with reagents such as hydrochloric acid, acetone, and ether. At each step, the volume of the product is much reduced, making shipment and secrecy progressively easier (P. H. Smith 1992), while the value increases by roughly a total of two orders of magnitude. Thus, a gram of cocaine worth $80 in the United States or Europe (Clawson and Lee 1996) requires inputs of 3.75 grams of cocaine paste, worth about $3.50 in Peru (Morales 1989). This amount of cocaine paste is made from approximately 430 grams of coca leaves (Morales 1989), worth to the farmer perhaps 65 cents (Clawson and Lee 1996). This means that slight increases in demand overseas can result in huge changes in land use in the supply countries like Peru. Unfortunately, another consequence is that dramatic changes in supply do little to control price or demand.

Geopolitics and the Spread of Coca/Cocaine in Peru

There are many nefarious consequences of the illicit portion of the coca/cocaine phenomenon. For one thing, it distorts and complicates state-to-state relationships between and among the drug-supplying and drug-using countries (e.g., García-Sayán 1989; George 1992; Malamud-Goti 1992; Bagley and Walker 1996; Clawson and Lee 1996; Menzel 1996; Riley 1996; Rossi 1996; McClintock 1998; Chepesiuk 1999; Cotler 1999; Luca de Tena 2000; Arnson 2001). Debt relief, humanitarian and technical assistance, military advice, political coordination—all become subsumed under a "drug war" discourse. The United States frequently conditions investment and assistance on the perceived sincerity of the drug-supplying countries in narcotics control efforts. Although less visible in the news media, the European countries utilize similar strategies. For example, the citizens of Colombia, Peru, and Bolivia have particular difficulties in acquiring travel visas for countries of the European Community.

Within Peru, state-to-people relations have become distorted in profound ways (e.g., Morales 1989; Poole and Rénique 1992; Cotler 1999), affecting indigenous peoples and other social groups. In the early years of the most recent coca/cocaine boom, Peru was under a military government (1968–1980). The initial goals of the state were to implement a land reform policy and to nationalize the portion of the economy controlled by foreign companies, particularly in the mining, fishing, manufacturing, and banking sectors (Klarén 2000). Land tenure changed in the sense that the properties of some large landowners were redistributed (McClintock and Lowenthal 1983), but this coincided with an abandonment of infrastructure and investment in rural areas and the start of massive migrations to urban areas and the Amazon basin. The economy was mismanaged, and both internal and external forces convinced the military to allow elections in 1979. It was during this time that the money entering Peru to pay for coca leaves and cocaine paste became a significant economic force (Poole and Rénique 1992). Coca cultivation increased on the eastern slopes of the Andes where farmers knew how to grow and harvest coca and where the state had little presence. Probably the government's attitude at this time can be best characterized as indifference or ignorance to what was going on in the Amazon basin hinterland.

This changed dramatically with the second government of Fernando Belaúnde (1980–1985), when these very areas were made the centerpieces of his stated goal to colonize the Amazon by building roads and promoting new settlements, under initiatives begun during his first government (1963–1968) (Denevan 1966; Belaúnde 1994; Santos and Barclay 1995). The rhetoric used by his administration suggested that the end pursued was to unify the country and provide opportunities for the rural poor. This was an attractive prospect for developed countries, international donor agencies, and banks, all of which invested tens of millions of dollars in the Carretera Marginal venture and associated colonization projects (Bedoya and Klein 1996). Of course, the lands opened to settlement were not uninhabited—they were the territories of indigenous groups not consulted by national or international planners (Remy 1994). And it was clear that all the roads built ended in the capital city of Lima, increasing the central government's power and providing most of the economic benefits to those who chose to live and work in that rapidly growing metropolis. Narcotic control efforts began during this time period but were soon rendered inefficient by the proliferation of coca fields and coca/cocaine wholesalers. Klarén (2000: 374) reports that cocaine was Peru's largest export rubric in

1982, of about $700 to $800 million, but not tabulated in official economic data. The area planted in coca increased, according to INEI (1997), as follows: 1980, 39,861 hectares; 1981, 48,085 hectares; 1982, 56,153 hectares; 1983, 57,694 hectares; 1984, 60,163 hectares; 1985, 77,139 hectares.

This was also the time when two armed guerrilla groups began to be a significant source of social unrest, both to the country as a whole and to local residents of particular areas (Gonzales 1992; Poole and Rénique 1992; Kent 1993; Tapia 1997; Stern 1998). The MRTA (Movimiento Revolucionario Tupac Amaru) carried out kidnappings and other violence in urban areas, but they also soon found a significant geographic space where they could operate on the eastern slopes, primarily near Qullabamba and Satipo and eventually in the Huallaga Valley also. They were frequently accused of being accomplices of the drug wholesalers from Peru and Colombia. The other armed group was the Shining Path (Sendero Luminoso), originally located in the central highlands of Ayacucho but, by 1982, also beginning to operate in the Amazon lowlands of central Peru. This put them into contact with the drug wholesalers, with whom they had an adversarial and competitive relationship in the early years. Later, it became clear that they were tolerant of the drug trade, despite philosophical objections, because of the large sums of money involved and the strategic advantages of using the Peruvian Amazon and Andean foothills to retreat, regroup, and train their adherents. The negotiations and alliances between these groups and the drug middlemen was called narco-terrorism (Tarazona-Sevillano 1990).

Armed social actors thus surrounded local people who lived in the coca-producing areas (Menzel 1996; Palmer 1996; Taylor 1997). From 1982 and throughout the administration of Alan García (1985–1990) there were violent conflicts among the Peruvian police, the Peruvian armed forces (army and navy), the MRTA, and the Shining Path. Some of these conflicts involved government versus guerrilla groups. However, others were between the guerrilla groups for control of the Ene and Huallaga Valleys (Strong 1992). Also, there was increasing evidence of official corruption, with elements of the armed forces accepting the presence of or even benefiting from the drug wholesalers. The local people were the principal victims of this complexity (Poole and Rénique 1992). There were more than 25,000 civilian fatalities during this period in Peru. Spatially, the worst violence was in coca-growing areas—the same places made attractive for colonization in the 1970s and early 1980s. In addition, the reprisals and massacres against rural communities that became widespread in the highlands of Peru, and which were perpetrated by the armed forces, began in about 1988 and were common throughout Alberto Fujimori's first administration (1990–1995). This violence forced tens of thousands of refugees to the coastal and highland cities or down to the Amazon lowlands.

Efforts by the state to control social unrest thus became intertwined with the increasingly important economic role of coca/cocaine, which by 1987 represented 40 percent of Peru's exports and about $1 billion annually (Klarén 2000). According to INEI (1997) reports, areas of coca were planted as follows: 1986, 88,397 hectares; 1987, 108,837 hectares; 1988, 138,231 hectares; 1989, 137,640 hectares; 1990, 137,184 hectares. Because of poor economic management, Alan García was forced to accept international demands to open the Peruvian economy to foreign investment. The Fujimori administration accentuated this trend by opening the economy further, especially in the sectors nationalized by the military government and in relation to cheap imports of foods and manufactured goods. One implication of this "neoliberal" strategy in Peru was that the economy was further dollarized. Because many of the dollars entering Peru were being used to buy coca and cocaine paste, this was a national policy, with international acceptance, of legalized money laundering. This coincided with national and international schemes (De Soto 1986) to utilize the resources found in Peru's informal economy, much of which was also financed by money originating in narcotics. The second administration of Fujimori (1995–2000) further institutionalized many of these efforts, taking advantage of the disappearance of most of the activities of the guerilla groups. Estimates in the news media at the time of this writing (April 2001) suggest that there are now between 35,000 and 45,000 hectares of coca in Peru. However, because of increased productivity by coca growers, smaller areas now produce more coca per unit of area then several decades ago.

Currently, there seems to be a social amnesia in Peru about the power and control exerted by coca/cocaine, with little discussion of it in regard to the areas affected in the eastern slopes and little notice of its consequences for people in both rural and urban areas. This also occurs internationally. For example, the role of illicit drugs in Peru's political crises was overlooked by Tulchin and Bland (1994), and their part in creating negative effects on the rural poor was neglected in Gwynne and Kay's (1999) and Loker's (1999) overviews of globalization.

Social Consequences and Local Landscapes

It is difficult to find detailed published reports on what the local people experienced and thought during the decades of the most violence and social unrest in Peru. It would be important to know the following: What were the effects on family and on local demography? What were the associated changes in land use and land cover? What were the effects of ethnicity on their responses?

Of course, it is not clear how much of the social difficulties can be blamed on coca/cocaine. That would require an imaginary Peru—one where the Shining Path and MRTA appeared but where there was no money entering the economy from the drug trade. Here, I collect recent accounts by social researchers in areas affected by coca/cocaine or in other areas where coca could be cultivated. I consider first, the indigenous groups and then others, mostly colonists. I begin in northern Peru and move to the south.

Indigenous Peoples

Coca is principally grown in the foothills of the eastern slopes of the Andes. It is there where most impact has occurred, although some social groups have been relatively little affected. For example, the lowland indigenous groups least affected by coca/cocaine in this region are the Jívaro and related groups such as the Shuar, Mayna, Aguaruna, Achuara, Candoshi, and Huambisa, who are found in northern

Peru (and across the border into Ecuador). They live in areas potentially cultivatable for coca, but they do not traditionally use the plant (Brown 1986; Descola 1994) and their lands (in Peru) are still remote from colonization efforts. Furthermore, the guerrilla groups were not active in this part of Peru. All of these factors have resulted in little penetration of coca/cocaine.

Rather different are the Lamas (Lamistas), a Quechua-speaking group on lands that form an enclave surrounded by areas colonized by settlers from the Andes during the last 40 years in the Huallaga River valley. Coca is widely grown by these settlers in the Tarapoto area and to some extent by the Lamas, particularly those who are most closely tied to the cash economy. Just to the south of their lands is the upper Huallaga River valley, which became the world's principal source of cocaine during the 1980s. This area had been largely depopulated of indigenous people several centuries earlier because of disease and other consequences of the Spanish colony (Maskrey et al. 1990).

It was in central Peru where the most unrest that affected indigenous people occurred in lowland areas. Some of the Asháninka (Campa) and related groups (Nomatsiguana, Ashinanca, Pajonalino, Caquite, Piro, and Ucayalino) were drawn into the armed conflict (Brown and Fernández 1991; Rojas Zolezzi 1994; Santos and Barclay 1995; Manrique 1998). This had to do with attempts by the Shining Path and MRTA to occupy lands of the Asháninka or at least to make an alliance or to obtain permission to pass through their lands. These efforts were rejected, and images of Asháninka men posing with bows and arrows became common on television or in Peruvian newspapers. Shining Path members killed many with modern weapons. There was also displacement of refugees: For example, some moved into the Palcazu River Valley (upper Pachitea River Valley) in the late 1980s and early 1990s, causing in turn displacement of some of the Amuesha (Yanesha) to more isolated locations (figure 11.4). The armed forces provided limited armament and organization to the Asháninka under Fujimori's first administration, and their fighters eventually forced a withdrawal of the Shining Path. This is mostly a story of power and fighting and not one directly tied to coca/cocaine, although coca is grown traditionally by the Asháninka (Rojas Zolezzi 1994). But it bears mentioning that the entire Ene River Valley, although within historical Asháninka areas of influence, was opened to colonization in the 1960s, and many lowland and foothill areas were deforested and some planted to coca in the 1970s and 1980s. This is the area where the Shining Path is still active to this day, in remote parts of the valley. Based on firsthand experience, del Pinott (1998) compares the treatment of the Asháninkas there by the Shining Path to the effects of Nazi concentration camps.

The general violence associated with the guerrilla groups spread out from the Andes of central Peru into the Amazon as far east as Pucallpa. Indigenous groups there were not drawn into fighting like the Asháninka, but they were living in landscapes where incursions by the Shining Path or MRTA and retaliatory actions by the armed forces became common from about 1986 to 1993. The largest groups affected by this social unrest were the Shipibo and Conibo, as well as the Cashibo, Cocama, and Pishquibo. Coca is not used traditionally by the Shipibo or Conibo, based on my interpretation of descriptions by Bergman (1980) and Eakin et al. (1986).

Figure 11.4. This Amuesha family is posing in their finest clothes. They live in the Is-cozacin are of central Peru (photo by Kenneth R. Young).

In southern Peru, the Machiguenga (Matsiguenga) occupy lands in the upper parts of the Urubamba River and the Madre de Dios River watersheds. The influence of coca/cocaine, at least in terms of where coca is planted and harvested, appears to stop just about where their lands begin, perhaps because of their fierce reputation toward outsiders. In addition, their lands are generally not accessible by road and are on remote portions of the waterways. They cultivate coca traditionally for use as an anaesthetic, according to Johnson (1983). Baksh (1995) described a decline in their quality of life with increased integration into the market economy.

The smaller indigenous groups further to the south probably have been more affected by roads and colonization than directly by coca/cocaine, based on descriptions in Gray (1996b). This includes the Arakmbut (Harakmbut, Amarkeri) and others. Gray (1996a) describes the ritual importance of coca to the Arakmbut. Several places near Puerto Maldonado have been used for transshipment of cocaine or cocaine paste toward Brazil or Bolivia. In general, border areas, especially between Peru and Colombia, have become unsafe to local people because of drug processing and shipping.

Indigenous peoples in the Andean highlands were also affected during these years of violence, although the causes are only indirectly or distantly attributable to coca/cocaine. Most of the casualties were in the Ayacucho highlands (Manrique 1998). This and other areas were depopulated because of the fleeing of refugees. Coca used for traditional purposes by highland people still had to be acquired from

Figure 11.5. A colonist is standing amid a field he recently cut and burned from tropical forest in central Peru (photo by Kenneth R. Young).

the lower elevations, where it is grown. The shipment of leaves within Peru was restricted (C. J. Allen 1988), but there have not been active programs to discourage this traditional use in the highlands (although this use is forbidden in the coastal cities).

Others

Coca/cocaine distorts the values and goals of colonists (figure 11.5) and long-time settlers. To start, life is difficult in the foothills of the Andes—the climate is rainy, fertile soils on gentle slopes are scarce, and markets for agricultural products are distant or unreachable. Ironically, the roads or rivers that allow for transportation and increased communication also permit the arrival of the bulky materials needed for conversion of coca leaves to cocaine paste. For example, the point on the Andes where low-gradient Amazon rivers become turbulent Andean streams or rivers, at about 700 to 1,000 meters of elevation, is also the place at which rivers can no longer be used by boats to bring in barrels of chemicals and sacks of lime. Coca can be grown at much higher elevations, but the illicit processing of the leaves needs to be done nearer to large rivers or within several hours of a road. Thus, every attempt to better conditions for settlers in the Peruvian Amazon by improving infrastructure paradoxically augments the ease and attractiveness of participating in the drug trade. Coca leaves are harvested throughout the year and so can provide a steady income in an area characterized by seasonality of climate, harvests, and the need for paid laborers. The drug wholesalers will even pay cash in the field to farmers with coca leaves, eliminating the need to take a harvest to a distant market for a possible sale. In some localities, the wholesalers have replaced the typical function of the state in buying extra agricultural production and providing loans that permit plantings of new crops.

Most people living in the coca-producing areas do not want to participate in an illicit activity. Certainly, they would avoid the risk and associated violence if given a choice. However, at least 50,000 people have become actively involved in cultivation, transportation, or some other aspect of coca/cocaine (Alvarez 1992). Many more people have benefited indirectly as they provided goods or services to those who had money, often dollars, that came from outside the community. The town of Tingo Maria had about 5,000 inhabitants and one dusty street in the late 1970s. In the early 1990s, there were tens of thousands living in and around Tingo Maria, which had several new car dealerships: Coca fields could be seen on the hills surrounding the town.

Effective local and regional governance, with national oversight, could accompany improved conditions for settlers. This has not happened in the eastern slopes, where salaries of public employees are less than in the big cities. While generals were paid $500 a month during the García and Fujimori administrations, a single drug flight allowed to leave from a clandestine airfield was worth $10,000 to $15,000 to the local authority. There were hundreds of such flights a year, with the income going to whoever exerted control locally, whether a guerrilla group or a governmental entity.

Cocaine paste is addictive but much cheaper and easier to produce than cocaine. It is also bulkier and less valuable, so the presence of nearby markets is an advantage. It is now the most commonly used illicit drug among the middle and lower classes in the cities of Peru. Although cocaine use in Peru is limited to a small urban elite, mimicking the behavior of peers in developed countries, the presence of cocaine paste creates neighborhoods of fear in Lima (Riofrío 1996), Pucallpa, and other cities. It economically ties coca-producing areas to demand inside Peru or in cities of neighboring countries and further complicates control efforts.

Environmental Consequences

In Young (1996), I evaluated how much biological diversity was at risk from land use practices associated with coca cultivation in Peru. For just one department, San Martín, and only considering plants found growing below 1,500 meters of elevation, I showed that 3,375 species could be negatively affected by the clearing of forests to establish fields of coca. Of these, 521 are national endemics, species unique to Peru, and 161 of these species are only known from San Martín's forests, growing in the same kind of environment that has been deforested for coca. If a similar analysis was done for the butterflies, frogs, birds, mammals, and other animal groups with much diversity that are found in the native forests at 500 to 1,500 meters in eastern Peru, the biodiversity potentially at risk would be high indeed, approaching the national totals of smaller tropical countries. Davalos (2001) recently analyzed the biodiversity issues for a similar area in Colombia.

Of course, not all the deforestation is caused by coca: There are also pastures and maize fields and oil palm plantations. Roughly a third of Peru's deforestation is in places where coca is grown, which would mean 700,000 to 1 miillion hectares of tropical forest cut as a result. What coca/cocaine has done as an economic and social phenomenon is to provide the financial means and motives for deforestation. It has also inverted typical spatial expectations of deforestation. People tend to clear forests near roads and choose first the flattest lands with the best soils (Rudel 1993). This logic is reversed with coca/cocaine: The best coca fields are those that are most inaccessible to narcotic control efforts, that is, on isolated sites in hilly areas. Thus, coca-related deforestation affects forests that otherwise would not have been attractive to colonists.

Also, coca fields are often created on areas that are 0.25 to 1.0 hectare in size, leaving forest margins around the field. The patchwork landscapes that result (figure 11.3) suggest that even forests not directly cut will be influenced indirectly by the forest edge conditions that can limit or prevent the survival of plant and animal species that require large tracts of undisturbed forest (Schelhas and Greenberg 1996; Laurence and Bierregaard 1997). In addition, new fields tend to be established in more isolated sites, thus creating even more forest fragmentation.

There seems to be little likelihood of ecological restoration of these deforested and degraded landscapes. If, in addition, these lands cannot be used sustainably or economically for legal crops, the environmental tragedy is increased. If these lands were or are used by indigenous peoples, the environmental consequences are compounded by social disruption and loss.

Because coca is grown on steep slopes with no ground cover and often with heavy applications of pesticides, concerns have been expressed about soil erosion, pesticide contamination, and impact on water quality (Dourojeanni 1989). Where processing of cocaine paste occurs, chemicals are released into the environment through dumping in rivers or drainage into the soil. MacGregor (1990) estimates that this input is on the order of 50,000 tons of kerosene and 2,000 tons of sulfuric acid each year.

The coca/cocaine deforestation front is now quite near the boundaries of several national parks: Río Abiseo and Yanachaga-Chemillén (Echavarria 1991; Young 1996). This front engulfed Tingo Maria National Park in the 1980s. It would only take a little more international demand to pull farmers into those forested areas. For that matter, it would only take more concerted control efforts in the Huallaga and upper Pachitea valleys to push farmers onto more isolated hill slopes, some of which are nominally protected by being within the legal limits of national parks or on lands designated for use by indigenous peoples.

Conclusions

Environmental Degradation

Numerous species of plants and animals are potentially at risk in Peru from the loss of forest cover and the increase in forest fragmentation that results from coca/

cocaine. Critical habitat is being lost, especially in the foothills of the eastern slopes of the Andes. Species dependent on large tracts of undisturbed forest are most threatened, as are those that have very limited distributions or use the forests seasonally. In addition, the streams and rivers of the foothills provide habitat and spawning grounds for fish and other aquatic organisms. Pesticides and the chemicals used for the processing of cocaine paste enter these bodies of water, although measures of ecotoxicity have not been made.

That is perhaps the most perplexing part of evaluating the environmental consequences of coca/cocaine: No relevant data are being systematically gathered. Despite large investments in satellite technology and despite the publicizing of measurements of hectares of coca in Peru, given to three significant digits by the different government agencies, no accurate published maps show where coca grows. There are no yearly accounts of where and why forest was cut. No research is being done on forest fragmentation in the coca-growing areas. No field studies are published about the plants and animals most at risk. There are no monitoring stations on the streams and rivers to measure water quality. For that matter, coca/cocaine is erroneously not listed as an important environmental concern for Peru in the overviews by Dinerstein et al. (1995) and Mittermeier et al. (1999), and the areas used for coca cultivation are not targeted for any special conservation programs by governmental and nongovernmental organizations.

Needed are monitoring programs that keep track of the location and causes of forest losses; that gather data on the presence and abundance of plants and animals, especially of the species most at risk; and that measure the quantity and quality of water moving through the foothills and into the Amazon. Needed are special efforts to restore degraded forests, to slow down the advance of deforestation, and to protect the lands designated for biodiversity conservation or for the use of indigenous peoples. Needed is the answer to the question, Why is so little being done?

Social Costs

The social costs borne by innocent people caught in the middle of coca/cocaine have been quite visible in the news media: massacres, abandonment of their lands, and loss of basic human rights. This is not to say, however, that the violence has been well documented or understood. The scientific approach is obviously limited if no relevant data have been gathered. Starn (1991) criticized social scientists for not paying more attention to the effects of the Shining Path, although researchers with long-term ties to indigenous communities are indeed beginning to publish detailed accounts of what those people lived through in the 1980s and 1990s (Mitchell 1991, 1999; Kirk 1997; Stern 1998). There are hidden economic ties that must be traced, from the violence and uncertainty of the eastern-slope foothills near Uchiza to the grimy streets of Lince in Lima. These economic forces and the social networks that develop also potentially link Amazonian groups to drug-use fashions in the United States and Europe. These ties have real consequences for land-use practices and planting decisions by farmers. They also affect the livability of urban areas and the behavior of people hoping to improve their lot in life (Medina-Mora and del Carmen Mariño 1992).

These social concerns have national and international consequences. It is easy for politicians in the North to shift blame for narcotics to the South (Mabry 1996; Morales 1996). The annual ritual of counting how many hectares of coca are present (even though the methods used are not clarified) becomes the critical step in how bilateral and multilateral relations among countries are viewed. Within Peru, economic assistance becomes tied to "crop substitution" programs, which supposedly offer new crops, new products, and new markets in return for not planting coca. Despite near universal negative evaluations of their success (McClintock 1989; OTA 1993), these are the only visible governmental programs in the coca-growing areas of the eastern slopes, with the exception of military and police activities. Sadly, the programs also include the building of roads in tropical forests, thus perpetuating the road-deforestation-coca linkage.

To add complexity, a holistic approach would also need to include the other illicit drugs that are readily grown in any warm place in Peru with enough rainfall or access to irrigation. Marijuana is grown on a small scale for domestic sale, and opium is now planted in small hidden fields in virtually every highland department. In addition, any dramatic change in supplies of cocaine paste or cocaine originating from Peru will affect demand, as perceived by local people in Bolivia and Colombia. More control in one place simply shifts the supply and associated deforestation and environmental degradation to other places. For that matter, coca has been a cultivar for several millennia. There is little to stop its cultivation in any warm place in the world.

The social research needed is of all kinds: from more work on the economics, especially the microeconomic consequences in rural communities, to a pursuit of a better understanding of geopolitics, based on internal documents and the recollections of retired administrators. To understand local communities, research that uses a political ecology approach would be particularly revealing.

Political Ecology of Coca/Cocaine

Coca is an example of a traditionally used plant that can be modified into a derivative of international importance. That product, cocaine, can change global and national economies. The term coca/cocaine includes the entire social complex, from the planting of the coca in eastern Peru to the delivery of illicit cocaine to users in New York City, for example. A political ecology approach would help delineate the economic and power connections that activate and maintain this complex. It also provides a conceptual framework to analyze the situation of people living in particular areas and kinds of landscapes. Perhaps the understanding that originates from this approach can be used to suggest policy alternatives that could mitigate some of the negative environmental and social costs.

Political ecology has several definitions and applications (Blaikie and Brookfield 1987; Atkinson 1991; Painter and Durham 1995; Peet and Watts 1996; Bryant and Bailey 1997; Stott and Sullivan 2000). Here, I use it in the sense of a research approach that clarifies the relationship between political and economic power and the use of natural resources in particular landscapes. As a recent example, Turner (1999) shows how local processes are driving most of the regional changes in land use in the Sahel. In practical terms, this usage refers to the ties between the dynamics of political processes and the dynamics of land use. In addition, many authors use political ecology to explore issues of environmental justice (Dobson 1998; Low and Gleeson 1998); I will briefly mention some of those implications also.

Illicit drugs, particularly those that generate international demand and involve large amounts of money, appear to be an important topic to address in terms of political ecology. The linkages I have mentioned in this chapter connect the lifestyles of people in the North with the land-use decisions of people in the South. In between are a series of social actors, intermediaries in the economic flows, and representatives of the states' interests and those of other parts of society. Because of these linkages, decisions on what crops to produce on a humid hillside in eastern Peru eventually have consequences for those who work to control the availability of drugs. But fairness demands that the opposite also be considered: that the decisions made by recreational and habitual drug users have consequences for the economic and political realities of Andean farmers. In turn, those farmers affect land cover and directly and indirectly alter the environments of native peoples and native plants and animals.

The asymmetry of the power relations involved with illicit drugs is probably the most conspicuous feature of the linkages between the source and consuming countries. There is little power and there are few alternatives for colonists in eastern Peru. Certainly they are mostly victims, despite the fact that their collective actions also make victims of other people and other species. Contrast that fact with the billions of dollars associated with both the control and purchase of illicit drugs by and within the consuming countries. Imagine the resources that could be brought to bear against a producer of a traditional crop, which provides a harvest that other individuals transform into an illegal product. No doubt this is what has motivated some analysts to champion the coca growers. For example, Bryant (1997: 13) states that "forest clearance linked to illegal cultivation . . . or forbidden crops (eg. coca), may all be examples of weaker grassroots actors asserting their perceived right to shape local environmental conditions."

In the parts of Peru where coca is commonly grown, much of the shaping of local environmental conditions by colonists has taken place in frontiers created by the state to attract those colonists. Colonization, whether explicitly or indirectly encouraged by the state, has taken place with massive subsidies in the form of roads and other infrastructure, plus services for health and education. Initially, many of these costs were covered by foreign and international lenders. Today, Peruvians continue these subsidies in the form of interest and principal payments of about $2 billion each year, originating from a foreign debt of more than $30 billion. The colonization, however, did not take place on a blank slate but rather in Peru's most biodiverse region (Young 1996; Young and León 1997) and in the traditional lands of numerous indigenous peoples. That the degree and kind of environmental degradation are amplified and altered by the effects of illicit drugs is perverse and sad. Forests are degraded and native people displaced for a benefit that seems illusionary.

Unfortunately, I found a paucity of relevant local narratives recorded by social researchers. The violence of the 1980s and 1990s in Peru, associated with the drug trade and the guerrilla groups, has prevented the in-depth, local immersion that is required. The environmental injustices, similarly, can only be identified at a distance, without the fine-grained detail necessary to pinpoint impacts on biodiversity in particular places or toxicity effects on people in particular watersheds. The documentation and exploration of these topics need to be research priorities. This kind of information would help to disaggregate colonists into a variety of social groups, differing in their knowledge and interests in and effects on the tropical forests, allowing more nuanced generalizations. Certainly there are local and regional differences among the colonists and their effects on the forests (Barclay et al. 1991; Santos Graneros and Barclay 1995). It would also help to further characterize the multiple paths of resistance and accommodation chosen by the different indigenous groups (e.g., Roldán and Camayo 1999).

Gibson et al. (2000) delineate some of the controls acting upon assessments of local resource users in terms of costs and benefits of the use of nearby forests. For colonists and native groups, long-term use of forest resources requires that forest still be present, of an extent that warrants utilization, and suitable for providing a resource (other than merely serving as potential land to be used someday for farming or grazing). In turn, the forest users must (1) view the forest as important for them, (2) have a shared interest in its continued existence, and (3) have shared values and thus rules for continued use. It is possible to imagine scenarios where these features could be true of some colonized areas, for example, if forests remained nearby, if there was some form of communal or shared use, and if colonists came from similar backgrounds. Certainly, these would generally be features to be expected in many indigenous communities, especially in those cases in which property rights to their lands had been recognized by the state.

The rapid development of coca/cocaine in the 1970s and 1980s in Peru as an economic phenomenon is reminiscent of the boom-bust resource cycle that characterized rubber in the Amazon (Barham and Coomes 1994) and other economic cycles of natural resources (Topik and Wells 1998). As a further parallel, the Asháninka have been victims of both the rubber and the coca/cocaine booms (Brown and Fernández 1991). Of course, the biggest contrast is that we are still living through the coca/cocaine cycle. From this perspective, it is clear that these cycles have not only a temporal component but also a strong spatial parameter. As drug enforcement efforts and military control of the countryside of Peru increased in the 1990s, coca was shifted to more isolated areas. In addition, the processing to paste and cocaine was further delinked spatially, with operations moving to border areas or into neighboring countries. In fact, the rise in coca/cocaine in Colombia in the 1990s (Steinberg 2000) accompanied flattening or even declining trends for Peru.

The causal link for coca/cocaine today is the rise in international capitalism, globalization, and increased sophistication in the transshipment process. Bryant (1997) points out that too much environmental research remains focused on proximate, rather than ultimate, causation. His proposed solution is to focus on how power relations are linked to environmental problems. The suggested methods are to document the role of powerful actors and to examine how grassroots actors can be encouraged to develop alternatives (e.g., Bebbington and Bebbington, 2001). I have provided evidence for the former in this chapter, and in the final section I examine the latter.

Policy Alternatives

In Peru, there is a striking spatial and temporal relationship between colonization initiatives in the Amazon and coca/cocaine. Another example would be in lowland Bolivia, where the Yuquí are threatened by loss of game and land to colonists who are growing three crops of coca leaves each year (Stearman 1995; see also Sanabria 1993 and Léons and Sanabria 1997). One policy approach would be to make even more investment in these areas by foreign donors, by NGOs (nongovernmental organizations), and by the national government. This could be implemented with rural agrarian banks to make small loans, by providing reasonable salaries for public employees, by constructing and maintaining decent roads and communications to allow for the marketing of agrarian products, and by staffing agricultural extension agents to provide information on appropriate crops. Some of these are elements of the crop substitution programs, although their current funding is only a tiny portion of the investment that would be necessary. More to the point, policy that encourages settlement in the Amazon appears to be counter to the lessons (supposedly) learned from 4 decades of failures to occupy tropical, humid environments in socially and ecologically sustainable ways (e.g., Moran 1981; N. Smith 1981; Bunker 1985; Barclay et al. 1991; Schmink and Wood 1992; Ruiz 1993).

The rethinking of conventional wisdom and the recognition of policy alternatives begin by acknowledging that the lands discussed are not empty of their original inhabitants, whether native plants and animals or indigenous people. In Peru, there are two main areas in the eastern slopes that, as a generalization, have not been converted by coca/cocaine: protected landscapes and lands where traditional indigenous groups are found. The exceptions are areas where recently colonized lands surround an enclave (e.g., the Lamas, Tingo Maria National Park), where roads provide access (e.g., the Huallaga River Valley), or where violence has come from outside by the arrival of armed groups (e.g., the Ene River Valley).

The national parks and nature reserves that are still intact in eastern Peru are not in that condition because of active protection programs. Instead, it is their isolation in remote places that has protected them so far. Just a handful of park guards is employed in these areas (with monthly salaries of about $40), and there is little budget for or interest in patroling or even delineating park boundaries. The future of these protected areas depends to a great extent on the future of coca/cocaine. More interest by the conservation NGOs in the foothills of the eastern slopes could be an important element for hope. They could help implement park-people programs that provide benefits to neighbors of the protected areas (Wells et al. 1990; Western and Wright 1994; Stevens 1997).

In addition, it should be possible to benefit from and promote the resistance shown by indigenous groups to the arrival and land transformations of coca/cocaine. My survey has revealed that the groups least affected have been those with one or more of the following characteristics: no traditional use or cultivation of coca, a strong ethnic identity, ownership of large tracts of land, isolation from the road and river transportation network, and little interest in the market economy. Thus, programs of land rights and preservation of aspects of indigenous cultures (Clay 1988; Reed 1995; Brohman 1996; Sponsel et al. 1996; Bodley 1999; Tresierra 1999; Stonich 2001) might be the best investment possible to slow or stop the expansion of coca/cocaine. Other benefits are obvious: Native peoples remain on their lands and make their own decisions on how to interact with the outside world.

I do not believe that it is wise to spend great sums of money to make conditions better for the recent colonists of the Peruvian Amazon. That can only serve to pull more settlers to these areas and will fuel more inappropriate or illicit land use. As an alternative, investments in the protected areas and for indigenous rights have many beneficial aspects, not the least that they reduce the size of areas potentially available for coca/cocaine expansion. This shift in policy should be accompanied by increased efforts to understand the natural and the inhabited landscapes of eastern Peru. The inclusion of these topics in discourse about tropical deforestation is long overdue.

References

Allen, C. J. 1986. Coca and cultural identity in Andean communities. In *Coca and Cocaine: Effects on People and Policy in Latin America*, ed. D. Pacini and C. Franquemont, pp. 35–48. Cultural Survival Report 23. Cambridge, MA: Cultural Survival.

———. 1988. *The Hold Life Has: Coca and Cultural Identity in an Andean Community.* Washington, DC: Smithsonian Press.

Allen, F. 1994. *Secret Formula: How Brilliant Marketing and Relentless Salesmanship made Coca-Cola the Best-Known Product in the World.* New York: Harper Business.

Alvarez, E. 1992. Coca production in Peru. In Drug Policy in the Americas, ed. P. H. Smith, pp. 72–87. Boulder, CO: Westview Press.

Anderson, A. B., ed. 1990. *Alternatives to Deforestation: Steps Toward Sustainable Use of the Amazon Rain Forest.* New York: Columbia University Press.

Aramburú, C. E. 1989. La economía parcelaria y el cultivo de coca: El caso del alto Huallaga. In *Pasta Básica de Cocaína: Un Estudio Multidisciplinario*, ed. F. León and R. Castro de la Mata, pp. 231–259. Lima: Centro de Información y Educación para la Prevención del Abuso de Drogas.

Arnson, C., ed. 2001. *The Crisis of Democratic Governance in the Andes. No. 2. Woodrow Wilson Center Reports on the Americas.* Washington, DC: Woodrow Wilson International Center for Scholars.

Atkinson, A. 1991. *Principles of Political Ecology.* London: Belhaven.

Bagley, B. M., and W. O. Walker III, eds. 1996. *Drug Trafficking in the Americas.* Miami, FL: North-South Center Press.

Baksh, M. 1995. Changes in Machiguenga quality of life. In *Indigenous Peoples and the Future of Amazonia: An Ecological Anthropology of an Endangered World*, ed. L. E. Sponsell, pp. 187–205. Tucson: University of Arizona Press.

Barclay, F., M. Rodríguez, F. Santos, and M. Valcárcel. 1991. *Amazonia 1940–1990: El extravío de una illusion.* Lima: Terra Nuova.

Barham, B. L., and O. T. Coomes. 1994. Reinterpreting the Amazon rubber boom—investments, the state, and Dutch disease. *Latin American Research Review* 29: 73–109.

Barraclough, S. L., and K. B. Ghimire. 2000. *Agricultural Expansion and Tropical Deforestation: Poverty, International Trade and Land Use.* London: Earthscan.

Bebbington, A. J., and D. H. Bebbington. 2001. Development alternatives: Practice, dilemmas and theory. *Area* 33(1): 7–17.

Bedoya, E., and L. Klein. 1996. Forty years of political ecology in the Peruvian upper forest: The case of the upper Huallaga. In *Tropical Deforestation: The Human Dimension*, ed. L. E. Sponsel, T. N. Headland, and R. C. Bailey, pp. 165–186. New York: Columbia University Press.

Belaúnde, T. F. 1994. *La Conquista del Perú por los Peruanos*, 3d ed. Lima: Editorial Minerva.

Bergman, R. W. 1980. Amazon economics: The simplicity of Shipibo Indian wealth. Ph.D. dissertation, Syracuse University, Syracuse, NY.

Blaikie, P., and H. Brookfield. 1987. *Land Degradation and Society*. London: Methuen.

Bodley, J. 1999. *Victims of Progress,* 4th ed. Mountain View, CA: Mayfield.

Brohman, J. 1996. *Popular Development: Rethinking the Theory and Practice of Development*. Oxford: Blackwell.

Brown, K., and D. W. Pearce, eds. 1994. *The Causes of Tropical Deforestation*. Vancouver: UBC Press.

Brown, M. F. 1986. *Tsewa's Gift: Magic and Meaning in an Amazonian Society.* Washington, DC: Smithsonian Institution Press.

Brown, M. F., and E. Fernández. 1991. *War of Shadows: The Struggle for Utopia in thePeruvian Amazon.* Berkeley: University of California Press.

Bryant, R. L. 1997. Beyond the impasse: The power of political ecology in Third World environmental research. *Area* 29(1): 5–19.

Bryant, R. L., and S. Bailey. 1997. *Third World Political Ecology*. London: Routledge.

Bunker, S. G. 1985. *Underdeveloping the Amazon: Extraction, Unequal Exchange, and the Failure of the Modern State*. Chicago: University of Chicago Press.

Chepesiuk, R. 1999. *Hard Target: The United States War Against International Drug Trafficking, 1982–1997*. Jefferson, NC: McFarland.

Clawson, P. L., and R. W. Lee, III. 1996. *The Andean Cocaine Industry*. New York: St. Martin's.

Clay, J. W. 1988. *Indigenous Peoples and Tropical Forests: Models of Land Use and Management from Latin America*. Cambridge, MA: Cultural Survival.

Cotler, J. 1999. *Drogas y Política en el Perú: La conexión norteamericana*. Lima: Instituto de Estudios Peruanos.

Davalos, L. M. 2001. The San Lucas Mountain range in Colombia: How much conservation is owed to the violence? *Biodiversity & Conservation* 10: 69–78.

Denevan, W. M. 1966. The Carretera Marginal de la Selva and the central Huallaga region of Peru. *Geographical Review* 56: 440–443.

Descola, P. 1994. *In the Society of Nature: A Native Ecology in Amazonia*. Cambridge: Cambridge University Press.

De Soto, H. 1986. *El otro Sendero: La revolución informal*. Lima: Instituto Libertad y Democracia.

Dinerstein, E., D. M. Olson, D. J. Graham, A. L. Webster, S. A. Primm, M. P. Bookbinder, and G. Ledec. 1995. *A Conservation Assessment of the Terrestrial Ecoregions of Latin America and the Caribbean*. Washington, DC: World Wildlife Fund and World Bank.

Dobson, A. 1998. *Justice and the Environment: Conceptions of Environment and Sustainability and Theories of Distributive Justice*. Oxford: Oxford University Press.

Dourojeanni, J. J. 1989. Impactos ambientales del cultivo de la coca y la producción de cocaine en la amazonía peruana. In *Pasta Básica de Cocaína: Un Estudio Multidiscipli-*

nario, ed. F. León and R. Castro de la Mata, pp. 281–299. Lima: Centro de Información y Educación para la Prevención del Abuso de Drogas.

Dove, M. R. 1993. A revisionist view of tropical deforestation and development. *Environmental Conservation* 20: 17–24.

Duke, J. A., D. Aulik, and T. Plowman. 1975. Nutritional value of coca. *Botanical Museum Leaflets, Harvard University* 24: 113–119.

Eakin, L., E. Lauriault, and H. Boonsta. 1986. *People of the Ucayali: The Shipibo and Conibo of Peru.* Dallas: International Museum of Cultures.

Echavarria, F. R. 1991. Cuantificación de la deforestación en el valle del Huallaga, Perú. *Revista Geográfica* 114: 37–53.

Gagliano, J. 1994. *Coca Prohibition in Peru: the Historical Debates.* Tucson: University of Arizona Press.

García-Sayán, D., ed. 1989. *Coca, cocaine y narcotráfico: Laberinto en los Andes.* Lima: Comision Andina de Juristas.

George, S. 1992. *The Debt Boomerang: How Third World Debt Harms Us All.* Boulder, CO: Westview Press.

Gibson, C. C., E. Ostrom, and M. A. McKean. 2000. Forests, people, and governance: Some initial theoretical lessons. In *People and Forests: Communities, Institutions, and Governance*, ed. C. C. Gibson, M. A. McKean, and E. Ostrom, pp. 227–242. Cambridge, MA: MIT Press.

Goldsmith, F. B., ed. 1998. *Tropical Rain Forest: A Wider Perspective.* London: Chapman & Hall.

Gonzales, J. E. 1992. Guerrillas and coca in the upper Huallaga Valley. In *The Shining Path of Peru*, ed. D. S. Palmer, pp. 105–125. New York: St. Martin's.

Gray, A. 1996a. *The Arakmbut: Mythology, Spirituality, and History in an Amazonian Community.* Providence, RI: Berghahn Books.

———. 1996b. *Indigenous Rights and Development: Self-Determination in an Amazonian Community.* Providence, RI: Berghahn Books.

Gwynne, R. N., and C. Kay, eds. 1999. *Latin America Transformed: Globalization and Modernity.* London: Arnold.

Horta, K. 2000. Rainforest: Biodiversity conservation and the political economy of international financial institutions. In *Political Ecology: Science, Myth and Power*, ed. P. Stott and S. Sullivan, pp. 179–202. London: Arnold.

INEI (Instituto Nacional de Estadistica e Informática). 1997. *Perú: Estadisticas de producción, trafico y consumo de drogas, 1994–96.* Lima: Instituto Nacional de Estadistica e Informática.

Isbell, B. J. 1985. *To Defend Ourselves: Ecology and Ritual in an Andean Village.* Prospect Heights, IL: Waveland Press.

Jepma, C. J. 1995. *Tropical Deforestation: A Socio-Economic Approach.* London: Earthscan.

Johnson, A. 1983. Machiguenga gardens. In *Adaptive Responses of Native Amazonians*, ed. R. B. Hames and W. T. Vickers, pp. 29–63. New York: Academic Press.

Kent, R. B. 1993. Geographical dimensions of the Shining Path insurgency in Peru. *Geographical Review* 83: 441–454.

Kirk, R. 1997. *The Monkey's Paw: New Chronicles from Peru.* Amherst: University of Massachusetts Press.

Klarén, P. F. 2000. *Peru: Society and Nationhood in the Andes.* Oxford: Oxford University Press.

Laurence, W. F., and R. O. Bierregaard, Jr., eds. 1997. *Tropical Forest Remnants.* Chicago: University of Chicago Press.

Léons, M. B., and H. Sanabria, eds. 1997. *Coca, Cocaine, and the Bolivian Reality.* Albany: State University of New York Press.

Loker, W. M., ed. 1999. *Globalization and the Rural Poor in Latin America.* Boulder, CO: Lynne Rienner.

Low, N., and B. Gleeson. 1998. *Justice, Society and Nature: An Exploration of Political Ecology.* London: Routledge.

Luca de Tena, B. B. 2000. *La Guerra de la Cocaína: Drogas, geopolítica y medio ambiente.* Madrid: Editorial Debate.

Mabry, D. J. 1996. The U.S. military and the War on Drugs. In *Drug Trafficking in the Americas,* ed. B. M. Bagley and W. O. Walker III, pp. 43–60. Miami, FL: North-South Center Press.

MacGregor, F. E. 1990. *Cocaína: Problema y soluciones andinos.* Lima: Asociación Peruana de Estudios e Investigaciones para la Paz.

Malamud-Goti, J. 1992. *Smoke and Mirrors: The Paradox of the Drug Wars.* Boulder, CO: Westview Press.

Manrique, N. 1998. The war for the Central Sierra. In *Shining and Other Paths: War and Society in Peru, 1980–1995,* ed. S. J. Stern, pp. 193–223. Durham, NC: Duke University Press.

Martin, R. T. 1970. The role of coca in the history, religion, and medicine of South American Indians. In *The Coca Leaf and Cocaine Papers,* ed. G. Andrews and D. Solomon, pp. 20–37. New York: Harcourt Brace Jovanovich.

Maskrey, A., J. Rojas, and T. Pinedo, eds. 1990. *Raices y Bosques: San Martín, modelo para armar.* Lima: Tecnología Intermedia.

McClintock, C. 1989. The war on drugs: The Peruvian case. *Journal of Interamerican Studies and World Affairs* 30: 127–142.

———. 1998. *Revolutionary Movements in Latin America: El Salvador's FMLN and Peru's Shining Path.* Washington, DC: United States Institute of Peace Press.

McClintock, C., and A. F. Lowenthal, eds. 1983. *The Peruvian Experiment Reconsidered.* Princeton, NJ: Princeton University Press.

Medina-Mora, M. E., and M. del Carmen Mariño. 1992. Drug abuse in Latin America. In *Drug Policy in the Americas,* ed. P. H. Smith, pp. 45–56. Boulder, CO: Westview Press.

Menzel, S. H. 1996. *Fire in the Andes: U.S. Foreign Policy and Cocaine Politics in Bolivia and Peru.* Lanham, MD: University Press of America.

Mitchell, M. P. 1991. *Peasants on the Edge: Crop, Cult, and Crisis in the Andes.* Austin: University of Texas Press.

———. 1999. Detour onto the Shining Path: Obscuring the social revolution in the Andes. In *Deadly Developments: Capitalism, States and War,* ed. S. P. Reyna and R. E. Downs, pp. 235–278. Amsterdam: Gordon and Breach.

Mittermeier, R. A., N. Myers, P. Robles Gil, and C. G. Mittermeier, eds. 1999. *Hotspots: Earth's Biologically Richest and most Endangered Terrestrial Ecoregions.* Mexico City: CEMEX, Agrupación Sierra Madre.

Morales, E. 1989. *Cocaine: White Gold Rush in Peru.* Tucson: University of Arizona Press.

———. 1996. The Andean cocaine dilemma. In *Drug Trafficking in the Americas,* ed. B. M. Bagley and W. O. Walker III, pp. 161–177. Miami, FL: North-South Center Press.

Moran, E. F. 1981. *Developing the Amazon.* Bloomington: Indiana University Press.

Myers, N. 1993. Tropical forests: The main deforestation fronts. *Environmental Conservation* 29: 9–16.

Osborne, H. 1973. *Indians of the Andes: Aymaras and Quechuas.* New York: Cooper Square Publishers.

OTA (Office of Technology Assessment). 1993. *Alternative Coca Reduction Strategies in the*

Andean Region. Office of Technology Assessment. Washington, DC: Congress of the United States.

Painter, M., and W. Durham, eds. 1995. *The Social Causes of Environmental Destruction in Latin America*. Ann Arbor: University of Michigan Press.

Palmer, D. S. 1996. Peru, drugs, and Shining Path. In *Drug Trafficking in the Americas*, ed. B. M. Bagley and W. O. Walker III, pp. 179–191. Miami, FL: North-South Center Press.

Peet, R., and M. Watts, eds. 1996. *Liberation Ecologies: Environment, Development, Social Movements*. London: Routledge.

del Pinott, P. 1998. Family, culture and "revolution": Everyday life with Sendero Luminoso. In *Shining and Other Paths: War and Society in Peru*, ed. S. J. Stern, pp. 159–192. Durham, NC: Duke University Press.

Piperno, D. R., and D. M. Pearsall. 1998. *The Origins of Agriculture in the Lowland Neotropics*. San Diego: Academic Press.

Place, S. E. 1993. *Tropical Rainforests: Latin American Nature and Society in Transition*. Wilmington, DE: Scholarly Resources.

Plowman, T. 1984a. The ethnobotany of coca (*Erythroxylum* spp., Erythroxylaceae). *Advances in Economic Botany* 1: 62–111.

———. 1984b. The origin, evolution, and diffusion of coca, *Erythroxylum* spp., in South and Central America. In *Pre-columbian Plant Migration*, ed. D. Stone, pp. 125–163. Papers of the Peabody Museum of Archeology and Ethnology 76. Cambridge, MA: Harvard University.

———. 1986. Coca chewing and the botanical origins of coca (*Erythroxylum* spp.) in South America. In *Coca and Cocaine: Effects on People and Policy in Latin America*, ed. D. Pacini and C. Franquemont, pp. 5–33. Cultural Survival Report 23. Cambridge, MA: Cultural Survival.

Poole, D., and G. Rénique. 1992. *Peru: Time of Fear*. London: Latin America Bureau.

Reed, R. 1995. *Prophets of Agroforestry: Guaraní Communities and Commercial Gathering*. Austin: University of Texas Press.

Remy, M. I. 1994. The indigenous population and the constitution of democracy in Peru. In *Indigenous Peoples and Democracy in Latin America*, ed. D. L. Van Cott, pp. 107–130. New York: St. Martin's.

Riley, K. J. 1996. *Snow Job? The War Against International Cocaine Trafficking*. New Brunswick, NJ: Transaction Publishers.

Riofrío, G. 1996. Lima: Mega-city and mega-problem. In *The Mega-City in Latin America*, ed. A. Gilbert, pp. 155–172. Tokyo: United Nations University Press.

Rojas Zolezzi, E. 1994. *Los Ashaninka, un pueblo tras el bosque: Contribución a la etnología de los Campa de la Selva Central Peruana*. Lima: Fondo Editorial Pontificia Universidad Católica del Perú.

Roldán, R., and A. M. Camayo. 1999. *Legislación y derechos indígenas en el Perú*. Lima: Centro Amazónico de Antropología Práctica.

Rossi, A. 1996. *Narcotrafico y Amazonia ecuatoriana*. Quito: Ediciones Abya-Yala.

Rostworowski de Diez Canseco, M. 1988. *Conflicts over Coca Fields in XVIth Century Peru*. Memoirs of the Museum of Anthropology 21. Ann Arbor: University of Michigan.

Rudel, T. 1993. *Tropical Deforestation: Small Farmers and Land Clearing in the Ecuadorian Amazon*. New York: Columbia University Press.

Ruiz, L., ed. 1993. *Amazonia: Escenarios y conflictos*. Quito: Centro de Investigación de los Movimientos Sociales del Ecuador and Abya-Yala.

Rury, P. M., and T. Plowman. 1983. Morphological studies of archeological and recent coca leaves (*Erythroxylum* spp.). *Botanical Museum Leaflets, Harvard University* 29: 297–341.

Sanabria, H. 1993. *The Coca Boom and Rural Social Change in Bolivia.* Ann Arbor: University of Michigan Press.

Santos Granero, F., and F. Barclay Rey de Castro. 1995. *Ordenes y desórdenes en la Selva Central: Historia y economía de un espacio regional.* Lima: Instituto de Estudios Peruanos.

Schelhas, J., and Greenberg, R., eds. 1996. *Forest Patches in Tropical Landscapes.* Washington, DC: Island Press.

Schmink, M., and C. H. Wood. 1992. *Contested Frontiers in Amazonia.* New York: Columbia University Press.

Smith, N. 1981. Colonization lessons from a tropical forest. *Science* 214: 755–761.

Smith, P. H. 1992. The political economy of drugs: Conceptual issues and policy options. In *Drug Policy in the Americas*, ed. P. H. Smith, pp. 1–21. Boulder, CO: Westview Press.

Spillane, J. F. 2000. *Cocaine: From Medical Marvel to Modern Menace in the United States, 1884–1920.* Baltimore: Johns Hopkins University Press.

Sponsel, L. E., T. N. Headland, and R. C. Bailey, eds. 1996. *Tropical Deforestation: The Human Dimension.* New York: Columbia University Press.

Starn, O. 1991. Missing the revolution: Anthropologists and the war in Peru. *Cultural Anthropology* 6: 63–91.

Stearman, A. M. 1995. Neotropical foraging adaptations and the effects of acculturation on sustainable resource use: The Yuquí of lowland Bolivia. In *Indigenous Peoples and the Future of Amazonia: An Ecological Anthropology of an Endangered World*, ed. L. E. Sponsel, pp. 207–224. Tucson: University of Arizona Press.

Steinberg, M. K. 2000. Generals, guerrillas, drugs, and Third World war-making. *Geographical Review* 90: 260–267.

Stern, S. J. 1993. *Peru's Indian Peoples and the Challenge of Spanish Conquest: Huamanga to 1640*, 2nd ed. Madison: University of Wisconsin Press.

———, ed. 1998. *Shining and Other Paths: War and Society in Peru, 1980–1995.* Durham, NC: Duke University Press.

Stevens, S., ed. 1997. *Conservation Through Cultural Survival: Indigenous People and Protected Areas.* Washington, DC: Island Press.

Stonich, S. C., ed. 2001. *Endangered Peoples of Latin America: Struggles to Survive and Thrive.* Wesport, CT: Greenwood Press.

Stott, P., and S. Sullivan, eds. 2000. *Political Ecology: Science, Myth and Power.* London: Arnold.

Strong, S. 1992. *Shining Path: Terror and Revolution in Peru.* New York: Times Books.

Tapia, C. 1997. *Las Fuerzas Armadas y Sendero Luminoso: Dos estrategias y un final.* Lima: Instituto de Estudios Peruanos.

Tarazona-Sevillano, G. 1990. *Sendero Luminoso and the Threat of Narcoterrorism.* New York: Praeger.

Taylor, L. 1997. Counter-insurgency strategy, the PCP-Sendero Luminoso and the civil war in Peru, 1980–1996. *Bulletin of Latin American Research* 17: 35–58.

Topik, S. C., and A. Wells, eds. 1998. *The Second Conquest of Latin America: Coffee, Henequen, and Oil During the Export Boom, 1850–1930.* Austin: University of Texas Press.

Tresierra, J. C. 1999. Rights of indigenous peoples over tropical forest resources. In *Forest Resource Policy in Latin America*, ed. K. Keipi, pp. 135–160. Washington, DC: Inter-American Development Bank.

Tulchin, J. S., and G. Bland, eds. 1994. *Peru in Crisis: Dictatorship or Democracy?* Boulder, CO: Lynne Rienner.

Turner, M. D. 1999. Merging local and regional analyses of land-use change: The case of livestock in the Sahel. *Annals of the Association of American Geographers* 89: 191–219.

Wells, M., K. Brandon, and L. Hannah. 1990. *People and Parks: Linking Protected Areas Management with Local Communities*. Washington, DC: World Bank.

Western, D., and R. M. Wright, eds. 1994. *Natural Connections: Perspectives in Community-Based Conservation*. Washington, DC: Island Press.

Wood, W. B. 1990. Tropical deforestation: Balancing regional development demands and global environmental concerns. *Global Environmental Change* 1: 23–41.

Young, K. R. 1996. Threats to biological diversity caused by coca/cocaine deforestation in Peru. *Environmental Conservation* 23: 7–15.

Young, K. R., and B. León. 1997. Eastern slopes of Peruvian Andes, Peru. In *Centres of Plant Diversity: A Guide and Strategy for Their Conservation. Vol. 3. The Americas*, ed. S. D. Davis, V. H. Heywood, O. Herrera-MacBryde, J. Villa-Lobos, and A. C. Hamilton, pp. 490–495. Cambridge: World Wide Fund for Nature and The World Conservation Union.

12

Modern Use and Environmental Impact of the Kava Plant in Remote Oceania

Mark Merlin
William Raynor

The kava plant, *Piper methysticum* Forst. f., is an attractive shrub in the pepper family, Piperaceae (figure 12.1). Known by various names in tropical Pacific, such as *yagona*, *kava*, *kava kava*, *'awa*, *seka*, and *sakau*, it is propagated vegetatively, as are most of the traditional crops in the region. Kava has been used for many centuries to produce psychoactive preparations. Its active principles, several lipidlike substances known as kavalactones, are concentrated in the rootstock and roots. These psychoactive chemicals are ingested traditionally by Pacific islanders as cold-water infusions of chewed, ground, pounded, or otherwise macerated kava stumps and roots. Mind-altering kava preparations are, or once were, imbibed in a wide range of Pacific Ocean societies. These include peoples living in some lowland areas on the large Melanesian island of New Guinea in the western Pacific to very isolated islands such as those in Polynesian Hawai'i, 7,000 kilometers to the northeast (figure 12.2).

Beyond this widespread local use in the tropical Pacific, utilization of kava in parts of Europe as a plant source for medicinal preparations has a relatively lengthy history. In Europe it has been used as a sedative, tranquilizer, muscle relaxant, relief from menopausal symptoms, and treatment for urinary tract and bladder ailments (Lebot et al. 1999). Over the past decade, there has been rapidly increasing interest in kava well beyond the areas of traditional use among Pacific Islanders (figure 12.3). This includes a huge surge in the use of kava products in Europe, North America, Australia, and elsewhere. Within the past 3 to 5 years there has been widespread recognition of its potential to emerge as a mainstream herbal product.

Modern cultivation and use of kava in the Pacific has significantly expanded in some traditional use areas such as Vanuatu, Fiji, Tonga, Samoa, and Pohnpei. There

Figure 12.1. Kava, *Piper methysticum* Forst. f., with its characteristic heart-shaped leaves and spike of tiny flowers that do not produce seed. The plant may reach heights of up to 3 meters and is always reproduced vegetatively using stem cuttings (photo courtesy of W. A. Whistler).

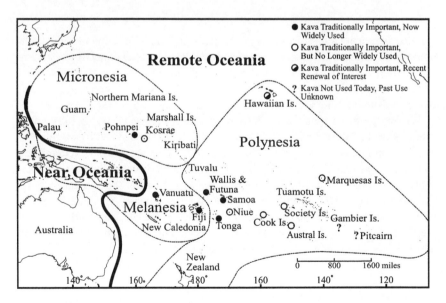

Figure 12.2. Map of Remote Oceania.

Figure 12.3. A Pohnpei Islander strains pounded kava rootstock and water through hibiscus fiber to make the traditional psychoactive drink *sakau* (photo by Mark Merlin).

are also significant signs of rejuvenated interest in kava cultivation in some traditional areas of use where it had been abandoned because of depopulation, political prohibition, or zealous missionary denunciation. Increasing use and cultivation of kava on these Pacific islands has been stimulated by local consumption rates and rising demand for commercial export.

Whereas its cultivation and use have risen rapidly in recent decades, the cultural role of kava has shifted radically. On some islands kava has been freed, more or less, from its position as a tradition-bound, sacred, drug plant with strict controls on its use. In parts of Vanuatu, Fiji, and Pohnpei, kava has become a source of mind-altering substances consumed by a greatly expanded part of the population, with both societal and environmental consequences. In this chapter we focus largely on its extensive cultivation and consumption on the high volcanic island of Pohnpei, in the Federated States of Micronesia, with a special emphasis on the environmental impact of its broadening use on that island and elsewhere.

Origins and Dispersal of Kava in Remote Oceania

Since all kava, known scientifically as *Piper methysticum*, is reproduced vegetatively and is not known to produce viable seeds, this plant is considered to be fully domesticated and completely dependent upon humans for its continued existence. Indeed, from a botanical point of view, *P. methysticum* is not a true species but rather a series of cloned cultivars—the cumulative result of artificial selection over many centuries. It has been suggested that these cloned cultivars are probably all derived from *Piper wichmanii* C. DC., a truly wild species that has a native range extending over much of the humid region of New Guinea through the Solomon Islands, and as far east as the archipelago of Vanuatu, formerly known as the New Hebrides (Lebot et al. 1992).

Many botanists still differentiate *P. wichmannii* from *P. methysticum*. However, it has been argued that the most convincing morphological, chemical, and genetic evidence supports the assumption that these two taxa of *Piper* are, respectively, the truly wild and the cultivated forms of the same species (Chew 1972; Lebot et al. 1986). Although some Pacific Islanders grow and use some parts of species that botanists recognize as *P. wichmannii*, in this chapter, the kava plant or the kava drink refers to those cultivars still known as *P. methysticum*. The word *kava* is used here synonymously to refer to both the plant itself and the mind-altering beverage made from its rootstock.

It is assumed here that it was within the native region of *Piper wichmanii*, in one or more places, that humans probably began cultivating this wild species or a closely related wild member of the pepper family. Over time, through an extended process of trial and error, selection for useful cultivars developed. The domestication process may have begun in a number of different areas within the native range of the wild pepper progenitor. However, a strong case can be made that it began in northern Vanuatu, approximately 3,000 to 4,000 years ago, or perhaps more recently, when subsistence farmers first began to use stalk cuttings to grow the wild pepper species that is the ancestor of many, if not all, modern kava plants. Over time, selection of traits desirable for human use led to the development of clones with different ecological adaptations and chemical compositions. Some of these clones were subsequently spread to southern Vanuatu; westward to areas in western Melanesia; north to a few small, high islands in Micronesia; and east to various volcanic islands in Polynesia (Lebot et al. 1992; Luders 1996).

Until recently, scholars and scientists divided the massive area of the Pacific region beyond Southeast Asia and Australia into three subregions, or categories— Melanesia ("the dark islands"), Micronesia ("the small islands"), and Polynesia ("the many islands"). Based on linguistics, degree of insular isolation, adaptation to relatively small islands, and additional factors, Green and others have suggested a two-part regional division of Near Oceania and Remote Oceania (Green 1991; cf. Pawley and Green 1973; see figure 12.2).

Human settlement of Near Oceania (essentially western Melanesia) and Australia occurred at least 40,000 years ago. The islands of Remote Oceania, which include the Santa Cruz group (the easternmost Solomons Islands), Vanuatu, New Caledonia, Fiji, and all the islands lumped into Polynesia and Micronesia, were first discovered and settled by humans only 1,000 to 3,800 years ago (Kirch 2000).

The remarkable human achievement of reaching the very isolated islands of Remote Oceania in the late Holocene involved many difficult exploratory or accidental discoveries, made by peoples collectively referred to as Austronesians or, in the earlier phases, the Lapita peoples (Kirch 1997). They had a common heritage of language and several other culture traits. These included their relatively similar transported landscapes of agroforests, irrigated swamps, and/or dry field agriculture, as well as their portmanteau biota of consciously and accidentally introduced organisms, including a number of domesticated species (cf. Anderson 1952; Crosby 1986; Kirch 1997). Evidence suggests that the domestication process did not end when people entered the Pacific but continued through experimentation and artificial selection of species found in both Remote and Near Oceania (e.g., Yen 1985, 1991, 1998). Based on morphological, genetic, and linguistic research, it has been suggested that kava was first cultivated and most elaborately selected in Vanuatu (Lebot et al. 1992). Therefore, it is assumed that its domestication began in Remote Oceania, where it became a highly important cultural source of religious inspiration, social status identification, and traditional medicine.

In Oceania, the traditional mind-altering use of kava can be contrasted geographically with that of another customary psychoactive drug plant, the betel nut palm, *Areca catechu* L. This palm almost certainly has a longer history of human use than kava. It was probably first cultivated in South or Southeast Asia and then spread, along with other domesticated crops, to the western Pacific (Marshall 1987). The fruits of the betel nut palm are generally chewed, along with lime and one or more leaves of a vine, *Piper betle* L., which incidentally is in the same genus as the kava shrub. This *Piper* vine and the betel nut palm were among those species carried purposefully out into the Pacific. However, with the exception of a few high islands in western Micronesia (i.e., Palau and Yap), *A. catechu* and *P. betle* were restricted traditionally in their distribution and use to Near Oceania. Betel nut has long been consumed for its stimulating effects and is strongly integrated into the social customs of many areas of Southeast Asia and the western Pacific. However, there is very little if any geographical overlap in the traditional use of betel nut and kava, which with the exception of some lowland areas in New Guinea, is traditionally limited in its range to the more remote parts of the tropical Pacific.

Traditional Uses

The first European explorers who landed on the islands of Remote Oceania encountered societies in which kava drinking was an essential part of religious, political, and economic life. Cultivation and use of the plant have virtually disappeared from almost all of eastern Polynesia and Kosrae Island in Micronesia. On the other hand, within Remote Oceania, kava is still an important psychoactive drug in parts of the "new," or eastern, Melanesia (e.g., Vanuatu and Fiji); in most of the islands of western Polynesia (including Samoa and Tonga); and on Pohnpei Island in Micronesia (figure 12.2).

Scientific observations of kava use began with the earliest European exploration of the Pacific region. In the eighteenth century, Captain James Cook recorded information given to him by members of his crew, who sampled heavy doses of kava and compared its effects to that of opium. The comparison was inaccurate, for kava, or at least the mind-altering infusions made from most cultivars, is neither a hallucinogen nor a stupefacient. Rather, the psychoactive effects of kava are, in general, mildly narcotic, soporific, diuretic, and muscle relaxing.

Indeed, the rather subtle psychoactivity of kava is not easy to categorize according to common drug classification schemes. Schultes and Hoffman (1979) follow Lewin (1924) and typify kava as both a narcotic and a hypnotic. Siegel (1989) refers to the plant as a sedative hypnotic. The mind-altering potency of kava can vary greatly, from very weak to quite strong. The drug may generate sociability, a sense of peace and harmony, and in large doses, extreme drowsiness or sleep. On the other hand, instead of producing relaxation, kava may provoke nausea, although usually it produces feelings of ease and agreeable sociability among drinkers. Although some writers use terms such as *intoxication, drunkenness,* and *inebriation* to describe the human physiological reaction to kava, "the mental state differs from that induced by ethanol or other familiar drugs found in the Western world" (Lebot et al. 1992).

Present Use by Indigenous Peoples in Remote Oceania

For centuries, kava has had strong cultural significance for people in many Pacific Island societies, especially those in Remote Oceania. Many have believed, and some still do, that kava has sacred powers and therefore can be classified as a "plant of the gods" (e.g., Schultes and Hofmann 1979). The recent, rapidly growing interest in its use, often more recreational than sacred, and its cultivation as a cash crop are important contemporary issues in a number of tropical islands of Remote Oceania. Although here we focus primarily on the rising use and cash cropping of kava on Pohnpei, we will also comment on its present use and impact in other areas in the region.

Vanuatu

Vanuatu (formerly New Hebrides) is a group of 83 islands located northeast of New Caledonia and northwest of Fiji in the southwestern portion of Remote Oceania (figure 12.4). The total land area covers 12,190 square kilometers (4,707 square miles). An independent republic established in 1980, Vanuatu is now governed by its indigenous people. Consumption of kava is very widespread in these islands. Traditionally it was drunk on special occasions, to bind agreements, and to celebrate births, deaths, and marriages.

Although Vanuatu is most likely the homeland of kava, missionaries and former colonial rulers suppressed its consumption for many years. Since independence in 1980, however, kava drinking has been promoted as a means of strengthening traditional customs. Strict codes of behavior may be involved in its use in traditional village *nakamal* or other meeting places. On Tanna Island in Vanuatu, kava drinkers traditionally separate from each other and sit apart around the edge of the kava-drinking area, focused on the "voices" of their kava. Talking among the kava consumers on Tanna is generally discouraged because "noise spoils the kava." However, on other islands in Vanuatu, where no such restrictions exist, a talkative

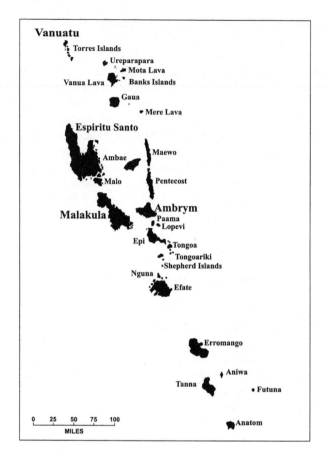

Figure 12.4. Map of Vanuatu.

atmosphere may develop. Indeed, today there is an increasing number of informal kava bars in Vanuatu, where very little if any ceremony occurs.

Kava produced in Vanuatu is generally regarded to be much stronger than that produced elsewhere in the Pacific. For example, analyses of the active ingredients (kavalactones) of the Vanuatu kava cultivars indicates that they are two to five times more psychoactive than those of the common Fijian varieties (Lebot et al. 1986, 1992). In addition, by far the greatest variety of kava cultivars is found in Vanuatu, with very strong differences in strength among many of them (Lebot et al. 1992). Some are regarded as simply too strong to drink, and they are used solely for medicinal purposes. In Vanuatu the practice of pulping freshly harvested kava is very prevalent; however, in most other areas in the Pacific, dried kava is generally used today.

Cultivation has greatly expanded in some areas of Vanuatu in response to growing local consumption, especially in kava bars, and for the export market, which has grown extremely fast over the past decade or so. The impact on the forest environments of Vanuatu needs to be studied, especially in light of what has been happening in the upland watersheds of some other islands such as Pohnpei, which is discussed below.

Fiji

The Republic of the Fiji Islands is an independent island nation in the southern Pacific Ocean. It comprises more than 800 islands, of which about 100 are inhabited. The islands cover a total land area of 18,376 square kilometers (7,095 square miles). Fiji, as the group of islands is generally known, achieved independence from the United Kingdom in 1970.

In Fiji, kava (*yagona*) drinking is still the centerpiece of many elaborate and important rituals. For others it is simply the focal point of social gatherings, where people consume the drink and exchange stories as they take turns sipping bowls of their watery mix. In Fiji, as it is in much of Vanuatu and in the island of Pohnpei, kava is essentially the national beverage. It is presented as a traditional gift or consumed with its special ritual to welcome visitors, bless construction of boats and house foundations, invoke magical spells, make agreements, settle disputes, and most often to converse.

Although kava remains central in Fijian cultures, there is controversy over how healthy it is for economic growth. As in other areas of traditional use in Remote Oceania, until more modern times kava use was restricted to ceremonial purposes by chiefs or priests. Today it is drunk abundantly in villages, some would argue to the detriment of families and social life, as well as at the expense of gardening, fishing, or other "productive activities" (Parker 1994). In several areas of Fiji, kava is planted instead of food crops because it is more lucrative. Because of the negative side effects of excessive drinking—which, as some suggest, include loss of industriousness—some Fijian officials have asked if immoderate kava drinking is really good for the nation.

By 1995 kava had developed into a profitable export crop. According to the Fiji Department of Information (1998), if the "continuity of supply and quality was vigorously maintained, growers and sellers had set a target for 2000 to increase kava acreage from 3,000 ha to 6,000 ha and to increase its export earnings from $6 million to $15 million." Although, the recent coup attempt (May–July 2000) and related political instability have taken their toll on the economy, kava cultivation remains relatively high because of increased local consumption in recent decades. Thaman (personal communication 2000) states that kava "has really been an increasing money spinner [in Fiji], and has expanded on the islands of Taveuni, Ovalau, Kandavu, and on the wet side of Viti Levu."

In Fiji, cultivated kava thrives at altitudes of between 150 and 300 meters and grows to a height of 3.5 meters at full maturity. Although very little, if anything, has been published about the environmental impact of kava cultivation, recent observations in the late 1990s on the larger islands of Viti Levu, Vanua Levu, and Taveuni indicate that "the expansion of kava planting along roads and into higher elevations has led to increasing deforestation and the opening up of new agricultural lands. Furthermore, its cultivation in the uplands of Fiji, also opens up areas for colonization by invasive, alien weeds" (Thaman, personal communication 2000).

Tonga

The archipelago of Tonga, located in western Polynesia, was united into a kingdom in 1845. It acquired its independence from Britain in 1970 and remains the only monarchy in the Pacific. The archipelago comprises 170 islands (36 inhabited), with a total land area of 748 square kilometers (292 square miles).

In the islands of Tonga, as in other areas in Remote Oceania, the traditional use of kava and its ceremonial ritual function psychologically as a symbol of elaborate social stratification. Kava drinking in Tonga occurs in two principal sets of circumstances: Private *faikava*, which function as a part of courtship ritual and as a social gathering; and the *kalapu kava*, or what can be called the Tonga kava club. A *faikava* is initiated by a specific person, who provides the kava to be consumed. A *kalapu* provides kava for a fee to anyone who may come to drink.

Increasing demand for kava in the islands of Tonga, along with an expanding export market, have stimulated more widespread kava cultivation. On Tofua, one of the high volcanic islands (still active) in Tonga, this cultivation has apparently had significant impact on the upland environment. Tofua is in fact the one island in Tonga that still has areas with extensive native forest. Unfortunately, "the expansion of kava planting into the upland forests by people who do not reside on the island has reportedly led to some rapid deforestation and associated erosion" (Thaman, personal communication 2000). Even on Tafahi, another small, high volcanic island of about 650 meters of elevation, kava plantations were beginning to cut into the native montane rain forest at least 10 years ago (Whistler, personal communication 2000). It is uncertain whether the relatively small area of cloud forest at the summit of this isolated Tongan island is still intact. This island and others in Remote Oceania with documented native upland forest need to be monitored for the possible impact produced by rapid expansion of kava cultivation.

Hawai'i

Traditionally there were a number of kava (*'awa*) cultivars in Hawai'i, and as in other parts of Remote Oceania, the ritualistic and restricted uses of Kava were a significant part of the local culture. Kava use was largely abandoned because of missionary and other pressures in the nineteenth century. However, air-dried kava rootstock was an early export crop, with shipments amounting to about 8 tons over the 14 years that the trade existed (Kepler 1983). After a lengthy period of disuse, during the 1990s a kava industry began to redevelop in Hawai'i. And with the reemergence of kava as a potential mainstream herbal product on the mainland United States and in Europe, by the end of the twentieth century cultivation of the plant was thriving and expanding. By that time, according to Ed Johnson (personal communication 2000), past president of the Hawaiian Kava Growers Association, about 200 acres in Hawai'i were being used to cultivate kava commercially, and tons of dried kava rootstock were being shipped to Germany. Jerry Konanui (personal communication 2000), president of the Association for Hawaiian 'Awa, indicated that he and other officials in his organization

have realized from the start about the responsibility that has to accompany the cultivation as well as the marketing of *'awa*. We have put [in an] immense amount of time
with workshops, symposiums as well as one on one with people interested in *'awa*.
Through our education program and delivering of the "consciousness" or the *pono*
[righteous] of it, I feel we have been successful. We don't expect to see the same clear
cutting of the native forest and recklessness of soil erosion as what has happened in
Ponape [Pohnpei]. And this may be due to the abundance of land available due to the
demise of the sugar industry and the terrible negative impact that the papaya ring spot
virus has inflicted on the papaya industry.

Konanui was raised in the Puna district of Hawai'i Island, which was traditionally
famous for its kava. He blames the Papaya industry, which "brought in the bull-
dozers," for clearing the once extensive native forest. He suggests that expanding
kava cultivation is at least "helping to eradicate the undesirable foreign invasive
species." This, he asserts, will help allow native plants like *'Ohi' a* [*Metrosideros*]
and others "to make a comeback." He believes that the kava industry "is still in the
wait and see stage for many potential growers and farmers as it is only quite recently that harvesting and marketing has taken place on cultivated *'awa* in a big
way. Many are watching eagerly to see how it does."

Case Study of Pohnpei Island, Federated States of Micronesia

Pohnpei, a high volcanic island in the Federated States of Micronesia, is the only
Micronesian island where kava (*sakau*) is still cultivated and consumed (figure
12.5). Until 1980, kava was consumed mainly in connection with feasts, funerals,
and other cultural events. However, over the last 2 decades, kava has grown in importance as a major cash crop, both for the local market (mainly in kava bars) and
for export to Pohnpeians overseas. Over a million pounds of kava entered the commercial economy in 1996, generating at least $3 million for local growers and busi-
ness people. Unfortunately, this astronomical growth in kava production has led to
widespread forest clearing: Nearly two-thirds of Pohnpei's intact native forests, or
10,000 hectares, have been degraded since 1975, mainly through kava cultivation
(figure 12.6). Major details about the historical and cultural trends surrounding the
emergence of kava as both Pohnpei's major cash crop and principal environmental
threat are discussed in the following sections, along with reports on local efforts to
build a more sustainable *sakau* (kava) industry.

For centuries, kava has been a central feature of the social and cultural life of
Pohnpei. The kava plant is still considered sacred by many of the island's inhabitants today. Kava is used to recognize many new titles or ranks, celebrate the opening of the seasons of major crops (breadfruit and yam), ask forgiveness, honor and
welcome visitors, seek a marriage, celebrate birthdays, bring together villagers, seal
agreements, and bury the dead (Reisenberg 1968; Merlin et al. 1992; Raynor 1994).
Originally consumed only by the *soupeidi* (chiefly ranks), since World War II kava
consumption has become more widespread and today is a nightly ritual for a large
percentage of the island's population.

Figure 12.5. Ariel view of humid, tropical Pohnpei Island, Federated State of Micronesia (photo by Mark Merlin).

However, recent trends in local kava use, combined with a quickly growing commercial demand for the crop in both local and export markets, have led to increased cultivation, much of it at the expense of Pohnpei's native forests. The recent movement of kava cultivation into the upland rainforests is of much concern. The forests and coral reefs of Pohnpei are still relatively intact, unlike those in neighboring islands. Pohnpei is one of only three islands in the Pacific more than 5 million years old that still has substantial natural forest cover (Pauley 1994). In fact, Pohnpei has the largest intact native upland rainforests and mangroves in the Federated States of Micronesia, with some of the most diverse and unique vegetation and wildlife in the Pacific region. The forests of Pohnpei contain over 270 species of plants, of which 110 (41 percent) are endemic to Pohnpei (Merlin et al. 1992). Sixteen percent of the island's 50 bird species are also endemic to Pohnpei. In addition, at least 25 species of terrestrial tree snails, 3 species of fish, and a skink species are endemic to the island. Pohnpeians depend on some of these species for subsistence and income. Moreover, Pohnpei's forests provide important watershed benefits—storing, filtering, and slowly releasing water into the island's numerous springs, streams, and rivers, while protecting the island's lowlands, lagoon, and reef from sedimentation and degradation.

Although Pohnpeians have always used their forest resources (Raynor 1994), these are in greater danger today than ever before. The accelerated forest loss, brought on mainly from agricultural clearing, chiefly for kava, has recently prompted conservation efforts based on the islanders' concern for their natural heritage. Below we describe the development of the natural resource management program that has resulted from this concern.

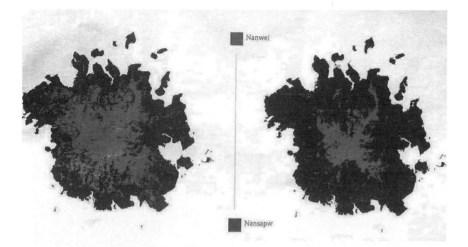

Figure 12.6. Two maps of Pohnpei (1975, left; 1995, right) showing widespread forest clearing as a result of kava cultivation.

History of Kava Use on Pohnpei

Recent scientific work has revealed much anecdotal evidence on the origin and introduction of kava into Micronesia. Based on genetic evidence, including an absence of variation in cultivar isozymes, the limited variation in morphotypes, and chemotypes in the region, kava appears to be a rather late introduction to the Micronesian islands of Pohnpei and Kosrae (Lebot et. al. 1992). This evidence suggests that kava was probably introduced directly from Vanuatu or via the Admiralty Islands. Only two cultivars are recognized on Pohnpei, *rahmwanger*, a common variety with spotted stems, and the rarer *rahmedel*, a smooth-stemmed variety traditionally reserved for the chiefs. This paucity of cultivar variation suggests a relatively recent introduction of kava to Pohnpei Island.

In both Pohnpei and Kosrae, cultural elements associated with kava drinking also suggest relations with the Admiralties to the south and Vanuatu to the more distant southeast. Pohnpei and the Admiralty Islands are the only places where kava is prepared by pounding the roots on large, flat basalt slabs (figure 12.7). The Pohnpei word for kava, *sakau*, and the Kosraean word, *seka*, appear cognate with the word *kau* in Balaun Island, located in Manus Province of Papua New Guinea. It is not possible to determine whether the plant was initially introduced to the Admiralty Islands from Kosrae and Pohnpei or vice versa. However, other genetic distribution work on Pacific plants (Ragone 1991; Lebot et al. 1992) indicates a movement of plant clones (e.g., taro and breadfruit) from Vanuatu to the eastern Caroline Islands of Micronesia.

According to legend, *sakau* (kava) fell to earth in several areas of Pohnpei's forest and began to grow. In these areas, known as *diwi*, *sakau* grew wild and often reached a tremendous size. Traditionally, people would visit these areas to harvest small amounts for personal use and collect planting materials for growing on their lands. Over the last few decades, most of the *diwi* has been destroyed by greedy commercial harvesters.

Figure 12.7. Dried kava rootstock powder processed in Vanuatu is now sold on the global market (photo by Mark Merlin).

Another popular legend recounts the introduction of *sakau* to Pohnpei from Katau Peidak (Katau of the east), which many believe to be Kosrae. The evil foreign rulers of Pohnpei at the time, the Saudeleur, had banned *sakau* from Pohnpei and would not allow its cultivation or use. However, since the plant was so important to the island's indigenous culture, a woman smuggled in her vagina a small branch of *sakau* from Kosrae to Pohnpei, which was then secretly planted and multiplied. One informant claims that this Kosrae introduction was actually a reintroduction, and most agree, usually with a certain amount of humor, that this legend explains to this day the difference in taste between Kosraen and Pohnpeian *sakau*.

Regardless of source, kava became an integral part of the island's religious, economic, political, and social life centuries ago and has been extensively cultivated and consumed on Pohnpei for a very long time. Informants agree that kava is an extremely special plant since it actually exceeds all other plants and animals, including humans, in its *wahu* (respect) value. Kava is the central element of the ritual feasts (*kamadipw en wahu*) held each year for the paramount chiefs to celebrate the opening of the yam season, and it accompanies all *nopwei* (ceremonial first offerings to the gods and chiefs) of both major seasonal crops—breadfruit and yams. Because of its respect value, kava is presented and prepared whenever one meets with chiefs or senior lineage members. This protocol is followed when requests are made for favors or forgiveness for particularly serious transgressions, for marriage ceremonies, and on various other occasions when a commoner needs to meet with higher ranked people or the paramount chiefs (Ashby, 1990; Anson and Raynor, 1993). Despite recent trends in commercialization, kava continues to hold its central place in the cultural and social system of Pohnpei.

Commercialization

Traditionally, consumption was reserved mainly for the higher ranking members of the culture. During the Japanese mandate (1914–1945), kava use was highly restricted and strict punishments were dealt to offenders. Since World War II, however, consumption has increased steadily among the general populace. Before the opening of the first kava bar in the Kitti district in 1972, kava was neither bought nor sold. Generally, each Pohnpeian man had his own kava, and the plant itself was considered a prestige crop, useful only in the traditional and social realm. Being able to provide kava at all family and community events marked a man as productive and successful, able to provide for his family and community at all times. Following the opening of the first markets, the commercial sale of kava began to increase, especially in the urban center of Kolonia, where drinkers rapidly outnumbered growers as the island's urban center doubled in population over 2 decades from 1970. As the cash economy has continued to grow, fewer people have the time to grow kava, although everyone who participates in the local culture needs it. Subsequently, a cash market also appeared in the mid-1970s for whole kava plants (with branches intact), preferred for cultural use.

The event that really increased the commercialization of kava, however, was the severe 1982–1983 El Nino drought, the worst ever recorded on Pohnpei. By the second month of the drought, much of the island's lowland kava crop was dying in the fields, and desperate farmers sold what they could to avoid total loss. At the same time, observant farmers noticed that the forests remained moist during the drought. Concerns about the future reliability of rainfall drove planting into the forest, where rainfall is more consistent and reliable and soil fertility is higher. It did not take growers long to also find that kava grew faster in the newly cleared forest areas, and as the local demand picked up, this became a key factor in stimulating upland kava farming. Since 1983, most new kava planting has been carried out in the island's upland forests, mainly in public lands. However, the distance and effort required to walk up through the steep, wet, forested terrain to cultivate the crop and then to carry out the harvested kava from the interior forests are quite burdensome. Consequently, the typical kava growers have gradually shifted from *Ohl en Pohnpei* (mature Pohnpeian men) to young men between 15 and 30 years of age. Kava cultivation is the most lucrative option open to rural young men, who are mostly uneducated, unskilled, lack access to family lands, and have only limited knowledge of traditional farming. The pull of the upland forests is further strengthened because having large quantities of kava not only provides a sizable income in a rather stagnant economy but also enhances the grower's status in his family and community.

Because of the use of public lands and the increased focus on the production of larger plants in a shorter time frame, cultivation methods have also gradually shifted to those favoring commercial production. These include such forest-destroying practices as total canopy clearing and clean-weeding. These practices may increase production in the short term but often cause long-term environmental problems. Whereas these ecologically unsustainable practices are rarely carried out on private lands, they are now the rule for kava plots in public forest regions.

Kava is now the major income source for much of the island's rural population, generating more than $3 million per year in the rural economy. Four thousand to 5,000 people (15 percent of the population) are engaged in kava production. For most, this is their primary source of income. The domestic market for kava is made up of about 50 licensed kava bars, a number of retail stores, and numerous unlicensed, temporary kava bars. By the mid-1990s, this commercial market utilized an estimated 477,000 kilograms per year (Yakana 1996). Local demand focuses mainly on fresh plant material, fresh pounded and squeezed roots, bottled extract, and frozen pounded roots. An export market also exists, mainly to supply the demand of expatriate Pohnpeians living in Guam, Saipan, Hawai'i, and the U.S. mainland. This overseas export market, made up of frozen pounded roots and liquid extract, is estimated at 40,000 kilograms per year. The annual harvest for customary use and personal consumption by farmers and their extended families on Pohnpei amounts to another 660,000 kilograms per year. Approximately 2,500 to 5,000 hectares are planted in kava, most in the island's upland forests, where soils are richer and kava grows relatively quickly to a marketable size.

Early Conservation Interventions

The impressive growth in kava production for commerce and personal consumption on Pohnpei has had a substantial negative impact on the island's natural environment. Beginning in 1982, island foresters and scientists began to notice an increase in deforestation. The Pohnpei State Division of Forestry and the United States Forest Service cooperated closely to facilitate the passage of the Pohnpei Watershed Forest Reserve and Mangrove Protection Act of 1987. The act stated that the central upland forest and coastal mangrove areas (about one-third of the island) were to be managed and enforced by the Pohnpei Department of Resource Management and Development. However, attempts by government officials to map the boundaries of the Watershed Forest Reserve (WFR) in 1990 were opposed by local villagers who considered the reserve to be a government land grab, in direct conflict with traditional Pohnpei resource use and authority:

> This opposition and similar incidents led to the formation of the Watershed Steering Committee in 1990, an interagency task force made up of representatives of government agencies, community leaders, and Non-governmental organizations (NGOs). In over 200 meetings, local communities unanimously requested that the Watershed Steering Committee institute two major changes: (1) Paramount and Village Chiefs (*Soumas*) need to become partners in the resource management process; and (2) environmentally sustainable resource management must be extended beyond the watershed reserve to encompass the entire island, from the mountains to the reefs.

In 1994, The Nature Conservancy (TNC), the South Pacific Regional Environmental Program (SPREP), and the Asian Development Bank began working with government agencies and communities to develop a detailed watershed management plan focused on community-based approaches to natural resource management. The plan was entitled Pohnpei's Watershed Management Strategy: Building a Sustainable Future: 1996–2000 (The Nature Conservancy, 1996). Aerial photography, part of the strategy, revealed that the intact, native forest cover on Pohnpei had been reduced from 42 percent of the island (15,008 hectares) in 1975 to just 15 percent (about 5,169 hectares) in 1995. Further analysis of the photos verified that most of the forest loss could be attributed to the drastic increase in upland cultivation of kava (Trustrum 1996).

Addressing a "Killer Threat"

By 1996, the staffs of most government and NGO resource management agencies on Pohnpei agreed that kava production in the upland forests was the major, or "killer," threat to the island's long-term environmental health. In January 1997, TNC, the College of Micronesia, Keidanren Nature Conservation Fund (Japan), and SPREP jointly launched a project to directly address the threat of upland kava cultivation by establishing a sustainable lowland kava industry. This strategy was supported by the recognition that prior to the severe drought of 1983, most of the kava in Pohnpei was grown in the lowlands as an agroforestry crop, intermixed with breadfruit, bananas, and coconut trees. The goal of joint project has been to return kava production to the local agroforests, which in many cases are already suffering from neglect and loss of crop diversity because of the increasing importance of cash and the migration from rural areas to seek paying jobs. Adding kava back to the system provides cash and prestige opportunities that may actually reverse the growing abandonment of subsistence agroforestry systems, which has already caused negative economic and health trends (Raynor 1991a, 1991b). Furthermore, there has been growing interest among many farmers to relocate kava cultivation back to the lowlands, where plantings are more accessible, can be protected from theft, and produce a more potent though slower growing product.

The lowland kava project has several strategies. The principal objective is the implementation of a "grow low" campaign to help local farmers create a supply of kava that is grown in a sustainable manner, without negative impact on the native upland forest. By the year 2000 the project was working with approximately 600 farmers and had established 2000 farmer-managed small nurseries around Pohnpei. Altogether these farmers had planted more than 1 million plants within less than two years.

In addition, the lowland kava project is working with different organizations and groups to further the campaign, including the College of Micronesia, the Pohnpei State Department of Resource Management and Development, and traditional leaders in the village communities outside of Kolonia. It is hoped that these efforts will further the education of natural resource management and encourage the recruitment and training of community conservation officers in each community to monitor and limit any further cultivation in upland forests.

The Pohnpei State and Municipal governments are also being encouraged to revise the 1987 WFR legislation to recognize and support community-based management. This involves efforts to obtain funding and technical assistance to delineate the WFR boundary, where most of the remaining intact forests are located.

Existing and potential kava exporters are being counseled when possible to help ensure recognition of environmental issues related to kava and to encourage "grow low" support from this business sector. Furthermore, radio programs, public meetings, posters, videos, and village ceremonies are among the activities that are being used to raise public awareness of the impact of clearing upland forest for kava cultivation.

As the project matures, this "green," kava cultivation model will be shared with other Pacific islands since the rapidly expanding kava export market is also threatening natural forests of several other Pacific islands, including Tonga, Fiji, Samoa, Vanuatu, and Kosrae (where it is not consumed but is clandestinely cultivated in the native forests for export to Pohnpei). Other compatible enterprises will be tested and promoted. In close partnership with the municipal governments, as well as with the Pohnpei Visitors Bureau and the Marine and Environmental Research Institute of Pohnpei (MERIP), the project team will work with rural communities to promote alternative compatible enterprises. These will include ecotourism, vegetable production for local and export markets, handicrafts production, and marine enterprises such as sponge farming and giant clam culture.

Conclusions

The growth of kava cultivation over the last two decades has had a mixed impact on the economy, environment, and culture of Pohnpei (figure 12.8). A greatly increased demand for kava has been stimulated by the strong move toward a cash economy and preference for wage labor. Expanded and intensified cultivation of kava in response to this rising demand has increased the income of rural Pohnpeians substantially, especially for younger, uneducated men. At the same time, however, significant environmental damage has occurred as growers have moved onto public lands in the island's upland forests, where conditions favor commercial production, at least in the short term, because of sufficient natural moisture and high, but transient, fertility. Stereoscopic analysis of recently updated aerial photography, supplemented by field reconnaissance, indicates that in only 27 years (1975–2002), approximately three-quarters of Pohnpei's intact native forests, about 12,000 hectares, have been heavily disturbed or destroyed (Newsome et al. 2003). It is safe to say that no greater environmental disaster has befallen the island in the more than 2,500 years that Pohnpei has been inhabited.

The "grow low" kava campaign designed to encourage lowland cultivation of the traditional drug plant, which began in 1997, has slowed but not yet stopped the relentless clearing of Pohnpei's remaining upland forests. The first round of funding for this campaign, provided to the Federated States of Micronesia through the Compact of Free Association with the United States, expired in late 2001. Funding sources had to be identified to replace this important assistance, which by 2001 made up more than two-thirds ($60 million per year) of the country's GNP. In 2002, the Pohnpei State Legislature approved $120,000 to complete the survey and delineation of Pohnpei Watershed Forest Reserve (Anon. 2003). This was, by far, the Pohnpei State Government's largest financial contribution to the management of the reserve since it was established in 1987. This commitment, and the slowing rate of modification of intact forest due to *sakau* cultivation (493 hectares/year between 1975 and 1995) to 153 hectares/year between 1995 and 2002 (Newsome et al. 2003), are positive indications

Figure 12.8. A common sight in the urbanized area of Kolonia and other parts of Pohnpei Island is a pickup truck containing large quantities of harvested kava plants (photo by Mark Merlin).

of a willingness of state government to work with traditional district political organization, as well as the progress of the "grow low" campaign and general education of the Pohnpeian people. The latter has come from the government and NGOs such as The Nature Conservancy, the Conservation Society of Pohnpei, and others.

Prior to the "grow low" campaign, the conventional bureaucratic approach to closing the forest through legislation had failed. In addition, diminishing external aid and government downsizing further undermined the government's ability to manage Pohnpei's natural resources during the latter part of the twentieth century. However, recent efforts by both public and private organization have raised hopes that upland watershed resources can be preserved. Nevertheless, it will ultimately be up to the island's rural leaders to bring kava cultivation out of the public watershed forests and back onto lowland agroforests on private land. Change in opinion during the last 13 years, from bitter opposition to general support of resource management, is currently the most visible sign of the impact of the Pohnpei Watershed Program (under which the campaign is being conducted). The challenge facing all Pohnpeians in the next decade will be to build a truly sustainable island economy that is not dependent to any significant degree on "illegal" and unsustainable kava cultivation on public lands. For the government, NGOs, and community participants in the project, developing the "grow low" campaign has been a valuable learning experience through which a uniquely "Pohnpei-style" approach—suited specifically to the island's social and political conditions—is being developed.

Finally, it should be noted here that alleged health issues provoked governmental bans on the legal use of kava products in parts of Europe in early 2002, which stimulated review of its legal use by governments elsewhere. These bans greatly limited the exportation of kava from the tropical Pacific countries where it had only recently become so important to the local economies. Whether these bans are sustained, and even spread geographically, remains to be seen; they certainly could have an important impact on the economies and environments of Vanuatu, Tonga, Samoa, Hawai'i, and Pohnpei. At the end of 2003, there was still no substantial resolution to the putative health issues regarding the supposed liver-damaging effects of kava consumption. However, indigenous consumption remains high in the remote tropical Pacific societies where kava has been a very important drug plant for thousands of years.

References

Anderson, E. 1952. *Plants, Man, and Life*. Berkeley: University of California Press.

Anonymous. 2003. "Watershed Management Gains House Support from Pohnpei State Legislature and Governor." *The Messenger-Serehd, Conservation Society of Pohnpei* 5(1): 1–2.

Anson, H., and W. Raynor. 1993. "Traditional Resource Management and the Conservation of Biological Diversity on Pohnpei Island, Federated States of Micronesia." In *Ethics, Religion and Biodiversity: Relations Between Conservation and Cultural Values*, ed. L. Hamilton, pp. 122–146. Cambridge: White Horse Press.

Ashby, G. A. 1990. *Guide to Pohnpei: An Island Argosy*. Eugene, OR: Rainy Day Press.

Chew. W. L. 1972. "The Genus Piper (Piperaceae) in New Guinea, Solomon Islands and Australia." *Journal of the Arnold Arboretum* 53: 1–25.

Crosby, A. W. 1986. *Ecological Imperialism: The Biological Expansion of Europe, 900–1900*. Cambridge: Cambridge University Press.

Dahl, C., and B. Rayor. 1996. Watershed planning and management: Pohnpei, Federated States of Micronesia. *Asia Pacific Viewpoint* 37(3): 235–253.

Fiji Department of Information. 1998. Fiji Today. Department of Information, Ministry of National Planning and Information. Suva, Fiji.

Green, R. C. 1991. "Near and Remote Oceania: Disestablishing 'Melanesia.'" In *Essays in Pacific Anthropology and Ethnobiology in Honour of Ralph Bulmer*, pp. 491–502. Auckland: Polynesian Society.

Iriarte, I. S. 1997. Pohnpei Paramount Chiefs' Council Meeting, Pohnpei Island.

Johnson, E. 2000. Past president of the Hawaiian Kava Growers Association. Personal communication.

Kepler, K. 1983. *Hawaiian Heritage Plants*. Honolulu: Oriental Publishing Company.

Kirch, P. V. 1997. *The Lapita Peoples: Ancestors of the Oceanic World*. Oxford: Blackwell.

———. 2000. *On the Road of the Winds: An Archaeological History of the Pacific islands Before European Contact*. Berkeley: University of California Press.

Konanui, J. 2000. Past president of the Hawaiian Kava Growers Association. Personal communication.

Lebot, V., P. Cabalion, and J. Levesque. 1986. "Le kava des ancêstres est-il l'ancêtre du kava?" *Naika, Journal of the Vanuatu National Science Society* 23: 1–11.

Lebot, V., E. Johnston, Q. Y. Zheng, D. McKern, and D. M. McKenna. 1999. "Morphological, Phytochemical, and Genetic Variation in Hawaiian Cultivars of 'Awa (Kava, Piper methysticum, Piperaceae." *Economic Botany* 53: 407–418.

Lebot, V., M. Merlin, and L. Lindstrom. 1992. *Kava: The Pacific Drug*. New Haven, CT: Yale University Press.

Lewin, L. 1924. *Phantastica: Narcotic and Stimulating Drugs*. London: Routledge, Kegan, Paul, Trench, Trubner.

Luders, D. 1996. "Legend and History: Did the Vanuatu-Tonga Kava Trade Cease in A.D. 1447?" *Journal of the Polynesian Society* 105: 287–310.

Marshall, M. 1987. "An Overview of Drugs in Oceania." In *Drugs in Western Pacific Societies: Relations of Substance*, ed. L. Lindstrom. Association for Social Anthropology in Oceania Monograph no. 11. Lanham, MD: University Press of America.

Merlin, M., D. Jano, B. Raynor, T. Keene, J. Juvik, and B. Sebastian. 1992. *Tuhke en Pohnpei; Plants of Pohnpei*. Honolulu: East-West Center, Program on Environment.

Nature Conservancy. 1996. "Pohnpei's Watershed Management Strategy 1996–2001: Building a Sustainable and Prosperous Future." Unpublished manuscript, Kolonia, Pohnpei.

Newsome, P. F., M. J. Page, and H. A. Hekil. 2003. *Vegetation Map of Pohnpei 2002, FSM*. Unpublished contract report. Palmerston North New Zealand: Landcare Research New Zealand, Ltd.

Parker, S. 1994. *Pacific Islands Monthly*, May, p. 17.

Pawley, A. K., and R. C. Green. 1973. "Dating the Dispersal of the Oceanic Languages." *Oceanic Linguistics* 12: 1–67.

Ragone, D. "Genetic Variation in Breadfruit (*Artocarpus altilis*)." 1991. Ph.D. dissertation, University of Hawaii. Honolulu, Hawai'i.

Raynor, W. C. 1991a. "Agroforestry Systems on Pohnpei: Practices and Strategies for Development." *Field Document 4*. South Pacific Forestry Development Programme.

———. 1991b. "Economic Analysis of Indigenous Agroforestry: A Case Study on Pohnpei Island, Federated States of Micronesia," In *Financial and Economic Analyses of Agroforestry Systems*, ed. G. Sullivan, S. Huke, and J. Fox, pp. 243–258 Paia, HI: Nitrogen Fixing Tree Association.

———. 1994. "Resource Management in Upland Forests of Pohnpei: Past Practices and Future Possibilities." *ISLA: A Journal of Micronesian Studies* 2 (Rainy Season): 47–66.

———. 1997. "Towards Community-Based Resource Management: The Pohnpei Watershed Project." Paper presented at the Eighth Pacific Science Inter-Congress, Suva, Fiji.

———. 2000. "*Sakau en Pohnpei*: Building a Sustainable *Sakau* Industry." Unpublished manuscript.

Reisenberg, S. 1968. *The Native Polity of Ponape*. Washington, DC: Smithsonian Institution Press.

Schultes, R. E., and A. Hofmann. 1979. *Plants of the Gods*. New York: MacGraw-Hill.

Siegel, R. K. 1989. *Intoxication: Life in Pursuit of Artificial Paradise*. New York: Dutton.

Thaman, R. R. 2000. Professor of Pacific Islands Biogeography, University of the South Pacific, Suva, Fiji. Personal communication.

Trustrum, N. 1996. "Pohnpei's Watershed Spatial Plan and Management Guidelines." In *Consultant's Reports: T.A. No. FSM-1925 Watershed Management and Environment*, ed. Nature Conservancy. Manila: Asian Development Bank.

Whistler, W. A. 2000. Professional Botanist, adjunct professor, University of Hawaii at Manoa, Honolulu. Personal communication.

Yakana, J. 1996. Unpublished raw data. Nature Conservancy, Kolonia, Pohnpei.

Yen, D. E. 1985. "Wild Plants and Domestication in Pacific Islands." In *Recent advances in Indo-Pacific Prehistory*, ed. V. N. M. Misra and P. Bellwood. New Delhi: Oxford University Press.

———. 1991. "Polynesian Cultigens and Cultivars: The Questions of Origin." In *Islands, Plants, and Polynesians*, ed. P. Cox and S. Bannack. Portland, OR: Disocorides.

———. "Subsistence to Commerce in Pacific Agriculture: Some Four Thousand Years of Plant Exchange." In *Plants for Food and Medicine*, ed. H. D. V. Prendergast. Kew, Eng.: Royal Botanic Gardens.

13

The Global Nexus of Drug Cultivation and Consumption

Joseph J. Hobbs

I t is a pleasure to write the closing chapter for this volume. My tasks are to present some common themes in these diverse studies, point out the unique features, and reflect on our roles as researchers of plant-based drugs and the people who produce, distribute, and use them.

The research behind this volume is extraordinary. Doing fieldwork about drugs is risky. Almost every situation described here involves illicit activities. Growers, traffickers, and merchants of these substances have every reason to be suspicious about the researcher, and they have been both generous and trusting in revealing their worlds to us. In turn we hope that our interpretations will benefit these people, not by condoning what is illegal, but by offering enlightened counsel to decision makers who should act with the best information on the human dimensions and costs of their policies, thereby reducing some of the harm done by actions based on ignorance or incomplete information.

Regardless of whether or not we approve of what they do, we must marvel at the extraordinary resourcefulness of these people, particularly the peasant farmers at the base of the drug enterprise. As Steinberg (chapter 6) notes, these seemingly conservative people are amazingly flexible and adaptable to the changing world around them. And one cannot help but admire the fortitude in their labors. Westermeyer (chapter 3) describes the work of Laotian opium harvesters as "pressured, repetitive, prolonged, and grueling. Thousands of bulbs rapidly incised and scraped, incised and scraped every day, day after day, from twilight to dusk—sometimes even at night by torch—for weeks." Their efforts are typical.

This is a volume about indigenous peoples and drugs, and it is much more. It offers insight into the drugs themselves, their production and marketing, their unique place in the process of globalization, the physiological impact of their use, their spiritual and perceptual dimensions, their impact on landscapes, and their role in social and political change, as well as the drug war and alternatives to conventional drug warfare. These studies represent work that, as Mathewson (chapter 1) has written, is "immense, compelling, and critically important."

The Beauty and the Beast

The chapters in this volume show us that drugs are the quintessential mixed blessing, brimming with paradox. To seek them out and to use them is part of what distinguishes us from other species—they make us human. But some of them rob us of our humanity. We can credit drugs, some say, with the development of cognition itself, with the evolution of religious beliefs, and with the alleviation of disease and suffering. But we can also blame drugs for impaired mental abilities, for the rejection of mores that maintain cohesion in cultures, and for sickness and death. They reduce pain; they cause even more pain. We take them to explore and discover; we take them to hide. They promote social cohesion; they isolate us from others and induce paranoia. Drugs in part define some ethnic groups; drugs have been used to destroy cultures. They facilitate hard work, perhaps contributing to national productivity; they keep people from working. Some drugs can be harvested from natural landscapes; the cultivation of others destroys unique ecosystems. Farmers grow them for rational reasons; the choice to grow drug crops is dangerously irrational. They help prop up governments; they bring governments down.

Drugs are a huge force behind social and environmental changes, many of them—but not all of them—negative. There are compelling arguments in this volume that drugs have long been an essential component in the formation and perpetuation of ethnic identity (see Mathewson), and ethnicity is certainly to be celebrated. Numerous ethnic groups have developed religious practices and beliefs that employ and even revere drugs, particularly the psychotropic ones. Andean peoples have long left offerings of coca leaves to petition safe passage through high mountain passes (Young, chapter 11). Kava continues to be held sacred by many people on Pohnpei (Merlin, chapter 12). The consumption of peyote is literally a sacrament for members of the Native American Church, who regard the cactus as a god (Kimber, chapter 7). Between the 1950s and 1970s, the spread of peyote through this growing movement "gave hope to the hopeless," writes Kimber. Hallucinogens have also given secular, nonindigenous users a pathway to a perceptual world previously experienced only by select ethnic groups and religious communities. These substances have given individuals an opportunity to view the world in unique ways and have sometimes led to collective social and spiritual movements that have had lasting and not always deleterious effects on the broader culture.

The chapters here suggest that most of the drugs with which indigenous peoples are involved are, at the stage they work with them, relatively benign compared with the value-added products that some of them become. Marijuana, peyote, coca leaf, and perhaps opium (though this is in a class of its own) have few of the debilitating and even fatal consequences of cocaine and heroin. The synthetic drugs, such as the amphetamines, that have no roots in indigenous societies are outside the scope of this volume, but they, too, are more destructive.

Indigenous Peoples and Drugs

This volume demonstrates that there is no neat or predictable correlation between indigenous or ethnic groups and drugs. Dominant cultures and media often collectively blame minorities—the Bedouin, the Maya, the Chechens—for drug problems. The realities are more complex. In some cases, indigenous peoples are the last or least likely to cultivate drugs. Young shows that this is the case with many Indians of eastern Peru. Coca cultivation has been introduced by mestizos, whose activities only compound the social disruption and loss already experienced by the indigenous people. But there are also numerous cases in this book of drug cultivation taking place in the homelands of traditional peoples marginalized from the national process of economic development. Westermeyer describes the poppy growers of Laos, for example, as minority groups disadvantaged in education, job opportunities, advancement, and political power, and Steinberg's Maya marijuana farmers likewise lived in the most economically depressed region of Belize. Lacking a national process of development, the Afghanistan described by Allan (chapter 4) was fertile ground for poppies.

So there is often an intersection between indigenous peoples and drug crops. Environmental determinism is not at work: Remote mountain locations where there are indigenous people are not inevitably drug strongholds. However, the fact that this intersection exists suggests that we need to pay close attention to the processes and consequences underlying it. We need especially to understand the root economic causes that draw indigenous people to the drug enterprise, a theme taken up below.

Even within a single country or region, ethnic groups span a continuum of involvement with drugs. Zhou (chapter 10) surveys the range of interactions in postrevolutionary China. Some groups had no involvement with drugs. Some groups had large proportions of opium addicts but did not produce or trade opium; others grew poppies and supplied raw opium without using it or moving it farther down the pipeline; still others grew poppies and consumed and trafficked in opium.

This volume reveals that a single indigenous group rarely follows the chain vertically from cultivation through trafficking. Typically, the ethnic group that grows a drug crop passes it on to a merchant from one or more different ethnic groups. In Zhou's China, for example, Tibetans grew and Han and Hui were the merchants. The drug lord in Steinberg's Kechi Maya village in Belize was non-Maya. Westermeyer's opium merchants in Laos are ethnic Lao or Chinese, whereas the poppy farmers are mountaineer minorities.

On down the chain, diasporas of ethnic groups often form links of drug transmission across international borders. McCoy (chapter 2) cites Kosovars scattered from Geneva to Macedonia, Turks from Berlin to Kazakhstan, Armenians from Moscow to Lebanon, Azerbaijanis from Sumgait to Kyrgyzstan, and Chechens from Baku to Kazakhstan, all of them cooperating in trafficking. Allan addresses the roles of Israeli crime syndicates and the particular geographical importance of Poland in funneling drugs to their destinations.

Why Users Use; Why Growers Grow; Why Traffickers Traffic

The chapters in this book show that people use drugs mainly in the pursuit of pleasure. That pleasure may be mainly physiological or cognitive, and it may be ostensibly recreational or religious, but it is pleasure. There is the pleasure of counteracting a hard day's physical labor with a palliative (McCoy's opium and Mills's, chapter 9, ganja); the pleasurable socializing of Indians from all walks of life while passing their *ganja* and *charas* pipes (Mills again), of Fijians sipping bowls of kava (Merlin), and of Andean peasants coming together to chew coca (Young); and the pleasurable disconnection from ordinary perception, including the "physical and mental exhilaration" and "long fits of laughter" induced by peyote (Kimber). Adherence to religious obligation through the use of peyote in the Native American Church is also a form of pleasure, as are the uses of substances such as kava to strengthen traditional customs and cement business arrangements or celebrate births, deaths, and marriages (Merlin). The most sinister drug is said to be the most pleasurable. No author in this book describes the heroin rush that has enslaved so many, but Linda Yablonski (1997) does in her novel *The Story of Junk*: "It's not easy to describe this euphoria—a sublime nausea, a flushed meeting of mortal and immaterial all at once, a leap beyond fate, a divine embrace."

Growers grow drugs sometimes for their own limited consumption, but mainly they do so because there are paying users elsewhere who seek such pleasures and because they believe that supplying that market is in their economic interest. Few growers are traumatized morally by what they do, and many may be unaware of the destructive end results of their harvests. Steinberg describes the Maya of southern Belize: "These are economically poor farmers who perceive psychoactive plants as cash crops, much like coffee or cacao, that are consumed in distant lands by unknown peoples. Certainly some farmers worry about the ultimate consequences of their dangerous harvest, but most have immediate economic needs to fulfill, and drug plants often help meet these needs." Likewise, Westermeyer points out that minorities in Laos who grow and smuggle poppies see their endeavors as legitimate commercial activites, not criminal or immoral acts: "With poppy, even farmers in remote areas can participate in an international cash economy . . . they could store wealth, purchase food and medicine, send their children to school, purchase kerosene lamps and bicycles. . . . In a country with few exportable products, opium was a primary means of participating in the economy of nations." Why grow kava on Pohnpei? Merlin's answer is a familiar refrain: "Kava cultivation is the most lucrative option open to rural young men, who are mostly uneducated, unskilled, lack access to family lands, and have only limited traditional farming knowledge . . . having large quantities of kava . . . provides a sizable income in a rather stagnant economy." Allan describes the impoverishment and destitution of Afghans who have remained in Afghanistan, and it is easy to appreciate McCoy's explanation for why poppy production exploded there in the 1990s: 3 million impoverished refugees return to a wartorn homeland, desperate to earn cash; what would they turn to but poppies?

Nowhere in this volume is there a portayal of drug crop growers who become wealthy—though Allan shows that poppies are clearly more profitable to the Afghan farmer than wheat—and none seem to be motivated by greed. Despite the retail value of heroin, poppies, for example, have only limited profitability for their farmers, and growing them involves hard labors and many risks (Westermeyer). It is rather the simple goal of maintaining some degree of social and economic security that motivates growers. Westermeyer has offered comparative figures for a period when Laotian poppy growers earned 50 cents to $1 per day, compared with the urban wage rate of $1 for unskilled or semiskilled labor. Such nonfarming wages were seldom available in the rural areas, so growing poppies was the only means of earning comparable capital.

Unique demographic, political, and other conditions also stimulate drug crop cultivation. In Laos, for example, wartime conditions in the 1970s gave people less land to work with in increasingly crowded areas, and poppies were the only viable alternative to more extensive slash-and-burn subsistence agriculture (Westermeyer). The warring parties in Afghanistan's civil conflict placed landmines in irrigation works, compelling farmers to grow a high-value crop with limited demands on land and water: opium poppy (Allan). Still others grow drug crops because mafia-style tactics force them to. Mexican drug traffickers, for example, use the threat of harming a peasant's family or taking away his land to force him to grow poppies or cannabis (Perramond, chapter 8). During the first half of the twentieth century, Han Chinese sometimes forced Tibetans to grow poppies (Zhou).

There are drawbacks to growing drug crops. Poppies are vulnerable to flooding, drought, hail, and depredations by livestock, wild animals, and aerial spraying (Westermeyer). But for most farmers there are advantages that compensate for such drawbacks. Poppies can be grown in different seasons from food crops, and they produce yields more rapidly than perennial fruit trees, tea, or coffee. Opium is lightweight, and therefore easier to get to market, and can be stored indefinitely, unlike most fruits, vegetables, and flowers (Westermeyer). Coca leaves can be harvested throughout the year, providing steady income, whereas seasonal factors restrict other crops (Young). The marketer actually comes to the coca leaf producer and even provides him with loans to plant new crops. Buyers also supply technical support and cash upon delivery to Maya marijuana farmers in Belize (Steinberg). These growers enjoy the advantage of being able to intercrop marijuana with their food staple, maize. Perramond describes a similar pattern in Mexico, where farmers interplant marijuana with maize, beans, squash, sunflowers, and tomato plants. For farmers in Peru, coca is just one part (although the most important) of an agricultural landscape and cycle that includes maize, beans, coffee, oil palm, and cattle pasture (Young). In nineteenth-century Bengal, cannabis was the most valuable asset in the crop portfolio (Mills). It was grown in a given field once every 4 years, in a cycle that included the cultivation of jute and mustard. In noncannabis years, potato, turmeric, tobacco, rice, and ginger were grown.

In sum, in environments of uncertainty, where people lack secure land tenure and livelihoods, drug crops are a valuable form of insurance.

Some of the same elements that make drug crops so perfect for cultivation also make them desirable to traffickers. Dried peyote buttons, for example, are an ideal trade good because they are lightweight, can be compressed, and can be stored for long periods (Kimber). Heroin, Westermeyer writes, is the smuggler's dream: difficult to detect, odorless, powdery and easily hidden in small volumes. He also points out that the raw material for heroin—opium—in contrast is bulky, odoriferous, and not easily disguised. Indeed, most of the raw materials for the drugs described in this volume stay close to home; cannabis is the exception, and it is unsurprising that it dominates drug interdiction statistics in both percentage and volume.

This book deals little with the logistics and geography of trafficking; only Perramond and McCoy discuss these issues at length. Perramond brings our attention to the need to avoid thinking of trafficking as a web of interlinked horizontal strands. Only the small-scale producers and smugglers, such as those he researched who work with cocaine and marijuana across the U.S.-Mexico border, are organized horizontally, with specialists in transportation, transborder shipment, reception, and storage. The larger industries are organized and integrated vertically.

Although not concerned with the mechanics of trafficking, this volume offers many illustrations of the geography of the global drug trade and shows that drugs are on the cutting edge of the process of globalization. There are some discussions here of traditional drug economies: The exchange of products to obtain coca leaves, for example, historically tied Andean highland and lowland communities together (Young), the Pushtuns of Afghanistan had a historically important regional niche in growing opium poppies (Allan), and kava was always important in the traditional economic sector in Oceania (Merlin). Today, however, coca, kava, and most of the drugs discussed here can best be viewed as belonging in the interconnected web of ideas, monies, and materials that is globalization.

The first drug to make its appearance as a global commodity was opium, under British stewardship in the nineteenth century. McCoy shows how Britain controlled opium vertically, from cultivation through processing to export. Opium was a leg in Britain's triangular trade, in which Indian opium and cotton went to China, Chinese tea to Britain, and British textiles and machinery back to India. This mercantile enterprise was enormously profitable for Britain; and having successfully forced China to legalize opium in 1858, Britain was assured of a large and captive market of addicts. The subsequent prohibition of drugs, and much later the fall of the Iron Curtain, gave rise to new expressions of globalization. In the 1990s, McCoy explains, heroin became a world drug as the result of the weakening of national and international controls and the strengthened factionalization of religion, region, race, and ethnicity.

Each case in this book illustrates clearly how drugs sweep local people, traditional and indigenous peoples in particular, into the vortex of global economic and cultural forces, at least those well beyond their traditional boundaries. Steinberg warns us against thinking of the Mopan and Kekchi Maya as traditional, isolated societies. Instead we should recognize how, especially through the marijuana trade, they have come to interact with economies far beyond the village level. Young shows how coca, a traditionally used plant, is modified into a derivative of international importance that affects national and global economies. Economic forces and social networks link remote Amazonian groups to drug-use fashions in the United States and Europe, and these ties have "real consequences for land-use practices and planting decisions by farmers." Perramond's trans-Mexico-U.S. border traffickers are an unlikely but certain model of effective international commerce, "the perfect business people" who have "begun to flexibly produce and move their products, in some ways imitating the corporate strategy of 'just in time' production, perhaps becoming the most timely of capitalist enterprises."

Drugs are big business. In this volume, McCoy relates that in the late 1990s the global drug traffic was a $400 billion annual industry, representing 8 percent of the world's trade and involving 51 million users. That value exceeds the worth of the world's iron and steel industries and the automobile industry and is comparable with the value of the global textile trade. Is this business good or bad for economies? It would be hard to deny that coca cultivation has pumped much-needed revenue into impoverished Peru, for example. Young reports that at least 50,000 people make money from the cultivation, transport, and other aspects of coca and cocaine, and many more benefit financially by providing goods and services to those 50,000. Whatever apparent benefits derive from this source of funds, however, it sends ominous ripples through the global system. The heroin trade comes in a particularly devastating package. McCoy states that "wherever this invisible commerce touches ground for processing, packaging, or exchange, the illicit enterprise quickly ramifies—encouraging drug production, official corruption, mass addiction, and HIV infection. Through the alchemy of capitalism, wherever this commodity comes to rest, mafias form, ethnic separatists arm, and a culture of criminality crystallizes."

Social and Material Changes

As drug cultivators are drawn into broader, even global economic networks, their lives change. For the "simple" peasant farmer—if that person ever was simple—drug money, although modest, creates both an ability to buy nontraditional goods and the belief that these goods are essential. In some circumstances it is less appropriate to envision a peasant farmer who feels compelled to grow drug crops just to get a place at the economic table than to think of the farmer who would like to buy what Steinberg calls the "perceived necessities" of modern life. The extra income from drug crops can purchase a radio, television, or motorcycle or replace a traditional thatch and dirt-floor dwelling with a modern concrete, two-story, electrified house, thus enhancing the farmer's perceived quality of life and social status.

Westermeyer shows how opium was actually a vehicle out of the Stone Age into the Iron Age in Laos. As recently as the 1960s, tribespeople who did not grow opium boiled water by dropping heated stones into bamboo containers, whereas their counterparts who had some cash from opium sales could, for the first time, afford to buy pots, cloth, footwear, dyes, guns, and more. Eventually such goods came to be perceived as essential items rather than luxuries, and they also served to enhance the social status of those who bought them. Typically the adoption of such material innovations has been accompanied by internal changes in social structures, mores, and behaviors. Steinberg reports a rejection of traditional social structures by the Maya in Belize, in favor of more Western models, especially among the young.

New material appetites also involved new relationships with others. In Belize, marijuana buyers provided marijuana growers with "free" vehicles, which would remain free only as long as the grower continued to grow. Among the Liangshan Yi in southwestern China, opium revenue brought a massive influx of rifles and handguns by 1950. This new firepower allowed the black Yi to consolidate their authority over smaller, weaker ethnic groups and to swell the ranks of slaves whom the Yi had conscripted from those groups (Zhou). Revenue from opium also brought guns and other new materials to the Tibetan area of Sichuan and succeeded in transforming a regional capital from a small village into a thriving and more ethnically diverse commercial center. Drugs thus act as major agents of social and landscape change.

The Drug Landscape

As geographers and allies of geography, the authors in this volume are particularly interested in the impact of drugs on the landscape. Drug landscapes are not ordinary landscapes. They either are or are meant to be hidden landscapes, concealed in sometimes unique and creative ways. Mills, for example, describes the "series of elaborate environmental interventions" that cannabis farmers in nineteenth-century India used to disguise their crop: "In seeking to use these landscapes in surreptitious ways they transformed them imaginatively, as they began to look at their local environments in novel ways for the new purpose of avoiding the state's planned interventions." Mills sees that not only cropped fields but also the entire landscape took on new meanings and uses for the production and trafficking of *ganja*:

> Peasants began to see river systems as smuggling routes, outhouses as contraband storerooms, and peripheral land as full of potential for concealed cultivation. The landscape was transformed through the preparation of hemp for the narcotics markets, both in the real world of field systems and irrigation systems and in the imaginative world of those who lived in the rural areas and who began to see their local environments in new and powerful ways.

Because of their relatively high economic value, drug landscapes are beloved landscapes to their cultivators. They are also despised landscapes, targeted for destruction by national authorities. They are landscapes of fear, for they are almost always illicit landscapes. Their cultivators are poised to defend, to fight, and to flee; they can become landscapes of conflict and violence. They are ephemeral landscapes. A drug raid, a change in market conditions, or environmental pressures can quickly change the face of the drug land. Perhaps the greatest turnaround in drug history is the astounding (but, according to Allan, dubious) apparent eradication of poppies in Afghanistan between 2000 and 2001.

Some patterns of likely drug landscapes emerge from this collection. Favored landscapes for drug growing are remote, isolated, often mountainous areas, far from the practical reach of security and other government forces or, conversely, where governments extend their reach to encourage and protect drug production (Zhou, Steinberg, Westermeyer, and McCoy). Both ends of the spectrum of the state's presence on the drug landscape may be seen in rugged Afghanistan, from the lawlessness that followed the withdrawal of Soviet forces to the Taliban's well-coordinated use of opium revenues (McCoy).

Whereas some studies in this volume point us to isolated regions as those mostly likely to have drug crops, others point to integrated regions: Where new roads, airports, and other infrastructure have sprung up to promote development, drug cultivation and processing often surge. The connection is obvious: The new links make it easier to get the goods to market. In Young's Peru, "without exception, every area with new roads and colonists became centers of coca leaf production for the illicit market." Sanabria (chapter 5) explains that it was not merely infrastructure but also the entire development process that encouraged illegal coca growing in Bolivia. National political-economic policies discouraged peasant household economics in favor of capital accumulations by agroindustrial elites. It was also in the interest of national authorities that peasants, particularly those settling in new regions, be provided with secure cash incomes. These positions, along with increasing involvement by the Bolivian elite in drug trafficking and growing demand for coca abroad, led to an explosion in coca cultivation in the 1980s and 1990s.

Drug crop cultivation has environmental impacts that are generally detrimental, arguably far more so than the cultivation of conventional food and other commercial crops. There are few examples in this volume of positive impacts on landscapes of drug cultivation, and none are sustainable. The only semipristine drug landscape is that of the south Texas peyote described by Kimber. In this case, the crop occurs naturally, and its successful propagation depends upon transforming the landscape as little as possible. However, *peyoteros* have begun to harvest the buttons before maturity and have exerted so much pressure on the resource that its populations are declining.

Landscapes elsewhere have to be cleared of original vegetation to make way for the drug crop. There is nothing new or inherently sinister about that, and this pattern could be viewed as just another cultural-agricultural landscape. Westermeyer portrays poppy cultivation in Laos as almost benign, at least in comparison with crops, such as corn, rice, wheat, and millet, that are also grown in slash-and-burn agriculture. The poppy is far less nutrient-demanding than these crops and therefore can be successfully grown in a single plot over a period of many years or even decades before the farmer needs to move on and clear a new field.

Much more disturbing is the pattern in which a drug crop requires extensive, regular clearing of natural vegetation, often in wilderness areas that otherwise would have remained untouched, and often with the additional environmental hazards of chemical pollution. Merlin discusses how kava cultivation in Fiji opens up new agricultural lands, especially in highland areas, with deforestation and the invasion of exotic weeds. Likewise, in Tonga, kava planting in upland forests has led to rapid deforestation and erosion. Most striking, kava cultivation has been the main force behind the clearing of two-thirds of Pophnei's intact native forest since 1975. Merlin does cite an argument favoring kava over papaya cultivation on the island of Hawaii. In this case, kava growing is helping to eradicate foreign, invasive species and allowing some native plants to make a comeback.

The most extreme environmental impacts are associated with coca cultivation in the foothills of the eastern slopes of the Peruvian Andes, as described by Young. In just a single district in Peru, and merely in elevations below 1,500 meters, 3,375 plant species, including 521 national endemics, are threatened by deforestation for coca cultivation. The inference is that the number of animal species and endemics threatened is far higher. Unlike the conventional food and commercial crops in the system, coca inverts the typical spatial expectations of deforestation by shunning flat, accessible areas in favor of remote, steep areas. Coca deforests areas that should not have been attractive for human modification. Its cultivation requires heavy use of pesticides, and its processing into cocaine paste requires the use of toxic chemicals. Destructive agents thus diffuse through the system, threatening habitat, species viability, and water quality.

Finally, with respect to drugs on the landscape, the case studies cite several examples of drug places as pilgrimage destinations. Kimber describes the Mustang Plains region of South Texas as a sacred landscape for both Native American Church members and the white American adventurers who have "followed the peyote road" to this area. Within this greater sacred landscape are specific places of reverence, such as Amada's shrine. Yet another form of pilgrimage is drug tourism. The pilgrimage shrines in these cases are not the hallowed ground where crops grow but both the exotic off-the-beaten-track destinations of the developing world (see Allan's Kabul, where in the golden age of the 1970s virtually anyone's drug of choice could be obtained) and the tolerant metropolis of the West (Amsterdam) where one may even today indulge in one's favorite euphoric to one's heart's content, with varying degrees of risk.

The Hydra

This volume reveals a remarkably consistent feature in the history of drugs: They are very elastic. That is, patterns in their production, transportation, marketing, and consumption change fundamentally, rapidly, and regularly. A user can change his or her drug of choice, often in response to the war on drugs and often with unforeseen negative consequences. Cut off from a customary drug, a user will find a substitute. The UN-sponsored suppression of opium in Thailand, for example, led to an explosion in the use of heroin imported from Burma. Not only was this opium substitute far more addictive and deleterious, but also needle sharing by its intravenous users led to an epidemic of HIV/AIDS in Thailand (McCoy). In Laos, pressure from the United States forced the government to implement an antiopium law in 1971. The result was an immediate surge in heroin use across the country (Westermeyer). The profile of user groups can change or widen rapidly, too. For example, peyote spread from Amerindian religious groups to U.S. artists, intellectuals, and hippies (Kimber).

Drug crop farmers are also flexible or elastic. There are no descriptions in this volume of a particular ethnic group that has always chosen to or been obliged to grow drug crops. Circumstances and opportunities favoring cultivation come and go, and people respond to them by adopting and abandoning drug crop agriculture. Whatever inherent difficulties there are in growing a particular drug crop, the knowledge and technology of its cultivation is spread easily, rapidly, and in predictable patterns. McCoy explains how the poppy culture spread through Afghanistan in the 1990s: The jobless young man became an itinerant harvester in an older opium district, learned how to grow the crop there, and then returned to plant poppies in the family plot of his home village, where neighbors emulated his success. Importantly and most encouraging for those looking for alternative ways to wage war on drugs, economic activities that are more profitable, less difficult, and less risky do lure farmers away from drug crops (Westermeyer).

For drug warriors, the downside of this picture is that the slack in drug crop production in one place is inevitably taken up in another, most likely where better alternatives do not exist. Almost all the authors refer to this dimension of elasticity. Of coca in Peru, Young writes, "More control in one place simply shifts the supply and associated deforestation and environmental degradation to other places." Likewise, Steinberg observes, "When one production area is either targeted or shifts to another crop, in this case marijuana production in Colombia, production is stimulated and shifts to a region where the political, legal, and economic conditions are right for an expansion of an illegal crop, in this case southern Belize." Zhou sees how opium cultivators in China's Han area were under pressure and turned to the Tibetan area as a safe haven for planting. The primary cause of such shifts is seldom environmental; it is the war against drugs.

McCoy offers such a startling and important analysis of the relationship between the war on drugs and the consequent growth of the global drug trade that it is worthwhile to recount it here in detail. The conventional drug war, he argues, has relied on repression and suppression of drug growers, traders, smugglers, and users. This law enforcement model assumes that the drug industry is inelastic and that coercion can crush it. At the local level, coercion, repression, or suppression may be effective; law enforcement can successfully clamp down on the dealers and users in a particular neighborhood, for example. However, McCoy points out, when the same model is applied to the international heroin trade, the effort fails because there are no limits to supply and demand. Both are elastic, and the coercion is incomplete or, as McCoy describes it, imperfect: "As the vice jaws of coercion tighten, supply and demand slip sideways into a spatial infinity." Opium cultivation, for example, when suppressed in one part of Asia is almost instantly taken up elsewhere on the continent, or it may even jump hemispheres, as it did to Mexico and Colombia. The source area of demand can also turn quickly. When the Drug Enforcement Agency (DEA) cracked down on exports of heroin from Thailand to the United States, the exports were deflected to Europe and Australia, which had been heroin-free for decades, and production shifted to Burma. McCoy argues that the conventional law enforcement model of suppressing drugs ignores the complex market dynamics of the illicit trade, with astonishing results. A sudden supply reduction in one area increases the value of these already high-value-added products (see also Perramond), encouraging production elsewhere. The Nixon war on drugs eradicated poppies in Turkey, for example, causing the world price of illicit opium to soar and prompting Southeast Asia to step into the production vacuum.

McCoy's sobering conclusion is that instead of reducing drug availability, repression may actually stimulate global opium production and contribute to a rapid increase of heroin supply in the United States and elsewhere. He blames four U.S. drug wars in 25 years for quadrupling the world's opium supply: "With such elastic constraints, the baton of repression becomes instead a prod, pushing consumption and production into ever-widening spheres and compounding the global drug problem." He offers these forecasts:

> In a few years, we may look back on the Cold War—with its Asian drug lords, Colombian cartels, and 5 million American narcotics addicts—as halcyon days, when we had the situation under some semblance of control. . . . Any attempt at solving America's heroin problem by reducing global opium production through a war on drugs seems unrealistic. . . . Significant increases in the world's opium supply will, quite clearly, subvert these attempts at a supply-side solution to the global drug problem. . . . There is no reason that world opium supply cannot reach, or even surpass, its historic 1906 high of 41,000 tons by 2027.

In sum, from production through distribution to consumption, drugs and the people involved with them are remarkably resilient. And so it is that we can securely forecast that drugs will always be with us. McCoy reminds us that "the human brain's chemistry makes all humanity potential addicts."

Drugs, Laws, and the State

To better understand the failures of the conventional war on drugs and to underscore some of the authors' alternative recommendations, it is useful to survey the authors' views on relationships between drugs and the state. This volume describes and analyzes the tensions between states and drug producers, consumers, and traffickers in ways that are both familiar and innovative.

There are two fresh perspectives on how indigenous or local peoples who cultivate drug crops express resistance to the state: through "subaltern" strategies and "moral geographies." Mills offers insight into subaltern groups, which are those that experience subordination in their society. These include the nineteenth-century cannabis growers of India's Ganga Mahal region who resisted compliance with British colonial control over their crop, but not by revolt or riot. Instead, the locals used their knowledge of the landscape to outwit surveillance by the colonial state's machinery, for example, by distributing the harvested crop so widely that it could not be accounted for and by creating the pretense that large quantities had been lost in "accidental" fires. Mills thus writes of the *ganja* growers that by "seeking to use these landscapes in surreptitious ways they transformed them imaginatively, as they began to look at their local environments in novel ways for the purpose of avoiding the state's planned interventions." Bolivian coca growers, as Sanabria describes, also used their intimate knowledge of landscape and other nonviolent means to successfully maneuver around national antidrug efforts through the mid-1990s. A closely related but more flexible concept is Mathewson's "moral geography," referring to the actual and symbolic terrain upon which traditional societies elaborate their livelihood and belief systems and the spaces in which they defend these practices and perceptions. Mathewson argues that for some indigenous cultures, drugs become defining elements in their relations with dominant cultures and political systems. In these and in any indigenous system in which drugs play a role, drugs serve as mechanisms of subordination or modes of resistance or both. Mathewson urges us to look for both the oppressive and the emancipatory potential of drugs for the promotion of cultural identity.

In the post–Cold War world, there are numerous instances of rebel groups — often ethically based — that are using drugs to fight one another or the state. McCoy offers a laundry list of regional rebels who, armed with drug money from sales of opium and heroin, are fighting for power. These struggles are particularly concentrated along the southern frontiers of the former Soviet Union, where, McCoy documents, "state control and civil society are weakening before the power of these new narco-mafias with their superior firepower, wealth, and political influence." In the Western Hemisphere, Young reports, the armed revolutionary groups MRTA and Shining Path found geographic refuge in Peru's eastern Andes and Amazon lowlands, where they came into contact with drug wholesalers. Once rivals and even enemies, in the 1980s the resistance groups and drug middlemen teamed up to form a significant new threat to national authorities that came to be labeled narco-terrorism. Local people in coca-growing areas were often caught in the crossfire, resulting in tens of thousands of civilian deaths and the flight of tens of thousands of refugees.

Who are the good guys and the bad guys in conflicts involving drugs, and indeed in the greater drug war itself? The boundaries are often blurred. All too often lawlessness pervades law enforcement. Westermeyer, for example, traces the career of opium in Laos from its legal days, before 1971, when virtually no corruption was associated with it, to the pervasive corruption that came with its prohibition. The law itself laid the foundation for corruption, Westermeyer argues, at both low and high levels. The highest levels of military and civilian authority involved themselves as essential players in the trade. Army officers arranged for its shipment and protection, and some Laotian diplomats conveyed heroin to Europe.

Sanabria warns that nothing is quite what it seems in the drug war; there is no simple distinction between good and evil, black and white. In his examination of the Bolivian case alone, the drug war matrix is revealed as impossible to disentangle and the war's rationale fundamentally flawed:

> To view the coca conflict as essentially one between "evil" or "criminal" coca growers and traffickers, on the one hand, and enlightened, law-abiding authorities and citizens, on the other — precisely the criminal justice perspective that ideologically informs, guides, and justifies current anticoca policy by the United States and U.S.-funded counternarcotics agencies and programs — is not only not enlightening but also fundamentally counterproductive.

Sanabria's chapter shows how

> the contest over coca in Bolivia reflects and embodies numerous and inherently con-
> flictive claims and counterclaims (social, political, economic, and ideological) by dif-
> ferent segments of Bolivian society, many of which entail (or involve) fundamental
> questions about legitimacy, hegemony, and challenges (or resistance) to the exercise
> of power by elites and state elites.

When, in the 1990s, Bolivian authorities finally capitulated to the terms of the U.S.-
sponsored drug war, it was only in their self-interest. The campaign to eradicate
coca intersected with elite interests in investments and capital accumulation in the
coca-growing regions. Sanabria foresees a landscape where tens of thousands of coca
cultivators are compelled to flee, to be replaced by industrial parks, military zones,
and a $5 million country club and golf course—financed in good part by multina-
tional companies and foreign governments, particularly the United States.

Skepticism about the drug war arises in large part from a long and tawdry history
of the United States and other governments using drugs for strategic leverage
abroad. Zhou describes how, during their occupation of China in the 1930s, Japanese
authorities encouraged opium addiction among Mongolia's ethnic Erlunchun. Addicts that provided the Japanese with information on the enemy were rewarded with
opium. McCoy reminds us that in 1950 the CIA-backed Nationalist Chinese forced
Burmese hill tribespeople to grow poppies to finance Nationalist resistance against
the Communist Chinese government. This pattern was followed in the 1980s when
the CIA assisted Afghan resistance to the Soviet invasion. As they regained ground
in Afghanistan, the mujaheddin pressed their supporters to grow poppies as a "revolutionary tax." Afghanistan's opium production tripled during these war years, and
laboratories for refining heroin sprouted up all along the Afghan-Pakistan frontier.
These labs also had, at least by extension, United States government links, as the
CIA funded the Pakistan intelligence service that defended the facilities. The end of
Cold War involvement in Afghanistan's affairs did not bring an end to the drug business however, as both sides in the country's civil war continued to support their war
efforts with revenue from opium and heroin (see Allan).

Thus the geopolitical dimension not only of drug production, distribution, and
consumption but also of the drug war itself is considerable. Young discusses the "nefarious consequences" of the illicit coca trade: "It distorts and complicates state-to-
state relationships between and among the drug-supplying and drug-using countries.
. . . Debt relief, humanitarian and technical assistance, military advice, political coordination—all become subsumed under a drug war discourse." In ways that are seldom even-handed or based on a country's record in human rights and other important issues, the United States often makes investment and assistance contingent upon
a country's narcotics control efforts —— the so-called certification effort.

Meanwhile, Back in the Fields . . .

Whatever its shortcomings, is the drug war being won? In some cases, at first
glance, yes. In Steinberg's Belize, Drug Enforcement Administration cooperation

with national authorities resulted in marijuana—formerly tolerated and grown and sold more or less openly—being criminalized, with harsh penalties. Farmers had their fields defoliated, so their maize was destroyed along with their marijuana. The farmers gave up—or did they?

No, Steinberg answers, and the war was not won. The Maya will go back to growing marijuana when the conditions are right. No, insists McCoy, nothing short of "perfect coercion" around the globe could destroy the drug trade. In this volume, perfect coercion has been seen to succeed only in China with the eradication of what was once the world's largest center of opium production, and only then because China was able to effectively seal its borders. It is not a model for the globalized world of today. The war on coca was not won in Bolivia, Sanabria insists. The DEA-backed efforts there, involving an all-out saturation of growing areas with "troops and other instruments of repression and surveillance," have all but destroyed illicit coca, but only for the time being:

> Long-term or permanent eradication of coca in the Chapare would necessarily entail ongoing, sustained ideological, political, and economic cohesiveness, and history suggests that such prospects are quite unlikely. As a result, if given the chance, and assuming little change in the international (but primarily U.S. and European) demand for cocaine and in national policies aimed at redressing the profound economic, political, ideological, and cultural cleavages in Bolivian society, we can expect that peasants in the Chapare and elsewhere will once again take up the cultivation of coca.

If you turn to the other chapters in this volume and substitute the relevant drugs and regional names for Sanabria's coca and Chapare, you will have a good idea of how the contributors view the ongoing, conventional war on drugs.

Recommendations

What, then, do the authors propose to reduce the fallout from drugs? Aside from the obvious solution of eliminating demand in the major consuming countries, the collective answer is to wage war on poverty and inequity, not on drugs.

Steinberg argues that national and international bodies intent on effective, long-term success in combating drugs must address the social and economic conditions that have made drug crops attractive to farmers. These include supplying financial incentives and initial subsidies for nontraditional crop plants, developing eco-tourism, creating greater access to regional and national markets for agricultural produce, and allowing greater political autonomy and control of local resources. Crop substitution could be a part of these efforts but should not be their centerpiece. Maya cultivation of marijuana was a logical follow-up to years of failed development ventures centered on increasing the production of honey, maize, rice, and beans. These failed because of insufficient demand, low prices, and marketing difficulties, whereas marijuana overcame all these obstacles. The past failures cannot simply be repackaged and brought back as new alternatives to drug crops unless the earlier problems are sufficiently researched and, if possible, corrected. Young dismisses the value of crop substitution for Peruvian coca growers, citing near universal negative evaluations of its effectiveness.

McCoy uses his broad historic and geographic perspective to argue that the 150-year record of failed drug prohibition offers an opportunity to learn from the past and to develop strategies for minimizing the negative impact of drug control. He looks to the role of the state, arguing that long-term eradication of drugs depends upon a strong, committed state that exerts itself forcefully in the absence of corruption. Increasing state control over drug-growing regions and the restraint of corruption might then be helpful.* In light of the state's centrality in drug control, argues McCoy, U.S. and UN efforts to ostracize "outlaw" states where drugs are grown —such as Burma—should be carefully rethought. Logic says that the United States and United Nations should cooperate with the national governments of the countries that are leaders in global opium production.

One recommendation notable by its absence in this volume is legalization of what are now illegal drugs. Not surprisingly, there is little discussion of how drug crops could be cultivated in more sustainable fashion. The exception is Merlin, whose subject, kava, is not an illicit drug. He is encouraged by the "grow low" campaign to urge kava farmers in Pohnpei to redirect the crop away from the highlands, where it causes so much deforestation, and back to the lowlands, where it can be intercropped with breadfruit, bananas, and coconut trees.

And what about preventing the need to wage war on drugs in new areas? Young proposes that safeguarding the integrity of an ethnic group may be the best means to ensure that its territory is not used for drug crop production. He does not advocate the continued and expanded support of development efforts that encourage settlement in the Amazon as a means of combating coca; he believes that this will only promote more colonization and more illicit land use. Instead, his focus is on what can be done to prevent coca's spread into new areas. Generally, these drug-free zones are protected natural areas and lands where traditional groups are found. To ensure that drugs do not spread into the wilderness areas, he urges more interest and funding by conservation nongovernmental organizations in the foothills of the eastern slopes. As for the traditional groups, his survey of communities in Peru found that those least affected by the coca/cocaine business had one or more of these characteristics: no traditional experience with coca, a strong ethnic identity, ownership of large tracts of land, isolation from road and river transport, and little involvement in the market economy. "Programs of land rights and preservation of indigenous cultures might be the best investment possible to slow or stop the expansion of coca/cocaine," Young proposes. His conclusions should not be taken to mean that enforced "primitivization" of remote communities should be encouraged or that these peoples should be discouraged from joining the market economy. Instead, governmental recognition and encouragement of their existence as rightful

---

* Perhaps, in this light, the Colombianization of Mexico, as described by Perramond, is a setback for the drug business there, at least for a while. Perramond's informants in Mexico explained how the successes of the drug war in Mexico—with stronger suppression of the trade and less corruption on the part of the local authorities—have dramatically increased levels of violence (this is what they call the Colombianization of Mexico). Unable to rely on corrupt officials, traffickers intimidate and use violence to ensure that their product and transport lines remain intact.

nationalities, as well as legislation to ensure their property rights, are likely to stave off the forces that have led other peoples to cultivate drug crops.

There are some glimmers of enlightened policy to be found in this volume. Even the giant bureaucratic machinery of the United States is capable of recognizing that not all scheduled substances and their uses must be fought in uniform fashion; the roles of religion and ethnicity can be considered. Thus the United States tolerates peyote use by the Native American Church (see Kimber). The collection, sale, and use of peyote are constrained by federal and state laws, with enforcement largely left to the states, in an effort to ensure that peyote reaches only registered NAC members.

Zhou's chapter suggests that Communist China also provided a model for handling questions of ethnicity and drugs, although it was a model China dropped. In the 1950s, Chinese authorities recognized that it would be fruitless to try to eradicate poppy cultivation without making an effort to introduce either crop substitutes or other means by which farmers could earn a living. They also recognized that the minority groups that were growing poppies constituted special cases that needed to be weaned from opium cautiously, lest they turn against the state. Chinese authorities therefore instituted a go-slow, generally lenient approach to drug eradication among these groups and even treated each group differently, according to its special cultural and economic circumstances. They soon abandoned this approach and took a more uniform, hardline position on opium eradication, but the earlier strategy could be revisited as new ways to wage the drug war are considered.

Where to from Here?

As would be expected, the academics coming together in this volume conclude that more research remains to be done. Young accuses us of being myopic in our views of drugs: Why have we not recognized their tremendous impact on natural landscapes? We ignore illicit drugs in the literature on deforestation. There are no relevant, systematically gathered data to evaluate the environmental consequences of coca/cocaine. No accurate maps show where coca grows, and there are no yearly accounts of where and why forest has been cut. There are no field studies being done on forest fragmentation in the coca-growing areas or on the plant and animal species at risk. There are no monitoring stations to measure water quality. There are no efforts to target coca-growing areas for nature conservation. Young calls upon us to use the knowledge and technological tools we have to take up these important studies. I would add that we have not sufficiently studied the fascinating geographical threads of the drug market, what McCoy calls the "cat's cradle of trafficking routes." And nowhere in this volume is there a discussion of how farmers of now-illegal crops might be licensed to produce coca leaf and opium for legitimate pharmaceutical and other needs (enterprises now limited to a very few countries), but certainly this avenue should be explored because it would take advantage of existing peasant resources and provide much-needed revenue to poor communities.

This volume has, as Mathewson wrote, been an important first step toward a more comprehensive geography of indigenous peoples' relations with drugs. He reminds us of the need to do much more mapping at many scales and modes, from conventional mapping of diffusion and distribution to the cognitive terrains of moral geographies. He appeals for more theorizing of "one of the last great untheorized topics" and for detailed empirical studies of specific cases. The academic community represented in this volume could do more and will, I hope, inspire others to provide more enlightened data and interpretation to decision makers in the war on drugs. It looks as if the nexus of that conflict will be around for a long time.

Reference

Yablonsky, L. 1997. *The Story of Junk*, p. 57. Boston: Little, Brown.

Index

Note: page numbers in *italics* refer to figures

Aba Tibetan Autonomous Prefecture, China, 240–242
addiction to opium, in Laos, 122–127
Admiralty Islands, 285–286
Afghanistan
  alcohol in, 137–138
  British creation of, 140
  civil war and opium economy, 64–69, 143–144
  European opium demand, 140–141
  human ecology, 67
  international aid, 82–83
  market relations, 71–73
  mountain cropping systems, 134–136
  opium and heroin production trends, 52–55, 133–134, 148
  opium bans and eradication, 78–81, 82–84, 133–134, 149–150
  opium cultivation distribution, *135,* 144–146, *146,* 150
  opium traffic, 147
  poppy varieties and harvesting methods, 146–147
  post-Taliban, 81–84, 133–134
  prospects, 148–150
  refugees, 149
  Taliban movement, 69–71, 78–81
  trade networks, historical, 138–140
  trafficking routes and networks, 43, 73–78
  United States, war with, 80
  UN opium studies, 69, 71–73
African Americans, 57
Afridi, Haji Ayub, 63
Afridi, Malik Waris Khan, 63
Aga Khan Rural Support Project (AKRSP), 142
Agaricaceae, 183
agricultural alternatives, 67, 119–120
agricultural systems. *See* cropping systems
Ahmed, Mehmood, 64
AIDS and HIV, 51, 52, 62, 73–74
aid to Afghanistan, international, 82–83
Albanian exiles, 77, 78
Albright, Madeleine, 61, 93
alcade legal-political system, 178
alcohol use, 137–138, 234, 243
Ali, Hazarat, 81–82
Al Qaeda, 74

amphetamines
  Burmese production of, 59–60
  commercial history, 33
  heroin import declines and, 49
  local manufacture of, 32
  markets in Indonesia and Philippines,
    60–61
  See also synthetic drugs
Andean coca/cocaine. *See* Bolivia;
    Colombia; Peru
Anglo-Oriental Society for the Suppression
    of the Opium Trade, 39
animals, drug use in, 19
Anjia, 237
Ann Arbor Sun, 199
Anti-Drug Abuse Acts (1986, 1888), 57
antidrug campaigns. *See* prohibition, inter-
    diction, and eradication programs
Apache, 192, 195
Arakmbut (Harakmbut, Amarkeri), 258
Areca catechu, 278
Arkan (Zeljko Raznatovic), 78
Arlacchi, Pino, 24, 70, 85
Armenia, 77
Army for the Liberation of the Albanian
    Population of Presevo, Medvedja, and
    Bujanovac (UCPMD), 78
Asháninka (Campa), 257, 265
Asian opium zone
  Cold War and, 44–45
  creation of, 34
  Iron Curtain and, 43
  share of world opium, 32
  See also Southeast Asia; Southwest Asia
Aung San Suu Kyi, 61
Australia, 49
'awa, 282–283
Aymara-speaking peasants, 162
Azerbaijan, 77

Badakhshan Province, Afghanistan, 75, 82,
    145, *146*
Balkans, 77–78
Baluchi tribes, 73, 75
Bangkok Drug Enforcement Administra-
    tion, 48
Bánzer, Hugo, 89, 159, 161, 162
bazaars, in Afghanistan and Pakistan, 73,
    84, 136
Belaúnde, Fernando, 254

Belize. *See* Maya marijuana cultivation
    in Belize
Bengal, 35–36
Bennett, William J., 58
Berkeley Barb, 199
Berlandier, Jean Louis, 192
betel nut palm, 278
bhang, 137, 221, 223
Bhutto, Benazir, 63, 64
big business, drugs as, 300
bin Laden, Osama, 75
biological diversity, 260
bodies, human, 20, 21
Bolivia
  coca federations, 163–164
  coca harvest declines, 86, 158–159
  colonization initiatives, 266
  domestic public opinion, 163
  eradication programs, 56–57, 157–163
  future prospects, 164
  history of coca cultivation, 154–156
  map, *155*
  political-economic context and social
    conflict, 155–158
borders, opium trade and, 43
Bosnia, 77, 78
Brent, Charles, 40
Britain
  in Kabul and the Hindukush, 140
  opium trade history, 35–37, 39
  resistance in India, 225–230
  tea, economic and social impact of, 26–27
British East India Company, 35–36
Browne, Sir Thomas, 13
Buddhist-orient addiction treatment,
    126–127
Buddhist Women's Auxiliary, Laos, 126
Bureau of Indian Affairs, 201
Burma
  CIA covert warfare, 43–44, 45
  contradictory impacts of U.S. policy,
    62–93
  government drug alliances (1990s),
    59–61
  heroin increases (1980s), 51–52
  opium eradication program, 61–62
  opium trafficking, 45, 85
  See also Southeast Asia
Bush, George H. W., 58
Bush, George W., 90

cacao, 21
caffeine, 136
Cali cartel, 86, 88
California, 48
Cannibis indica, 223
Cannibis sativa. See marijuana
Cárdenas, Amada, 194, 199
Cárdenas, Claudio, 194, 199
cargo system, 177
Caroline Islands, 286
Carrizo, 192
Carter, Jimmy, 49–50
Casey, William, 143
cash economy, 168, 178–179
Cashibo, 257
Castaño, Carlos, 87
Casteel, Steven, 79
Central Asia, 73–78, 84, 91
Central Intelligence Agency. *See* CIA
Chamroon Parnchan, Pra, 126–127
chandu, 120
Chapare region. *See* Bolivia
charas, 137, 221
Chichimeca, 195
Chihuahua, Mexico, 209, *210, 213, 214*
chillums, 221
China
    Aba Tibetan area, and opium suppres-
        sion, 240–242, 243
    Burma and, 45, 61, 85
    "democratic reforms," 236, 239, 241, 243
    eradication campaigns, 42–43, 61, 233,
        235–236, 237–243
    Erlunchun communities, and opium,
        233–236, 243
    Liangshan Yi, and opium, 236–240, 243
    minority nationalities, and ethnic stratifi-
        cation, 232, 233, 241, 242–243
    opium, effect on minority communities,
        232–233
    opium trade history, 33–39
"China white" heroin, 51
CIA (Central Intelligence Agency)
    in Afghanistan, 53–54, 81
    alliances with drug lords, 31–32, 43–44
    Nationalist Chinese, support for, 45
    in Peru, 85–86
Clark, David, 194
Clay, Jason, 15
Clinton, Bill, 90

coca/cocaine
    botany, 250
    chewing of, 250
    cocaine paste, 253, 260
    commercial history, 33, 250–251
    crack, racial factor in, 57
    environmental impacts, 260–262
    federations, coca, 163–164
    in Inca empire, 14
    plantation production, 21–22
    policy alternatives, 266–267
    political ecology, 263–266
    processing, 253
    production increases, 26
    race and, 57
    social significance, 250
    war on drugs and, 24, 55–58
    See also Bolivia; Colombia; Peru
Coca Cola, 17
Cocama, 257
Cochabamba, Bolivia, 159, 160, 162
coffee, 38
Cogan, Charles, 53, 65
Cold War, 42–46, 58
Colombia
    alliance with Mexican cartels, 56
    coca shift from Peru and Bolivia,
        86–88
    FARC executions, 22
    heroin, shift to, 87
    Plan Colombia, 88–89
    Reagan-Bush drug war, 55, 57–58
    Thrush-65 defoliation program, 56
colonialism, 14, 221, 225–230
colonization initiatives, 259–260,
    264–265, 266
Commanche, 195
commodification
    drug tourism and, 21
    globalization and, 299–300
    heroin chic, 51
    of opium, 26–27, 34
communities and locales, scale of, 21
conflicts, drug connection of, 20
Conibo, 257
control and prohibition of drugs. *See* prohi-
    bition, interdiction, and eradication
    programs
Controlled Substances Act (1970), 194
control of drugs, as identity assault, 14

Convention for Limiting the Manufacture
of Narcotic Drugs, 41
Cook, James, 278
corruption, 30–31, 89, 127–128, 306–307
country liquor, 137
covert warfare. *See* CIA
crack cocaine, 57
credit, to Afghan farmers, 71–72
criminal syndicates, 32, 41, 74, 77–78
Croatia, 77, 78
crop alternatives, 67, 119–120
cropping systems
   milpas in Belize, 171–173, *172*
   montane, in Southwest Asia, 134–136
   opium swidden, in Laos, 117
crop substitution strategy
   aid tied to, in Peru, 263
   developmental ventures, 308
   in Laos, 119–120
   in Thailand, 48, 179
Cuellar, Parmenio, 88
cultivation of drugs, reasons for, 297–299.
   See also specific locations
cultural identity, indigenous
   drugs as essential component in, 295
   external drug control as assault on, 14
   and moral geographies, 20–22
   promotion of, through drug use, 11–12,
   17
cultural identity, modern, 17
cultural roles of psychoactive plants, 3–4
Cultural Survival, 15
cupping, 126

DEA (Drug Enforcement Administration),
   175. *See also* prohibition, interdiction,
   and eradication programs
defoliation, 56, 86, 87, 88
deforestation, 260–261, 262, 285, *285,*
   302–303
deghans (sharecroppers), 147
demand for drugs
   elasticity of supply and demand, 25–26,
   29–30, 173, 303–304
   eradication programs, impact of, 89
   European youth travels and, 140–141
   growth and spread of, 26, 30
   reasons for drug use, 297
Deobandi, 137, 139
determinism, environmental, 296

diasporas, ethnic, 74, 77–78, 296–297
diet, 38–39, 136
Dignity Plan *(plan de dignidad),* 160
Diguet, Leon, 196
diwi, 286
domestication, of kava, 277
Doors of Perception (Huxley), 197
Dostum, Abdul Rashid, 81
Drug Abuse Control Act Amendments, 194
drug lords, CIA alliances with, 31–32,
   43–44
drugs, categorization of, 17–18
drugs, defining, 16–17
drugs, significance of, 3–4, 295–296
drug tourism, 21, 141, 303
drug trafficking. *See* trafficking
drug use. *See* demand for drugs; medicinal
   use of drugs; *specific locations*
Dubai, 139
Durand Line, 147
Dutch East India Company, 35

economic rationality, 169, 179
economies, indigenous, 11, 178–179
economy, moral, 20
Ecstasy, 89, 198–199
elasticity of supply and demand, 25–26,
   29–30, 173, 303–304
elite-centered projects, in Bolivia, 160
Ellis, Havlock, 196
endogenous drugs, 17
Ene River Valley, Peru, 255, 257
England. *See* Britain
enlightenment, 196
environmental determinism, 296
environmental impacts
   defoliation, 86, 87, 88
   general patterns, 302–303
   of kava, 281–282, 285, *285*
   of Peruvian coca/cocaine, 260–262
eradication programs. *See* prohibition, interdiction, and eradication programs
Erlunchun communities of China, 233–236,
   243
Errant Journeys (Zurick), 141
Escobar, Pablo, 86, 88
ethnic cropping patterns, 134–135
ethnic diasporas, 74, 77–78, 296–297
ethnic minorities. *See* minorities
Eugene Augur, 199

euphorica, 17
Europe
    heroin trafficking, 77
    kava use, 274
    Nixon's drug war and, 48–49
    opium trade history, 34–38
    youth travels, and drug demand, 140–141
excitantia, 17

Fahim, Muhammad, 84
faikava, 282
Faiz, Faiz Ahmed, 78–79
faquirs, 222–223
FARC (Fuerzas Armadas Revolucionarios
    de Colombia), 22, 87, 88
Federated States of Micronesia, *275,* 277,
    283–287, *284*
federations, coca, 163–164
fieldwork issues, 167, 294
Fiji, 281–282
fire, and resistance in India, 229
Florida, 56
food, drugs used as spices with, 136
food crops, ethnic patterns of, 134–135. *See
    also* crop substitution strategy
forest fragmentation, 261, 262
Frahi, Bernard, 80
Frankfurt Resolution (1990), 90
Frank Takes Gun, 194
freedom of religion, and peyote, 194–195,
    201, 202
free trade, 26–27, 72–73
Fujimori, Alberto, 86, 255, 256

ganja, 221, 224, 225–230
Ganja Mahal, India, 224, 225–230
Gansu Province, China, 240–241
García, Alan, 255
geopolitical dimension of drug wars,
    253–254, 307
Georgia, 77
Ghani Kel, Afghanistan, 73, 81, 84
Ghaus, Mullah Mohammed, 70
Ghost Dance, 192
globalization, 4, 58, 299–300
Golden Triangle, emergence of, 45. *See
    also* Southeast Asia
guerilla and rebel groups, 255, 257, 306
Gul, Hamid, 64, 65
guns, 237

habitat loss, 262
hallucinogens, 17, 18, 196. *See also* peyote
Han Chinese, 232, 238–239, 241–242
Haq, Fazle, 55, 63
Haq, Shamshul, 80
Harrington, Raymond, 196
Harrison Narcotics Act, 40
Hastings, Warren, 35
Hauatla, Oaxaca, Mexico, 21
HAVA (Helmand-Arghandab River Author-
    ity), 144
Haw, 38
Hawai'i, 282–283
Heilongjiang Province, China, 234
Hekmatyar, Gulbuddin, 53–54, 55, 65–66,
    75, 143
Helmand Valley, Afghanistan
    heroin processing, 55, 70
    irrigation in, 67, 72
    opium bans and, 79, 83
    opium economy, 150
    opium production, 75, 144, 146, *146*
    Taliban opium ban and, 81
    warlords, post-Taliban, 82
Helms, Richard, 52
hemp. *See* India; marijuana
herbal medicine, 126. *See also* medicinal
    use of drugs
Hermoza, Nicolas, 86
Hernández, Francisco, 195
heroin
    amphetamines as replacement for, 49
    Burmese, 51–52, 59–62
    Central Asian coalitions, 63
    "China white," 51
    in Colombia, 87
    Eurasian trafficking network, 73–78
    globalization of, 58
    Golden Triangle, 42
    heroin chic, 51
    in Laos, 61–62, 124, 129
    Nixon's drug war and, 47–49, 52
    origins of, 32
    in Pakistan, 52–55
    shift from opium to, 41
    users, increase in, 26
    See also opium
Hezb-i-Islami, 53, 75
highland-lowland divisions, 91–92
Hindukush mountains, 137, 139–140

hippie movement, and peyote, 185, 187, 197
Hitler, Adolf, 196
HIV and AIDS, 51, 52, 62, 73–74
Hmong, 45, 116
Hofmann, Albert, 197
Holbrook, Richard C., 83
Homo sapiens, 19
Huallaga River Valley, Peru, 255, 257
Huichole, 196, 198
human beings, as species, 19
human trafficking, 216
hunter-gatherers, 18
Huxley, Aldous, 197
hydromanagement systems, in India, 224
hypnotica, 17

identity. *See* cultural identity
immigration, illegal, 216
Inca empire, 14
India
    Afghanistan as British frontier, 140
    consumption of hemp, 222–223
    cultivation of hemp, and landscape,
        223–224
    hemp preparations, 221–222
    opium trade history, 33–39
    Pushtuns, historical presence of, 139
    resistance to British, 225–230
indigenous peoples and cultures
    belief systems, 202
    colonialism, 14
    cultural identity, and drug use, 11–12
    definitions and designations, 13–14
    distributions of, 15–16
    drugs, complex relationship with,
        296–297
    identity (*See* cultural identity,
        indigenous)
    marginalization and cash economy,
        178–179
    number of, 15
    traditional uses of drugs, 3–4
    See also specific countries
Indochina, 37–38, 45. *See also* Southeast
    Asia
Indonesia, 60–61
inebriantia, 17
Inner Mongolia Autonomous Region,
    China, 233–234
insurgencies, 91, 94

intercropping of marijuana, 171, 210
international norms, compliance with, 93
International Opium Convention, 40–41
International Work Group for Indigenous
    Affairs (IWGIA), 15
International Year of the Indigenous
    People, 16
Inter-Service Intelligence, Pakistan (ISI),
    53, 63–64, 66
intoxicants, taken with food, 136
Inuit, 19
Iran, 42, 46, 75. *See also* Southwest Asia
Irkutsk, Russia, 74
Iron Curtain, 43, 58
irrigation works, destruction of, 143
Islamic Hadd Ordinance, 148
Islamic Movement for Uzbekistan (IMU),
    76
Isma'ili (Sevener) Muslims, 137, 142, 145
isolation policy, 91
Israel, 138
itinerant harvesters. *See* seasonal workers
Iu Mien, 116

Japan, 234
Java, 35, 38
Jiaxi, 237
Jiayin County, China, 234–236
Jívaro, 256–257
Johnson, Ed, 282

Kabul, 139–140
kalapu kava, 282
Kandahar Province, Afghanistan, 82
Karzai, Hamid, 82, 144
kau, 285
kava in Remote Oceania
    botany, origins, and dispersal, 276–278
    commercialization, 283, 287–288
    conservation efforts, 288–290
    cultivation and ecology, 274, 276, 282,
        284, 287, 290
    cultural identity and, 17
    description, 274–276, *275*
    drug classification, 279
    environmental impacts, 281–282
    local and traditional uses, 278–283
    map, *275*
    on Pohnpei Island, 283–291, *284, 285,
        291*

Kekchí Maya. *See* Maya marijuana cultivation in Belize
Kerr, Hem Chunder, 224, 226–229
Khan, Ismail, 81
Khan, Jehangir, 53
Khin Nyunt, 59, 60
Khun Sa, 51, 59, 61–62
Kiowa, 192
KLA (Kosovo Liberation Army), 77
Kluever, Heinrich, 196
Konanui, Jerry, 282
Kosovo, 77, 78
Kosrae Island, Micronesia, 285–286
Kuhestanis, 137, 143
Kurd, Mohammad Asim, 64
Kyrgyzstan, 73–74, 76, 84

La Barre, Weston, 18–19, 193, 197
Lamas (Lamistas), 257
landscape factors
    Belize, 173, *174*
    general patterns, 301–303
    highland-lowland divisions, 91–92
    Peru, 261
    peyote gardens, 185
    resistance and transformation, in India, 225–230
    satellite visibility, 150
land settlement programs, in Bolivia, 154–155
languages, 15
Laos
    addiction to opium, 122–127
    agroeconomics of opium, 117–118
    antiopium efforts, 62, 129, 130
    CIA covert warfare, 43, 45–46
    commerce in opium, 121–122
    farm economics, 120–121
    heroin production, emergence of, 61–62, 129
    politicoeconomic factors, 115–117
    politics of opium, 127–129
    pros and cons of opium farming, 119–120, 127
    See also Southeast Asia
Latin America. *See* Bolivia; Colombia; Peru
law enforcement model, 29
League of Nations, 40–41
Leahy, Patrick, 88

legalization of drugs, 309
Lewin, Louis, 17–18, 196
Liangshan Prefecture, China, 236–240
licensing, in British India, 225
Lin Minxian, 60
Lippan Apache, 192
loans to Afghan opium farmers, 71–72
Lophophora williamsii. See peyote
lowland-highland divisions, 91–92
LSD, 197, 198–199
Luhan, Mabel Dodge, 196–197

Machiguenga (Matsiguenga), 258
madrasahs (religious schools), 137, 139
Maerkang, China, 240
majum, 221–222
The Making of the English Working Class (Thompson), 20
Manchuria, 233–234
manteqa ("place"), 138, 143
maps
    Bolivia, *155*
    Mexico, northwestern, *210*
    Native American Churches, *186*
    opium in Southwest Asia, *135*
    Peru, *252*
    peyote, *184*
    Remote Oceania, *275*
    southern Belize, *171*
    Vanuatu, *280*
marginalization, economic, 178–179
marijuana
    in California, 48
    environmental requirements, 223–224
    intercropping of, 171, 210
    Operation Condor (Mexico), 48
    in Pakistan, 137
    preparations of, 221–222
    Thrush-65 defoliation program (Colombia), 56
    See also India; Maya marijuana cultivation in Belize; Mexico
Masood, Ahmad Shah, 143
Mathewson, Kent, 201
Maung Aye, 60
Maya marijuana cultivation in Belize
    boom economy, 170
    criminalization and economic bust, 174–177
    cultural consequences of boom, 177–178

Maya marijuana cultivation in Belize
(*continued*)
cultural economic background, 168–169
history of marijuana economy, 169–174
map, *171*
marginalization and cash economy,
178–179
milpas, 171–173, *172*
production of marijuana, 170
Mazatec community, 21
McDonald, Darrel, 189
McIntosh, Ian, 13
Medellin cartel, 86, 88
medical metaphor, 96–97
medicinal use of drugs
coca, 33, 250
kava, 274
marijuana, 222
peyote, 196, 200
Melanesia, *275, 277*
Mercado, Leo, 199
mercantilism, 34–35
mescal, 183
"Mescal, a New Artificial Paradise" (Ellis),
196
mescal bean, 182–183
"Mescal Bean Eaters," 193
mescaline, 187
methadone, 125
methamphetamine, 59–60. *See also*
amphetamines
Mexico
alliance with Colombian cartels, 56
drug warfare, 216–217
Operation Condor (1975), 48
peyote use, 191–192
physical geography, *210*
poppy vs. marijuana cultivation,
209–210
Rarámuri marijuana cultivation, 211–213
Tohono transshipment trafficking, 211,
213–216
Micronesia, *275, 277,* 283–290, *284, 285*
militarization, 4
military corruption, in Laos, 128. *See also*
corruption
milpas, 171–173, *172*
miners in Bolivia, 156–157
minorities
in China, 232–233, 241, 242–243

in Laos, 115–116
in United States, 57
Mintz, Sidney, 21, 26
modernity, 17
modern moralists, 20
Mong Yawn, 60
montane agricultural systems, 134–136
Montesinos, Vladimiro, 85–86, 89
Mooney, James, 193, 196
Mopan Maya. *See* Maya marijuana cultivation in Belize
moral economy, 20
moral geography of drugs, 11–12, 20–22,
305–306
moralists, modern, 20
morning glory seeds, 197
morphine, 77. *See also* opium
mountain cropping systems, 134–136
Movers and Shakers (Luhan), 196–197
Movimiento Revolucianario Tupac Amaru
(MRTA), 255, 257, 306
moxybustion, 126
MRTA (Movimiento Revolucianario Tupac
Amaru), 255, 257, 306
muddat, 222
Mughal empire, 34
mujaheddin, 54–55, 65
mulberry, 137
Multidisciplinary Association for Psychedelic Studies, 200
Murali, Atluri, 227–228
Muscat, 139
Musharraf, Pervez, 64
mushrooms, psychoactive, 21
Muslims, alcohol use by, 137–138
Muslims, Isma'ili (Sevener), 137, 142, 145
Mustang Plains, Texas, 183, 185

Namangani, Juma, 75, 76
Nangarhar Province, Afghanistan
opium bans and, 70, 71, 79, 80–81, 84
opium cultivation, 144–145, *146*
opium trafficking, 74
Pushtun dominance, 150
warlords, post-Taliban, 81–82
narco-nationalists, 74
narco-states, 31
Nasim Akhundzada, Mullah, 54
National Detoxification Center, Laos, 124,
127

National Drug Control Strategy, 24, 58
national parks, in Peru, 261, 266
Native American Church (NAC)
    ceremony and ritual, 189–191
    history of peyote use, 182
    incorporation of, 193–194
    locations, *186*
    membership growth, 185
    non-Indians in, 199–200
Native American Religious Freedom Act
    (1978), 195
Native American Rights Fund, 194
Native Americans, drug use among. *See*
    peyote
Near Oceania, *275, 277*
New York City, and heroin chic, 51
Nixon, Richard, 46–50, 52
nongovernmental organizations (NGOs), 266
Northern Alliance (Afghanistan), 75,
    78–79
North West Frontier Province, Pakistan
    (NWFP), 53, 54, 134, 147, 148

Oceania. *See* kava in Remote Oceania
oloiuhqui, 197
Oman, 139
Omar, Mullah, 69, 78
opción cero (zero option plan), 158, 161
opium
    addiction, natural courses of, 123–124
    addiction, treatment for, 125–127
    advantages and disadvantages as crop,
        69, 119–120
    as appetite suppressant, 38
    Asian opium zone, 32, 34, 43, 44–45
    Cold War policies and actions, 42–46
    commercial history, 32
    dens, 123
    early antiopium movement, 39–42
    elasticity of production, 29–30
    epidemiology, 122–123
    illicit economy created by prohibition,
        28–30
    insurgencies and, 91
    monocrop, 62–63, 66
    muddat, 222
    Nixon's drug war and, 47–48
    policy history, modern, 26–27
    poppy varieties and harvesting methods,
        146–147

production increases, 26
prohibition policy, 24, 27
sacred and profane use of, 4
Soviet breakup, effect on trafficking,
    62–63
trade history, 33–39
See also specific locations
opportunity cost, 69
outlaw states, 93–94
Oxy-Contin, 89–90

Pacific Islanders. *See* kava in Remote
    Oceania
Pakistan
    Afghanistan involvement, 64, 66
    Aga Khan Rural Support Project, 142
    alcohol in, 137–138
    cannabis in, 137
    eradication efforts, 148, 149–150
    European opium demand, 140–141
    heroin production increases (1980s),
        52–55
    mountain cropping systems, 134–136
    narco-politics, 63–64
    opium cultivation, distribution of, *135*
    opium production, 148
    opium traffic, 147
    See also Southwest Asia
Palestine, 138
Panthays, 38
Pao Yuchang, 60
Papago (Tohono), 211
Papaver somniferum. See opium
Pashtuns, 81, 134, 138, 149. *See also*
    Taliban
Pastrana, Andres, 87
Patterson, Anne, 88
People's Republic of China. *See* China
Peru
    CIA involvement in, 85–86
    coca cultivation and production, 89, 251,
        252
    colonists, 259–260, 264–265, 266, 267
    environmental impacts, 260–262
    foreign relations, and coca/cocaine,
        253–254
    guerilla groups, 255, 257
    indigenous peoples, 254, 256–259
    map, *252*
    policy alternatives, 266–267

Peru (*continued*)
  political ecology of coca/cocaine,
    263–266
  political-economic history, 254–256
  social impacts of coca/cocaine, 256–261,
    262–263
peyote
  botany, 182–183
  ceremonies and rituals, 189–191, 201
  cult and religion, creation of, 192–196
  history and diffusion of, 182, 186–187,
    191–192, 201–202
  intoxication physiology, 187–189
  non-Indian *peyotists,* 199–200
  nonritual, profane uses, 182, 185,
    195–199
  peyote gardens of Mustang Plains, 183,
    185
  peyoteros (distributors), 183, 185, 194,
    198, *198*
  pilgrimages and trade, 183, 185
  populations and ranges, *184*
  prohibitions and sanctions, 187, 194–195
  religious freedom and, 194–195, 201,
    202
  as symbol, 200–201
The Peyote Cult (La Barre), 197
Peyote Foundation, 199
peyote mushrooms, 183
The Peyote Religion (Slotkin), 197
phantastica, 17, 18
*Phantastica: Narcotic and Stimulating
    Drugs—Their Use and Abuse* (Lewin),
    17–18, 196
Philippines, 39–40, 60–61
pilgrimages, 183, 185, 303
Piot, Peter, 74
Piper betle, 278
Piper methysticum. See kava, in Remote
    Oceania
Piper wichmanii, 277
Pishquibo, 257
place, as *manteqa,* 138
Plan Colombia, 88–89
plan de dignidad (Dignity Plan), 160
plantation production, 21
Pohnpei Island, Micronesia, 283–290, *284,*
    285, 291
Pohnpei Watershed Forest Reserve and
    Mangrove Protection Act (1987), 288

police corruption, 30–31. *See also*
    corruption
political ecology of coca/cocaine,
    263–266
Polynesia, *275, 277*
poppies, opium. *See* heroin; opium
Powell, Colin, 79
power relations, asymmetry of, 264, 265
Pretzsche, Ernst, 196
production of drugs, effects of prohibition
    policy on, 25–26
profitability, 32, 298
prohibition, interdiction, and eradication
    programs
  Afghanistan, 78–81, 82–84, 133–134,
    138, 149–150
  Aga Khan Rural Support Project, 142
  Andean eradication and defoliation
    programs, 85–90
  antiopium programs, and heroin shift,
    129
  Bolivia, 56–57, 157–163
  boom-bust cycle and, 177
  Burma, 61–62
  China, 42–43, 233, 235–236, 237–243
  coercive capacity, declining, 29
  Cold War policies and actions, 42–46
  Colombia, 55, 57–58, 88–89
  corruption and, 30–31, 89, 306
  demand, impact on, 89
  early antiopium movement, 39–42
  eradication strategy, 24–25
  future prospects, 33, 94–97
  geopolitical effects, 253–254
  isolation policy, 91
  Laos, 62, 129, 130
  market response, and undesired out-
    comes, 25, 27, 28–32, 95–96
  Mexico, 48, 216–217
  militarization, 4
  Nixon's drug war, 46–50, 52
  Pakistan, 148, 149–150
  Peru, 85–86
  peyote, 187, 194–195
  policy history, 20th century, 27
  political and military shields, 176
  political-economic implications, 90–94
  public skepticism, 90
  racial inequities, 57
  Reagan-Bush drug war, 50, 55–58

social costs, 89
socioeconomic conditions and, 180
Southeast Asian opium eradication
   (1990s), 61–62
success of, 307–308
Psilocybe, 183
psychedelics, 197. *See also* peyote
Pushtuns. *See* Pashtuns; Taliban

Qadir, Abdul, 82, 84
Qiang, 240, 241
Qing dynasty, China, 234, 236, 240
Qunuo, 237

race, 57
Rachikul, General, 128–129
Rahman, Akhtar Abdul, 55
rahmedel, 285
rahmwanger, 285
Rarámuri (Tarahumara), 195, 211–213
Rashid, Abdul, 69, 80
Rasul, Mohammed, 54
rationality, economic, 169, 179
Reagan, Ronald, 50
rebel and guerilla groups, 255, 257, 306
recommendations, 308–310
religion, 202, 222–223. *See also* Native
   American Church (NAC)
religious freedom, and peyote, 194–195,
   201, 202
Religious Freedom Restoration Act (1993),
   195
Remote Oceania. *See* kava, in Remote
   Oceania
Republic of the Fiji Islands, 281–282
resistance
   in Bolivia, 158
   in British India, 225–230
   to colonialism, 221
   moral economy and, 20
   Rarámuri farmers, in Mexico, 212
   subaltern groups, 221, 226, 307–308
river systems, and smuggling, 228
RLG (Royal Laotian Government),
   116–117
Rockefeller, Nelson, 47
rogue states, 93–94
Rohilkhand, 139
Rosen, Winifred, 19
Roy, Olivier, 79–80

Royal Northern Project, 179
Russia, 74

sakau, 283, 285–286
Salinas de Gotari, Carlos, 56
Samper, Ernesto, 86–87
San Antonio, Belize, 168
Sangin, Afghanistan, 73, 81, 83–84
San Pedro cactus, 199
San Pedro Columbia, Belize, 168, 170, 177
satellite imagery, 150
scale, 12, 21–22
school attendance, 170, 178
Schultes, Richard Evans, 197
Scott, James C., 20
searches for drugs, in shamanistic tradi-
   tions, 18
seasonal workers, 72
security agencies. *See* CIA (Central Intelli-
   gence Agency)
seka, 285
semisynthetic drugs, 17
Sendero Luminoso (Shining Path), 255,
   257, 262, 306
Serbia, 77, 78
shabu, 60
shamanistic traditions, 18. *See also* peyote
Shanghai commission, 40
Shan States, 59–60
sharecroppers, 147
Sharif, Nawaz, 64
Shipibo, 257
Shirzai, Gul Agda, 82
Siam, 37, 38. *See also* Thailand
Sichuan Province, China, 236, 240, 241
Sierra Madre, 209, *210,* 211–213
slash-and-burn agriculture, 117, 171–172,
   172, 173
slaves, in Yi society, 236–237, 239
Slotkin, J. S., 197
Smoking Opium Exclusion Act, 40
smuggling. *See* trafficking
social and material changes, 300–301. *See
   also specific locations*
socioeconomic conditions, and drug culti-
   vation, 180
Solarz, Stephen, 142
Sonora, Mexico, 209, *210,* 213–216
Sorrenti, Davide, 51
Souphanna Vong, 117

South America. *See* Bolivia; Colombia;
  Peru
Southeast Asia
  amphetamine markets, 60–61
  antiopium movement, 41–42
  Golden Triangle, 42, 45
  Nixon's drug war and, 47, 48
  opium and heroin production increases,
    50–52
  opium trade history, 37–38
  turn-of-the-century transition, 62
  See also specific countries
Southwest Asia
  Cold War opium trafficking, 42, 46
  heroin production trends, 52–55
  opium, possible future proliferation of,
    84
  opium cultivation distribution, *135*
  Soviet breakup and opium traffic,
    62–63
  See also Afghanistan; Pakistan; Turkey
Souvanna Phouma, 116, 128
Soviet Union, 62–63, 138
Spanish colonialism, 14
speed. *See* amphetamines
spices, 136
state formation, 91–92
state power, and drug wars, 90–91
Stevens, Stan, 13
Stewart, Omer C., 192
stimulants, taken with food, 136
strategic leverage, using drugs for, 307
subaltern groups, 221, 226, 307–308
sugar, 38
Sun Dance cult, 202
supply and demand, elasticity of, 25–26,
    29–30, 173, 303–304
suppression of drugs. *See* prohibition, inter-
    diction, and eradication programs
Sweetness and Power (Mintz), 26
swidden agriculture (slash-and-burn), 117,
    171–172, *172, 173*
syncretic religions, 202
syndicates, criminal, 32, 41, 74, 77–78
synthetic drugs, 17, 33, 89. *See also* am-
    phetamines

Tafahi Island, Tonga, 282
Taft, William Howard, 40
Tajikistan, 75–76

Taliban
  opium ban, 78–81
  and opium trade, 69–71
  Pakistani support for, 64, 66
  vineyard eradication, 138
Tanna Island, Vanuatu, 279
Tarahumara (Rarámuri), 195, 211–213
taxation, in British India, 225–227
tea, 26–27, 38, 136
teepees, and peyote ritual, 189, 190, *190*
temperance movement, 27, 39, 201
teonanacatl, 183
terrorism, war on, 217
Texas. *See* peyote
Texas mountain laurel, 182–183
Thailand
  amphetamine use, 59
  Nixon's drug war and, 48, 52
  opium trade in Kingdom of Siam, 37, 38
  Royal Northern Project, 179
Thompson, Edward P., 20
Thrush-65 defoliation program, 56
Tibetans, in China, 240–242, 243
Tingo Maria, Peru, 260
tobacco, 21
Tofua Island, Tonga, 282
Tohono O'odham, 211
Toledo, Alejandro, 86
Tomsen, Peter, 65
Tonga, 282
tourism, drug, 21, 141, 303
trade, international, 33–39, 138–140
trafficking
  Asian Opium Zone caravans, 43
  Burma, 45, 85
  China, 85, 238
  Cold War and, 42, 46
  Eurasian network for Afghan opium,
    73–78, 147
  prohibition, effect of, 30, 49
  reasons for, 299–300
  sectors within, 211
  smuggling, in British India, 228
  Soviet breakup and, 62–63
  Tohono transshipment trafficking, 211,
    213–216
transhumance, 67
Transmigration and Human Settlements
    plan, 160
travel, and drug tourism, 21, 141, 303

Trout's Notes on Sacred Cacti (Trout), 200
Truman, Harry, 45
Turkey, 42, 46, 47, 77. *See also* Southwest
    Asia
Turkmenistan, 76

Ullah, Mullah Naquib, 82
UNDCP (United Nations Drug Control
    Program), 24–25, 61, 70, 150
Union Church, 193
United Nations, 14, 27, 69
United Nations Drug Control Program
    (UNDCP), 24–25, 61, 70, 150
United Nations Fund for Drug Abuse Con-
    trol, 48
United States, drug policy history, 27–28. *See
    also* prohibition, interdiction, and erad-
    ication programs; war on drugs, U.S.
United States, opium trade history, 36
United Wa State Army (UWSA), 59–60
universality of drug use, 11, 18–20
Uruzgan Province, Afghanistan, 146, *146*
use of drugs. *See* demand for drugs; medic-
    inal use of drugs; *specific locations*
Uzbekistan, 76

Valbuena, Armando, 88
Vang Pao, 46, 128
Vanuatu, 277, 279–281, *280,* 285, 286
Vavilov, Nicolai, 135
vertical integration, 72–73
Vladivostock, Russia, 74

Wa Alternative Development Project, 61
Walters, John, 90
warfare, covert. *See* CIA
war on drugs, U.S.
    Andean eradication and defoliation pro-
        grams, 85–90

corruption and, 306
geopolitical effects, 253–254
medical metaphor as alternative, 96–97
militarization, 4
Nixon's drug war, 46–50, 52
prohibition strategy, 24
public skepticism, 90
Reagan-Bush drug war, 50, 55–58
social costs of, 89
success of, 307–308
See also prohibition, interdiction, and
    eradication programs
war on terrorism, 217
wars and conflicts, drug connection of, 20
Wasson, R. Gordon, 197
Wa warlords, 59–60
Wei Hseuh-kang, 60
Weil, Andrew, 19
Wright, Hamilton, 40

Xhemajli, Muhamed, 78
Xichang Prefecture, China, 236, 237–238,
    239

yaba, 59
yagona, 281
Yankee traders, 36
Yi society, in Liangshan, China, 236–240,
    243
youth drug market, 89, 140–141
Yugoslavia, 77–78
Yungas region, Bolivia, 154, 162
Yuquí, 266

Zadran, Padsha Khan, 82
Zahid, Abdur Rahman, 78
zero option plan *(opción cero),* 158, 161
Zia ul Haq, 55, 63
Zurick, David, 141